ITALIANISSIMO one

NEW EDITION

Denise De Rôme
Former Principal Lecturer and Head of Italian
University of Westminster

BBC

New Edition published 2004

Published by BBC Languages,
BBC Worldwide Ltd, Woodlands
80 Wood Lane, London W12 0TT

ISBN 0 563 51906 1

Developed by BBC Languages
Designed by Andrew Oliver
Edited by Sarah Boas
Illustrated by Linda Smith, Michaela Stewart, Robina Green, Gary Wing, Jeremy Oliver and Kathy Baxendale
Maps by Linda Smith
Studio photographs by Benedict Campbell
Audio Producer for new edition Martin Williamson, Prolingua Productions
Project Editor for new edition Joanna Kirby
Production Controller for new edition Man Fai Lau

Also available:
- Language Pack (course book and 4 audio CDs)
- Language Pack (course book and 4 audio cassettes)
- CD Pack (4 audio CDs)

- *Italianissimo* TV series is broadcast on the BBC TWO Learning Zone
- Free online activities at **www.bbc.co.uk/languages**

The author and publisher would like to thank Giulio Einaudi Editore for permission to quote a poem by Gianni Rodari from *Il secondo libro delle filastrocche* (1985) and part of a poem by Pier Paolo Pasolini from *La nuova gioventù* (1975); Garzanti Editore for permission to quote the poem 'Lunedì' by Primo Levi from *Ad ora incerta* (1982); and Arnaldo Mondadori Editore for permission to quote two poems by Giuseppe Ungaretti from *Vita d'un uomo* (1966).

This book is set in Bembo Roman by
Selwood Systems, Midsomer Norton
Printed and bound in Great Britain by
Butler & Tanner Ltd, Frome, Somerset

Contents

Course menu

Course menu

v

Using the Course

In each unit you'll be able to:

Interactions
Hear the language in action.

Key phrases
Look at some basics.

Patterns
See how the language is used.

Practice
Practise what you've just learned.

Vocabulary
Reinforce and widen your vocabulary.

Troubleshooting
Avoid common pitfalls.

At the end of Units 5 and 10 you'll be able to:

Systems
Look at the grammar – see how the language works.

Reinforcement
Do some more exercises.

Review
Check up on what you know and assess your progress.

Working on your own
Focus on language learning strategies.

Profile
Reinforce your listening and reading.

Culture
Enjoy some paintings and poems.

At the back of the book you can:

Answers
Find the answers to the exercises.

Basics
Sort out some basic grammar terms.

Reference
Find useful verb lists and other detailed information.

Index to Grammar
Find out where grammar points are explained.

Lexis
Check up on words you don't know.

Italianissimo 1 is a multimedia language learning package designed to meet the varying needs of the beginner or near beginner, whether studying alone or in a group. The course consists of:
- a book comprising 10 units
- 4 audio cassettes or CDs

The course is complemented by online activities at **www.bbc.co.uk/languages** and a 10-part TV series. This course takes between six months and one year to complete and takes learners to GCSE level standard. *Italianissimo 2* follows on from *Italianissimo 1* and takes learners up to roughly A-level standard. It has a similar structure and components.

Aims and Modes of Study

The course is suitable for all learners as it offers them the opportunity to study at their own pace and in the way that suits them best: the various components of the course make it possible for learners to study the same material from different angles and with different degrees of complexity. The course features:
- A choice of two ways of learning
- Plenty of reinforcement and repetition
- Help on how to develop language learning skills

Twin track approach

The learner has the option of choosing to follow one of two tracks:
- **Track 1** is the 'core' course, aimed at learners for whom basic communicative needs are most important. All the language needed for this is presented in the Patterns section. This gives learners the opportunity to absorb some of the key language and to extend it a little in conjunction with extra vocabulary and some exercises.
- **Track 2** is for intensive learners requiring more in-depth knowledge, who need to learn to communicate more independently in a wider variety of situations. In addition to the core material, there are extra grammatical explanations in the **Systems** and additional exercises in the **Reinforcement** sections.

The keynote of *Italianissimo 1* is flexibility: a comprehensive system of cross-references makes it possible for learners following Track 1 to dip selectively into Track 2 and for all learners to use the **Reference** section at the end of the book. After completing 5 units, learners have the opportunity to assess their progress in the **Review** section and change tracks if they wish.

Using the Course

Cassettes/CDs, Online, TV

Whichever track you choose to follow, you are encouraged to get used to hearing the language from the start, in conjunction with the cassette or CD. You will find that the books and cassettes/CDs are closely integrated. Cassette/CD symbols in the text indicate when there is an accompanying recording; a number is also given so you can find the right track quickly on the cassette/CD.

The TV gives additional dialogues and information about Italy as well as the core dialogues in the book. You can record the TV programmes, which are broadcast on the Learning Zone on BBC Two.

Free online activities based on video clips from the TV programmes are available on:
www.bbc.co.uk/languages

Getting Going

Italianissimo 1 provides varied, adaptable material which can be tailored to your individual learning goals. To make the most of the course, you need first to define what these are.

Define your goals

Whatever has prompted you to embark on this course, whether work, study or general interest, you'll find that to stay motivated you need to set yourself precise short-term aims. Think about what you will be using your Italian for and try to prioritise the four basic language skills involved. Although these skills are all interrelated, if you can grade the relative importance of each one for your

	Vital	*Important*	*Quite Important*	*Unimportant*
Speaking				
Listening				
Reading				
Writing				

particular purposes, you'll be able to focus more precisely on your goals and use the course more effectively.

Organise your time

Don't be over-ambitious. You must have realistic expectations. Decide how much time you can regularly devote to learning and stick to it. Bear in mind that most people need plenty of time and practice to build up confidence and proficiency. Research shows that on average learners forget about 80% of what they have studied within a mere twenty-four hours unless they use or review what they have learned!

Structure of the Course

Units 1–5 Introductions and personal information. Basic socialising, enquiries, requests and needs.
Units 6–10 Making arrangements, suggestions and invitations. Expressing basic feelings.

Working through a unit

Each unit is designed to provide material for several hours of learning and is divided into two main parts, with a **Cultura e parole** section in the middle and a short reference section at the end.

Additional grammar and exercise sections (called **Systems** and **Reinforcement**) are provided after every five units.

1 **Interactions 1** – dialogues
  Patterns 1 – language explanations and references to the **Systems**
  Practice 1 – exercises and activities

  Cultura e parole – the culture and the language

2 **Interactions 2** – dialogues
  Patterns 2 – language explanations and references to the **Systems**
  Practice 2 – exercises and activities

  Vocabulary
  Troubleshooting

Using the Course

Interactions

To start with we recommend you listen to the Interactions without first reading the text. If you are not used to this approach don't be daunted, as the dialogues are meant to be listened to several times to help you build up your listening skills.

Use the **First Time Round** questions to focus your attention. Make sure that you have understood the meaning of the words given at the beginning and that you understand the context by reading the introduction and questions carefully. You can also listen to the introductory material or bypass this and start your listening with the Interactions. With practice you will gain a great deal of confidence by realising you can grasp the gist through guesswork and by building on what you know. Listen as often as you wish. Then move on to:

Key Phrases

Study them and then see if you can pick them out on the recording. Once you are confident that you have got as far as you can by listening, study the written text to fill in any gaps in your comprehension. You can also use it to practise pronunciation in conjunction with the recording. To see how the language fits together, move on to:

Patterns

These provide basic explanations of the Key Phrases, often in conjunction with new vocabulary. If you are following **Track 2**, the in-depth approach, make use of the cross-references in Patterns to the grammar in the Systems section: those following **Track 1** may also find these helpful at times.

Practice

This section provides lively follow-up activities, some of them on cassette/CD, in which you can use and begin to adapt the language presented so far. As realistic as possible and often humorous, they are designed to give practice in all language skills. You'll find the answers at the back of the book. Some of the vocabulary is introduced in **Patterns**, so please look back at those if you get stuck for a word.

Suggested study plans

It's a good idea initially to devote two or even three sessions to each of the main parts of a unit. Your sessions can be quite brief and, as you progress through the course, you will develop your own study routines.

For **Part 1**

Track 1	Session 1	Session 2	Session 3
Approach A	Interactions & Patterns 1	Learn some vocabulary	Practice 1
Approach B	Interactions 1	Patterns & Practice 1	Learn some vocabulary

Repeat the process for **Part 2**.

Track 2

Vary your approach until you determine what works best for you. Aim at four or even five sessions to take account of Systems and Reinforcement exercises.

Vocabulary

This section is intended to aid gradual, systematic vocabulary acquisition by listing additional words on topics which come up in the unit. Any irregular or unusual stress on a word is marked by a dot so that you can pronounce new words correctly from the start. There are notes on vocabulary learning in the **Working on your own** sections of the book.

Learning to Learn

If you have never studied a language before, dip into the **Working on your own** and the **Basics** section before you start. These will help you gain the confidence you need to manage your own learning and experiment with the material in the course. Don't forget that there is plenty of material for extending your knowledge at leisure, both in the book, on the cassette/CDs and, of course, in the TV programmes and in the online activities. Do exploit everything to the full and make the most of *Italianissimo*! You don't have to be a linguist to achieve this, so persevere and enjoy the experience. **Buon lavoro e buon divertimento!**

SVIZZERA

AUSTRIA

UNGHERIA

FRANCIA

▲ Monte Blanco

VALLE
D'AOSTA

▲ M. Rosa

Bernina ▲

TRENTINO-
ALTO ADIGE

▲ Marmolada

• Aosta

LOMBARDIA

• Trento

FRIULI-
VENEZIA
GIULIA

• Milano

VENETO

• Torino

PIEMONTE

EMILIA ROMAGNA

• Venezia

• Trieste

Golfo di Venezia

LIGURIA

Po

• Genova

• Bologna

SAN
MARINO

Golfo di Genova

Arno

• Firenze

MAR LIGURE

TOSCANA

MARCHE

• Ancona

I. Capraia

MARE ADRIATICO

I. d'Elba

• Perugia

UMBRIA

CORSICA

Tevere

▲ Gran Sasso d'Italia

• L'Aquila

• **Roma**

ABRUZZO

LAZIO

MOLISE

• Campobasso

MAR
DI SARDEGNA

MAR TIRRENO

CAMPANIA

• Napoli

PUGLIA

• Bari

SARDEGNA

I. d'Ischia

• Potenza

BASILICATA

• Cagliari

▲ M. Pollino

Canale d'Otranto

Golfo di Taranto

CALABRIA

I TALIA

I. d'Ustica

• Catanzaro

Isole Eolie

Isole Egadi

• Palermo

Stretto di Messina

MAR IONIO

SICILIA

▲ M. Etna

TUNISIA

Simeto

MAR MEDITERRANEO

ix

Unità 1

Immagini
First impressions

Il Ponte Vecchio, Firenze

Part 1
(Interactions 1–6, Patterns 1, Practice 1)

Learn how to:
Say hello and goodbye
Say who you are
Ask for a ticket
Order a drink and a cake
Use numbers 1–20
Practise the sounds of Italian

Part 2
(Interactions 7–11, Patterns 2, Practice 2)

Learn how to:
Identify places and objects
Ask simple questions
Buy an ice-cream and order a snack
Say where you are
Spell your name

Grammar

Nouns and adjectives ending in **-o** and **-a**
Plurals of nouns and adjectives
Articles **un**, **una** – *a, an*
Articles **il**, **la**, **i**, **le** – *the*

questo, **questi** – *this*, *these*
di, **a** and **in**
Simple questions and negatives
essere – the verb *to be*

Want to take it further?
Grammar: see Systems 1, pp. 79–80   *More practice:* do Reinforcement 1, pp. 81–2

1

Interactions

1   [cc]   [CD] 2

Some of the people in the series say hello and Anna Mazzotti, the presenter, introduces herself.

First time round

Listen out for two ways of saying hello.

Ciao . . . **ci**ao. . . . **Buongiorno** . . . **buo**ngiorno. Buon**gi**orno, **io sono** Anna Ma**zz**otti.

> ### Key phrases
>
> **ciao**   *hello [familiar]*
> **buongiorno**   *good morning*
> **io sono**   *I am*

As you listen, look at the text and notice how the highlighted letters **ci**, **buo**, **gi** and **zz** are pronounced.

2   [cc]   [CD] 3

Next, some familiar Italian words and a way of saying cheers!

First time round

How many of the following would you eat?

Chianti   spa**ghe**tti   gorgon**z**ola   parmi**gi**ano fettu**cci**ne   Fras**ca**ti   Gu**cci**   Lan**ci**a **cin cin!**

> ### Key phrase
>
> **cin cin!**   *cheers!*

Read the text as you listen. How are the highlighted letters pronounced?

3   [cc]   [CD] 4

A few more hellos from a beach in Liguria and people saying who they are.

First time round

Cover up the text below! You'll hear four girls saying their names. Listen to the cassette/CD. What are they called? If necessary, press the pause button after each one and try to write down the name.

Ciao – io sono Marilina.
Ciao – io sono Giovanna.
Ciao – io sono Stefania.
Ciao – io sono Elisabetta.

4   5

Finally, two more names and a way of saying 'how do you do?'.

First time round

How is the name Walter pronounced in Italian?

Io sono Fran**ce**sca.
Io sono **W**alter Ta**gli**aferri.
Ciao – **piacere**.

Key phrase

piacere	*how do you do?*
	pleased to meet you

Look at the text as you listen. Three new sounds have been highlighted. How are they pronounced?

5   6

L'Italia in Miniatura is a large amusement park just outside Rimini on the Adriatic coast. As its name suggests, the park contains models in miniature of the main sights of Italy from all its twenty regions.

First time round

---

un biglietto	*a ticket*
una guida	*a guide*

Listen to the cassette/CD without looking at the text. Anna buys a ticket and a guide.
Can you pick out the Italian words for *please* and *thank you*?

Anna   **Un biglietto** e **una guida, per favore.**
Ragazza   Ecco il biglietto e la guida.
Anna   **Grazie.**
Ragazza   Grazie.

ecco   *here is*

Key phrases

un biglietto, per favore	*a ticket, please*
una guida, per favore	*a guide, please*
grazie	*thank you*

---

6   7

A couple go to the ticket-office at the Italia in Miniatura park.

First time round

---

ventidue	*twenty-two*

What do you think the word for *two* is?

Uomo   Due biglietti e due guide.
Donna   Ecco i biglietti e le guide, ventidue euro.
            Grazie.
Uomo   **Buongiorno.**
Donna   Buongiorno.

ecco   *here are*

Key phrase

buongiorno   *good morning.* [Here; *goodbye* not
                 hello.]

Patterns I

i) Saying hello

How you say *hello* depends on how formal your relationship is and on the time of day.

Ciao!   *Hello [inf. – friends only, all times of day]*
Buongiorno   *Good morning [lit. good day]*
Buonasera   *Good afternoon, good evening [lit. good evening]*

The word for *afternoon* is *pomeriggio*, but it is rarely used in greetings.

If you've already been introduced, you can say:

Piacere   *How do you do? [lit. pleasure]*

ii) Saying goodbye

This also depends on the degree of formality and on the time of day.

Ciao   *[inf.]*   Buonanotte   *Good night [inf. and form.]*
Buongiorno   Arrivederci   *Goodbye*
Buonasera

The intonation of **ciao, buongiorno,** and **buonasera** can be different when you say *goodbye*: the voice often falls at the end of the word. However, among native speakers you will find many differences in intonation.

iii) Saying who you are

The key verb is **essere** *(to be)* [see Systems, note 6, p. 80].

[Io] sono | Anna Mazzotti, sono italiana   *I am* | *Anna Mazzotti, I am Italian*
          | Walter Tagliaferri, sono italiano | *Walter Tagliaferri, I am Italian*

[noi] siamo | Anna e Francesca, siamo italiane   *We are* | *Anna and Francesca, we are Italian*
            | Walter e Carlo, siamo italiani | *Walter and Carlo, we're Italian*

For the changes in the word **italiano**, see Systems, note 4, p. 79.

iv) Asking for things

If you ask for one thing, the key words are **un** or **una** *(a, an)* and **per favore** *(please)*.

Un biglietto, per favore   *A ticket, please*   Ecco **il** biglietto   *Here is the ticket*
Un cappuccino, per favore   *A cappuccino, please*   Ecco **il** cappuccino   *Here is the cappuccino*
Una guida, per favore   *A guide, please*   Ecco **la** guida   *Here is the guide*
Una birra, per favore   *A beer, please*   Ecco **la** birra   *Here is the beer*

If you ask for more than one of anything, the endings of the words change:

Due cappuccini, per favore.   Ecco **i** cappuccini
Due birre, per favore.   Ecco **le** birre

Accepting: if you want to say *'Yes, please'*, use **grazie** not **per favore**:
Sì, grazie   *Yes, please*

See Systems, p. 79 for: plurals (note 1); *the* – **il, i, la, le** (note 2); *a/an* – **un, una** (note 3).

Patterns I

v) Numbers

Below are the numbers 1–20. There is a complete list of numbers in Ref. I, 1, p. 239.

uno	due	tre	quattro	cinque	sei	sette	otto	nove	dieci	undici	dodici
1	2	3	4	5	6	7	8	9	10	11	12

tredici	quattordici	quindici	sedici	diciassette	diciotto	diciannove	venti
13	14	15	16	17	18	19	20

vi) Sound-systems: spelling and pronunciation

To help your pronunciation, irregular stress has been marked by a dot [See Patterns 2, note vi, p. 13]. It is not difficult to pronounce Italian and the spelling is quite easy because the same sounds are always spelt in the same way. Start by noticing the differences – and similarities – with respect to the English:

a) Sounds with 'c'
Ci and ce correspond to the English *ch* sound:

> ciao   cin-cin   Lancia   camicia *(shirt)*   cibo *(food)*   Masaccio
> piacere   Francesca   Botticelli   dolcelatte   cena *(supper)*

But c followed by any other vowel is a hard *k* sound as in English:

> caffè *(coffee)*   pesca   *(peach)*   camera *(room)*   scarpe *(shoes)*
> ecco   pecorino *(pecorino cheese)*   albicocca *(apricot)*
> cupola *(dome)*   cucina *(kitchen)*   cugino *(cousin)*

Beware: chi and che are always hard *k* sounds:

> Chianti   Pinocchio   De Chirico   macchina *(car)*   finocchio *(fennel)*   radicchio *(radicchio)*
> Michelangelo   Marche   *[Italian region]*

b) Sounds with 'g'
Gi and ge have a soft *j* sound:

> parmigiano   Giotto   giacca *(jacket)*   Genova   gelato *(ice-cream)*   generoso *(generous)*

But g followed by any other vowel is a hard *g* sound as in English:

> Galles *(Wales)*   garage *(garage)*   collega *(colleague)*
> gorgonzola   gonna *(skirt)*   Gucci   laguna *(lagoon)*   Liguria *[region]*

Beware: ghi and ghe are always hard *g* sounds:

> Lamborghini   Ghirlandaio   Inghilterra *(England)*   spaghetti   traghetto *(ferry)*

c) Sounds with 'gli'
This is a characteristically Italian sound. You don't pronounce the *g*: the sound is more like the beginning of the word liaison:

> Modigliani   tagliatelle   biglietto *(ticket)*   maglia *(jumper)*   famiglia *(family)*   figlio *(son)*

d) Sounds with 'bu' + vowel and 'gu' + vowel

Words with this spelling correspond to an English *bw* and *gw* sound:

buongiorno   **buo**no *(good)*   **gui**da *(guide)*   **gua**nti *(gloves)*   li**ngua** *(language, tongue)*

e) Sounds with 'w'

The letter *w* is not strictly speaking part of the Italian alphabet – along with *j k x* and *y*. These letters are found nowadays in words of foreign origin. *W* is pronounced like *v*, so that the *W* in **W**alter is pronounced like the *V* in **V**alentino. See also:

water *(toilet)*   **w**altzer *(waltz)*

But the words *weekend* and *whisky*, also used in Italian, are pronounced with the English *w* sound.

f) The 'z' sound

Z can be pronounced in two ways, *tz* or *dz*:
zz tends to have the *tz* sound:

Ma**zz**otti   pi**zz**a   pia**zz**a   mo**zz**arella   indiri**zz**o *(address)*   raga**zz**o/a *(boy/girl)*

But a single **z** can also be pronounced *tz*:

Gra**z**ie   stan**z**a *(room)*   pran**z**o *(lunch)*   Ti**z**iano *(Titian)*   La**z**io *[region]*   Sco**z**ia *(Scotland)*

Words with the **dz** sound include:

gorgon**z**ola   **z**an**z**ara *(mosquito)*   **z**ucchine *(courgettes)*

Words beginning with **z** tend to have the *dz* sound.

g) The 'f' sound

In Italian there is no equivalent of the English *ph* sound, hence the spelling of words like:

Ra**ff**aello *(Raphael)*   **f**otogra**f**ia *(photograph)*   tele**f**ono *(telephone)*

vii) The alphabet   🔲 💿 14

To pronounce this properly, listen to it on the cassette/CD and practise saying it out loud.

A	B	C	D	E	F	G	H	I	L		
a	bi	ci	di	e	effe	gi	acca	i	elle		
M	N	O	P	Q	R	S	T	U	V	Z	
emme	enne	o	pi	cu	erre	esse	ti	u	vu	zeta	

The 'missing' letters of the Italian alphabet are: J, known as **i lunga**; K – **cappa**; W – **doppio vu**; X – **eex**; Y – **ipsilon** or **i greca**. They exist in foreign words adopted in Italian: **jazz, karatè, whisky, yoga.**

The vowels are pronounced approximately as follows:

a as in *car*   **e** as in *bed*   **i** as in *bead*   **o** as in *got*   **u** as in *souvenir*

e and **o** can vary depending on spelling and regional accents.

Practice I

caffarel

Cioccolato d'Autore dal 1826

3

L'AMARO DI ERBE MEDICINALI
CHE IN PIU' AIUTA IL FEGATO.

1

2

4

5

Caffè Segafredo Zanetti. Calore di casa.

What's on offer?

Can you pronounce the words in these adverts?
Think about the **c**, the **g, gli, z** and **buo** sounds.

1 Amaro medicinale Giuliani. L'Amaro di erbe
 medicinali che in più aiuta il fegato.
2 Select. Fagioli borlotti. I buoni legumi.
3 Caffarel. Cioccolato d'Autore dal 1826.
4 Scavolini. La cucina più amata dagli italiani.
5 Segafredo Zanetti. Tradizione rossa. Caffè
 Segafredo Zanetti. Calore di casa.

Odd one out   8

Below are four sets of words. Practise reading each
word aloud. Can you find the odd one out each
time?

1 chianti   cinzano   cin cin   vodka
2 Lamborghini   Lancia   Olivetti   Ferrari
3 Tiziano   vermicelli   Botticelli   Caravaggio
4 gorgonzola   dolcelatte   dolcevita   mozzarella

Places

Look at the map. Fill in the names of the three countries you've come across so far in Patterns. What's missing? Unscramble the word below to find out.

D R A I N A L

Nationalities

Now say which of the four countries you come from, using **sono** and one of these nationalities:

scozzese, irlandese, inglese, gallese.

If none of these apply to you, look up Ref. III, 5, pp. 242–3, for more examples.

Spot the city

Here are some people and things associated with five famous Italian cities. Can you name them in Italian?

1 Il papa Michelangelo il Colosseo
2 I Medici Botticelli il Ponte Vecchio
3 Caravaggio Maradona la pizza
4 Il Doge Tiziano la gondola
5 Juventus Fiat *La Stampa*

Hello or goodbye?   8

Listen to the people on the cassette/CD. Are they saying hello or goodbye? Remember to listen for the intonation. Tick your answer on the chart.

	Hello	Goodbye
1 Buongiorno		
2 Buongiorno		
3 Ciao		
4 Ciao		
5 Arrivederci		

Buying breakfast 8

Now test yourself and do some talking. See if you can ask for what you want, not forgetting the words for please and thank you. It's early morning. You go to a **pasticceria** – a cake shop – to buy a cake, that's **una pasta**.

You	*[Say, 'Hello'.]*
Commessa	Buongiorno. Desidera?
You	*[Say, 'A cake please'.]*
Commessa	Sì. Va bene questa?
You	*[Say, 'Yes'.]*
Commessa	Ecco la pasta, due euro e venti.
You	*[Repeat the price to check you've understood and say, 'Thank you, goodbye'.]*

How many?

Look over the numbers in Patterns, p. 5. Then answer these questions in Italian.

1 How many wheels on a car?
2 How many fingers on a hand?
3 How many days in a week?
4 How many legs has a spider got?
5 How many lives does a cat have?
Now for some Biblical clues:
6 How many Wise Men were there?
7 How many Commandments are there?

Phone numbers

You have to give someone your phone number in Italian so you practise it in advance. Write it down and say it aloud in single digits (n.b. 0 = zero).

Ordering Drinks   8

There's a group of you in a bar. Can you order the drinks? It's early evening.

You	*[Say, 'Good evening'.]*
Cameriere	Buonasera.
You	*[Say, 'A coffee and three beers, please'.]*
Cameriere	Sì, subito.

[You've forgotten to order two cappuccinos. Wait until the waiter comes back . . .]

Cameriere	Ecco il caffè e le birre.
You	*[Say, 'Thank you, two cappuccinos, please'.]*
Cameriere	Subito.

Cultura e parole

Most people, whether they have studied Italian or not, know a few words of the language, from **pizza, spaghetti** and **cappuccino** to **dolce vita** and **così fan tutte**. Italy and its language, however, are deceptively familiar. The stereotypes and images – **immagini** – tell us little about this varied and surprising country.

Bilingual signposts in the Alto Adige region

Italy has an ancient and influential civilisation and yet as a nation it is a relative newcomer – until 1861 it was a collection of separate states with individual traditions and cultures. This in part helps to explain Italy's **plurilinguismo** – its multilingualism. When Italy became a single nation it is estimated that only 2.5 per cent of the population spoke Italian as their mother tongue – **la lingua madre**. Even the new king, Vittorio Emanuele II, and the Prime Minister, Conte Camillo Cavour, were more at ease in French or Piemontese. Written Italian has existed for centuries – its foundations were laid by the poet Dante Alighieri in the early 14th century – and yet it was only spoken by a minority until the advent of television and mass education in the 1950s. At that time only about a third of Italians spoke it as their mother tongue. The other two thirds spoke various dialects – **i dialetti** – or even minority languages – **le lingue minoritarie** – at home and among friends, and used Italian in more formal situations. In many cases these dialects and languages were, and still are, very different from one another and from standard written Italian.

Nowadays, of course, **l'italiano standard** – standard Italian – is spoken by the overwhelming majority of people, but the dialects and minority languages have not died out. On the contrary, they can be heard on local radio or accessed on the websites developed by their supporters, who have conducted a longstanding campaign to improve their legal standing. Some five per cent of Italians still do not speak Italian as their mother tongue, while about two thirds are bilingual – **bilingue** – in Italian and a dialect or another language.

Since 1948 these minority languages have been protected by article 6 of the Italian Constitution. They include: Albanese, Catalan, Greek, Slovene, Croat, Franco-Provençal, Friulian, Ladino and Sardinian. French and German are especially protected, French in the Val d'Aosta region and German in the Bolzano province of the Alto Adige, where they are official languages together with Italian. In 1999 a new law – **la legge 482** – was passed to strengthen this protection. For the first time the minorities were all named and referred to as **popolazioni,** while provision for teaching minority languages in local schools was also mentioned. So far, however, the full implementation of the new law is still being discussed.

Mi contenti	**Mi accontento**
Ta la sera ruda di Sàbida	Nella nuda sera del Sabato
mi contenti di jodi la int,	Mi accontento di guardare la gente
fôr di ciasa ch'a rit ta l'aria	Chi ride fuori di casa nell'aria
Encia il me côr al è di aria	Anche il mio cuore è di aria
E tai me vuj a rit la int	E nei miei occhi ride la gente
E tai me ris a è lus di Sàbida ...	E nei miei ricci è la luce del Sabato ...

Part of a poem by Pier Paolo Pasolini in Friulian (left) with an Italian translation (right)

Interactions

7   🔳 💿 9

In the Italia in Miniatura park, Anna gets a preview of some of the places she'll be visiting in the series.

First time round

> i Trulli   *ancient conical houses*

Before listening, study the map of the regions on p. ix. Now listen without the text.

How many towns and regions can you spot?

È un monumento famoso. È il duomo di Firenze.
Questi sono i Trulli di Alberobello **in Puglia**.
Questo è un villaggio alpino.
Qui siamo **a Bologna in Emilia Romagna**.

qui   *here*

Key phrases

è	*it is*
questi sono	*these are*
questo è	*this is*
in Puglia,	*in Puglia,*
Emilia Romagna	*Emilia Romagna*
a Bologna	*in Bologna*

---

8   🔳 💿 10

In L'Italia in Miniatura Anna spots two of the sights you can see in Rome.

First time round

How can you tell Anna is asking questions and not making statements?

È la basilica di San Pietro?
È il Colosseo?

Key phrase

è . . .?	*is it . . .?*

9   🔳 💿 11

Anna goes to buy some postcards of Portofino: she ends up with pictures of the neighbouring village. San Fruttuoso.

First time round

> le cartoline   *postcards*

Apart from asking for the postcards, what else does Anna ask?

Anna	Buongiorno.
Signora	Buongiorno.
Anna	Queste cartoline . . .
Signora	**Sì**, va bene.
Anna	**Questo è** Portofino? *[she points to a postcard]*
Signora	**No, questo non è** Portofino, è San Fruttuoso.

va bene   *fine*

Key phrases

sì	*yes*
questo è . . .?	*is this . . .?*
no, questo non è	*no, it isn't*

10   🔲   📀   12

Anna chooses an ice-cream in a **gelateria** – an ice-cream shop.

First time round

un gelato	*ice-cream*
il cono	*cone*
cocco	*coconut*

What flavours does Anna choose?

Giovane	**Buonasera.**
Anna	Buonasera. Un gelato, per favore.
Giovane	Sì – il cono?
Anna	Sì, grazie. E, questo è cioccolato?
Giovane	*[pointing to another container].* No, questo è cioccolato e questo è cioccolato bianco.
Anna	Ah, allora, cioccolato e cocco.
Giovane	Sì.
Anna	Grazie. **Buonasera.**
Giovane	Buonasera.

allora   *then*

Key phrase

buonasera   *(1) good afternoon*
                     (2) goodbye

II   🔲   📀   13

The scene is a bar in Florence. Anna's friend, Gianna, wants a quick lunch, **un panino** – a roll, and **una pizzetta** – a mini pizza. She also wants an expresso – **un caffè**. First she needs to place her order and pay at the till.

First time round

prosciutto	*ham*
formaggio	*cheese*

a What does the woman at the till say when Gianna thanks her?
b What does the barman ask to find out what Gianna wants?

Gianna	Un panino, una pizzetta e un caffè, per favore.
Cassiera	Un panino, una pizzetta e un caffè… , sono sette euro.
Gianna	Ecco a Lei. *[Gianna hands her a ten euro note.]*
Cassiera	Tre euro di resto, grazie a Lei. *[She hands Gianna the receipt and then the change.]*
Gianna	Grazie.
Cassiera	**Prego**.
	[Gianna goes to the counter and holds out her receipt.]
Barista	**Prego?**
Gianna	Un panino, una pizzetta e un caffè.
Barista	Un panino con prosciutto o con formaggio?
Gianna	Con formaggio per piacere.
Barista	Va bene. Allora … un panino, una pizzetta e … un caffè.
Gianna	Grazie.
Barista	**Prego**.

Key phrases

prego	*don't mention it*
prego?	*what will you have?*

Patterns 2

i) This is a ..., these are ...

The key word is **questo**, and the key verb **essere** *(to be)* [Systems, note 6, p. 80].

quest**o** è	**un** monument**o** famos**o**	*this is*	*a famous monument*
	un quadr**o** famos**o**		*a famous picture*
quest**a** è	**una** chies**a** famos**a**	*this is*	*a famous church*
	una cappell**a** famos**a**		*a famous chapel*

quest**i** sono monument**i** famos**i**	*these are*	*famous monuments*
quest**e** sono chies**e** famos**e**		*famous churches*

See Systems, notes 4 and 5, pp. 79 and 80 for the changes in the endings of the words.

ii) It is a ..., they are (the) ...

There is no word used for *it* or *they*: the verb is sufficient. [See Systems, notes 2 and 3, p. 79 for **un, una; il, i, la, le**]

È un disegno meraviglioso	*It's a marvellous drawing*
È il capolavoro di Leonardo da Vinci	*It's Leonardo da Vinci's masterpiece*

Sono cappelle meravigliose	*They are marvellous chapels*
Sono le Cappelle Medịcee	*They are the Medici Chapels*

iii) Asking and answering questions

When you ask a question the word order doesn't change, but the intonation often does. Practise your intonation with these examples:

Questo è il treno per Nạpoli?	*Is this the train for Naples?*
Sì, è il treno per Nạpoli	*Yes, it's the train for Naples*
No, non è il treno per Nạpoli	*No, it's not the train for Naples*

Questa è la strada per Firenze?	*Is this the road for Florence?*
No, non è la strada per Firenze	*No, it's not the road for Florence*

iv) Saying where you are

The key words are **in** and **a**: **a** is for towns, **in** for countries and regions. The other expressions are best learned gradually.

Sono/siamo a	Bologna	*I am, we are in*	*Bologna*
	casa	*at*	*home*
	scuola		*school*
Sono/siamo in	Itạlia	*I am/we are in*	*Italy*
	Inghilterra		*England*
	biblioteca		*the library*
	bagno		*the bathroom*
	cucina		*the kitchen*
	giardino		*the garden*
	piscina	*at*	*the swimming-pool*

See Systems, note 8 ii, p. 80.

Patterns 2

v) Sound-systems

a) The -gn- sound
This is pronounced like the beginning of the word 'new' in English. It's a familiar sound if you are in the habit of eating lasa**gn**e!

> Bolo**gn**a   Emilia Roma**gn**a   Gran Breta**gn**a (*Great Britain*)
> si**gn**ore (*Mr/man*)   si**gn**ora (*Mrs/lady*)   si**gn**orina (*Miss/young lady*)
> Mante**gn**a   monta**gn**a (*mountain*)   ba**gn**o (*bathroom*)

b) 'qu' + vowel, 'du' + vowel
As with **bu** and **gu** + vowels, you make a *w* sound – *kw* and *dw*:

> **que**sto (*this*)   **qua**dro (*picture*)   **qui** (*here*)   **duo**mo (*cathedral*)

The same applies to most words where **u** + another vowel follow a consonant:
> s**cuo**la (*school*)   **fuo**co (*fire*)   l**uo**go (*place*)   **nuo**vo (*new*)   s**uo**no (*sound*)   **vuo**to (*empty*)

c) 'Sci', 'sce': the -sh- sound
This is easy to pronounce, but confusing on paper.

> pro**sci**utto (*ham*)   pi**sci**na (*swimming-pool*)   **sci**arpa (*scarf*)   cu**sci**no (*cushion*)
> pe**sce** (*fish*)   **sce**lta (*choice*)   **sce**na (*scene*)

Beware: **schi** and **sche** are hard *sk* sounds:

> **sche**rzo (*joke*)   **sche**letro (*skeleton*)   **schi**fo (*disgust*)   ri**schi**o (*risk*)   **schi**ena (*back*)

d) Double consonants
In Italian double consonants should be stressed more than single consonants, which is not always easy for foreigners. Sometimes, though, the difference is easy to make clear:

> ro**ss**a (*red*)   rosa (*pink*)   ca**ss**a (*till*)   casa (*house*)

The single **s** in the middle of words is pronounced like an English *z*. But with other double consonants it's less straightforward. The important thing is to listen and you'll get the hang of it. A double consonant means the vowel sound is shorter and more open than with single consonants.

> pro**sci**utto (*ham*)   conosciuto (*well-known*)   se**rr**a (*greenhouse*)   sera (*evening*)
> se**tt**e (*seven*)   sete (*thirst*)   so**nn**o (*sleep*)   sono (*I am*)

vi) Stress patterns

In most words the stress occurs on the last vowel but one. But many common words are exceptions:

> telefono   camera   numero   macchina

The stress falls on the end of a word where there is an accent: città (*town*)   nazionalità (*nationality*)
If a word ends in two vowels the stress pattern varies:

> Lucia   Lombardia   Lucio   Liguria

You'll find irregular or difficult stress patterns marked in the vocabularies at the end of the units and in the Lexis at the back of the book.

Practice 2

Regions

Look at the map of Italy on p. ix with the twenty regions marked. Try to pronounce them. Be careful with the ones ending in **-ia**. Only one has the stress on the final **-i** – Lombardia. Read them aloud.

Where?

Can you say where you are, using **in** or **a** as appropriate?
e.g. [giardino]   Sono in giardino.

1 [bagno]   **2** [cucina]   **3** [casa]
4 [biblioteca]   **5** [scuola]

What's this?

Imagine you are teaching some new vocabulary to a child. You've come across all the words you need in this unit. You'll need to decide which form of **questo** to use.
e.g.   Questo è ...
        Questa è una birra.

What are these?

Make the above sentences plural, using **questi** or **queste**.
Now practise saying these sentences as questions. Don't change anything except the intonation.

Buying an ice-cream   14

Listen to the cassette/CD and play your part in the conversation.

Whet your appetite!

Which Italian dish do you think you would prefer? Read through the ingredients given below. Try and pronounce each item and then make your choice. The Vocabulary on p. 15 will help, but you don't need to understand every word.

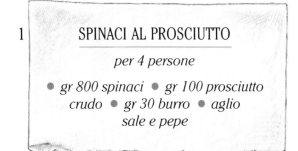

1
SPINACI AL PROSCIUTTO
per 4 persone

● *gr 800 spinaci* ● *gr 100 prosciutto crudo* ● *gr 30 burro* ● *aglio*
sale e pepe

2
AGNELLO IN SALSA
per 6 persone

● *kg.1 agnello* ● *gr. 350 pomodori maturi* ● *aglio, prezzemolo, maggiorana* ● *vino bianco secco* ● *strutto*
sale e pepe

What's in a name?

Here are the surnames of some well-known Italians:
Marconi   Mussolini   Pavarotti   Ferrari

1 Here, in the wrong order, are their first names:
Benito   Enzo   Guglielmo   Luciano
Can you match them up with their surnames?
2 What do you associate each of them with?
a) la lirica   b) la radio   c) la macchina   d) il fascismo
3 These people all have something in common. Do you happen to know what it is?

Identikit   ⌈c̄c̄⌉ ◎ 14

Listen to the cassette/CD and the sounds of the Italian alphabet.
Can you say who you are? Start with **Sono** ...
Now give your nationality. **Sono** ...
Try and spell your surname.
Next give your phone number ...

Vocabulary

Food

il cibo	food
l'agnello	lamb
la bistecca	steak
il pollo	chicken
il prosciutto	ham
la salsiccia	sausage
il vitello	veal
il formaggio	cheese
la verdura	vegetables
l'aglio	garlic
il basilico	basil
la carota	carrot
la cipolla	onion
i fagiolini	green beans
il finocchio	fennel
i funghi	mushrooms
la patata	potato
il pomodoro	tomato
il prezzemolo	parsley
il radicchio	radicchio
le zucchine	courgettes
gli spinaci	spinach
i fagioli	dried beans
la frutta	fruit
la banana	banana
la mela	apple
la pera	pear
la pesca	peach
il gelato	ice-cream
la panna	cream

il finocchio

la cipolla

il radicchio

la cappella

Places

il luogo	place
il posto	place
la biblioteca	library
la cappella	chapel
la casa	house, home
la città	town, city
la chiesa	church
il duomo	cathedral
il giardino	garden
il parco	park
la piscina	swimming-pool
la scuola	school

Meals

il pasto	meal
la prima colazione	breakfast
il pranzo	lunch
la cena	supper, dinner

Drinks

la bevanda	drink
la birra	beer
analcolico	non-alcoholic
il caffè	coffee
il cappuccino	cappuccino
il tè	tea
il vino	wine

People

la persona	person
il bambino [m]	child, baby
la bambina [f]	child, baby
il cameriere	waiter
la commessa	shop assistant
la donna	woman
la signora	Mrs, lady
il figlio	son
la figlia	daughter
i figli	children
il giovane	young man
il ragazzo	boy
la ragazza	girl
l'uomo	man
gli uomini	men

Everyday objects

la borsa	bag
il libro	book
la macchina	car
la matita	pencil
la penna	pen
il portafoglio	wallet
il taccuino	notebook
il quaderno	exercise-book

Rooms

la stanza	room
il bagno	bathroom
la camera da letto	bedroom
la cucina	kitchen
la sala da pranzo	dining-room
il salotto	sitting-room

Adjectives

buono	good
bello	beautiful
meraviglioso	marvellous, wonderful
nuovo	new
vecchio	old
antico	old, ancient
fresco	fresh
lungo	long
stanco	tired
pronto	ready
caldo	hot
freddo	cold

Troubleshooting

Culinary confusion

In most languages there are words with several meanings. In Italian this is especially true when it comes to food.

Don't confuse the following:

la pasta	*pasta/small cake*

il pasto	*meal*

Tongue-twisters   14

Try pronouncing the Italian word for *tongue-twister*.

Scioglilingua

Now try pronouncing this well-known Italian tongue-twister. It means, *'Thirty-three people from Trento entered Trento all thirty-three on the trot!'*

Trentatré trentini entrarono dentro Trento tutti e trentatré trotterellando.

Sound systems

Can you make the difference between *supper, scene* and *back* clear?

cena	scena	schiena
CH	SH	SK

Unità 2

In famiglia e fra amici
Meeting family and friends

Una famiglia italiana a pranzo

Part 1 (Interactions 1–3, Patterns 1, Practice 1)	**Part 2** (Interactions 4–8, Patterns 2, Practice 2)
Learn how to: Ask where something or someone is Ask what something is Ask who someone is Ask a person their name and say what you're called Find out what's available	*Learn how to:* Introduce friends and family Ask and say what objects are called Ask someone what they are doing Say what you are doing Say where you live

Grammar	
Nouns and adjectives ending in **-e** Articles **l'** and **un'** **il mio, il tuo, il suo** – *my*, *your*, *his/her/its* **c'è, ci sono** – *there is, there are*	**dove? chi? che cosa? come?** – *where? who? what? how?* **-are** and **-ere** verbs, present tense **-are** reflexive verbs: **chiamarsi** Using **tu, lei, voi**, the right word for *you*

Want to take it further?
Grammar: see Systems 2, pp. 82–5   *More practice:* do Reinforcement 2, p. 86

Interactions

 16

Valentino Muratori, a financial consultant by profession, owns a small vineyard in the Colli Albani hills, not far from Rome. At harvest time his family and friends turn their hands to the picking and get invited to a picnic lunch. In his villa Valentino sorts out the provisions with his wife, Valentina, and a friend, Rossella.

First time round

Pick out the four items of food and drink being discussed.

Valentino	Tesoro, **dove sono** le bottiglie di vino?
Valentina	Sono qui.
Rossella	E qui cosa c'è?
Valentina	**C'è** il pane.
Rossella	La pasta, **dov'è**, Valentina?
Valentina	È qui. **Ecco** la pasta.
Valentino	**Cos'è questo?**
Rossella	È il caffè, Valentino.
Valentino	Allora, c'è tutto. Possiamo andare?
Valentina	Andiamo.

e qui cosa c'è?	*and what's this here? (lit. here what is there?)*
c'è tutto	*that (there)'s everything*
possiamo andare?	*can we go?*
andiamo	*let's go*

Key phrases

dove sono?	*where are?*
c'è	*there is*
dov'è?	*where is?*
ecco	*here is*
cos'è questo?	*what is this?*

Dov'è, dove sono? 16

Listen to the cassette/CD and ask where certain things are.

18

2   17

Anna greets Valentino Muratori in the vineyard as the grape-picking gets under way.

First time round

molto lavoro	*a lot of work*
oggi	*today*
sua moglie	*your wife*

What two things does Anna want to know?

Anna	Buongiorno, signor Muratori.
Valentino	Buongiorno, Anna.
Anna	**C'è** molto lavoro oggi?
Valentino	Sì, moltissimo.
Anna	E sua moglie, dov'è?
Valentino	Mia moglie è là.

là   *over there*

> **Key phrase**
>
> **c'è?**   *is there?*

3   18

In the vineyard Anna meets some of the grape-pickers. She introduces herself and talks to four girls.

First time round

| mia sorella | *my sister* |
| una mia amica | *a friend of mine* |

a Can you spot how to say 'My name is'?
b Pick out their names.

Anna	Ciao!
Daniela	Ciao!
Anna	Io **mi chiamo** Anna. Tu, **come ti chiami?**
Daniela	Io mi chiamo Daniela.
Anna	E **lei, chi è?**
Daniela	Questa è mia sorella.
Anna	Ciao! Tu, come ti chiami?
Rosanna	Mi chiamo Rosanna.
Anna	Lei, **come si chiama?**
Cristina	Io mi chiamo Cristina e lei è Eliana, una mia amica.
Eliana	Piacere!

> **Key phrases**
>
> | **mi chiamo** | *I'm called* |
> | **come ti chiami?** | *what are you called?* |
> | **lei, chi è?** | *who is she?* |
> | **come si chiama?** | *what are you called? [formal 'Lei' form]* |

Phone-in   19

Can you spot the names of the callers to a radio phone-in programme and also where they are ringing from?

Patterns I

i) Naming yourself and others

To say *'My name is'* you use the verb **chiamarsi** *(to be called, lit. to call oneself)*.

> [Io]. mi chiamo ... Anna   *My name is Anna*

When you ask someone their name it's literally *'How do you call yourself?'* [**Come** means *how*].

> [Tu,] come ti chiami?   *what's your name? [informal]*
> [Lei,] come si chiama?   *what's your name? [formal]*
> [Voi,] come vi chiamate?   *what's your name? [plural]*

If you've already introduced yourself you don't need to ask the full question to find out what someone else is called. **E tu? E Lei? E voi?** *(lit. and you?)* is sufficient.

Io mi chiamo	Anna, e tu?	My name is	Anna, what about you?
	Gianni, e Lei?		Gianni, what about you?
	Rosanna, e voi?		Rosanna, what about you?

See Systems, note 6 ii, p. 85 for **chiamarsi**.

ii) Identifying people

The key word is **chi?** *(who)*.

Chi è?	*Who is it?*	È	mio fratello/mia sorella	*It's*	*my brother/sister*
			mio cognato/mia cognata		*my brother-/sister-in-law*
			mio figlio/mia figlia		*my son/daughter*
			mio marito/mia moglie		*my husband/wife*
			mio padre/mia madre		*my father/mother*
			mio suocero/mia suocera		*my father-/mother-in-law*

See Systems, note 3, p. 84 for **mio, mia**.

Chi è?	*Who is it?*	Sono io	*It's me*	Siamo noi	*It's us*
		È lui, è lei	*It's him, her*	Sono loro	*It's them*

iii) Identifying objects

The key phrase is **che cosa?** *(what?)*. This literally means *what thing?* **Cosa** is often used on its own, without **che**. In front of **è, cosa** becomes **che cos'è** and is pronounced as one word.

[Che] cos'è?	*What is it?*	È	un digestivo	*It's*	*an after-dinner drink*
			un dolce		*a dessert*
			una macedonia		*a fruit salad*
			un' insalata		*a salad*

[Che] cosa sono?	*What are they?*		digestivi	*They're*	*after-dinner drinks*
		Sono	dolci		*desserts*
			macedonie		*fruit salads*
			insalate		*salads*

Patterns I

iv) Asking and saying where things are

The key words are **dove?** *(where?)* and **ecco** *(here is, here are).*

In front of **è, dove** becomes **dov'è** and is pronounced as one word.

Dov'è	il libro?	*Where is*	the book?	Ecco il libro	*Here is the book*
	il giornale?		the newspaper?		
	la bottiglia?		the bottle?		
	la chiave?		the key?		
	l'aranciata?		the orangeade?		

Dove sono	i libri?	*Where are*	the books	Ecco i libri	*Here are the books*
	i giornali?		the newspapers?		
	le bottiglie?		the bottles?		
	le chiavi?		the keys?		
	le aranciate?		the orangeades?		

See Systems, note 1 ii, p. 83 for singular endings in **-e** and **l', un'**.

v) Describing what there is

The key phrases are **c'è** (there is) and **ci sono** (there are).
In front of **è, ci** becomes **c'è** and is pronounced as one word.
You can use **c'è** and **ci sono** for describing:

C'è	il bagno	*There is*	the bathroom
	la cucina		the kitchen

Ci sono	i coltelli	*There are*	the knives
	le forchette		the forks

vi) Making enquiries

You can turn **c'è** and **ci sono** into questions to make enquiries:

C'è	una banca qui vicino?	*Is there*	a bank near here?
	una farmacia qui vicino?		a chemist's near here?

Ci sono	ristoranti buoni qui?	*Are there*	good restaurants here?
	trattorie buone qui?		good trattorias here?

vii) Finding out what's available

If you add **[che] cosa,** to **c'è** and **ci sono**, you can find out what's available, in a restaurant, for example:

Oggi, che cosa c'è? *What is there today?*
C'è la minestra casalinga e il risotto *There is home-made minestra and risotto.*
Ci sono fettuccine e lasagne *There are fettuccine and lasagne.*

Practice I

What's your name?

Using the clues given in the answers, choose the right question form to ask the following people their names.

1 – Ciao, mi chiamo Nicola.
2 – Buongiorno, piacere, mi chiamo Aldo Bernini.
3 – Io mi chiamo Carla e lei si chiama Rosanna.

What about you?

Now introduce yourself to each of the following people, and then find out what they're called.

1 You meet someone older than yourself on a train.
2 You're at a party given by old friends and meet their young nephew.
3 You come across a young couple in a bar.

Who is it?

Look at the family tree and read the statements made by five of its members. They're all talking about the same person: who is it? – **Chi è?** Check in Patterns 2, note ii, on p. 20 if you've forgotten a word.

Angela	X è mio figlio.
Marco	X è mio padre.
Maria	X è mio fratello.
Giovanni	X è mio cognato.
Bianca	X è il fratello di mio padre.

Spot the relations

Below are all the names of the Cicognani family. Reading downwards, can you discover the words for father-in-law and aunt?

S U S A N N A	P A T R I Z I O
L U C I A	M A R I A
M A R C O	B I A N C A
G I A N C A R L O	
A N G E L A	
B A R B A R A	
G I O V A N N I	

Now try to use each word in a sentence.

Guess who?

Can you identify four other members of the Cicognani family from what they say about themselves? Use the family tree.

1 Io sono la sorella di Marco e la figlia di Patrizio e Susanna. Chi sono?
2 Io sono la madre di Barbara e Angela e la moglie di Giovanni. Chi sono?
3 Io sono il figlio di Giovanni e Angela e il marito di Susanna. Chi sono?
4 Io sono il cognato di Giancarlo e il padre di Barbara e Angela. Chi sono?

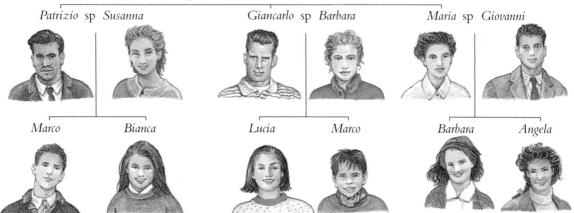

FAMIGLIA CICOGNANI

Giovanni sposato con *Angela*

Patrizio sp *Susanna*   *Giancarlo* sp *Barbara*   *Maria* sp *Giovanni*

Marco   *Bianca*   *Lucia*   *Marco*   *Barbara*   *Angela*

What's in it? 19

You've made a wonderful salad and your friend asks you what's in it – **che cosa c'è dentro?** Reply using the recorded cues.

Amico È buona quest'insalata. Che cosa c'è dentro?
You [*Tell him there are tomatoes.*]
Amico E poi, che altro?
You [*Say there's mozzarella.*]
Amico E il basilico, c'è?
You [*Tell him, yes, there's basil.*]

Looking for the bank 19

Listen to the cassette/CD and practise asking for some useful places.

House with all amenities

You are an estate agent trying to sell a house. During the visit to the house your client wants to know what amenities there are in the district. You tell him, picking your adjectives carefully from the list below. You've certainly got all the answers!
e.g. C'è una scuola qui vicino?
    Sì, c'è una scuola nuova.

1	C'è un parco qui vicino?	*vecchio*
2	C'è una piscina qui vicino?	*nuovo*
3	C'è una chiesa qui vicino?	*grande*
4	C'è una trattoria qui vicino?	*piccolo*
		bello

Now can you say what amenities you have in your area?

What's on today? 19

You're in a small family trattoria in the Lazio region. There's no menu, so talk to the owner and sort out what you're going to eat.

Il primo *(first course)*

Padrone Buongiorno.
You [*Say hello and ask him what there is today.*]
Padrone Oggi, per primo c'è la stracciatella e ci sono spaghetti all'amatriciana.
You [*Ask what stracciatella is*]
Padrone La stracciatella è una minestra in brodo con uova sbattute e formaggio.
You [*A clear soup with beaten egg, mmm. What about the spaghetti all'amatriciana; ask what that is.*]
Padrone È un piatto di spaghetti con pomodoro, vino bianco e peperoncino.
You [*Order spaghetti. Say, 'the spaghetti, please'.*] .
Padrone Va bene.

Il secondo *(main course)*

Padrone Per secondo c'è il pollo arrosto e ci sono i saltimbocca di vitello.
You [*Chicken or veal? Order the chicken.*]

Home cooking

Look at this advertisement for a family cookery book and answer the questions. Try and use guesswork rather than look words up.

1 The title of the book includes a member of the family: which one?
2 What do you think the sentence beginning 'Ecco . . .' might mean, roughly?
3 How many colour photographs are there?
4 How many pages are there?
5 How many recipes are there?

Cultura e parole

When parents register the name of their new-born baby in the registry office – **l'anagrafe** – they can call their child anything they like: there was a brief period under Mussolini when foreign names, or names deemed 'irreligious, ridiculous or subversive', were banned. Yet Italy has a tradition of foreign or politically-inspired names: Mussolini himself was named by his anarchist-republican father after Benito Juarez, a Mexican president; while in his native Romagna, names like Napoleone, Bruto, Spartaco or even Anarchico were not unknown! There are many ordinary names, however, which to a foreigner can cause confusion: these are the common boys' names ending in **-a**: Andrea; Battista; Gianmaria; Luca and Nicola. The last is especially confusing, as the stress comes on the **o**, not the **i**.

Universale Economica Feltrinelli

GAVINO LEDDA
PADRE PADRONE
L'educazione di un pastore

The closeness of the Italian family is proverbial and the excessively close attachment which can exist between mother and son has given rise to the derogatory term **mammismo**, for which there is no simple direct equivalent in English. However, the term **figli di papà**, which describes pampered children with no need to earn their living, is fairly easily recognisable as 'Daddy's boys'. But are all Italian children really spoilt? Not judging by recent statistics, which suggest that child abuse is as common in Italy as in Britain. And this is not a new trend. The existence even today in the Italian language of the term **padre-padrone** – 'father-owner' would point to that. It was coined and much used to describe the absolute legal power of the father over his children until the changes made in 1975 when the **Diritto di famiglia** came into force.

This law abolished the legal domination of men both inside and outside the home, giving partners in a marriage equal economic and legal rights. Divorce – **il divorzio** – was legalised in 1978 and abortion – **l'aborto** – in 1980. Since 2001, fathers as well as mothers are entitled to maternity and paternity leave – **il congedo di maternità e di paternità**, and **l'assegno di maternità** – a maternity grant – is payable to all mothers. With one of the lowest birth rates in the world, Italy now has very small families, but this does not make them less important. Despite the advent of a welfare state there remains an historic mistrust of the state and a reliance on the family structure as the pivot of society. There is truth in what the writer Leonardo Sciascia once said, namely that Italy is not so much a nation as a collection of families.

Interactions

4 [cc] [CD] 20

After the morning's grape-picking, Anna joins the guests at the picnic lunch inside the Muratori's chalet. She asks them what they're eating and drinking.

First time round

la torta	cake

Can you pick out how Anna asks the questions:
a What are you eating?
b What are you drinking?

Anna	**Cosa mangi?**
Ragazza	Mangio pane e formaggio.
Anna	Signora, **cosa mangia?**
Signora 1	Mangio torta di cioccolato e torta di crema.
Anna	**Cosa beve?**
Signora 2	Bevo acqua.
Anna	Signor Antonio, cosa beve?
Sig. Antonio	Bevo vino. Salute!
Anna	Cosa beve?
Uomo	Bevo caffè.

Salute! *to your health, cheers!*

Key phrases

cosa mangi?	*what are you eating?*
cosa mangia?	*what are you eating? [formal]*
cosa beve?	*what are you drinking? [formal]*

5 [cc] [CD] 21

Anna visits the local wine-making firm – **azienda vinicola** – and meets some pupils and teachers on a tour.

First time round

un po'	*a little*
qualche volta	*sometimes*

Anna is curious to know:
Do Lorenzo and Maria both drink wine?

Anna	Ciao!
Lorenzo	Ciao!
Anna	**Bevi vino?**
Lorenzo	Sì, un po' con l'acqua.
Anna	E come ti chiami?
Lorenzo	Mi chiamo Lorenzo e **questa è la mia maestra**.
Anna	Signora, Lei, come si chiama?
Maria	Mi chiamo Maria.
Anna	E **beve vino?**
Maria	Sì, qualche volta.

Key phrases

bevi vino?	*do you drink wine?*
beve vino?	*do you drink wine? [formal]*
questa è la mia maestra	*this is my teacher*

This is ... [cc] [CD] 21

Listen to the cassette/CD and see if you can understand who is being introduced.

6 [cc] [CD] 22

The wine factory is called the Cantine San Marco – the San Marco cellars. The co-owners, Signor Notarnicola and Signor Violo, greet Anna.

First time round

che tipo di?	*what kind of?*
il proprietario	*owner*
questa azienda	*this firm*

a What are the owners' first names?
b What type of wine does the San Marco firm produce?

Anna	Buongiorno.
Sig. Not.	Buongiorno a Lei.
Anna	Lei, come si chiama?
Sig. Not.	Umberto Notarnicola e sono il proprietario delle Cantine San Marco.
Anna	Che tipo di vino produce quest'azienda?
Sig. Not.	Quest'azienda produce un vino bianco e **si chiama Frascati DOC**.

[...]

Anna	Lei come si chiama?
Sig. Violo	Mi chiamo Bruno Violo e **sono anch'io** un proprietario di quest'azienda vinicola.
Anna	Questa macchina lava le bottiglie?
Sig. Violo	Sì, questa macchina lava le bottiglie e poi con un'altra macchina mettiamo il vino in bottiglia.

e questa macchina?	*and what about this machine?*
poi	*then*

Key phrases

si chiama Frascati DOC	*it's called Frascati DOC*
sono anch'io ...	*I'm also...*

7 ⌷ ◉ 23

The grape harvest is celebrated in the nearby town of Marino with a parade in Renaissance dress and the colourful costumes of the medieval guilds – **le Arti**.

portare	*to wear*
la gonna	*skirt*
il vestito	*costume, dress*

Anna speaks to a mother who introduces her little girl and to two young men.

One of the costumes is black and white. What's that in Italian?

[...]

Signora	**Questa è Silvia.**
Anna	Ciao Silvia.
Silvia	Ciao!
Anna	**Che cosa porti?**
Silvia	Un costume tradizionale di Marino, bianco e nero con la gonna a fiori.
Anna	Grazie.
[Anna	**Che cosa porta?**]
Signore	Porto il vestito verde dell'Arte dei Vascellari.
Uomo a cavallo	Porto un costume rinascimentale rosso e giallo.

l'Arte dei Vascellari	*the Vatmakers' Guild*
a fiori	*flowered*

Key phrases

questa è Silvia	*this is Silvia*
che cosa porti?	*what are you wearing?*
che cosa porta?	*what are you wearing? [formal]*

8 ⌷ ◉ 24

Finally, watching the parade, Anna comes across Stefano, his wife Stefania, and another person.

First time round

la figlia *daughter*	Who is she and what is she doing?

Anna	Buonasera.
Stefano	Buonasera.
Anna	Lei come si chiama?
Stefano	Stefano Bucciarelli e **questa è mia moglie.**
Anna	**Piacere.**
Stefania	**Piacere.**
Anna	Lei come si chiama?
Stefania	Io mio chiamo Stefania Vizzuti e **questa è mia figlia.**
Anna	Ciao!
Valentina	Ciao!
Anna	Come ti chiami?
Valentina	Valentina.
Anna	E cosa mangi?
Valentina	Un gelato.

Key phrases

questa è mia moglie	*this is my wife*
piacere	*how do you do?*
questa è mia figlia	*this is my daughter*

Photo call ⌷ ◉ 25

Listen and introduce various members of your family.

Patterns 2

i) Introductions

A simple way of introducing someone is to use **questa** and **questo**:

Questa è	Silvia	*This is*	*Silvia*
	mia moglie		*my wife*
	la mia vicina		*my neighbour*

Questo è	Lorenzo	*This is*	*Lorenzo*
	mio marito		*my husband*
	il mio vicino		*my neighbour*

Questa è la mia amica Paola e questo è suo cugino Marco   *This is my friend Paola and this is her cousin Marco*

Questo è il mio amico Sandro e questa è sua cugina Ida   *This is my friend Sandro and this is his cousin Ida*

For more on **mio, suo, mia, sua** see Systems, note 3, p. 84.

ii) Finding out what things are called

The key verb is **chiamarsi** *(to be called)*. [See Systems, note 6 ii, p. 85.]

Come si chiama il vino? Si chiama Frascati DOC.   *What's the wine called? It's called Frascati DOC*

Questo, come si chiama?   *What's this called?*
Questa si chiama zuppa inglese, è un dolce   *This is called trifle, it's a dessert*

Questi, come si chiamano?   *What are these called?*
Questi si chiamano crostini, sono antipasti   *These are called crostini, they're starters*

iii) What you are doing and what you do

To find out what people are up to, the key phrase is [**che**] **cosa?** Put this before the verb.

Che cosa	mangi? [tu]	*What are you eating?/what do you eat?*
	mangia? [Lei]	
	mangiate? [voi]	

Mangio	bruschetta	*I am eating/I eat*	bruschetta [garlic bread]
Mangiamo	torta	*We are eating/we eat*	cake

Some verbs have slightly different patterns:

Che cosa	bevi? [tu]	*What are you drinking?/do you drink?*
	beve? [Lei]	
	bevete? [voi]	

Bevo	vino	*I'm drinking/I drink*	wine
Beviamo	acqua	*We're drinking/we drink*	water

See Systems, notes 6 and 7, p. 84 and p. 85 for more on verbs.

The three forms of *you*:

Tu is informal. It's used with children and people you know well.
Lei is formal. It's used with people you don't know well.
Voi is used to talk to more than one person.

iv) Identifying with others: me too, you too

The key word is **anche** *(also, too)*. You can combine this with **io, tu, lui, lei, noi, voi** and **loro**.
In front of **io**, **anche** becomes **anch'io** and is pronounced as one word:

Sei	australiano anche tu?	*Are you*	*Australian too?*
È	anche Lei?		
Siete	australiani anche voi?		
Sono	americano anch'io	*I'm*	*American too*
Siamo	americani anche noi	*We're*	
È	canadese anche lui/anche lei?	*Is he/she*	*Canadian too?*
Sono	canadesi anche loro?	*Are they*	

You can use **anche** with other verbs:

Lavora in Inghilterra anche Lei? *Do you work in England too?*

Practice 2

What's this?

Can you identify the objects in the pictures? And can you say what they're called? The answers are in the text.

1 Che cos'è?

'"Orbis" è il nome di questo orologio da parete di DeAgostini in acciaio con fondo marmorizzato: **76 euro** nel diametro di cm 28.'

È un ...
Si chiama ...

2 Che cosa sono?

'Si chiamano "La cupola" e sono in fusione d'alluminio con manico e pomolo in poliammide nero, le caffettiere disegnate da Aldo Rossi per Alessi. Da una, tre, o sei tazze, costano rispettivamente, €55,00, €69,50 e €80,00.'

Sono ...
Si chiamano ...

2

Odd one out

Read these sets of words aloud and see if you can spot the odd one out. To help your pronunciation all irregular stresses have been marked. Check any words you don't know in the Vocabulary on p. 31.

1 ụtile fạcile difficile elegante elefante importante
2 patata carota pomodoro pomerịggio cạvolo sẹdano peperone
3 banana uva mela pera pesce pesca arạncia
4 gonna camịcia vestito giacca giallo scarpa sciarpa
5 bicchiere piatto coltello forchetta cucchiạio acciạio

Where is everyone?

in camera	ascoltare la musica
in salotto	guardare la televisione
a scuola	studiare lingue
in cucina	preparare la cena
a casa	leggere un libro

Match up where everyone is and what they're doing, using the drawings as a guide.
e.g. Sua nonna, dov'è?

Mia nonna è a casa. Legge un libro.

1 Sua madre, dov'è?   2 Suo padre, dov'è?

3 Suo figlio, dov'è?   4 Suo nonno, dov'è?

Friends and neighbours

Imagine the people below are your friends and neighbours in Italy. Introduce them to your visitors from home.
e.g. Your neighbour Pietro and his wife Laura.
  Questo è il mio vicino Pietro e questa è sua moglie Laura.

1 Your friend Gina and her brother Paolo.
2 Your neighbour Sandra and her friend Susanna.
3 Your friend Giuseppe and his brother Enrico.
4 Your neighbour Manlio and his cousin Cristina.

Now introduce your real friends from home to your friends and neighbours in Italy.

I too ...

Say what you have in common with other members of your group.
e.g. Studio l'italiano.
  Anch'io studio l'italiano.

1 Abito in Gran Bretagna.
2 Lavoro molto.
3 Sono di nazionalità britannica.

You too?

Find out whether your new acquaintances have anything in common with you.
e.g. Io abito qui vicino. Anche Lei abita vicino?

1 Io abito a Bologna.
2 Io lavoro in via Cavour.
3 Io studio lingue.

Now ask a couple the same questions.

29

Colour associations 📼 💿 25

How well do you know your colours?

bianco   nero   giallo   rosso   verde   azzurro

Below are some clues to the colours given here.
You'll also hear them on the recording. Listen and
answer aloud in Italian.

1 What are the colours
of the Italian flag
shown here?
Answer in Italian: La
bandiera italiana è ...

2 What colour is linked to Italian international
sport?
3 What colour is synonymous with a detective story
or film?
4 Finally, write down the colours you associate with
the following (they are not on the cassette/CD):
a) being in debt; **b)** being in credit; **c)** surrender;
d) ecology?

Identikit

Below is a form for a free catalogue. Check if there
are words you don't know, then fill it in, putting your
house number after the street name. Leave **C.A.P.**
and **Prov.** blank. They stand for the postal code –
codice di avviamento postale, and the province –
la provincia.

PER RICEVERE IL CATALOGO ILLUSTRATIVO,
SCRIVETE A:
SNAIDERO R. S.p.A. 33100 MAJANO [UD]

NOME

COGNOME

INDIRIZZO

TEL   **C.A.P.**

CITTÀ   **PROV.**

FIRMA

📼 💿 25

Now imagine giving your details over the phone to
a hotel or campsite. Rehearse your name and address
in Italian.

Mi chiamo ...
Abito a ... *[town]*, in ... *[country]*
Il mio indirizzo è ...

If you need help with the street number, look up
Ref. I, 1, p. 239.

Vocabulary

Family

il cognome	surname
il nome	name
la famiglia	family
il cognato	brother-in-law
la cognata	sister-in-law
il/la cugino/a	cousin
il genero	son-in-law
la nuora	daughter-in-law
il fratello	brother
la sorella	sister
il marito	husband
la moglie	wife
il nipote	nephew/grandson
la nipote	niece/granddaughter
il nonno	grandfather
la nonna	grandmother
il suocero	father-in-law
la suocera	mother-in-law
i/le gemelli/e	twins
l'amico/a	friend
il fidanzato	fiancé
la fidanzata	fiancée
il signore	Mr, man
la signorina	Miss, young lady

Meals

l'antipasto	starter
il primo	first course
il secondo	main course
il dolce	sweet, dessert

Food

la carne	meat
il maiale	pork
il manzo	beef
il fegato	liver
il pesce	fish
il cavolo	cabbage
l'insalata	salad
il peperone	green pepper
il peperon-cino	chili pepper
i piselli	peas
il sedano	celery
l'albicocca	apricot
la fragola	strawberry
il lampone	raspberry

il limone	lemon
il melone	melon
l'uva	grapes
il pane	bread
il burro	butter
la marmellata	jam
il pepe	pepper
il sale	salt

Drinks

l'acqua	water
il digestivo	after-dinner drink
il latte	milk

Tableware

il bicchiere	glass
il coltello	knife
il cucchiaio	spoon
la forchetta	fork
il piatto	plate
la tazza	cup

Places

la capitale	capital
il capoluogo	regional/provincial capital
l'edicola	news-stand
l'isola	island
il mercato	market
il paese	country, village
la nazione	nation
il ristorante	restaurant
l'ufficio	office
la via	street

Verbs

abitare	to live
ascoltare	to listen
assaggiare	to taste
bere	to drink
guardare	to look, watch
firmare	to sign
lavorare	to work
imparare	to learn
leggere	to read
mangiare	to eat
portare	to wear; bring

provare	to try [on]
scrivere	to write
studiare	to study
vedere	to see

Adjectives

grande	big
piccolo	little
simpatico	nice/pleasant
antipatico	nasty/unpleasant
simile	similar
diverso	different
facile	easy
difficile	difficult
utile	useful
elegante	elegant
gratis	free

Colours

arancione	orange
azzurro	blue
bianco	white
giallo	yellow
grigio	grey
marrone	brown
nero	black
rosso	red
verde	green

Clothes

la camicia	shirt
la camicetta	blouse
il cappello	hat
il cappotto	coat
la giacca	jacket
la gonna	skirt
la maglia	jumper
la maglietta	T shirt
i pantaloni	trousers
le scarpe	shoes
la sciarpa	scarf
il vestito	dress, costume

Troubleshooting

Don't confuse the following:

È, sono   C'è, ci sono

è	it is	c'è	there is
è?	is it?	c'è?	is there?
sono	they are	ci sono	there are
sono?	are they?	ci sono?	are there?

C'è is short for **ci è**. The word for *there* is **ci** but in front of **è** it becomes **c'** and is pronounced as one word.
The verbs **è** and **sono** on their own mean *it is* and *they are*.
Words for *it* and *they* do exist **(esso/a; essi/e)**, but they are no longer used in spoken Italian.

Chi è? Chi sono?   Chi c'è?

Chi è/chi sono are used for identifying people; **chi c'è** is used for finding out who's around:

Chi è?	*Who is it?*	È Anna.	*It's Anna.*
Chi sono?	*Who are they?*	Sono Anna e Maria.	*They're . . .*
Chi c'è?	*Who's here?*	C'è Anna.	*Anna's here.*
[lit.	*Who is there?*]	Ci sono Anna e Maria.	*Anna and Maria are here*

Cos'è? Cosa sono?   Cosa c'è?

Cos'è/cosa sono are used for identifying objects; **cosa c'è** is used for finding out what's available.

Cos'è	*What is it?*	È	*It's a*
Cosa sono?	*What are they?*	Sono	*They're*
Cosa c'è?	*What is there?*	C'è	*There's*
		Ci sono	*There are*

Dove?   dov'è?

Finally notice the difference between:

Dove?	*where?*	Dov'è?	*where is?*

Dov'è? means **dove è?** In front of the verb **è**, **dove** drops the final **-e** and is pronounced as one word.

Unità 3

Il tempo libero

Leisure time

Sciatori a Livigno nella Valtellina, Lombardia

Part 1
(Interactions 1–4, Patterns 1, Practice 1)

Learn how to:
Say where you are from
Ask someone how they are
Say how you are
Ask and talk about your family and
   their ages
Talk about the things and activities
   you prefer
Ask why and give reasons

Part 2
(Interactions 5–8, Patterns 2, Practice 2)

Learn how to:
Make introductions
Offer food and drink
Say how long you've been doing
   something
Say what you need
Express pleasure and admiration

Grammar

Articles **l'**, **lo**, **gli** and **uno**
nostro, **vostro**, **loro** – *our, your* [pl.],
   their
quanto? quanti? – *how much?*
   how many?
da with the present tense – *how long for,*
   how long since

Using **vero?** – *isn't it? aren't you? didn't*
   we? etc.
-ire verbs: **preferire**, **offrire**
-ire reflexive verbs: **divertirsi**
stare and **avere**

Want to take it further?
Grammar: see Systems 3, pp. 87–8   *More practice:* do Reinforcement 3, pp. 89–90

Interactions

I 〔cc〕 〔◎〕 27

In the nineteenth century, Liguria was the haunt of the wealthy British and a favourite leisure spot. Today that past survives in the thriving Anglo-Ligurian club, which meets every Thursday in the seaside town of Bordighera and holds an annual garden party on the Queen's birthday. Anna meets some of the guests.

First time round

inglese	English
le alunne (f)	pupils

Read the questions below, then listen without the text.

a What are the names of the four people Anna speaks to?

b What is the relationship between the first person she speaks to and the other three girls?

[...]

Anna	Signora, piacere, sono Anna Mazzotti.
Carla	Piacere. Io sono Carla Pira. Insegno inglese qui in Liguria. Queste sono le mie alunne e questa è mia figlia.
Anna	Ciao.
Bianca	Ciao.
Anna	Come ti chiami?
Bianca	Io mi chiamo Bianca.
Anna	E **quanti anni hai?**
Bianca	Ho otto anni.
Anna	Come ti chiami?
Angela	Io mi chiamo Angela.
Anna	E **di dove sei?**
Angela	Sono d'Imperia.
Anna	Da quanto tempo studi l'inglese?
Angela	Studio inglese da otto anni con la mia professoressa.
Anna	Come ti chiami?
Chiara	Mi chiamo Chiara.
Anna	Chiara, **hai fratelli?**
Chiara	Sì, ho un fratello.
Anna	Sei qui con la tua famiglia?
Chiara	No, non sono qui con la mia famiglia ma sono qui con la mia professoressa d'inglese.

da quanto tempo ...?   *for how long ...?*

Key phrases

quanti anni hai?	*how old are you? [inf.]*
di dove sei?	*where are you from? [inf.]*
hai fratelli?	*have you any brothers or sisters?*

2 ⌐⌐⌐ ◎ 28

Along the coast from Bordighera is Sanremo, famous not only for its song festival and flowers, but also for its beach and luxury yachts.

First time round

Anna talks to the captain of a large yacht. He isn't from Sanremo.
Where does he come from?

Anna	Buongiorno.
Capitano	Buongiorno.
Anna	**Come sta?**
Capitano	Io sto bene, grazie.
Anna	**Di dov'è?**
Capitano	Io sono d'Imperia. È una città qui vicino – a Sanremo.

> ### Key phrases
>
> | | |
> |---|---|
> | **come sta?** | *how are you?* |
> | **di dov'è?** | *where are you from?* |

3 ⌐⌐⌐ ◎ 29

On the beach Anna meets Mario and Luca.

> | | |
> |---|---|
> | sposato/a | *married* |

Are either of them married?

Anna	Mario, di dove sei?
Mario	Sono di Sanremo.
Anna	**Sei sposato?**
Mario	No, per fortuna non sono sposato.
Anna	Luca, di dove sei?
Luca	Sono di Sanremo e vivo qui.
Anna	E **sei sposato?**
Luca	No. **Non** sono sposato **neanch'io.**

per fortuna   *luckily*

> ### Key phrases
>
> | | |
> |---|---|
> | **sei sposato?** | *are you married? [inf.]* |
> | **non . . . neanch'io** | *me neither* |

4 ⌐⌐⌐ ◎ 30

Anna has four other brief encounters on the beach – with a mother and daughter on a pedalo, a teenage girl, another mother, and a teenage boy.

First time round

> | | |
> |---|---|
> | abbronzarsi | *to tan* |
> | divertente | *fun* |
> | riposarsi | *to rest* |
> | ascolto | *I listen* |

What are these people doing on the beach?

Anna	Ciao.
Ragazza	Ciao.
Anna	*[to the mother]* Buongiorno, signora. **Perché** siete qui?
Ragazza	Beh, **è** molto **divertente stare qui**, pedalare, andare sul mare, abbronzarsi.
Anna	Ciao, come stai?
Ragazza	Bene, grazie.
Anna	**Perché** sei qui?
Ragazza	Sono qui per divertirmi.
Anna	E **cosa preferisci fare?**
Ragazza	**Preferisco mangiare** il gelato [. . .].
Anna	Signora, lei **perché** è qui?
Madre	Sono qui **perché** ho bisogno di riposarmi . . . [. . .]
Marco	In spiaggia gioco a pallavolo, sto con gli amici, ascolto la musica e prendo il sole.

andare sul mare	*to go out on the sea*
per divertirmi	*to enjoy myself*
gioco a pallavolo	*I play volleyball*
sto con gli amici	*I spend time with my friends*

> ### Key phrases
>
> | | |
> |---|---|
> | **perché . . .?** | *why?* |
> | **perché** | *because* |
> | **è divertente stare qui** | *it's fun being here* |
> | **cosa preferisci fare?** | *what do you prefer doing?* |
> | **preferisco mangiare** | *I prefer eating* |

Sound effects   ⌐⌐⌐ ◎ 30

Listen to the cassette/CD and say what you prefer doing.

Patterns I

Exchanging personal information

i) Asking and saying how you are

The key verb is **stare** *(to be, to stay)* [see Systems, note 2, p. 87].

Come | stai?   *How are you?*   Come sta?   *How* | *is he/she?*
      | sta?
      | state?   Come stanno? | *are they?*

Sto/stiamo bene, grazie   *I'm/we're fine, thanks*
Sta/stanno bene, grazie   *He, she/they are fine, thanks*
Non c'è male – e tu?/e Lei?/e voi?   *Not bad – how about you?*
         – e lui?/e lei?/e loro?   *how about him/her/them?*

ii) Asking and saying where you're from

The key verb is **essere** *(to be)*. The question, literally, is *'of where are you?'*

Di | dove sei?   *Where are you from?*
   | dov'è?

You usually answer by naming your home town:

Sono di | Imperia   *I'm from* | *Imperia*
       | Manchester | *Manchester*

If there's an adjective for the inhabitants of a town or region it can be used instead:

Sono romano/sono di Roma   *I'm Roman/from Rome*
Sono ligure   *I'm Ligurian/from Liguria*

But to say what country you're from you always use your nationality and not **di** plus the country:

Sono inglese   *I'm English/from England*

There is a list of nationalities in Ref. III, 5, pp. 242–3.

iii) Talking about the family

Marital status

Sei | sposato/a?   *Are you married?*   Sì | sono sposato/a   *Yes* | *I'm married*
È | sposato/a? | siamo sposati/e | *we're married*
Siete | sposati/e?   No, non sono sposato/a   *No, I'm not married*

Children

The key verb is **avere** *(to have)* [see Systems, note 2, p. 87].

Hai | figli?   *Have you got any* | *children?*
Ha | dei bambini? | *young children?*
Avete |

Ho | due figli, un maschio e una femmina   *I've got* | *two children, a boy and a girl*
Abbiamo | *We've got* |

No, non ho figli   *No, I haven't got any children*

Patterns I

Brothers and sisters

Hai | fratelli?   *Have you got any brothers or sisters?*
Ha |

Sì, ho un fratello e una sorella   *Yes, I've got a brother and a sister.*
No, non ho fratelli,   *No, I haven't got any brothers and sisters,*
   sono figlio unico/sono figlia unica   *I'm an only child*

Age

When you ask someone's age you literally say *'How many years have you?'* The key question word is the adjective **quanto**.

Quanti anni hai/ha?   *How old are you?*   Ho sette anni.   *I'm seven.*

Quanti anni | ha | tuo figlio?   *How old is your son?*
      | | Suo figlio?
      | | vostro figlio?

Quanti anni | hanno | i tuoi figli?   *How old are your children?*
      | | i Suoi figli?
      | | i vostri figli?

See Troubleshooting, p. 48 and Systems, note 6, p. 89 for **Suoi/tuoi**, etc.
See Ref. I, 1, p. 239, for a complete list of numbers.

iv) Asking and stating preferences

The key verb is **preferire** *(to prefer)*. [See Systems, note 1, p. 87.]
To say what you like doing best, just use the infinitive after **preferire**:

Cosa | preferisci | fare?   *What do you prefer doing?*
    | preferisce |
    | preferite |

Preferisco | leggere e guardare la televisione | *I prefer* | *reading and watching television*
Preferiamo | chiacchierare e stare insieme | *We prefer* | *chatting and being together*

v) Asking why and giving reasons

The key words are **perché?** *(why?)* and **perché** *(because)*:

Perché | sei/è qui?   *Why* | *are you here?*
    | giochi/gioca a pallavolo? | *do you play volleyball?*

perché | è divertente   *because* | *it's fun*
    | è interessante | *it's interesting*

You can be more specific by adding a verb in the infinitive:

perché è divertente | stare in Italia   *because it's fun* | *being in Italy*
           | giocare | *playing/to play*

You can use other adjectives in the same way:

È	importante	imparare l'italiano	*It's*	*important*	*to learn Italian*
	necessario			*necessary*	
	essenziale			*essential*	

vi) Identifying with others: me neither, you neither

The key word is **neanche** *(neither)*. You can combine it with **io, tu, lui, lei, noi, voi** and **loro**. In front of **io**, **neanche** becomes **neanch'io** and is pronounced as one word.

Non sono sposato neanch'io   *I'm not married either*
Non hai fratelli neanche tu?   *Don't you have brothers and sisters either?*
Non ha figli neanche Lei?   *Don't you have children either?*

Practice I

How are you all?

You meet a friend, Roberto, in the street and ask him how he is. Complete the conversation using **stare**.

You	Ciao, Roberto. Come . . .?
Roberto	Bene, grazie. E tu?
You	. . . bene anch'io. E tua moglie?
Roberto	. . . bene anche lei.
You	E i figli?
Roberto	. . . bene anche loro.
You	Allora, voi . . . tutti bene!
Roberto	Sì, . . . tutti bene.

Getting to know you   31

You meet up with Luca in a bar one evening. Find out something about him and his family. You don't know him very well, so use **Lei**.

You	*[Say hello and ask how he is.]*
Luca	Buonasera. Bene grazie. E Lei?
You	*[Say you're fine too.]*
Luca	Lei, di dov'è?
You	*[Say you're from Rome and ask where he comes from.]*
Luca	Sono di Genova e abito a Sanremo.
You	*[Ask if he is married.]*
Luca	Sì, sono sposato.
You	*[Ask where his wife comes from.]*
Luca	Mia moglie è di Genova anche lei.
You	*[Ask if he has got any children.]*
Luca	Sì, ho una femmina e due maschi.
You	*[Ask how old his daughter is.]*
Luca	Mia figlia ha dieci anni.
You	*[Ask about his sons.]*
Luca	I miei figli hanno nove e sette anni.

Kindred spirits

You're single, an only child and no good at games!
At parties you tend to feel the odd one out. But the
conversation at this party is different . . .

> Non gioco a tennis

To which you can reply, expressing pleasant surprise:

> Ah, davvero? Non gioco a tennis neanch'io!

Here are some more phrases welcome to your ears:

1 Non ho fratelli
2 Non sono sposato
3 Non ho figli
4 Non gioco a golf

Can you give an appropriate reply, expressing
solidarity?

Tea or coffee?

You're entertaining Italian guests for the weekend.
First you need to know what refreshments your
guests prefer. Ask each person in turn using the
alternatives suggested below.
e.g. Patrizia, . . . tè o caffè?
Patrizia, cosa preferisci – tè o caffè?

1 Andrea, . . . vino bianco o vino rosso?
2 Signor Fante, . . . un Cinzano o un Campari?
3 Signori, . . . vodka o whisky?

What you'd rather do

Now you want to know what people would rather
do. The choice is not unlimited, so use the
alternatives given.
e.g. Patrizia, . . . stare a casa o vedere un film?
Patrizia, cosa preferisci fare – stare a casa o vedere
un film?

1 Andrea, . . . guardare la televisione o ascoltare la
radio?
2 Signor Fante, . . . mangiare adesso o aspettare?
3 Signori, . . . giocare a bridge o giocare a scacchi?

Priorities

The symbols below explain the amenities available
in various holiday resorts, being considered by you
and some Italian friends. Pick out a few and put
them in order of importance.
First what do you prefer to have; then what's
important; what's necessary; and, lastly, what's
essential for you.

e.g. In vacanza:
preferisco ottimi ristoranti
è importante avere divertimenti
è necessario avere una spiaggia attrezzata
è essenziale avere giochi per bambini

If you know other Italian speakers, discuss their
preferences too.

Parcheggio Ottimi ristoranti

In prossimità del mare Sports acquatici Piano bar

Piscina Tennis Giochi per bambini

Discoteca Spiaggia attrezzata Divertimenti

Choosing a holiday

Read these descriptions of different holiday resorts.

LA NOSTRA OPINIONE

«*Atmosfera cordiale ed informale per un soggiorno piacevole e divertente a contatto con la natura*».

a

famiglia

TRANQUILLITA' E VERDE, SICUREZZA NEGLI SPAZI ALL'APERTO PER BAMBINI, RICEVIMENTO FAMILIARE, PREZZO E OFFERTE STUDIATE PER GRUPPI FAMILIARI

LA NOSTRA OPINIONE

«*Vicinissimo al mare costituisce la soluzione ideale per una vacanza piacevole e rilassante*».

b

LA NOSTRA OPINIONE

«*Animazione, sports, megadiscoteca e un club giovane, frizzante per una vacanza folle*».

c

TESSERA CLUB

obbligatoria in hotel e in residence e per tutta la stagione 45 euro per persona per l'intero soggiorno (bambini 3/14 anni 35 euro), in loco. **Include**: uso del campo da tennis e bocce, windsurf, canoa, vela, catamarano, tiro con l'arco, pedalos, tuffi, nuoto, yoga, ginnastica aerobica, arte applicata, fotografia, mini e junior club, piscina olimpionica e per bambini, piscina con idromassaggi, lezioni collettive degli sports previsti, centro commerciale, discoteca, spettacoli musicali, giochi, feste, cabaret.

LA NOSTRA OPINIONE

«*Formula dinamica e divertente, ideale per una vacanza giovanile e sportiva*».

TESSERA CLUB

(obbligatoria dal 15/6 al 31/8) per entrambe le formule 50 euro per persona (bambini oltre 10 anni) per l'intero periodo di soggiorno, da pagare in agenzia. **Include**: servizio medico, parcheggio, ping-pong, deposito valori, campo calcio, servizio spiaggia, discoteca, piscina, pallavolo e animazione.

d

Decide which one you would go for: **a**, **b**, **c**, or **d**. There's no need to understand every word, but look things up if you want to. Be prepared to justify your choice:

preferisco … perché

Now unscramble the two words below. They each occur twice in the descriptions. One is linked to the word for saying 'How do you do?'. The other is connected with the verb for 'having fun'.

LEVOIPACE   TENTREVIDE

Your spare time

Can you think of ten words which will help you talk about your spare time? If you need help, there is a list of useful expressions in the Vocabulary on p. 47.

Golf in Italy

Read this article about the history of golf in Italy and for each of the years mentioned see if you can work out how many players and how many golf courses there were. How many are there today? For numbers see note 10, p. 90 and Ref. I, 1, p. 239.

Nel 1954 in Italia ci sono diciotto campi e milleduecento giocatori. Nel 1960 i duemilacinquecento golfisti hanno a disposizione venticinque campi da gioco. Nel 1970 gli iscritti alla Federazione sono già settemila con trenta campi.

Nel 1980 a giocare sono tredicimila persone, che diventano venticinquemila nel 1985.

In questi giorni i golfisti praticanti sono quasi quarantamila e i campi da gioco sono centotrentasette.

Cultura e parole

In Italy, as elsewhere, indoor leisure activities are centred on TV – **la TV** – and the Internet – **l'internet**. Italian television has over 600 channels, about a fifth of the world's terrestrial channels – **canali terrestri**. It is dominated by RAIUNO, RAIDUE and RAITRE, the main public channels of the **RAI (Radiotelevisione italiana)**, and by the private channels owned by Silvio Berlusconi: Canale 5, Rete 4 and Italia 1. These are all broadcast in both analogical – **analogico** – and digital – **digitale** – forms. Satellite TV – **la TV satellite** – is also extremely popular with viewers – **i telespettatori**: this is obvious from the number of satellite dishes – **antenne paraboliche** – to be seen everywhere. The main private satellite channels – **canali satellitari** – are provided by Sky, but the RAI also has five channels. In the world of television, Italians have adopted many English words, as can be observed by flicking through TV programmes. Amongst those on offer are **i soap opera, i reality show, i talk show, gli quiz,** and **i sit-com**. However, some English words in Italian have slightly different or unexpected meanings. **Una fiction** is often used for a TV drama, and **uno spot** is the word used for a TV advertisement.

The Internet also plays a major part in indoor leisure. Surfing the web – **navigare sul web** – is an important pastime, as is chatting online – **chattare online**. As with television, the language of the Internet is not difficult for English speakers: the meaning of **la home page, la password, la user-id, la directory, il browser** or **links** is obvious. Other terms, **il sito web** – website, or **cliccare** – to click, for example, are very similar, while a few, such as **cerca** – search, **vai** – go, **annulla** – cancel or **indietro** – back, are purely Italian.

Sport – **lo sport** – is an extremely important part of both outdoor and indoor leisure. The national sport, football – **il calcio** – from the Italian word for kick, is avidly followed by the fans – **i tifosi** – on TV, on the web and on Teletext – **il Televideo**, but of course they also flock to the stadium – **lo stadio** – to see the match – **la partita**. The best teams – **squadre** – are in the Premier League, known as **serie A** and they all compete in the national championships – **i campionati nazionali**. Perhaps because football is the national game, it has escaped the anglicising trend common in Italian sport, although English words are used, often in slightly adapted form. A goal is **un gol** but the actual goal on the pitch – **il campo** – is **la porta**. A penalty is **un rigore** or simply **un penalty**, while **l'allenatore** or **il coach** is the coach. Finally, **il Mister** is a term commonly used for the manager.

Interactions

5   [cc]   [◎] 32

The very first tennis club in Italy, Il Bordighera Tennis Club, was founded by the British residents of Bordighera in the last century. The club is now all-Italian, with a splendid new bar, gym and games room. Its young Vice President, Giulio Preti, meets Anna.

First time round

il circolo	club
i campi	courts
la terra rossa	clay

Read the words given here and use a bit of guesswork.

a Who else in Giulio's family plays tennis?
b How many courts does the club have?

Anna	Giulio, **da quanto tempo giochi** a tennis?
Giulio	Gioco a tennis da almeno quindici anni.
Anna	E la tua famiglia gioca?
Giulio	La mia famiglia gioca a tennis, i miei genitori, mio fratello . . .
Anna	E il circolo, **da quanto tempo esiste?**
Giulio	Il circolo esiste da cento anni. – Questi sono i campi da tennis.
Anna	Quanti campi avete?
Giulio	Abbiamo sei campi da tennis; quattro in terra rossa e due in sintetico. – Adesso possiamo andar a prendere qualcosa da bere al bar?
Anna	Sì, volentieri.

qualcosa da bere	*something to drink*
volentieri	*with pleasure*

Key phrases

da quanto tempo . . .	*how long . . .*
giochi?	*have you been playing?*
esiste?	*has it existed?*

6   [cc]   [◎] 33

In the bar Anna chooses a very Italian drink. She is introduced to two club members, Beppe and Gino, and also to Vincenzo . . .

First time round

il nostro	*our*
la spremuta	*fresh juice*
i soci	*members*

a Who is Vincenzo?
b How do you say 'What are you having?'

Giulio	Questo è il nostro bar. **Ti presento** il nostro barista, Vincenzo.
Vincenzo	Piacere, come sta?
Anna	Molto bene, grazie.
Giulio	**Cosa prendi** da bere, Anna?
Anna	Una spremuta con lo zucchero.
Giulio	Due spremute per favore, Vincenzo . . . Beppe? E Gino?
Vincenzo	Oh, eccoli.
Giulio	Ciao, Beppe.
Beppe	Ciao.
Giulio	Ciao, Gino.
Gino	Ciao, Giulio.
Giulio	Ti presento due soci del tennis.
Anna	Piacere.
All	Ciao, piacere.
Giulio	Beppe, cosa prendi?
Beppe	Un aperitivo.
Giulio	Gino, cosa prendi?
Gino	Anch'io, grazie.
Giulio	Due aperitivi, per favore.
Vincenzo	Subito.
[. . .]	

eccoli   *here they are*

Key phrases

ti presento	*let me introduce you to*
cosa prendi?	*what are you having?*

7 ⌜cc⌝ 🔘 34

Not far from Bordighera, near the French border, are the Hanbury Botanical Gardens, founded in 1867 by an English tea merchant, Sir Thomas Hanbury. Anna first meets Guido Novaro who's in charge, and then Luca, one of his assistants.

First time round

gestire	to manage
lo stato	the state
all'aria aperta	in the open air

Can you pick out:
a How long has Guido been working in the Hanbury Gardens?
b What does he like about his job?

Anna	Signor Guido Novaro, Lei è assistente tecnico dell'università di Genova. Chi gestisce questi giardini?
Sig. Novaro	Il giardino è proprietà demaniale, cioè, dello stato.
Anna	E lo gestisce . . .?
Sig. Novaro	Lo gestisce l'università di Genova.
Anna	Da quanto tempo lavora qui?
Sig. Novaro	Lavoro qui da ventinove anni.
Anna	È un lavoro piacevole?
Sig. Novaro	È un lavoro molto bello.
Anna	Perché?
Sig. Novaro	Eh . . . perché lavorare all'aria aperta è molto divertente con tante belle piante.
Anna	Avete molto lavoro?
Sig. Novaro	Sì, abbiamo molto lavoro tutto l'anno.
Anna	**Avete bisogno di** molto personale?
Sig. Novaro	**Abbiamo bisogno di** molto aiuto, sì.

[. . .]

Anna	Luca, da quanto tempo è che lavori qui?
Luca	Lavoro qui da solo sei mesi.
Anna	**È bello lavorare** qui?
Luca	Sì, è molto bello anche perché amo lavorare all'aria aperta.

cioè   *that is to say*

Key phrases

avete bisogno di?	*do you need?*
abbiamo bisogno di	*we need*
è bello lavorare qui?	*is it nice working here?*

8 ⌜cc⌝ 🔘 35

Walking round the gardens Anna meets a holiday-maker who is enjoying the weather.

First time round

il tempo	*the weather*

Can you work out why he is here?

Anna	**Che bella giornata, vero?**
Dott. Savini	Ah, oggi il tempo è splendido . . . meraviglioso.
Anna	Ma Lei, di dov'è?
Dott. Savini	Io sono ligure, di Imperia.
Anna	Ed **è qui in vacanza, vero?**
Dott. Savini	Sì, sono qui perché ho bisogno di riposare. [. . .]

Key phrases

che bella giornata, vero?	*it's a lovely day, isn't it?*
è qui in vacanza, vero?	*you're here on holiday, aren't you?*

Isn't it? Aren't you? etc.   ⌜cc⌝ 🔘 36

Listen to the cassette/CD and see how easily these common phrases are used in Italian. Try and see if you can use **vero**.

Patterns 2

i) Making introductions

Ti	presento	mia sorella	Let me introduce	my sister
Le		le mie sorelle		my sisters
		mio fratello		my brother
		i miei fratelli		my brothers

See Systems, note 6, p. 89 for **mie**, **miei**, etc.

The response is usually **piacere** or **molto piacere**.

ii) Offering food and drink

To find out what someone is having, you need the verb **prendere** *(to take)*:

Cosa prendi?/prende?   *What are you having?* [lit. *taking*]

If you want to be more specific you can ask:

Prendi qualcosa	da bere?	Are you having anything	to drink?
Prende	da mangiare?		to eat?

To say what you're having:

Prendo un'aranciata   *I'll have an orangeade*

iii) Saying how long for? how long since?

All you need is the word **da** and the present tense:

Da quanto tempo è qui?   *How long have you been here?*
Da quanto tempo studia l'italiano?   *How long have you been studying Italian?*

Da can mean *for* or *since*:

Sono qui da ieri   *I've been here since yesterday*
Studio qui da sei mesi   *I've studied here for six months*
Gioco a golf da due anni.   *I've played golf for two years*

iv) Checking and confirming

In Italian all you need is the word **vero?** – which means *true?* – on the end of the sentence.

Lei è qui in vacanza, vero?   *You're here on holiday aren't you?*
Lei parla italiano, vero?   *You speak Italian, don't you?*
Studia l'italiano da molto tempo, vero?   *You've been studying Italian for a long time, haven't you?*

v) Expressing need

The expression **avere bisogno di** literally means *to have need of*:

Hai/ha bisogno di aiuto?   *Do you need help?*

Ho bisogno di	riposare	I need	to rest
	divertirmi		to enjoy myself

Patterns 2

vi) Expressing pleasure

The key phrase is **è bello**, literally *it's beautiful*, followed by an infinitive:

È bello	stare qui	*It's nice/lovely*	*being here*
	essere in vacanza		*being on holiday*

To express admiration, use the phrase **che bello:**

Che bella giornata!   *What a lovely day!*   Che belle scarpe!   *What lovely shoes!*

In front of masculine nouns **bello** is shortened:

Che bel vestito!   *What a lovely dress!*   Che bei pantaloni!   *What lovely trousers!*

Che bello! on its own means   *How lovely, how nice!*

See Systems 10, note 4, p. 211, for a fuller explanation.

Practice 2

May I introduce . . .?

You've got plenty of people to introduce. Can you get it right? First introduce the following to your friend Danilo:

| 1 | your mother | 3 | your sisters |
| 2 | your brother | 4 | your neighbour |

Now introduce these people to dottor Rabbiotti:

| 5 | your parents | 7 | your girlfriend |
| 6 | your aunt | 8 | your grandparents |

How lovely!

Everyone likes getting compliments. Practise on the objects pictured here by admiring what you see! Then ask who they belong to, using the **Lei** form of address, and **suo, sua, suoi, sue** (without the article).

e.g. Che bei fiori! Sono Suoi?
   What lovely flowers? Are they yours?

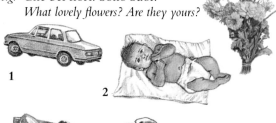

1

2

3

4

Refresh your memory

How many different drinks can you remember? The Vocabulary in Units 1–3 will help. Check out the words for different snacks at the end of this unit.

It's on me   [cc]   [CD] 37

You're buying the drinks and snacks for two people: Sandra, who's an old friend, and signor Giustini, whom you've only just met. Ask each of them what they're having.

You	*[Ask signor Giustini what he's having to drink.]*
Sig. G.	Un aperitivo – un Cinzano.
You	*[Ask him what he's having to eat.]*
Sig. G.	Un panino con formaggio.
You	*[Now ask Sandra what she's having.]*
Sandra	Un'acqua minerale, con limone.
You	*[Ask her if she's having anything to eat.]*
Sandra	Un tramezzino con prosciutto.
You	*[Say – me too and I'll have a Cinzano.]*

How long for?

What activities do the pictures represent? Check in the Vocabulary if you need help with the words. Practise saying how long you've been doing certain activities, starting with the ones shown here:

e.g. an hour; three weeks; eighteen months; seven years

Give your reasons!

Can you give two good reasons for doing each activity?
e.g. ... stare all'aria aperta
    Ho bisogno di stare all'aria aperta.
    È bello stare all'aria aperta.

1 imparare una lingua straniera
2 stare con la famiglia

Now say the following are (1) fun and (2) interesting to do:

3 lavorare in un paese straniero
4 essere socio di un circolo
5 giocare a scacchi

Questionnaire   37

Listen to the two people talking about how they spend their leisure time. As you listen, tick the chart below.

	Speaker 1	Speaker 2

ascoltare: la musica classica
    la radio
fare: ginnastica aerobica
    del giardinaggio
    yoga
giocare: a scacchi
    a tennis
guardare: la televisione
    un video
leggere: romanzi/riviste
stare: con gli amici
cucinare		

Identikit

Continue to draw up an identikit picture of yourself. Say the answers aloud in Italian, answering as fully as you can.
Di dov'è?   Ha fratelli?
È sposato?   Ha figli?
Ha animali domestici?
Da quanto tempo studia l'italiano?

3

Vocabulary

Free time

il passatempo	*pastime*
l'hobby	*hobby*
la gara	*competition*
il gioco	*game*
il torneo	*tournament*
la partita	*match*
lo sport	*sport*
lo svago	*entertainment*
	relaxation
preferito	*favourite*

Verbs

allenarsi	*to train*
ballare	*to dance*
cantare	*to sing*
cucinare	*to cook*
dipingere	*to paint*
disegnare	*to draw*
distrarsi	*to amuse oneself*
tenersi in forma	*to keep fit*
perdere	*to lose*
vincere	*to win*

Sports

l'alpinismo	*climbing*
le bocce	*bowls*
la canoa	*canoeing*
la corsa campestre	*cross-country running*
il ciclismo	*cycling*
il calcio	*football*
l'equitazione	*horse-riding*
la ginnastica aerobica	*aerobics*
il nuoto	*swimming*
la pallavolo	*volley-ball*
il pattinaggio	*skating*
il parapendio	*hang-gliding*
il tiro con l'arco	*archery*
lo sci	*skiing*
lo yoga	*yoga*

People

la zia	*aunt*
lo zio	*uncle*
lo straniero	*foreigner*
lo studente	*student*
l'amico	*friend*
il turista	*tourist*
l'atleta	*athlete*
il giocatore	*player*
il tifoso	*fan*
il maestro	*coach*

Idioms

avere fame	*to be hungry*
avere sete	*to be thirsty*
avere caldo	*to be hot*
avere freddo	*to be cold*
avere fretta	*to be in a hurry*
aver voglia di	*to feel like*
avere tempo di	*to have time*
avere bisogno di	*to need*

Drinks and snacks

la bibita	*cold drink*
l'amaro	*bitter digestive drink*
lo champagne	*champagne*
l'aperitivo	*aperitif*
la spremuta	*fresh fruit-juice*
lo spumante	*spumante*
il succo di frutta	*fruit juice*
il ghiaccio	*ice*
lo zucchero	*sugar*
fare uno spuntino	*to have a snack*
la brioche	*croissant*
il panino	*roll*
le patatine	*crisps*
il toast	*toasted sandwich*
il tramezzino	*sandwich*

Activities

passare il tempo/ trascorrere il tempo	*to spend time*
appartenere a un circolo	*to belong to a club*
a un coro	*a choir*
essere socio di un circolo	*to be a member of a club*
essere iscritto a un corso	*to be enrolled on a course*
frequentare un corso	*to attend a course*
seguire un corso	*to follow a course*
avere la tessera per ...	*to belong to, have a ticket for ...*
la biblioteca	*the library*
una palestra	*a gym*
avere un abbonamento a ...	*to have a subscription to ...*
una rivista	*a magazine*
praticare uno sport	*to play a sport*
giocare a squash/	*to play squash*
a calcio	*football*
a carte	*cards*
a scacchi	*chess*
fare del giardinaggio	*to garden*
lavorare a maglia	*to knit*

Troubleshooting

Whose is whose?

Getting possessives right can be difficult. The main thing to remember is that in Italian they agree with the *object possessed*, whereas in English they agree with the *owner*.

his/her		*their*	
il suo	libro	il loro	libro
i suoi	libri	i loro	libri
la sua	penna	la loro	penna
le sue	penne	le loro	penne

Questo è il libro di Marco? È il suo libro?   *Is it his book?*
Questo è il libro di Carla? È il suo libro?   *Is it her book?*
Questo è il libro di Marco e Carla? È il loro libro?   *Is it their book?*

The plural forms **suoi**, **sue** indicate *one* owner but *several* objects.

i suoi libri	*his, her books*
i loro libri	*their books*

Don't forget that **Suo** means *your* when you're using the polite form of address:

		your	
il Suo libro	i Suoi libri	la Sua penna	le Sue penne
il tuo libro	i tuoi libri	la tua penna	le tue penne
il vostro libro	i vostri libri	la vostra penna	le vostre penne

Possessives can also be used as pronouns, i.e., without the noun:
   È un bel libro. È tuo?/Suo?/vostro?
The article tends to be dropped in front of the pronoun, except when needed for clarification or emphasis.

Unità 4

I pendolari
Travelling and routines

Al lavoro in motorino, periferia di Roma

Part 1	**Part 2**
(Interactions 1–4, Patterns 1, Practice 1)	(Interactions 5–6, Patterns 2, Practice 2)
Learn how to:	*Learn how to:*
Talk about where you go	Say what job you do
Say what transport you use	Tell the time
Say how often you travel	Use the days of the week
Explain what you have to do	Say what time you leave and
Say what your day is like	when you arrive
	Talk about your working hours
	Say how often and how many times

Grammar	
Prepositions with definite articles, **a** + **il** = **al**, etc.	The preposition **da** and some of its uses
	andare, venire, uscire
Using **a** and **in** with places – *in* and *at*	**fare**
	dovere

Want to take it further?
Grammar: see Systems 4, pp. 93–4   *More practice:* do Reinforcement 4, pp. 95–6

Interactions

I  2

It's not much fun getting to work in the morning, especially if you have to commute – **fare il pendolare**. Anna talks to early-morning travellers at Ferrara station to find out what it's like.

First time round

il pendolare	*commuter*	You'll hear three
presto	*early*	views expressed – all
tardi	*late*	by women.

As you listen, match the views outlined below with the relevant speaker:

a Commuting is very stressful.
b Commuting is fairly tiring.
c A commuter's day is tiring and very long.

Voice 1	Voice 2	Voice 3

Anna	**Com'è** la vita del pendolare**?**
Signora 1	La vita del pendolare è faticosa e dura perché la giornata **è molto** lunga.
Signora 2	La vita del pendolare **è abbastanza** faticosa. Mi alzo al mattino molto presto e torno alla sera molto tardi.
Signora 3	È molto stressante [...]

Key phrases

com'è ...?	*what's it like?*
è molto ...	*it's very ...*
è abbastanza ...	*it's fairly ...*

2 [cc] [CD] 3

Two of the commuters explain how they get from home to work.

First time round

esco di casa	*I leave the house*
prendo	*I take*
vado	*I go*

As well as the car, there are three other means of transport mentioned. They don't sound too different from their English equivalents: can you guess what they are?

[*Anna*	**Come va da casa al lavoro?**]
Signora 1	Esco di casa, **prendo la macchina** perché abito in periferia, parcheggio in stazione, vicino alla stazione, che è difficile perché ci sono molte macchine e molta gente. Prendo il treno, arrivo a Bologna che è la città in cui lavoro e prendo un autobus e vado a lavorare.
Signora 2	Arrivo alla stazione **in macchina** poi in treno vado fino a Bologna e da Bologna **con la bicicletta** vado fino al lavoro.

molta gente	*many people*
in cui	*in which*
da	*from*
fino a	*to, as far as*

> ### Key phrases
>
> | | |
> |---|---|
> | **come va . . .** | *how do you get . . .* |
> | **da casa al lavoro?** | *from home to work?* |
> | **prendo la macchina** | *I take the car* |
> | **in macchina** | *by car* |
> | **con la bicicletta** | *by bike* |

How do you get there? [cc] [CD] 3

Listen to the cassette/CD and say how you get around.

3 [cc] [CD] 4

Silvia Malagò and Danilo Trabecca both live in Ferrara and travel to work together part of the way.

First time round

il treno delle sette e cinquantatré	*the 7.53 train*
il binario	*platform*

a Do they go to the station together?
b What platform does their train leave from?

Silvia	Mi chiamo Silvia e abito a Ferrara ma lavoro a Bologna. **Ogni mattina** dal lunedì al venerdì **vado in bicicletta alla stazione** di Ferrara e prendo il treno delle 7.53 per Bologna che parte dal binario numero tre.
Danilo	**Tutti i giorni**, tranne il sabato e la domenica, vado alla stazione di Ferrara in macchina e prendo il treno delle 7.53 per Bologna che parte dal binario numero tre.

dal lunedì al venerdì	*from Monday to Friday*
tranne	*except*
il sabato e la domenica	*on Saturdays and Sundays*

> ### Key phrases
>
> | | |
> |---|---|
> | **ogni mattina** | *every morning* |
> | **vado . . .** | *I go . . .* |
> | **in bicicletta** | *by bike* |
> | **alla stazione** | *to the station* |
> | **tutti i giorni** | *every day* |

Days of the week 4

Listen to the cassette/CD and try to learn the days of the week.

4 5

Silvia and Danilo meet up with Anna on Bologna station before work and sort out various arrangements. Anna is late and Danilo is in a hurry – he's got to get to his job in Imola, 33 km from Bologna.

First time round

ho fretta	*I'm in a hurry*
a pranzo	*at lunchtime*
fare colazione	*to have breakfast*

a When do Anna and Danilo plan to meet?
b Where do Anna and Silvia plan to meet and how will they get there?

Anna	Scusate, sono in ritardo.
Silvia	Ciao.
Danilo	Ciao, non importa. Come va?
Anna	Non c'è male, grazie.
Danilo	Anna, scusa, ma ho fretta, **devo prendere** l'altro treno per andare a Imola. Ci vediamo a pranzo, allora?
Anna	Sì.
Danilo	Ciao.
Anna	Arrivederci, a presto.
Silvia	Ciao.

Anna	Silvia, tu hai tempo di fare colazione adesso?
Silvia	Sì, volentieri. Ho una fame da lupo. Conosco un bar in Piazza Maggiore che si chiama Bar Giuseppe. Io però **devo andare** in bicicletta perché dopo devo andare al lavoro.
Anna	Beh, va bene.
Silvia	Va bene?
Anna	Tu vai in bicicletta e **io vengo** in autobus.
Silvia	Va bene.
Anna	Va bene? Andiamo.

scusate, scusa	*sorry*
non importa	*it doesn't matter*
l'altro	*the other*
hai tempo di . . .?	*have you got time to . . .?*
ho una fame da lupo	*I'm starving [I've got a wolf's hunger]*
a presto	*see you soon*
ci vediamo	*see you*

Key phrases	
devo prendere . . .	*I've got to catch . . .*
devo andare . . .	*I've got to go . . .*
io vengo . . .	*I'm coming/I'll come*

Odd one out   6

Listen to the cassette/CD. Which is the appropriate phrase to use in the circumstances?

Patterns I

i) Getting about

The key verbs are **andare** *(to go)* and **venire** *(to come)* plus the words for *to* – **in** and **a** [see Systems, note 1 i, p. 93]

vado/vengo	a casa	*I go/come*	home
	a scuola		to school
	a messa		to Mass

vado/vengo	in città	*I go/come*	into town
	in periferia		to the suburbs
	in chiesa		to church

It is largely a question of idiom whether you use **in** or **a**. However, there are some rules:

With towns it's always **a**:
Vado/vengo a Ferrara.   *I go/come to Ferrara*

With countries it's **in**:
Vado/vengo in Italia   *I go/come to Italy*

A often combines with **il, l', lo, la, i, le, gli** to form one word:

vado	al lavoro	*I go*	to work
	all'estero		abroad
	allo stadio		to the stadium
	alla fermata dell'autobus		to the bus-stop
	ai giardini pubblici		to the public gardens
	agli istituti di bellezza		to beauty salons
	alle manifestazioni per la pace		to peace demonstrations

At this stage use **a** with the definite article if you're in doubt about how to say *to*.

Look at Systems, note 4 i, p. 94 if you want to know more.

ii) Transport

In Italy, you travel *in* or *with* things: the key words are **in** or **con**:

| vado | in bicicletta | *I go* | by bicycle |
| andiamo | con la bicicletta | *we go* | |

| vengo | in autobus | *I come* | by bus |
| veniamo | con l'autobus | *we come* | |

| vai/va | in treno | *you go* | by train |
| andate | con il treno | | |

| vieni/viene | in metropolitana | *you come* | by tube |
| venite | con la metropolitana | | |

| va/vanno | in aereo | *he, she goes/they go* | by 'plane |
| viene/vengono | in motocicletta | *he, she comes/they come* | by motorbike |

If you walk it's **a piedi**:

vado/vengo | a piedi *I walk, I go/come* | *on foot*

You can also say how you travel by using
prendere *(to catch)* or *(to take)*:

| prendo | l'aereo | *I take* | *the plane* |
| prendiamo | un tassì | *we take* | *a taxi* |

iii) Saying how often things happen

The key word is **ogni** *(every)*.

Vengo qui	ogni mattina/giorno	*I come here*	*every morning/every day*
	ogni sera/pomeriggio		*every evening/afternoon*
	ogni settimana/mese		*every week/month*
	ogni lunedì/domenica		*every Monday/Sunday*
	ogni anno/estate		*every year/summer*
	ogni tanto		*every so often*

| Il treno parte | ogni ora/ogni due ore | *The train leaves* | *every hour/two hours* |
| | ogni dieci minuti | | *every ten minutes* |

iv) What you have to do

The key verb is **dovere** *(to have to)*. [See Systems, note 1 ii, p. 93.]
It is followed by an infinitive:

Devo	scendere qui	*I must*	*get out here*
Dobbiamo	aspettare l'autobus	*We must*	*wait for the 'bus*
	fare il biglietto		*get the ticket*

Devi	pagare un supplemento?	*Do you have to*	*pay a supplement?*
Deve	fare un abbonamento?		*get a season ticket?*
Dovete	prenotare un posto?		*book a seat?*

v) Asking and saying what it's like

In Italian you say, *'How is it?'* – **Come è? Come** is shortened to **com'** in front of **è** and pronounced
as one word:

Com'è	la vita del pendolare?	*What's*	*a commuter's life like?*
	la Sua giornata?		*your day like?*
	il Suo lavoro?		*your job like?*

È	una vita molto stressante	*It's*	*a very stressful life*
	una giornata tanto interessante		*an extremely interesting day*
	un lavoro abbastanza noioso		*a fairly/quite boring job*
	un lavoro poco piacevole		*not a very pleasant job*
	un lavoro un po' faticoso		*a somewhat boring job*

Practice I

Excuses! Excuses!

There is a particular chore you have been asked to do and you are busy explaining to your friend why you can't do it. You've written your regular appointments in your diary:
e.g. Ogni lunedì vado in ufficio.

lunedì	Ufficio
martedì	Piscina
mercoledì	Supermercato
giovedì	Ufficio
venerdì	istituto
sabato	Studio
domenica	

Perhaps Sundays are free? Say what *you* normally do on a Sunday.

Refresh your memory (1)   6

Listen again to the first part of Interaction 2 where a woman describes her journey to Bologna. Don't look back at the text, but listen as often as you need to answer these questions:

How does she say:

    I leave the house . . .   I take the car . . .
    I get to Bologna . . .   I catch a bus . . .
    I go to work . . .

Getting to work

Your friends are telling you how they travel. Francesca, for example, takes the train to work.
e.g. Vado in treno. Sì, prendo il treno.

What about the others?

1 Giancarlo

2 Giovanna

3 Luca

4 Stefania

How about you? How do you get to college or work?

How do you get there?   6

Now see if you can describe a journey to a friend.

Amico	Come vai da casa al lavoro?
You	*[Say you leave the house and go to the bus-stop.]*
Amico	Devi aspettare molto?
You	*[Say no, you don't have to wait long.]*
Amico	E poi, quando arrivi a Manchester?
You	*[Say when you arrive in Manchester you walk to the office.]*
Amico	Ah! L'ufficio è vicino alla stazione, allora . . .
You	*[Say yes, it's near the station.]*
Amico	Che fortuna!

Now describe a journey you make regularly, starting with leaving the house and ending with your final destination.

Where's everybody?

Where do members of the family go to do the following:

e.g. Per comprare un giornale, mio padre . . .
Va all'edicola.

1 Per giocare con i figli, gli zii . . .
2 Per comprare frutta e verdura, mia madre . . .
3 Per prendere un caffè, mio fratello e io . . .
4 Per prendere un autobus, mia sorella . . .
5 Per vedere un film, mio cugino e mia cugina . . .
6 And this evening everyone's going to the match.
   Tutti . . .

Memory test

How long does it take you to unscramble the days of the week below?

1 VERDIEN   5 ABATOS
2 LEOCRIDEM   6 VIGEDIO
3 LEUNDI   7 EDITRAM
4 NIDOMECA

What's it like?

Here's what life is like for some people. Read what they say and then make your own comment; use one of the phrases given here to describe each person's situation.

> **poco divertente   molto noiosa**
> **tanto interessante   poco stressante**

You don't need to understand every word to answer, so try to guess any words you don't know. You can, however, find them in the Vocabulary.

e.g. 'La mia giornata è piacevole: mi alzo tardi, mi lavo, mi vesto, prendo uno o due caffè, e leggo il giornale. Poi vado a trovare gli amici e pranziamo al ristorante. La sera andiamo al cinema o al bar.'
La sua vita è veramente . . . *(His life is really . . .)*
La sua vita è veramente poco stressante!

1 'La mia giornata è dura e faticosa. Mi sveglio prestissimo, mi alzo subito e vado a lavorare. Lavoro dalla mattina alla sera e torno a casa tardi. Sono stanco e vado a letto. Non ho molti amici.'
La sua vita è veramente . . .

2 'La mia giornata è monotona: mi alzo la mattina alla stessa ora, esco di casa alla stessa ora e prendo lo stesso autobus. Arrivo in ufficio, vedo le stesse persone e scrivo le stesse lettere. Ho lo stesso orario da vent'anni!'
La sua vita è . . .

3 'Ogni giorno è diverso. Viaggio molto e vado in tanti paesi diversi – in Giappone, in India per esempio. Incontro tante persone diverse e imparo sempre cose nuove.'
La sua vita è . . .

Now say what *you* do on: a boring day; on an interesting day.

Cultura e parole

Le Ferrovie

In a country as fragmented as Italy, the railways – **le ferrovie** – have always been an important means of communication. Italy's first Prime Minister, Cavour, was well known for his passionate belief in the power of the railways to unify the nation, while Mussolini's boast that he made the trains run on time is legendary. In fact the railways were efficiently run as early as the beginning of the 20th century when most of the 13,000 km of track were taken over by the State and they became one of Italy's first nationalised industries. Since 2000, however, they have largely been run by public-private partnership. There are now almost 20,000 km of track and, despite sometimes vociferous commuter complaints on the **trenoproblem** website, Italy's train service is generally acknowledged to give value for money.

Milan Central Railway Station

With the increase in commuting, one of the most positive developments has been the move to integrate transport within each region and make it possible to travel by train, bus and tube using the same ticket. The regional authorities are responsible for ensuring that different transport companies charge the same. Tickets are obtained at the **biglietterie** – ticket offices – in the main stations and there are also automatic options. You can buy ordinary tickets or season tickets – **abbonamenti** – online at the **biglietterie Internet** and collect your ticket at the **postazioni self-service** – self-service stations – found in the main concourses. In over 500 smaller stations there are **biglietterie automatiche** which give you a **ricevuta di credito** – a credit note – if there is insufficient change.

Il trasporto urbano

Public transport within cities is increasingly complex, and many of Italy's main cities plan to complete a major expansion and upgrading of their urban and intercity transport networks by 2010. Bologna, for example, plans to have a new underground station – **stazione sotterranea** – for high-speed trains – **i TAV (treni ad alta velocità),** leaving the old **stazione centrale** for urban and suburban services.

Travel around towns is mostly by bus, and often by tram – **il tram** – but also increasingly by tube – **la metropolitana**. In some places such as Naples, you can go by funicular – **il funicolare** – as well as by

trolleybus – **il filobus**, while in Venice public transport is, predictably, by boat; not so much the gondola as the **vaporetto** – the waterbus. Tickets for most of these services are bought in advance at tobacconists – **tabacchi** – or newspaper kiosks – **edicole**. You can get a single ride – **una corsa semplice** – or a book of tickets – **un blocchetto**. They are valid for a certain period of time, often 75 or 120 minutes and you have to stamp them – **convalidare** – before use.

Le autostrade

For those choosing not to use public transport there are the **autostrade**. First built in the 1920s, often along the old Roman roads, the Aurelia, the Flaminia, the via Emilia and the via Appia, the 7,000 km of motorways have unified Italy at least as much as the railways. Once completely State-owned, they are now under public-private ownership. The toll – **il pedaggio** – can be paid at the toll station – **il casello** – in cash or, more speedily, using a **Viacard** or **Telepass**. The **Telepass** is fixed to the windscreen and read electronically, the cost being debited to your account.

Interactions

5a   7

Anna and Silvia meet up again in the Bar Giuseppe. Anna learns about Silvia's job.

First time round

| spesso | *often* |
| devo uscire | *I have to leave* |

Anna wants to know if Silvia often has breakfast in the bar and how long she's been commuting.

a How does she ask Silvia what job she does?
b How long is Silvia's working day?

Anna   Vieni spesso qui a fare colazione?
Silvia   Ogni tanto quando ho tempo.
Anna   Da quanto tempo fai la pendolare?
Silvia   Faccio la pendolare da . . . da molto tempo, da cinque anni, però lavoro a Bologna solo da tre anni.
Anna   E **che lavoro fai** esattamente?
Silvia   **Lavoro** in un ufficio, **nel campo dell'informatica.**
Anna   È lunga la tua giornata?
Silvia   Sì, abbastanza. Lavoro **dalle nove alle cinque** del pomeriggio in ufficio, però devo uscire di casa **la mattina alle sette e mezza** e torno **la sera** alle sei e mezza.

Key phrases

che lavoro fai?	*what job do you do?*
lavoro nel campo	*I work in the field*
dell'informatica	*of computers*
dalle nove alle cinque	*from nine to five*
la mattina	*in the morning*
alle sette e mezza	*at half past seven*
la sera	*in the evening*

5b   8

Anna finds out a bit more about Silvia's journey to work. She asks Silvia if she lives far from the station.

First time round

lontano da	*far from*
quando piove	*when it's raining*
e c'è la nebbia	*and foggy*

a How does she get to work?
b Is there anything unusual about her journey?

Anna   Ma abiti lontano dalla stazione?
Silvia   No, abito in città, in centro, nel centro di Ferrara.
Anna   E come fai per andare a lavorare allora?
Silvia   Prendo la bicicletta per andare da casa alla stazione di Ferrara, poi prendo il treno e ho un'altra bicicletta vecchia alla stazione di Bologna per andare al lavoro. Ho due biciclette, insomma. E poi la sera per tornare a casa, faccio la stessa cosa.
Anna   Ma **d'inverno** quando piove e c'è la nebbia?
Silvia   Faccio quasi sempre la stessa cosa, non cambio programma.
Anna   Che coraggio!
Silvia   Anna, scusami, **sono** già **le nove** e sono in ritardo per il lavoro e devo scappare.

come fai per . . .?	*how do you . . .?*
non cambio programma	*I don't change my routines*
che coraggio!	*you're brave!*

Key phrases

| **d'inverno** | *in the winter* |
| **sono . . . le nove** | *it's nine o'clock* |

4

6 [cc] (CD) 9

After lunch with Danilo in Imola, Anna spends the afternoon in Bologna and then boards the train for Ferrara. She talks to a state employee who commutes regularly.

First time round

un impiegato dello stato	*a state employee*
. . . volte alla settimana	*. . . times a week*
verso che ora rientra?	*about what time do you return?*

How many times a week does this man travel?

[*Anna*   **Che lavoro fa?**
Signore   Sono un impiegato dello stato.]
Anna   E **quante volte** alla settimana, quindi, deve fare Ferrara – Bologna?
Signore   Beh, io viaggio praticamente dal lunedì al venerdì per cinque giorni alla settimana.

Anna   E verso che ora rientra la sera?
Signore   Per tre giorni alla settimana rientro **alle quindici e trenta** e per due giorni alla settimana **alle diciotto e trenta**.

fare Ferrara–Bologna *to make the Ferrara–Bologna trip*
praticamente *virtually, basically*

Key phrases

che lavoro fa?	*what job do you do?*
quante volte?	*how many times?*
alle quindici e trenta	*at 3.30 p.m.*
alle diciotto e trenta	*at 6.30 p.m.*

24-hour clock [cc] (CD) 10

Listen to the cassette/CD and revise the numbers from 10 to 30. Now listen to the station announcements and work out what they mean.

Patterns 2

i) Jobs

When you ask people what job they do, you need the verb **fare** *(to do)*. [See Systems 1 ii, p. 93.]

Che lavoro | fai? *What job do you do? [informal]*
           | fa? *[formal]*

The answer is literally, '*I do the . . .*'

Faccio | il medico   *I'm* | *a doctor*
       | l'assistente sociale | *a social worker*
       | la segretaria | *a secretary*

But you can also use **sono** and say '*I am*', with or without **un** and **una**:

Sono | (un/un') insegnante   *I'm* | *a teacher*
     | (un) postino | *a postman*

If you are in charge, the word varies according to the profession. Here's one expression:

È il capo *He's the boss*

Fare or **essere** are often used interchangeably with all the above professions (with the exception of **operaio**, generally used only with **essere**). However, **fare** is more specific and clearly indicates that you are actually practising your profession. Another way of stating your job is to use **mi occupo di**:

Mi occupo di | marketing   *I'm in* | *marketing*
             | pubbliche relazioni | *public relations*

To indicate what line you're in, you use **nel campo di** *(in the field of)*:

| Lavoro nel campo | dell'informatica | *I work in* | *computers* |
| | delle comunicazioni | | *communications* |

Sometimes you simply want to say where you work, or who you work for:

Lavoro	in un ospedale	*I work*	*in a hospital*
	alla posta		*at the post office*
	per una ditta		*for a firm*

ii) **Telling the time**

The 24-hour clock is used for timetables. 'O'clock' is expressed in terms of *'the hours'* – **le ore**:

8.00: le otto *2.15: le due e un quarto/e quindici* *4.30: le quattro e mezza/e mezzo/e trenta* *10.45: le undici meno un quarto/le dieci e quarantacinque*

Che ore sono?/Che ora è?   *What time is it?*

When you say the time, the word **ore** is dropped, leaving **sono + le +** number:

| sono | le otto | *it's* | *eight o'clock* |
| | le undici | | *eleven o'clock* |

But if you want to say *one o'clock* you use **è + l'**:

è l'una   *it's one o'clock*

And midday or midnight is simply:

| è | mezzogiorno | *it's* | *midday* |
| | mezzanotte | | *midnight* |

For time past the hour you need to know the numbers up to 60 [see Ref. I, 1, p. 239] and use the word **e** – *and*:

sono	le due e mezza/e trenta	*it's*	*half past two/two thirty*
	le tre e un quarto/e quindici		*quarter past three/three fifteen*
	le sette e cinquantatré		*seven fifty-three*

To say *half past,* Italians use **e mezzo** as well as **e mezza**.

iii) **Arrivals and departures: at what time?**

The key word is **a**, combined with **le** or **l'**:

Esco alle nove e torno all'una.   *I leave at nine and come back at one.*
Usciamo a mezzogiorno e torniamo a mezzanotte.   *We leave at midday and come back at midnight.*

See Systems, note 1 i, p. 93 for **uscire** *(to leave, to go out).*

Patterns 2

iv) From when to when?

The key words are **da** and **a**, combined with **le** and **l'**:

Lavoro dalle nove alle cinque   *I work from nine to five*

If it's a day of the week, **da/a** combine with **il** or **la**:

Lavoro | dal lunedì al venerdì
| dal sabato alla domenica

v) Saying how often you do things

Ogni quanto | vieni?   *How often do you come?*
Quanto spesso |
Vieni spesso qui?   *Do you often come here?*

Vengo … | sempre   *I come* | *always*
| spesso   *often*
| di solito   *usually*
| qualche volta, a volte   *sometimes*
| ogni tanto   *occasionally*

Non vengo mai   *I never come*

vi) Saying how many times

The key word is **volta** followed by **a**, which combines with **la**, **il**, and **l'**.

quante volte | alla settimana?   *how many times* | *a week?*
| al mese?   *a month?*
| all'anno?   *a year?*

una volta | alla settimana   *once* | *a week*
due volte | al mese   *twice* | *a month*
tre volte | all'anno   *three times* | *a year*

vii) Saying when

To express *on* and *in*, all you need are the words for *'the'* – **il**, **la**, etc.

quando? *when?* | la mattina | vado a lavorare | *in the morning* | *I go to work*
| il lunedì   *on Mondays*
| il pomeriggio | dormo   *in the afternoon* | *I sleep*
| la sera   *in the evening*
| il fine settimana | esco   *at the weekend* | *I go out*

However, for seasons it's **di** and **in**:

d'inverno | vado in vacanza | *in the winter* | *I go on holiday*
d'estate   *in the summer*
in primavera | rimango in città | *in the spring* | *I stay in town*
in autunno   *in the autumn*

Practice 2

I work for the State ⊙ 10

Find out what the Bianciardis do for a living.

You	*[Ask signor Bianciardi what job he does.]*
Sig. B	Sono un impiegato dello stato.
You	*[He works for the state, but ask him where he works.]*
Sig. B	Lavoro alle poste.
You	*[Ah, he could be a postman, then. Ask him if he's a postman.]*
Sig. B	No, non faccio il postino, sono il direttore delle poste in Emilia Romagna.
You	*[Oh, the boss . . .! Better luck next time . . . Now ask his wife, dottoressa Bianciardi what she does.]*
Dott.ssa B	Sono anch'io una dipendente statale. Lavoro in una scuola.
You	*[Well that's easy, she's a teacher of course. Ask her if she's a teacher.]*
Dott.ssa B	No, non insegno. Sono la preside di una scuola.
You	*[Oh, she's the headmistress. Well, nearly right. Now you tell her what you do.]*

What do you have?

For each day of the week say when you have a meal or drink. Take care how you express 'have'.

e.g. Il lunedì mattina al bar *(have a coffee)*
Il lunedì mattina prendo un caffè al bar.

1 Il martedì mattina a casa *(have breakfast)*
2 Il mercoledì a mezzogiorno *(have lunch)*
3 Il giovedì alle 4.30 *(have a snack)*
4 Il venerdì sera con i suoceri *(have an aperitif)*
5 Il sabato sera a casa *(have supper)*
6 La domenica alle 5 con amici inglesi *(have tea)*

Now say how frequently you do each of the above: always? often? usually? sometimes? occasionally?

Identikit

If you work outside the home answer the following:
Che lavoro fa? Dove lavora? Come fa per andare al lavoro? Quante ore lavora al giorno? A che ora comincia e a che ora finisce?

If you're not employed, answer the following:
Cosa fa durante il giorno? Com'è la Sua vita?

Timetables

Look at the Bologna-Ferrara timetable below.
[**IR**=Interregionale, **R**=Regionale, **ES**=Eurostar, **D**=Diretto]

a If you want to find out what time the train leaves, which word do you look for?
b What is the Italian word for *arrival*?
c What do you think **durata** means?
d You want to be in Ferrara by 10.15. Which is the quickest train?

BOLOGNA – FERRARA

Partenza	Arrivo	Treni	Durata
07:53	08:25	**IR**	00:32
08:18	09:07	**R**	00:49
08:53	09:25	**IR**	00:32
09:42	10:08	**ES**	00:26
09:53	10:25	**D**	00:32

What time?

On Silvia's clocks are the times she does certain things during the day. Can you say when she does what?

1 A che ora si alza? **2** A che ora fa colazione?

3 A che ora prende il treno la mattina? **4** A che ora va a letto?

4

Vocabulary

Time

quando	when
adesso	now
subito	at once
oggi	today
stasera	this evening
domani	tomorrow
già	already
dopo	afterwards, after
poi	then
presto	early
tardi	late

The time

l'ora	time, hour
il minuto	minute
il secondo	second
l'orologio	clock, watch
la sveglia	alarm
in ritardo	late
in anticipo	early
in orario	on time
avanti/indietro di x minuti	x minutes fast/slow

People jobs, and work

la professione	profession
il mestiere	trade, job
il/la collega	colleague
il capo	boss
il direttore	primary sch. head (m)
la direttrice	primary sch. head (f)
il proprietario	owner
l'autista	driver
l'avvocatessa	lawyer (f)
l'avvocato	lawyer (m)
la casalinga	housewife
il/la commesso/a	shop assistant
il/la dattilografo/a	typist
il/la dentista	dentist
il/la farmacista	chemist
il/la giornalista	journalist
l'idraulico	plumber
l'infermiere/a	nurse
l'ingegnere	engineer
l'insegnante	sec.-teacher
il/la maestro/a	primary teacher
il meccanico	meccanic
il medico	doctor (m/f)
l'operaio/a	worker (m/f)
il/la parrucchiere/a	hair-dresser (m/f)
il/la poliziotto/a	policeman/woman
il postino	postman
il/la preside	sec. sch. head
il/la ragioniere/a	accountant (m/f)
la segretaria	secretary
il tassista	taxi-driver
lo studente	student (m)
la studentessa	student (f)
disoccupato/a	unemployed
in pensione	retired
il lavoro	work
il posto	job, place, seat
lo stipendio	salary
il salario	wage
guadagnare	to earn
spendere	to spend
risparmiare	to save
fare sciopero	to strike

Going places

andare	to go
venire	to come
uscire	to go out, to leave
partire	to leave
fermarsi	to stop
aspettare	to wait (for)
attraversare	to cross
tornare	to go/come back
rientrare	to get back
salire	to get into, to go up
scendere	to get out of, to go down
viaggiare	to travel
andare a trovare	to visit [person]
visitare	to visit [place]
andare/venire a piedi	to walk
fare il biglietto	to buy a ticket
fare un viaggio	to make a journey
fare una passeggiata	to go for a walk

Everyday activities

svegliarsi	to wake up
alzarsi	to get up
lavarsi	to wash
pettinarsi	to do one's hair
farsi la barba	to shave
fare il bagno	to have a bath
fare colazione	to have breakfast
fare il bucato	to do the washing
fare i compiti	to do homework
fare la doccia	to have a shower
fare la spesa	to go shopping
pranzare	to have lunch
cenare	to have supper
andare a letto	to go to bed

Adjectives

stesso	same
diverso	different
monotono	monotonous
noioso	boring
interessante	interesting
divertente	fun, enjoyable
piacevole	pleasant
affollato	crowded
libero	free, vacant
alto	high
basso	low

Troubleshooting

Ora   tempo   volta

In the expressions below, the English word *time* translates three Italian words:

a che **ora**?	*at what time?*
non ho **tempo**	*I haven't got time*
quante **volte**?	*how many times?*

Ora is the word for hour but it is also used when you're asking the time:

che ora è?	*what time is it?*

Tempo is the general word for time, and is used for weather too:

il tempo passa	*time passes*
da molto tempo	*for a long time*
fa bel tempo	*the weather is good*

Volta is used in connection with events:

un'altra volta	*another time*
è la prima volta	*it's the first time*
due volte al giorno	*twice (2 times) a day*

molto   much, many   very

Molto can mean *much/many*. In this case it is an **adjective** agreeing with the accompanying noun:

ci sono molt**e** macchine	*there are many cars*

However, **molto** can also be an **adverb** meaning *very*, in which case it never changes its form:

la giornata è molt**o** lunga	*the day is very long*

Unità 5

Vivere in città
City living

Il Palazzo Comunale, Piazza Maggiore, Bologna

Part 1 (Interactions 1–4, Patterns 1, Practice 1)	**Part 2** (Interactions 5–7, Patterns 2, Practice 2)
Learn how to:	*Learn how to:*
Ask for a room in a hotel	Say what you want to do
Ask for goods in a shop	Say what needs to be done
Ask about prices	
Make simple requests and ask for permission	
Find out about opening times	
Ask if something is possible	

Grammar

Irregular nouns and their plurals	**potere**, **volere**
di + definite article – *some*	More uses of **da**
dare	

Want to take it further?
Grammar: See Systems 5, pp. 97–8   *More practice:* do Reinforcement 5, pp. 99–100

Interactions

1   🔲   ⓪ 12

Anna's friend Giorgio has arrived in Bologna for a conference on pollution. He finds a small hotel – **un albergo** – in the centre and goes in to ask for a room – **una camera**. He wants a single room with a bath – **una singola con bagno**.

First time round

una notte	*a night*
una doppia	*a double room*

a How long does he want to stay?
b Does he get the room he wants?

Receptionist	Buongiorno.
Giorgio	Buongiorno. **Ha** per caso **una** camera libera**?** – Una singola con bagno.
Receptionist	Per quante notti, signore?
Giorgio	Per tre notti.
Receptionist	Mmm, vediamo… Una singola con bagno, no, mi dispiace. Abbiamo soltanto una doppia con doccia.
Giorgio	E la doppia, **quanto costa**?
Receptionist	Cento euro al giorno compresa la prima colazione.
Giorgio	Ah, allora va bene. **La prendo**.
Receptionist	D'accordo. Una doppia per tre notti allora. **Mi dà** un documento per favore?
Giorgio	Certo. Ecco la mia carta di identità.
Receptionist	Grazie. E questa è la chiave per la camera numero dodici. La prima colazione è alle sette – dalle sette alle dieci.
Giorgio	Va bene, grazie! A più tardi.

la doccia	*shower*	la chiave	*key*

Key phrases

ha una ….?	*do you have a …?*
quanto costa?	*how much does it cost?*
la prendo	*I'll have it*
mi dà …?	*can I have…?*

Have you got a room?   🔲   ⓪ 12
Listen to the cassette/CD and find out if you can stay in this hotel.

2   🔲   ⓪ 12

Before seeing Anna, Giorgio goes to a chemist's.

First time round

i capelli	*hair*
il mal di gola	*sore throat*

a What does he buy?
b How much does he spend altogether?

Sig.ra Bruni	Buongiorno. Desidera?
Giorgio	Buongiorno. Mi dà uno shampoo per capelli normali per piacere.
Sig.ra Bruni	Sì, ecco. Abbiamo questo che è adatto per lavaggi frequenti e poi c'è questo qua per lavaggi settimanali.
Giorgio	Ho capito. Uhm, **quanto costano**?
Sig.ra Bruni	Costano lo stesso prezzo, signore, sei euro e trenta.
Giorgio	Va bene, prendo questo per lavaggi frequenti.
Sig.ra Bruni	Serve altro?
Giorgio	Ah, sì. **Ha qualcosa per** il mal di gola?
Sig.ra Bruni	Certo. Abbiamo queste pastiglie o lo sciroppo.
Giorgio	Preferisco lo sciroppo. **Quant'è**?
Sig.ra Bruni	Lo sciroppo … vediamo … Costa … quattro euro e quaranta.
Giorgio	Va bene, **lo prendo**.
Sig.ra Bruni	Basta così?
Giorgio	Sì, grazie, basta così. **Quant'è**?
Sig.ra Bruni	Allora, sono dieci euro e settanta centesimi in tutto.
Giorgio	Ecco a Lei.
Sig.ra Bruni	Grazie, buongiorno.

ho capito	*I see*	le pastiglie	*lozenges*
lo sciroppo	*syrup*	Ecco a Lei	*here you are*

Key phrases

quanto costano?	*how much do they cost?*
ha qualcosa per…?	*have you got something for…?*
quant'è?	*how much is it?*

At the chemist's   🔲   ⓪ 12
You want something for a stomach-ache. Listen and play your part in the conversation.

3 🖭 ◎ 13

Bologna's **Centro informazioni comunali** provides information on all the city's services: there's even a computer which records levels of pollution – **inquinamento.** When Anna visits the Centre she asks if she can try the computer.

First time round

> l'inquinamento *pollution*

a Is Anna allowed to use the computer?
b Is everyone allowed to use the computer when they want to?

Anna	**Scusi. Posso?**
Ragazza	Sì, sì, **prego.**
Anna	**Che cosa si può** vedere esattamente?
Ragazza	Questo computer permette di vedere il grado di inquinamento nelle varie zone della città di Bologna.
Anna	E chi può usare questo computer?
Ragazza	È a disposizione di tutti. La gente lo può usare quando vuole per sapere se l'aria è inquinata.
Anna	E lo consultano spesso?
Ragazza	Sì, molti cittadini sono curiosi di sapere il livello di inquinamento della zona dove abitano.
Anna	Ah, è un'ottima iniziativa.

la gente lo può usare quando vuole	*people can use it when they want to*
permette di vedere	*makes it possible to see*

Key phrases

scusi. Posso?	*excuse me, may I?*
prego	*go ahead*
che cosa si può...?	*what can you...?*

4 🖭 ◎ 14

The **Centro informazioni** also houses the tourist office. Anna checks she's in the right place and then enquires about opening hours.

First time round

aprire	*to open*
chiudere	*to close*

Use the words given here and what you studied in Unit 4.

a When is the office open?
b Are the Sunday opening hours the same?

Anna	Questo è l'ufficio turistico, vero?
Lucia	Certo.
Anna	Buongiorno.
Lucia	Buongiorno.
Anna	**Quando siete aperti?**
Lucia	Siamo aperti tutto il giorno. Non chiudiamo a mezzogiorno.
Anna	**A che ora aprite?**
Lucia	Apriamo alle nove e chiudiamo alle diciannove.
Anna	E siete aperti dalle nove alle diciannove anche di domenica?
Lucia	No, la domenica siamo aperti solo dalle nove alle tredici.
Anna	Ho capito. Qui vengono molti turisti?
Lucia	Sì, molti turisti italiani e anche stranieri.
Anna	Grazie, arrivederci.
Lucia	Arrivederci.

anche di domenica?	*on Sundays as well?*
ho capito	*I see*

Key phrases

quando siete aperti?	*when are you open?*
a che ora aprite?	*what time do you open?*

Patterns I

i) Asking for goods and services

You can use the verb **avere** and the singular or plural *you*:

Avete	una camera doppia?			a double room?
Ha	qualcosa per il mal di gola?	*Have you got*		something for a sore throat?

If you are asking for *some*, or *any*, use **di** combined with the definite article:

	della pomata antisettica?			antiseptic cream?
Avete	del dentifricio?			toothpaste?
Ha	delle pastiglie per la gola?	*Have you got any*		throat pastilles?
	dei cerotti?			plasters?

If you know that they have what you want, use the phrase **mi dà,** literally '*will you give me*':

Mi dà	un documento?			some identification?
	del dentifricio?	*Can I have*		some toothpaste?

[The verb **dare** (*to give*) is in Systems, note 1 ii, p. 97.]

Asking the price

All you need is the verb **costare** and the right word for *the:*

	la birra?			the beer?
	il succo di frutta?			the fruit juice?
Quanto costa	l'aperitivo?	*How much is*		the aperitif?
	l'aranciata?			the orangeade?

	le birre?			the beers?
Quanto	i succhi di frutta?			the fruit juices?
costano	gli aperitivi?	*How much are*		the aperitifs?
	le aranciate?			the orangeades?

If you want to know what everything adds up to, use the phrase **quant'è?**
(*how much is it? how much is that?*).

Quant'è?	Dieci euro e settanta centesimi	*How much is it?*	*10 euros 70 cents*
Quant'è?	Cento euro	*How much is it?*	*100 euros*

[For more on numbers see Ref. I, 1, p. 239.]

Saying you'll take it or them

The key verb is **prendere.** The words for *it* and *them* depend on the words they replace:

Va bene,	lo prendo (il vestito)		*Fine, I'll take it* [See Systems 3, note 8, p. 90.]
	la prendo (la giacca)		

Va bene,	li prendo (i fiori)		*Fine, I'll take them*
	le prendo (le rose)		

Patterns I

ii) Asking permission

The key verb is **potere** (*to be able to*) [See Systems, note 1, p. 97.]

Posso? *May I?*

Posso	entrare?	*Can I*	*come in?*
	guardare?		*look?*
	vedere?		*see?*

iii) Finding out what's possible

Again, the key verb is **potere**:

Che cosa si può	vedere	a Bologna?	*What can one/you*	*see*	*in Bologna?*
	fare			*do*	

iv) Asking someone to do something

Potere is useful for making requests:

Puoi ripetere, per favore? (*informal*)   *Can you repeat, please?*
Può parlare lentamente, per favore? (*formal*)   *Can you talk slowly, please?*

v) Opening and closing times

When making general enquiries, **voi,** the plural *you,* is often used:

Quando siete aperti?   *When are you open?*

Siamo aperti	tutto il giorno	*We're open*	*all day*
	tutti i giorni		*every day*
	i giorni feriali		*on weekdays*
	dalle 9 alle 19		*from 9 a.m. till 7 p.m.*

Siamo chiusi i giorni festivi   *We're closed on holidays*

To find out specific times the question to ask is:

A che ora	aprite?	*What time do you*	*open?*
	chiudete?		*close?*

Apriamo alle nove   *We open at 9 a.m.*
Chiudiamo alle diciannove   *We close at 7 p.m.*

If you are asking when other places open and close, you use these forms of the verbs **aprire** and **chiudere:**

A che ora	apre la posta?	*At what time*	*does the post office open?*
	aprono i musei?		*do the museums open?*

A che ora	chiude?	*At what time*	*does it close?*
	chiudono?		*do they close?*

Le torri Garisenda e Asinelli, Bologna

Practice I

The buildings of Bologna   15

You drop in to the tourist office and ask Lucia: What can one see in Bologna? Ask her in Italian. Listen to her answer. Now try to jot down the names of some of the buildings she mentioned.

Information seeking 15

Here are some other items that might be available in the tourist office:

posters (**i poster**), booklets (**gli opuscoli**), leaflets (**i dépliant**), information (**le informazioni**), map (**una pianta della città**).

Listen and repeat the words.

Now, ask if they have any of these items:

> i poster della città   i dépliant sugli alberghi
> gli opuscoli sui musei   le informazioni sugli
> autobus   le piante di Bologna

e.g. i poster della città:
> Ha/Avete **dei** poster della città?

[Look at Unit 4 Systems, note 4, p. 94 if you need any help combining **di** with **il, la, i, le,** etc.]

When is it open?

Now try to ask what time the following buildings open and close:
> la posta   le banche   i musei

Refresh your memory

Play Interaction 1 again. This time listen out for the key phrases: *have you got a . . . ?; can I have?; how much is . . . ?; that's all; I'll have it.*

How much?   15

Below are items of food you can buy in a market. The prices of the fruit and vegetables are marked, but the groceries are not. Ask the stallholder how much each grocery item costs and write the price underneath.

You'll find the following phrases helpful:
al chilo	*per kilo*
all'etto	*per 100 grammes*
al litro	*per litre*
mezzo chilo	*half a kilo*
mezzo litro	*half a litre*

L'alimentare   **Il fruttivendolo**

i pomodori
€0,90 kg

1 il prosciutto

. . . .

le pesche
€2,35 kg

2 il pane

. . . .

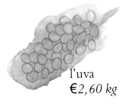

l'uva
€2,60 kg

3 il formaggio

. . . .

le mele
€2,30 kg

4 il burro

gli spinaci
€2,95 kg

. . . .

Il fruttivendolo ▱ ◎ 15

Listen to the cassette/CD and talk to the shopkeeper. The prices he quotes are from the price-list on the previous page.

Shopkeeper	Buongiorno. Desidera?
You	Buongiorno. *[Ask: have you got any peaches?]*
Shopkeeper	Sì, ecco.
You	*[Ask how much they cost.]*
Shopkeeper	Costano 2,35 al chilo.
You	*[Repeat the price. Ask for a kilo please.]*
Shopkeeper	Va bene. Desidera altro?
You	Sì, . . . *[Ask: can I have 2 kilos of spinach please?]*
Shopkeeper	Due chili di spinaci, sono 5 euro e 90. Serve altro?
You	Sì . . . *[Ask: have you got any grapes?]*
Shopkeeper	Sì. Costa 2 euro e 60 al chilo.
You	Va bene, . . . *[Repeat the price. Ask: can I have half a kilo please?]*
Shopkeeper	Mezzo chilo, va bene. 1 euro e 30. Basta così?
You	*[Say yes, that's all and ask for the total.]*
Shopkeeper	Sono 9 euro e 55 centesimi.
You	*[Repeat price.]* Va bene, grazie.

You can use this dialogue for further practice – with a fellow learner or on your own. Choose your own items and use the prices from the previous exercise.

I'll have it

For each of the items below, say you'll have it or them. Make it absolutely clear what you want by then naming the item and the colour.

e.g. Va bene, **la** prendo. Sì, prendo la maglia rossa.

Aguapark

Look at the information leaflet advertising the summer-time prices and opening hours of the Aguapark swimming pool complex. Answer the questions in Italian – aloud or in writing.

1 L'Aguapark è aperto tutto l'anno?
2 È aperto tutti i giorni da giugno a settembre?
3 È aperto tutto il giorno?
4 A che ora apre la mattina?
5 A che ora chiude la sera?
6 Per un adulto quanto costa l'ingresso la mattina?
7 E per un bambino di 10 anni, quanto costa?
8 Quanti tipi di abbonamenti ci sono?

Cultura e parole

he 1980s and 1990s saw enormous progress in environmental awareness in Italy, supported by a tenfold increase in government spending on the environment – **l'ambiente**. New legislation was passed, such as a tax on plastic bags – **i sacchetti di plastica**, a law obliging every region to install a set quota of petrol pumps selling lead-free petrol – **benzina senza piombo**, and the recycling – **il riciclaggio** – of urban waste – **i rifiuti urbani**. Recently, to the dismay of the many environmental associations – **associazioni ambientaliste** – there has been a decrease in public spending and a relaxing of some of the legislation. Much of the responsibility for implementing the legislation rests with the Environment departments – **gli Assessorati all'Ambiente** – of the provincial and municiple councils – **le province** and **i comuni**. Bologna and its surrounding province is universally acknowledged to have been a pioneer in this field. It continues to provide recycling points – **stazioni ecologiche** – where people can dispose of their waste in different coloured containers for separate collection – **la raccolta differenziata**, and it also provides online monitoring of air quality – **la qualità dell'aria**.

The city of Bologna is attached to green policies but the number of councillors from the **Federazione dei Verdi** – the Green Party – has drastically fallen in recent years. Traditionally Bologna is actually linked to the colour red. Known as **Bologna la rossa** for its longstanding left-wing political affiliations and also for the brick with which much of the city is built, the city is associated with efficiency and radical policies. However it is also famous for its culinary pleasures which can be sampled in a wide range of flourishing restaurants, trattorias and **osterie** – taverns or inns – some of which are located in Bologna's famous **portici** – arcades.

There are 37 kilometres of arcade in Bologna, more than in any other Italian city. The first ones were built in the 12th and 13th centuries to solve a student housing problem when Bologna's university – the first in Europe – attracted over 2000 students to the city. Faced with this influx, the **comune** hit on the idea of using the space over the arcades for extra accommodation. Nowadays the arcades are places to take a pleasant stroll – **una passeggiata** – and relax, whatever the weather.

Osterie: Osterie have gone up in the world. Originally they were sordid taverns associated with drunkenness and low life. Nowadays they are carefully done up in traditional regional decor and are amongst the 'in' places to go and enjoy a vast range of wines, beers and spirits (mainly grappa and whisky). Food is available and sometimes entertainment as well.

Interactions

On the outskirts of Bologna, in the **Parco dei Cedri** the Italian Worldwide Fund for Nature – **il WWF** – and the Bologna town council have set up a protected area within the park. Anna meets two people involved in the project and finds out what it's about.

First time round

le scuole elementari	*infant and junior schools*
le medie	*middle schools*
gli scopi didattici	*educational aims*
cercare di ottenere	*to try and achieve*

Remember to listen out for words which resemble English.

a Can you pick out who's the boss?
b What do they want people to learn about? Plants, or plants and animals?

Anna	Voi lavorate per il WWF, vero?
Fausto	Sì.
Anna	Lei come si chiama?
Fausto	Io mi chiamo Fausto Bonafede e sono il responsabile per il WWF di questo progetto.
Andrea	E io mi chiamo Andrea Sivelli e lavoro anch'io per il WWF.
Anna	Venite qui ogni giorno?
Andrea	Beh, ogni giorno no, però molto spesso.
Anna	E anche d'inverno?
Fausto	Anche d'inverno. Certo.
Andrea	Anche quando piove.
Anna	E cosa fate?

Fausto	Mah, accompagniamo spesso bambini e ragazzi delle scuole elementari e delle medie con scopi didattici.
Anna	E da quanto tempo esiste il progetto?
Andrea	Beh, questo progetto esiste dal novembre del 1989.
Anna	Che cosa cercate di ottenere con questo progetto?
Fausto	Cerchiamo di fare conoscere la flora ma anche la fauna caratteristiche di questa regione. E **vogliamo** studiare la natura abbandonata a sé stessa.

sono il responsabile . . . di questo progetto	*I'm in charge of this project*
che cosa cercate di ottenere?	*what are you trying to achieve?*
abbandonata a sé stessa	*left to itself*

Key phrase

vogliamo *we want*

Comune di Bologna
Assessorati all'Ambiente e alla Cultura

la Repubblica

Parchi e giardini bolognesi 8

**Parco
dei Cedri**

6   🔲   💿 17

When Fausto and Andrea have completed their work Anna finds out what still needs to be done.

First time round

tutelare l'ambiente	*to protect the environment*
cosa rimane da fare?	*what is left to do?*

What suggestions do Andrea and Fausto make for protecting the environment? Try to pick out two.

Anna   **Che cosa bisogna fare** per tutelare l'ambiente?

Andrea   Beh, **bisogna** imparare a vivere con la natura e non a combatterla.

Anna   Le persone che vengono qui, cosa fanno? Rispettano l'ambiente?

Andrea   Beh, in genere, sì, anche perché quando vengono qui per rilassarsi capiscono che la natura è indispensabile per vivere.

Anna   Che cosa rimane da fare per la conservazione della natura?

Fausto   Qui in Italia e anche in altri paesi rimane tanto da fare, bisogna, io credo, estendere queste esperienze di natura libera, senza l'intervento dell'uomo, in altre parti, in altre aree. E poi **bisogna usare meno la macchina,** utilizzare meno l'energia, eccetera.

Anna   Ma siete ottimisti per il futuro?

Andrea   Sì.

Fausto   Moderatamente ottimisti.

Anna   Grazie.

estendere queste esperienze di natura libera . . . in altre parti	*to extend these attempts at leaving nature alone . . . to other places*

Key phrases	
che cosa bisogna fare?	*what needs to be done?*
bisogna . . .	*you need to . . .*
bisogna usare meno la macchina	*you need to use cars less*

7   🔲   💿 18

The inhabitants of Bologna are enthusiastic about their town. Anna finds out from three of them why it's so nice living there.

First time round

pieno di	*full of*
punto di vista	*point of view*

Sort out what each person is keen on and put the correct letter in the boxes below:

a nightlife   **b** walking around town   **c** shopping

Voice 1	Voice 2	Voice 3

Anna   Perché è bello vivere a Bologna?

Ragazza   Bologna è bella perché ha un bel centro pieno di negozi, pieno di vetrine, è sempre illuminata. È una bella città!

Giovane   Bologna è una città che offre molto, diciamo, anche da un punto di vista della vita notturna. C'è una 'cultura' di osterie, una 'cultura' di posti dove si mangia bene e si beve bene!
[. . .]

Signora   È molto bello passeggiare anche sotto la pioggia a Bologna, perché abbiamo questi splendidi portici, che sono una delle caratteristiche principali di Bologna.

diciamo	*let's say*
si mangia bene	*you eat well*
si beve bene	*you drink well*
sotto la pioggia	*in [lit. under] the rain*

A meal out   🔲   💿 19

Bologna's night spots, in particular its restaurants, are much advertised on the local radio stations. There are two ads on the cassette/CD from Radio Sfera Regione. Listen for what's being advertised and then see if you can pick out the addresses.

Patterns 2

i) Saying what you want to do

The key verb is **volere** (*to want*) [see Systems, note 1 i, p. 97].

| Cosa | vuoi / vuole / volete | fare? | *What do you want to do?* |

| Voglio | studiare l'italiano | *I want* | *to study Italian* |
| Vogliamo | parlare italiano | *We want* | *to speak Italian* |

ii) Saying what must be done

The key verb is **bisognare** (*to be necessary*). The only form used when talking about the present is **bisogna** (*it is necessary, you/one must*).

Cosa bisogna fare?   *What must one do?*

| Bisogna | lavorare per la pace / condannare la guerra | *You must* | *work for peace / condemn war* |

Practice 2

A better world?

Can you unscramble the phrases below to form a series of slogans? There's one word too many.
**Per un mondo migliore
BISOGNA . . .**

ESSERE

la guerra!

RISPETTARE

tolleranti!

giovani!

LAVORARE

gli altri

CONDANNARE

per la pa

New Year resolutions

First choose each resolution for yourself and say what you must do. Use **volere** and **dovere** each time.

e.g. avere più tempo libero *to have more free time*

    Io **voglio** avere più tempo libero

    lavorare meno   *to work less*

    Devo lavorare meno.

1 perdere 5 chili   *to lose 5 kilos*
    mangiare pochissimo   *to eat very little*

2 fare più esercizio   *to take more exercise*
    praticare uno sport   *to take up a sport*

3 imparare il tedesco   *to learn German*
    andare a un corso serale   *to go to an evening class*

4 risparmiare soldi   *to save money*
    spendere di meno   *to spend less*

5 essere più tollerante   *to be more tolerant*
    ascoltare gli altri   *to listen to others*

Now pick a few for a member of your family or a friend:

e.g. essere più sano/a   *to be healthier*

    Mio fratello **vuole** essere più sano.

    smettere di fumare   *to give up smoking*

    Deve smettere di fumare.

★ You can work with a fellow learner and use the dictionary to make up your own resolutions.

At the tobacconist's   19

On the tape/CD you'll hear an interview with Valerio Venturi, who runs a tobacconist's in the historic centre of Bologna. Listen to the statements and check whether they are true or false.

Identikit   19

Describe your home town or a town you know well. There's some help given on the cassette/CD and below are some questions to guide you.

1 Di dov'è, Lei?
2 È grande, la Sua città?
3 Com'è la Sua città?
4 Che cosa c'è da vedere?
5 È bello vivere a . . . ?

Vocabulary

Time

tutto il giorno	all day
tutto l'anno	all year
durante	during
i giorni festivi	holidays
i giorni feriali	work days

People

l'abitante	inhabitant
il cittadino	citizen
il poliziotto	policeman
la poliziotta	policewoman
il sindaco	mayor

Il campanile

Cityscape

l'edificio	building
il palazzo	appartment block
il municipio	town hall
il museo	museum
il campanile	bell tower
la torre	tower
il ponte	bridge
i portici	arcades
la statua	statue
la strada	road
il marciapiede	pavement
il traffico	traffic
il semaforo	traffic light
il segnale	signpost
il parco	park
la biblioteca	library
la pinacoteca	art gallery

Shopping

il prezzo	price
l'acquisto	purchase
i soldi	money
gli spiccioli	small change
il resto	change
caro/costoso	expensive
il negozio	shop
il supermercato	supermarket
il magazzino	department store
la vetrina	shop window
l'alimentare (m)	grocer's
la cartoleria	stationer's
l'erboristeria	health shop
la farmacia	chemist's
il fruttivendolo	greengrocer
la libreria	bookshop
la macelleria	butcher's
la pasticceria	cake shop
la panetteria	bread shop
il parrucchiere	hairdresser
la tabaccheria	tobacconist

Verbs

parcheggiare	to park
fare caldo	to be hot
fare freddo	to be cold
comprare	to buy
vendere	to sell
spendere	to spend
risparmiare	to save

Seasons

la stagione	season
la primavera	spring
l'estate (f)	summer
l'autunno	autumn
l'inverno	winter

La statua

Weather

il tempo	weather
il clima	climate
l'aria	air
inquinato	polluted
pulito	clean
il cielo	sky
sereno	clear
nuvoloso	cloudy
la nuvola	cloud
il vento	wind
la nebbia	fog, mist
che tempo fa?	what's the weather like?
fa bel/brutto tempo	the weather's good/bad
c'è sole	it's sunny
tira vento	it's windy
il caldo	heat
il freddo	cold
l'afa	sultry heat
la pioggia	rain
piovere	to rain
la neve	snow
nevicare	to snow
la grandine	hail
grandinare	to hail
il lampo	lightning
il tuono	thunder
il temporale	storm

Troubleshooting

Aver bisogno di   bisogna

Don't confuse these two expressions.
Aver bisogno di literally means *to have need of.* (**il bisogno** means *need*). It is used like an ordinary verb:

ho bisogno di	*I need*	abbiamo bisogno di	*we need*
hai bisogno di	*you need*	avete bisogno di	*you need*
ha bisogno di	*he/she/it needs*	hanno bisogno di	*they need/you need*

Bisogna is part of the verb **bisognare** (*to be necessary*) but **bisogna** is the only form of the verb used. It can only be used in an impersonal, general sense:

bisogna studiare	*one/you must study/ it is necessary to study*

La gente è   people are

A singular form for a plural meaning.

La gente is used a lot in Italian. You need to remember to use singular verbs and adjectives with it, even though the meaning is plural. Look at these examples from Units 4 and 5.

molta gente [p. 51]	*lots of people*
la gente lo può usare quando vuole [p. 67]	*people can use it when they want*

Systems I

1 Nouns
i) Masculine and feminine

biglietto
gui**da**

Unlike English, all Italian nouns have a gender, – they are either masculine or feminine.
Nouns ending in **-o** are usually masculine:
formaggio   ragazzo   figlio   bagno

Nouns ending in **-a** are usually feminine:
pizza   ragazza   figlia   cucina

Other endings are possible. For example, masculine nouns can end in **-è**:
caffè   tè

Feminine nouns can end in **à**:
città   nazionalità

ii) Singular and plural

biglietto   bigliett**i**
gui**da**   gui**de**

Masculine nouns usually form their plural in **-i**:
formaggi   ragazzi   figli   bagni

Feminine nouns usually form their plural in **-e**:
pizze   ragazze   figlie   cucine

Nouns ending with an accented letter do not change their form in the plural.

2 Definite articles

il biglietto   **i** biglietti
la guida   **le** guide

Definite articles are words for *the.*
The form depends on whether the accompanying noun is masculine or feminine, singular or plural.

il	i
il formaggio il ragazzo	i formaggi i ragazzi

la	le
la pizza la ragazza	le pizze le ragazze

If the noun ends in an accented letter the article changes in the plural, even though the noun stays the same.
il tè   i tè   la città   le città
See also Unit 3, Systems, note 4, p. 88.

3 Indefinite articles

un biglietto
una guida

Indefinite articles are words for *a/an.*

un	una
un formaggio	una pizza
un ragazzo	una ragazza
un caffè	una città

As in English, there is often no need for an article in the plural:
un formaggio *(a cheese)*   formaggi *(cheeses)*
una pizza *(a pizza)*   pizze *(pizzas)*

To say *some* or *any* (the plural of *a*), see Unit 5, Systems, note 2iii, p. 98. See also Ref. I, 8 v, p. 240.

4 Adjectives

il	monumento famoso
i	monumenti famosi
la	basilica famosa
le	basiliche famose

Adjectives change their endings to agree with the gender and number of the noun they accompany. This is always shown by the form of the article, whereas the noun ending is not necessarily a reliable guide.
Unlike English, adjectives generally come *after* the noun, though quite a few common ones can also go before it. See Ref. V, 1, p. 244, for the position of adjectives.

Spelling note: Nouns and adjectives ending in **-ca**, **-ga** always add **h** before the plural ending:
basilica   basiliche   antica   antiche
lunga   lunghe

This is necessary to keep the original hard *k* sound of the singular ending.

The need for an **h** often applies to nouns and adjectives ending in **-co**, **-go**:

> tedesco   tedeschi   antico   antichi
> lungo   lunghi

There are a number of important exceptions:

> e.g. amico   amici   greco   greci

For more on spelling see Ref. VI, 1, p. 245.

5   Demonstrative adjectives

> quest**o** monument**o**
> quest**a** basilic**a**
> quest**i** monument**i**
> quest**e** basilic**he**

Questo always precedes the noun. Its ending changes according to the gender and number of the noun it accompanies.

6   Essere (to be)

> **sono** Anna
> **è** il Colosseo
> **sono** i Trulli

The present tense of **essere** is formed as follows:

(io)	sono	*I*	*am*
(tu)	sei	*you [informal]*	*are*
(lui, lei)	è	*he, she, it*	*is*
(Lei)	è	*you [formal]*	*are*
(noi)	siamo	*we*	*are*
(voi)	siete	*you [plural]*	*are*
(loro)	sono	*they*	*are*

i) Subject pronouns

In Italian the subject pronouns [*I, you, etc.*] are not strictly necessary to convey the meaning, whereas in English you have to use them. Italian subject pronouns are used mostly for emphasis or clarification:

> No, io non sono Stefano, lui è Stefano

ii) Understanding Lei

Lei means *she* and *you*. You use the same form of the verb and the same pronoun to talk about someone female and to talk formally to another person, whether female or male.

> Lei è inglese?   *Are you English?*
> *Is she English?*

The context will tell you whether it's *you* or *she*.

iii) Two meanings of sono

Sono can mean *I am* or *they are*. **Essere** is the only verb where the **io** and the **loro** forms coincide. The context will tell you which form is which.

7   Sentence structures

i) Affirmative and negative statements

> è una casa
> **non** è una casa

Making a sentence negative is easy. Put **non** in front of the verb.

> sono case   *they are houses*
> non sono case   *they aren't houses*

ii) Questions

> è una casa?
> **non** è una casa?

Remember, all statements can become questions with no change in word order. The rising intonation is all that's necessary.

> sono case?   *are they houses?*
> non sono case?   *aren't they houses?*

8   Prepositions

i) Di

> la basilica **di** San Pietro

One of the meanings of **di** is *of*. It can be used with places:

> i Trulli di Alberobello

and also with people:

> le cartoline di Anna   *Anna's postcards*

ii) A and in

> siamo **a** Bologna
> **in** Emilia Romagna

A and **in** are both used to mean *in*:
a is used with towns, small islands and with some set expressions which you need to learn:

> a Rimini   a Capri   a Elba   a casa   a scuola

In is used with continents, countries, large islands and many set expressions which you can learn gradually:

> in Europa   in Francia   in Sicilia   in Sardegna
> in città   in campagna   in montagna   in salotto

Reinforcement I

porta — lampada — finestra — quadro — pianta — vaso — camino — divano — poltrona — tavolo — tazza — piatto — sedia — tappeto

A Your sitting-room

1 The contents of your sitting-room have all been labelled. Can you point out the objects in it to a friend?

e.g. Ecco la porta . . .

2 There are more than one of some of these objects. Can you also point these out?

e.g. Ecco le piante.

B Apples or pears?

Here are some more objects for you to identify to your friend.

e.g. È una mela. È una pera.   **1** *penna   matita*

2 *portafoglio   borsa*   **3** *libro   quaderno*

4 *pomodoro   cipolla*   **5** *ragazzo   ragazza*

But your friend's a bit confused and gets the wrong one of each pair, so you patiently correct him . . .

e.g. È una mela?
No, non è una mela, è una pera.

1   È una matita?
. . . .

2   È un portafoglio?
. . . .

3   È un quaderno?
. . . .

4   È un pomodoro?
. . . .

5   È una ragazza?
. . . .

C The cathedral is famous

Match the adjectives to the phrases. Only one
adjective will fit each phrase.

e.g. Il duomo è . . .	fresca
Il duomo è famoso.	caldo

1 La frutta è . . .	famoso
2 Il cappuccino è . . .	fredda
3 La birra è . . .	questo
4 Il ragazzo è . . .	stanco
5 I giardini sono . . .	pronti
6 Le paste sono . . .	antiche
7 I caffè sono . . .	buone
8 Le città sono . . .	belli

The adjectives used are all in the Vocabulary on
p. 15.

D This is a car!

Look at the objects below. Identify them, using
questo and the word for *a*. Then define them
further by using the adjective indicated. Remember
to make any necessary changes to the ending.

nuovo

e.g. Questa è una macchina. È una macchina nuova.

1 *vecchio*   **2** *rosso*

3 *nuovo*   **4** *buono*

5 *freddo*   **6** *vecchio*

E Check out your spelling!

Make these sentences plural.

e.g. Il monumento è antico.
    I monumenti sono antichi.

1 La basilica è antica.
2 Il libro è lungo.
3 La strada è lunga.
4 La signora è stanca.
5 Il ragazzo è stanco.
6 La pesca è fresca.
7 Il pomodoro è fresco.

F I or they?

Which subject pronoun should be used in each of
these sentences: **io** or **loro**?

e.g. Sono italiani.
    Loro sono italiani.

1 Sono contento.
2 Sono australiana.
3 Sono americani.
4 Sono vecchie.

G Do you know your prepositions?

Complete the sentences using the prepositions **in**, **a**
and **di** correctly.

e.g. La scuola . . . lingue per stranieri è . . . Perugia
    . . . Umbria.
    La scuola **di** lingue per stranieri è **a** Perugia **in**
    Umbria.

1 Anna è . . . Rimini . . . Emilia Romagna
2 Diego è . . . Cagliari . . . Sardegna.
3 I figli . . . Sandra sono . . . Italia . . . Capri.
4 Il figlio . . . Maria è . . . scuola.
5 La tazza . . . Cristiano è . . . cucina.
6 Il portafoglio . . . Angelo è . . . casa . . . salotto.

Systems 2

I Nouns

i) Feminine nouns beginning with a vowel

l'amica
un'amica

When a feminine noun begins with a vowel, the definite article **la** and the indefinite article **una** are shortened to **l'** and **un'**. But the plural definite article, **le** does not change.

l'	un'	le
l'aranciata	un'aranciata	le aranciate
l'edicola	un'edicola	le edicole

ii) Nouns ending in -e

il padre
la madre

Some nouns ending in **-e** are masculine and others feminine. Although the endings are the same, the articles vary according to the gender of the noun.

il	i	la	le
il dolce	i dolci	la canzone	le canzoni
il signore	i signori	la chiave	le chiavi

un	una
un nome	una notte
un cognome	una televisione

With a feminine noun beginning with a vowel, use **l'** and **un'**:

l'	un'	le
l'opinione	un'opinione	le opinioni
l'arte	un'arte	le arti

Nouns ending in **-zione** are always feminine:
la lezione

Apart from this rule, there are no clues as to the genders of nouns ending in **-e**, and it is advisable to note them down as you come across them. This is particularly important if the noun begins with a vowel: **l'estate** (*summer*) is feminine but **l'esame** (*exam*) is masculine.

For masculine nouns beginning with a vowel, see Unit 3, Systems, note 4 i, p. 88.

2 Adjectives

i) Adjectives with -e nouns

il pane fresco
la chiave vecchia

The spellings of the noun and adjective endings do not necessarily need to match. The adjectives agree with the number and gender of the noun, which is shown by the article.

ii) Adjectives ending in -e

il costume tradizionale
il pasto tradizionale
la lezione tradizionale
la torta tradizionale

There is a large category of adjectives which have only two forms: a singular and a plural.

singular: -e	plural: -i
il nipote intelligente	i nipoti intelligenti
la nipote intelligente	le nipoti intelligenti
il ragazzo intelligente	i ragazzi intelligenti
la ragazza intelligente	le ragazze intelligenti

iii) -issimo endings

molto molt**issimo**
intelligente intelligent**issimo**

Many adjectives, irrespective of whether they end in **-o** or **-e**, can have **-issimo** on the end. This adds the meaning of *very/extremely* to the adjective.

3 Possessive adjectives

la mia maestra
il mio maestro

masc.	fem.	
il mio	la mia	*my*
il tuo	la tua	*your*
il suo	la sua	*his/her*
il Suo	la Sua	*your*

i) The words for *my, your, his* and *her* are adjectives, and agree with the thing or person they describe. Unlike English, the definite article usually precedes them:

questa è la mia amica
questo è il mio vestito

If a *single* family member is described, then the article is dropped:

questa è mia sorella
questo è mio fratello

However, if there is a second adjective, or a suffix is added to the noun, the article comes back again:

questa è la mia piccola sorella
questa è la mia sorellina

ii) To say *your*, use **tuo/tua** if you're using **tu**, and **Suo/Sua** if you're using **Lei**.

iii) **suo/sua** is also used for *his/her:*

questa è la sua gonna
questo è il suo vestito

For further information on possessives, see Unit 3, Systems, note 6, p. 89.

4 Using the article

Unlike English, articles are used in Italian with surnames or titles, when talking *about* people:

Il signor Muratori è qui   *Mr M. is here*
Il dottor Viola è qui   *Dr V. is here*
Il professor Carli è qui   *Prof C. is here*

However, if you are talking directly *to* someone, you don't use the article:

Buongiorno, signor Muratori
Dottor Viola, cosa beve?
Buonasera, professor Carli

In front of a name, **signore/dottore/professore** lose the **-e**.

For further uses of the article, see Unit 3, Systems, note 5, p. 89.

5 Formal and informal speech

Tu, Lei and **voi**

tu sei Anna?
Lei è la signorina Mazzotti?
voi siete Carlo e Maria?
voi siete i signori Manzi?

Tu (informal) and **Lei** (formal) both mean the singular *you*. **Voi** – the plural *you* – is used in informal and formal situations. There is a formal plural *you* – **loro**, but it is not used in everyday conversation.

Tu is always used with children, within the family and amongst friends. It is increasingly used amongst colleagues at work, although **Lei** is used by adults who don't know each other. It is best to use **Lei** when in doubt about the correct form of address.

6 Regular verbs

There are three main types of regular verbs: **-are**, **-ere** and **-ire**. The first two have appeared in this unit.

i) Present tense of -are and -ere verbs

The present tense is formed by substituting the **-are** and **-ere** endings with the following:

		-ARE	**-ERE**
		portare *to wear*	**mettere** *to put*
I	(io)	port**o**	mett**o**
you	(tu)	port**i**	mett**i**
he	(lui)		
she	(lei)	port**a**	mett**e**
you	(Lei)		
we	(noi)	port**iamo**	mett**iamo**
you	(voi)	port**ate**	mett**ete**
they	(loro)	port**ano**	mett**ono**

Systems 2

ii) Reflexive verbs: the present tense

These follow the pattern of regular present tense verbs, with the addition of **mi, ti, si, ci, vi, si**. These reflexive pronouns are essential to the meaning and cannot be omitted, unlike the subject pronouns. The easiest equivalent in English is the addition of 'myself', 'yourself', etc.

-ARE	**-ERE**
chiamarsi *to be called*	**mettersi** *to put (oneself)*
mi chiam**o**	**mi** mett**o**
ti chiam**i**	**ti** mett**i**
si chiam**a**	**si** mett**e**
ci chiam**iamo**	**ci** mett**iamo**
vi chiam**ate**	**vi** mett**ete**
si chiam**ano**	**si** mett**ono**

Other common reflexive verbs are: **addormentarsi** *(to fall asleep)*, **alzarsi** *(to get up)*, **coricarsi** *(to go to bed)*, **fermarsi** *(to stop)*, **lavarsi** *(to wash)*, **pettinarsi** *(to do one's hair)*, **trovarsi** *(to be [somewhere], to find oneself)*, **riposarsi** *(to rest)*, **svegliarsi** *(to wake up)*, **perdersi** *(to get lost)*.

7 Using the present tense

beve vino?

The present tense can be used to say what happens in general and what is happening now:

cosa beve?	*what do you drink? [in general]*
	what are you drinking? [now]
cosa mangia?	*what do you eat? [in general]*
	what are you eating? [now]

8 Irregular verbs

Present tense

bere   **bevo**
produrre   **produco**

Some verbs do not always conform to a regular pattern in all tenses. Take, for example, **bere** and **produrre**. In the present tense, the regular **-ere** endings are added to **bev-** or **produc-**.

bere *to drink*	**produrre** *to produce*
bevo	produco
bevi	produci
beve	produce
beviamo	produciamo
bevete	producete
bevono	producono

9 Sentence structures

Word order

e la pasta, dov'è?
dov'è la pasta?

Word order is more flexible in Italian than in English. When a word is being emphasised, it is frequently put in front of the verb:

qui cosa c'è?	*[lit.]*	*here what is there?*
e sua moglie, dov'è?		*and your wife, where is she?*
e tu, come ti chiami?		*and you, what is your name?*

Reinforcement 2

A Memory game
Using the definite article can you make these nouns plural?

1 amica autostrada attrice autorità
2 edicola entrata emigrazione età
3 isola idea immigrazione indennità
4 offerta opinione occasione opportunità
5 utopia uscita unione università

B About Italy
You have been faxed some information about Italy and its population, etc. but some of the text is illegible. Using the list of key words, put it back together.

[1] **popolazione** [a] **simile**
[2] **milione** [b] **grande**
[3] **abitante** [m] [c] **principale**
[4] **capitale** [d] **importante**
[5] **regione**
[6] **fiume** [m]

[1] d'Italia è [a] alla [1] della Gran Bretagna. Ci sono circa 58 [2] di [3]. [4] d'Italia si chiama Roma. A Roma ci sono circa 3 [2] di [3]. È la città più [b] d'Italia. In Italia ci sono 20 [5] e circa 100 province. [6] più lunghi sono il Po e il Tevere; le montagne [c] sono le Dolomiti, le Alpi e gli Appennini. Ci sono circa 37 isole italiane e 22 laghi. Le isole più [b] sono la Sicilia e la Sardegna. I laghi più [d] sono il Lago di Garda e il Lago Maggiore.

Note: più *most*; circa *about*

C My brother
Which of the following phrases require the article before the possessive adjective?

1 mia famiglia è grande
2 mia amica è simpatica
3 mio fratello è simpatico
4 mia cugina è antipatica
5 mio fratellino è intelligente

D It's all yours
Complete the sentences by supplying the appropriate word for *your*, not forgetting the article.

1 Maria, come si chiama . . . amica?
2 Antonio, dov'è . . . giornale?
3 Signor Tagliaferri, questa è . . . penna?
4 Signora De Amicis, . . . borsa non è qui.
5 Dottor Corti, ecco . . . chiave.
6 Ecco, . . . dolce, signorina.

E Get it right!
Choose which of the two forms of the verbs given in the sentences below is correct.

**abitare leggere scrivere
studiare produrre bere**

1 Sua figlia, che cosa [studia/studie]?
2 Suo figlio, che cosa [legga/legge]?
3 Dove [abitono/abitano] i signori Cialdi?
4 Che cosa [scrivono/scrivano] Giacomo e Aldo?
5 Chi non [beve/bevi] vino? I bambini non [bevano/bevono] vino.
6 Chi [produci/produce] più vino – i francesi o i tedeschi? I francesi ne [producono/producano] di più.

F Using reflexives
Use the reflexive verbs given to complete the text.

Note: presto *early*; tardi *late*

1 Mio padre [chiamarsi] Pietro. Lavora molto. [alzarsi] presto la mattina e [coricarsi] tardi la sera.
2 Noi siamo gemelle. [chiamarsi] Letizia e Patrizia. Siamo molto diverse. Io sono Letizia e la mattina [svegliarsi] presto. Poi [alzarsi, lavarsi e pettinarsi]. Patrizia [riposarsi] e non [alzarsi]!
3 I nonni [chiamarsi] Stefano e Stefania. Sono anziani e [riposarsi] molto. Qualchevolta [addormentarsi] dopo pranzo e [svegliarsi] solo per la cena!

G Try your hand at this multiple choice
Only one of the choices in the sentences below is correct: which is it?
1 [Dov'è/Dove] la pasta? [C'è/È] qui.
2 [C'è/È] molto lavoro oggi?
3 [Ci sono/Sono] molti bambini qui?
4 [Cos'è/Cosa c'è] qui? [Ci sono/C'è] gelati e torte

Systems 3

1 Regular verbs

i) Present tense of -ire verbs
There are two regular patterns. They are formed by substituting the **–ire** ending with the following:

preferire *to prefer*	**offrire** *to offer*
prefer**isco**	offr**o**
prefer**isci**	offr**i**
prefer**isce**	offr**e**
prefer**iamo**	offr**iamo**
prefer**ite**	offr**ite**
prefer**iscono**	offr**ono**

Other verbs like **preferire**: **capire** *(to understand)*, **finire** *(to finish)*, **gestire** *(to manage)*.
Offrire is like: **aprire** *(to open)*, **dormire** *(to sleep)*, **seguire** *(to follow)*, **servire** *(to serve)*.

Each time you come across a new **–ire** verb you need to learn which of the two patterns it follows. Refer to the list in Ref. VIII, A, 1i, p. 248.

ii) Reflexive verbs
You have come across **–are** and **–ere** reflexive verbs in Unit 2, Systems, note 6 ii, p. 85. The **–ire** reflexive verbs follow the pattern of verbs like **offrire**.

divertirsi *to enjoy oneself*
mi divert**o**
ti divert**i**
si divert**e**
ci divert**iamo**
vi divert**ite**
si divert**ono**

Vestirsi *(to get dressed)* is a common **–ire** reflexive verb.

2 Irregular verbs

i) avere and stare
The following are irregular in the present tense:

avere *to have*	**stare** *to be, to stay*
ho	sto
hai	stai
ha	sta
abbiamo	stiamo
avete	state
hanno	stanno

Avere is used with numerous basic idioms. [See Vocabulary, p. 47.]

There are fewer idioms with **stare**. Two important ones are: **stare attento** *(to be careful)*, **stare zitto** *(to be quiet)*.

ii) Other useful irregular verbs

rimanere *to stay, remain*	**tenere** *to keep, hold*
rimango	tengo
rimani	tieni
rimane	tiene
rimaniamo	teniamo
rimanete	tenete
rimangono	tengono

Tenere can be reflexive, as in **tenersi in forma** *(to keep fit)*:
> Mi tengo in forma perché nuoto
> *I keep fit because I swim*

Many verbs have the same pattern, e.g. **appartenere** *(to belong)*:
> appartengo a un circolo   *I belong to a club*

Rimanere can sometimes be used instead of **stare**:
> domani rimango a casa
> *tomorrow I'm staying at home*

3 Using the present tense

i) Saying 'for how long'

sono qui **da** un'ora

In Italian the present tense can be used with reference to the past to say for how long something has been going on. The word **da** means *for* and *since*:

> Sono in Italia da un mese
> *I've been in Italy for a month*
> Sono in Italia da settembre
> *I've been in Italy since September*

ii) Present + infinitive

è divertente **stare** qui
è bello **giocare** a golf

Many adjectives can be used with **è** in this way, followed directly by the infinitive, e.g.:
facile, difficile; possibile, impossibile; essenziale; necessario; interessante; noioso; utile; inutile

> È facile imparare l'italiano
> *It's easy to learn Italian*
> È impossibile capire tutto
> *It's impossible to understand everything*

ho bisogno **di** mangiare

Idioms which use **avere** need **di** in front of the infinitive:
> Ho tempo di giocare

iii) Present + Reflexive infinitive

ho bisogno di divertir**mi**
hai bisogno di divertir**ti**

If the verb you are using is reflexive you need to vary the infinitive ending as follows:

divertirsi *to enjoy oneself*	
ho bisogno di divertir**mi**	abbiamo bisogno di divertir**ci**
hai bisogno di divertir**ti**	avete bisogno di divertir**vi**
ha bisogno di divertir**si**	hanno bisogno di divertir**si**

With expressions using **è . . . bello/necessario**, etc, the reflexive infinitive stays the same:
> è bello divertir**si**
> è necessario tener**si** in forma

4 Nouns and articles

i) Masculine nouns beginning with a vowel

l'   gli   un

l' *(the)*	**gli** *(the)*	**un** *(a)*
l'amico	gli amici	un amico
l'esercizio	gli esercizi	un esercizio
l'ospedale	gli ospedali	un ospedale

ii) Masculine nouns beginning with s- + consonant, z, ps, gn and y

lo   gli   uno

lo *(the)*	**gli** *(the)*	**uno** *(a)*
lo straniero	gli stranieri	uno straniero
lo zio	gli zii	uno zio
lo psicologo	gli psicologi	uno psicologo
lo gnocco	gli gnocchi	uno gnocco

You now know all the definite and indefinite articles. Here is the complete list:

	Definite		Indefinite	Example
Masc.	il l' lo	i gli gli	un un uno	ragazzo amico zio, studente
Fem.	la l'	le le	una un'	ragazza idea, isola

Some and *any* is explained in Unit 5, p. 98 and Ref. I, 8v, p. 240.]

Systems 3

5 Using the article

In Italian, definite articles are needed with the following:

i) Places and languages
Continents:
L'Europa *Europe*; L'Asia *Asia*
Countries:
La Gran Bretagna *Great Britain*; L'Italia *Italy*
Regions:
La Liguria *Liguria*; Il Lazio *Lazio*
Large islands:
La Sicilia *Sicily*; La Sardegna *Sardinia*
Lakes:
Il lago di Garda *Lake Garda*
Languages:
Il giapponese è difficile. *Japanese is difficult.*
Studio l'italiano. *I study Italian.*
Note, however, that with **parlare** there is no need for an article:
Parlo italiano. *I speak Italian.*

ii) Nouns used in a general, collective sense
Gli amici sono necessari *Friends are necessary*
Le lingue sono importanti
Languages are important

iii) Abstract nouns
la musica   la vita   la primavera

iv) Substances, categories and species
Lo zucchero è dolce
Il tennis è uno sport popolare
I gatti sono animali domestici

For further uses of the definite article see Unit 2, note 4, p. 84.

6 Possessives

In Unit 2 you learnt **mio**, **mia**; **tuo**, **tua**; **suo**, **sua**, which accompany singular nouns. There are other forms to accompany plural nouns. Here is the complete list:

Masc. Sing.	Pl.	Fem. Sing.	Pl.	
mio	miei	mia	mie	*my*
tuo	tuoi	tua	tue	*your*
suo	suoi	sua	sue	*his/her/its*
Suo	Suoi	Sua	Sue	*your*
nostro	nostri	nostra	nostre	*our*
vostro	vostri	vostra	vostre	*your*
loro	loro	loro	loro	*their*

i) Possessives and the definite article
As we saw in Unit 2, Systems, note 3, p. 84, the definite article is normally used in front of possessive adjectives. It is omitted with a singular family member (e.g. **mia figlia**) unless modified by an adjective, a suffix or a prefix:
questa è **la** mia figlia più piccola
è **il** mio fratellino
è **la** mia bisnonna

Mamma and **babbo** are considered to be diminutives and are used with the article.
è **la** mia mamma

Loro always takes the article:
questa è **la** loro figlia

And in the plural the article is always used:
queste sono **le** mie figlie

ii) Omitting possessives
Possessives are often omitted with parts of the body:
Ho gli occhi azzurri
My eyes are blue, I've got blue eyes
Ho i capelli castani
My hair is brown, I've got brown hair

iii) Possessives as pronouns
You can use possessives as pronouns. The article tends to be dropped except when needed for clarification or emphasis.
Che bella macchina! È tua?
but:
Questo è il mio e questo è il tuo.

7 Interrogatives

> da **quanto** tempo?
> **quanti** anni hai?

Quanto/a? *How much?*
Quanti/e? *How many?*
These are adjectives and pronouns. They agree with the person or thing they refer to:
> Quanti libri e quante penne ci sono?

8 Object pronouns

> **lo**   **la**

Lo and **la** can mean *it* or *him* and *her*.
Lo is used if the noun is masculine singular:
> Lo prendo   [il portafoglio]
> Chi lo aiuta?   [Carlo]

La is for feminine singular nouns:
> La prendo   [la borsa]
> Chi la aiuta?   [Elisa]

9 Vero?

> è qui in vacanza, **vero?**

Vero – which means *true* – can also be used on the end of negative sentences:
> Non è difficile, vero?   *It isn't hard, is it?*
> Lei non è italiano, vero?
> *You're not Italian, are you?*

10 A note on numbers

Look at the numbers from 20 upwards in Ref. I, 1, p. 239.
Cento *(a hundred)* is invariable in Italian:
> 100 – cento   200 – duecento   300 – trecento

Mille *(a thousand)* and **milione** *(a million)* are not invariable:
> 1000 – mille   2000 – duemila
> 1000000 – un milione   2000000 – due milioni

A Which pattern?

Look at the verbs in the sentences below. They are all **-ire** verbs, but which pattern do they follow? Tick the appropriate box and fill in the infinitive of each verb. If you need help, check the list in Systems, note 1, p. 87.

	Infin.	**-isco**	**-o**
1 Oggi offrite voi da bere?			
2 Non capiamo neanche noi.			
3 Preferite la coca cola?			
4 Perché non aprite la porta?			
5 Seguiamo un corso d'inglese.			
6 Quando finite il lavoro?			
7 Pulite la vostra camera.			
8 Dormite molto?			
9 Partiamo domani?			
10 Adesso servite la minestra.			
11 Perché non bolliamo l'acqua?			
12 Sentite il telefono?			

Check the meanings if necessary and make sure you know all the forms of the verbs.

B Reflexives

Complete the sentences using the appropriate present tense form of these reflexive verbs.
e.g. Io *[vestirsi]* lentamente perché sono stanco.
     Io mi vesto lentamente perché sono stanco.

1   Mio figlio *[divertirsi]* in piscina.
2   Mio nonno *[riposarsi]* in giardino.
3   Le mie figlie *[divertirsi]* a scuola.
4   I miei genitori *[riposarsi]* in montagna.
5   Noi *[vestirsi]* rapidamente perché abbiamo fretta.

C Can you supply the questions?

Use the answers as clues.
e.g. Sì, rimango a Bordighera per una settimana.
     Rimani/rimane a Bordighera per una settimana?

1   …? Sì, rimaniamo in Italia per un anno.
2   …? Sì, appartengo a un circolo.
3   …? Sì, tengo animali domestici in casa.
4   …? Sì, mi tengo in forma!

Reinforcement 3

D Basic needs

Say what you need or want to do when you are hungry, thirsty, etc., and then enquire about others. Choose from the following:

mangiare una brioche; prendere un toast; fare uno spuntino; bere un'acqua minerale; prendere un succo di frutta; fare colazione

e.g. [Io] – aver fame – aver bisogno di –
Ho fame, ho bisogno di mangiare una brioche.

1 [Noi] – aver caldo – aver voglia di –
2 [Voi] – aver sete – aver bisogno di – ?
3 [Tu] – aver fame – aver voglia di – ?

Now say what you have or haven't time for:
4 [Io] – aver fretta – non aver tempo di –
5 [Noi] – non aver fretta – aver tempo di –

E How long for?

You want to ask how long your friends have been in various places. Use **stare** and **da**.
e.g. Lei – in Italia – 20 anni?
Sta in Italia da vent'anni?

1 Tu – a Sanremo – 15 giorni?
2 Voi – in montagna – 3 settimane?
3 Loro – al mare – 2 mesi?
4 Lei – in campagna – molto tempo?
Now say how long you have been in a particular place.

F What do you do and why?

Say what people do in their spare time and why they do it, using both **per** and **perché ho bisogno di**.
e.g. Gioco a carte. Mi diverto.
Gioco a carte per divertirmi.
Gioco a carte perché ho bisogno di divertirmi.

1 Mia moglie nuota. Si rilassa.
2 I miei parenti giocano tutti a bridge. Si divertono.
3 Ascolto la musica. Mi riposo.
4 Giocate a squash? Vi tenete in forma?
5 Prendi il sole? Ti abbronzi?
Now say what you do in your spare time and why.

G Using the definite article

1 Look at the names of these countries. Which ones do you think require one of the following articles: **l'**, **lo**, **gli**. Beware when it comes to the ones beginning with **S**!

Egitto Iran Iraq Stati Uniti Spagna
Zaire Zimbabwe Zambia Svezia Svizzera
Sri Lanka Sudafrica Afghanistan

There is a list of countries in Ref. III, 5, pp. 242–3.

2 Find the correct definite article for each noun below and then make each plural.

straniero straniera svago spiaggia suocero
spumante *(m)* zabaglione *(m)* zia zio
psicologo hobby animale *(m)* isola
uccello esercizio origine *(f)* ordine *(m)*
aperitivo stato

H There's only one!

Ask how many there are and say there's only one each time. Use **quanto** and **uno, un, una, un'**.
e.g. *[Quanto]* studenti ci sono?
– C'è ... studente soltanto.
Quanti studenti ci sono?
– C'è uno studente soltanto.

1 *[Quanto]* esercizi ci sono? – C'è ...
2 *[Quanto]* stranieri ci sono? – C'è ...
3 *[Quanto]* ragazze ci sono? – C'è ...
4 *[Quanto]* ragazzi ci sono? – C'è ...
5 *[Quanto]* isole ci sono? – C'è ...

I My friend Fabrizio

Insert articles where necessary.

mio amico Fabrizio ha occhi azzurri e capelli biondi. È italiano. Italia è un paese molto bello con tante montagne, Alpi, Appennini e Dolomiti. Il lago più grande d'Italia è lago di Garda. Fabrizio è ligure. Liguria è una regione che confina con Francia. Famiglia di Fabrizio non è grande: ha due sorelle. Sue sorelle studiano inglese, ma Fabrizio studia matematica. Suo padre è professore di matematica! Fabrizio ama molto sport e anche musica.

J Say it's yours

Using the cue in English, complete the sentences using possessive adjectives. As you do so, fill in the puzzle across. Can you spot an extra possessive and also a colour?

1 *[your – tu form]*
   Marco, ecco il . . . aperitivo.
2 *[your – Lei form]*
   Signora, dove sono i . . . figli?
3 *[your – voi form]*
   Signori, questo è . . . figlio?
4 *[our]*
   No, questo non è . . . figlio.
5 *[their]*
   Questo è Angelo e questa è Maria. Ti presento anche Marina, la . . . figlia.

n					
	t				
	v				
		s			
	1				

When you find the hidden words use them both in a short sentence.

K It and the

Each of the sentences below includes the words **lo** or **la**. Can you say which is a definite article *(the)* and which is an object pronoun *(it)*?
e.g. Nuoto perché lo trovo rilassante. *(pronoun)*

1 Dov'è Sandro? Non lo vedo.
2 Dov'è lo zucchero? Non lo trovo.
3 Ecco la pasta. La servo subito.
4 C'è Maria oggi? Non la vedo.

Systems 4

1 Irregular verbs

i) Andare, venire, uscire

vado a Bologna
vengo in autobus
esco di casa

andare *to go*	venire *to come*	uscire *to go out (of), to leave*
vado	vengo	esco
vai	vieni	esci
va	viene	esce
andiamo	veniamo	usciamo
andate	venite	uscite
vanno	vengono	escono

Andare, like many basic verbs, has a range of meanings. It crops up in a variety of common expressions:

   Come va?   *How's it going/how are things?*

Come va is an *informal* expression and is equivalent to **Come stai?**

   Va bene   *That's fine/all right [lit. it goes well]*

Using **uscire**: without a preposition it means to go out:

   Esco spesso la sera   *I often go out in the evening*

If you want to say what you go out and do, **uscire** can be used with the preposition **a**:

   Esco a fare la spesa   *I go out and do the shopping*

Uscire is used with the preposition **da** to mean *to leave, to go/to come out of.*

   Esco dall'ufficio alle cinque
   I leave the office at five o'clock
   Esco dalla stazione alle otto e mezza
   I come out of the station at half past eight

With the word **casa** *(home),* **di** is used in preference to **da**:

   La mattina esco di casa alle sette e mezza
   In the morning I leave the house at half past seven

ii) Fare and dovere:

   che lavoro **fa**?
   devo partire

fare *to do, to make*	dovere *to have to*
faccio	dovere *to have to*
fai	devo
fa	devi
facciamo	deve
fate	dobbiamo
fanno	dovete
	devono

Fare has a wide range of meanings and is used in many common idioms:

   fare una domanda   *to ask a question;*
   fare la spesa   *to shop*

Dovere is always used in conjunction with another verb in the infinitive:

   Devo andare al lavoro
   Dobbiamo fare il biglietto

2 Using the present tense

i) Summary of uses so far

As we have seen, the present tense is used to express what is happening now; what happens in general; how long something has been happening:

   Cosa fai? Vado al mercato
   What are you doing? I'm going to the market.
   Vado al mercato ogni venerdì
   I go to the market every Friday
   Vado al mercato da nove anni
   I've been going to the market for nine years

ii) The immediate future

   domani **vado** al mercato

The present tense is also often used to express the immediate future:

   Vengo in bicicletta   *I'll come/I'm coming by bike*
   Domani rimango a casa
   Tomorrow I'll stay/I'm staying at home

3 Prepositions

A or **in**?

sono/vado **a** Bologna
sono/vado **a** casa
sono/vado **in** centro
sono/vado **in** Italia

A and **in** each have two meanings: *in/at* and *to*. Here is a summary so far:

a) Use **in** with:

countries and regions:
Vado in Gran Bretagna   *I go to Britain*
Lavoro in Emilia Romagna   *I work in Emilia Romagna*

paese *country* and **posto** *place*:
Vado in molti paesi/posti diversi
I go to many different countries/places
Lavoro in posti diversi   *I work in different places*

streets, piazzas, etc.:
Vado in via Garibaldi   *I go to via Garibaldi*
Conosco un bar in Piazza Maggiore   *I know a bar in Piazza Maggiore*

set expressions:
vado in città   *I go to town*
studio in biblioteca   *I study in the library*

b) Use **a** with:

towns and small islands:
Vado a Capri   *I go to Capri*
Arrivo a Londra   *I arrive in London*

set expressions:
Torno a casa   *I go back home*
Studio a scuola   *I study at school*

There's more on **in** and **a** in Ref. III, 1–4, p. 242.

4 Prepositions and definite articles

dal lunedì **al** venerdì
il treno **delle** 7.53
un impiegato **dello** stato

When the prepositions **a**, **da**, **di**, **in** and **su** *(on)* precede a definite article, (the word for *the*), then they combine with it to form one word as follows:

	il	i	la	le	lo	l'	gli
a	al	ai	alla	alle	allo	all'	agli
da	dal	dai	dalla	dalle	dallo	dall'	dagli
di	del	dei	della	delle	dello	dell'	degli
in	nel	nei	nella	nelle	nello	nell'	negli
su	sul	sui	sulla	sulle	sullo	sull'	sugli

Not all prepositions combine with the article: **per** is never combined, and with **con** it's optional – you rarely see it in writing.
Never combine a preposition and an *indefinite* article:
La lettera è **nella** borsa   *The letter is in the bag*
but:
La lettera è **in una** borsa   *The letter is in a bag*

i) **A** and **in**

mangia **alla** mensa
abito **nel** centro di Ferrara

A is used with many other expressions of place, but with the article:
Mangio al ristorante/alla mensa
I eat at the restaurant/in the canteen
Faccio la spesa al supermercato
I shop at the supermarket

If a noun is modified by an adjective, or a specifying phrase, then you need the article:
Abito in centro   *but*
Abito **nel** centro di Ferrara
I live in the centre of Ferrara
Torno **alla** vecchia casa
I'm going back to the old house
Vado **nell**'Italia meridionale
I go to Southern Italy

Casa, however, modified by a possessive adjective, is an exception:
Torno a casa mia   *I'm going back to my home/house*
Abiti a casa sua?   *Do you live in his/her house?*

Systems 4

ii) Da

> parte **dal** binario 3
> parto **dall'**Italia

Unlike **in** and **a**, **da** *(from)* nearly always requires the article:

Vado a teatro	*but* Torno **dal** teatro
Vado in ufficio	*but* Esco **dall'**ufficio

The only exceptions are towns, **casa** and **scuola**:

Vado a Roma	Parto **da** Roma
Vado a casa	Parto **da** casa
Vado a scuola	Parto **da** scuola

Da is also used in expressions of place meaning *to* and *in/at*. See Unit 5, Systems, note 2, p. 97.

5 Variations in the use of prepositions

The use of prepositions can be quite flexible. It depends on a number of things, including the region someone is from and the degree of familiarity with the place:

> parcheggio alla stazione

is considered 'standard' Italian, but there are plenty of people who say:

> parcheggio in stazione

if they are talking about a familiar station.

Reinforcement 4

A   Which verb makes sense?

1 Dove *[vai/vieni]* domani? – Domani *[vado/vengo]* a casa di un amico.
2 Chi *[va/viene]* qui stasera? – Stasera *[vanno/vengono]* Lucia e Filippo.
3 *[Esco/parto]* sempre di casa presto la mattina.
4 Il treno *[esce/parte]* dal binario 3.
5 Domani *[usciamo/andiamo]* al ristorante.
6 Come *[va/fa]*? – Non c'è male.
7 Come *[va/fa]* per arrivare al lavoro?

B   Do you come here often?

You are at a party and you ask various people whether they come regularly to the following places:

e.g. *To a new acquaintance:* Italia – ogni estate?
Viene in Italia ogni estate?

> *To your friend Enrico:* Bologna – ogni mese?
> *To a group of children:* partita – ogni sabato?
> *To Marco and Elisabetta:* mercato – ogni venerdì?
> *To your boss:* ristorante – ogni sera?

C   I must go!

Rewrite the passage below using the appropriate form of the verb *dovere* plus the infinitive of the verbs marked.

Ogni mattina io e mio marito [**1** usciamo] di casa alle 7.15. Io [**2** vado] a Imola, mio marito [**3** va] a Cesena. Lui prende la macchina e io [**4** vado] a piedi alla stazione. Quando arrivo alla stazione [**5** faccio] il biglietto e poi [**6** trovo] un posto, che è difficile, perché il treno è sempre affollato. La sera torno tardi. [**7** vado] a letto presto perché [**8** mi alzo] alle 6.30.

D   Do you have to?

Answer the following questions using **fare**.
e.g. Dovete fare la spesa domani? *[sempre – il sabato]*
No, facciamo sempre la spesa il sabato.

1 Deve fare il bucato dopo pranzo? *[di solito – la mattina]*
2 Devi fare il bagno la mattina? *[sempre – dopo cena]*
3 Dovete fare colazione adesso? *[non . . . mai]*

E Think of a reason

Answer the questions below by choosing the most appropriate expression with **fare** or **uscire**.

e.g. Perché non siete in ufficio?

> Fare: il biglietto/il bucato/sciopero/la doccia

Non siamo in ufficio perché facciamo sciopero.

1 Perché non studiate mai?

> Uscire: ogni tanto/spesso/a volte

Non studiamo mai perché . . .

2 Tua figlia si diverte la sera?

> Fare: un viaggio/la pendolare/i compiti

No, non si diverte la sera perché . . .

F The engineer's wife

Here is an exercise to remind you how definite articles and propositions are combined. Below, to help, are the definite articles plus a completed chart for the preposition **a**:

	Sing.	Plu.	Sing.	Plu.
Masc.	il	i	al	ai
	l'	gli	all'	agli
	lo	gli	allo	agli
Fem.	la	le	alla	alle
	l'	le	all'	alle

Read the sentences below and separate the combined articles and prepositions used into their component parts.

e.g. È la moglie dell'ingegnere.   di + l' = dell'.

1 Il portafoglio è nella borsa.
2 La chiave è nella porta oppure sul tavolo.
3 Lavoro dal lunedì al venerdì
4 Ogni domenica vado a casa dell'avvocato Bianchi.
5 Lo stipendio delle infermiere è molto basso.
6 Lo stipendio dei medici è abbastanza alto.

G From dawn to dusk

Now combine the prepositions given below with the definite article:

1 Mio fratello studia [da] mattina [a] sera.
2 La vita [di] studenti è dura.
3 La giornata [di] pendolare è lunga e faticosa.
4 Il film dura [da] otto [a] dieci e mezzo.
5 I libri sono [in] studio, [su] scaffale.

H Where do you live and work?

Choose between **in** and **a**.

1 Abito *in/a* Italia, *in/a* Ferrara, *in/a* via Madama.
2 Vado spesso *in/a* Irlanda, *in/a* Dublino: il mio amico abita *in/a* periferia, ma lavora *in/a* centro.
3 Di solito vado *in/a* vacanza *in/a* Capri, ma quest'anno vado *in/a* Emilia Romagna, *in/a* montagna.
4 Il lunedì non vado mai *in/a* lezione, ma studio sempre *in/a* biblioteca.

I The house in Garibaldi street

Combine the prepositions **in, a, da** and **di** with the definite article where necessary.

1 Abito [in] una bella casa [in] via Garibaldi. È [in] centro della città.
2 Abito [in] periferia, [in] periferia di Roma, [in] un appartamento moderno.
3 Qualchevolta vado [in] Italia, a trovare mio zio [in] campagna. I miei amici abitano vicino [a] casa sua.
4 I nonni abitano [in] Italia del nord, [a] Milano. Vanno spesso [a] teatro, [a] cinema e [a] concerti.
5 Domani parto [da] Roma. Parto [da] stazione Termini per tornare [a] casa mia.
6 Vado [in] ufficio la mattina alle 9.00 e la sera esco [da] ufficio alle 18.00.
7 Io scendo [da] autobus vicino [a] stadio, poi vado [in] Piazza Giulio Cesare per fare la spesa [a] supermercato.

Systems 5

I Irregular verbs

i) potere and volere

posso vedere?
voglio vedere

potere *to be able to*	volere *to want*
posso	voglio
puoi	vuoi
può	vuole
possiamo	vogliamo
potete	volete
possono	vogliono

Potere is always used in conjunction with another verb in the infinitive:

Può ripetere, per favore?   *Can you repeat, please?*
(*Is it possible for you to repeat?*)

Use **potere** only for expressing possibility or requesting permission. In English 'I can see him now' expresses both possibility and the simple fact of seeing.

Lo posso vedere adesso, perché ho tempo
(i.e. *It is possible for me to see him now*)

But:

Lo vedo adesso, vicino alla finestra
(i.e. *I see him now, near the window*)

Volere is followed by another verb in the infinitive or by a noun. It can be preceded by a pronoun:

Voglio partire
Voglio un aumento *(a pay-rise),* lo voglio presto

ii) Other irregular present tenses

dare *to give*	dire *to say*	sapere *to know*	contenere *to contain*
do	dico	so	contengo
dai	dici	sai	contieni
dà	dice	sa	contiene
diamo	diciamo	sappiamo	conteniamo
date	dite	sapete	contenete
danno	dicono	sanno	contengono

Contenere is conjugated in the same way as other verbs formed from **tenere,** e.g. **ottenere** (*to obtain, achieve*).

2 Prepositions

i) Da

Its various meanings include:

from:	vado da casa al lavoro	[place]
	parte dal binario 3	
	lavoro dal lunedì al venerdì	[time]
for:	sono qui da un'ora	[time]
since:	sono qui da lunedì	[time]
to:	ho molto da fare	[purpose]
	cosa prende da bere?	

In conjunction with names of people **da** means *to* or *at* [See **ii)** below.]

to:	vado da Mario. (*. . . to Mario's*)	[place]
	vado dal signor Rossi	
at:	abito da mia sorella (*. . . at my sister's*)	[place]
	abito dalla signora Mancini	

Da is also used with the names of shopkeepers and professional people.

to: vado dal macellaio   (*. . . to the butcher's*)
vado dal medico   (*. . . to the doctor's*)

at: sono dal parrucchiere   (*. . . at the hairdresser's*)
sono dal dentista   (*. . . at the dentist's*)

Note: You can only use **da** with people, not with names of shops and places. [See below.]

ii) A and in

A and **in** are both used with shops and public places to mean *to* or *at*. **In** is used if the place ends in **–ia:**

vado in | macelleria   (*. . . to the butcher's*
| farmacia
| osteria

In all other cases use **a** combined with the definite article:

vado | al mercato
| all'alimentare
| alla Standa *[the name of a chain store]*

Note: For the other uses of **in** and **a** see Unit 4, Systems, note 3, p. 94.

iii) Di

So far the main meanings encountered are:

of:	il cugino	di Angela	[possession]
		del signor Brancati	
	l'orario	delle lezioni	[specification]
		dei treni	
	le strade	di Ferrara	[specification]
		della mia città	

Di dov'è, Lei? (*where from,* [place]
                 lit. *of where?*)
Sono di Edimburgo

some/any: [quantity]

There are two kinds of '*some*':

Some/a bit of	Some/a few
del burro della marmellata dell'olio dello zucchero	dei ragazzi degli studenti delle ragazze
un po' di	alcuni, alcune

Di + the *singular* definite article is needed when you mean *a part/a bit of* something. You can also say **un po' di** (*e.g.* un po' di burro). **Di** + the *plural* definite article is needed when you mean *several/a few.* You can also use **alcuni/e** (*e.g.* alcuni ragazzi).

Sometimes you can use both:

Oggi compro | del formaggio [= un po' di
            | formaggio]
            | dei formaggi [= alcuni
            | formaggi]

See Ref. I, 8vi and vii, p. 240 for *none/no, not any.*

3 Irregular nouns

i) Invariable nouns

These have the same form in the singular and the plural, but the articles change as usual. Some are foreign words:

il bar, i bar   lo shampoo, gli shampoo
il computer, i computer   l'autobus, gli autobus

You have also come across:

il golf, il dépliant, il poster, lo sport, il tennis
Accented words:
il caffè, i caffè
il tè, i tè
la città, le città
l'attività, le attività
la nazionalità, le nazionalità
l'università, le università

ii) Masculine nouns ending in -a

il programma, i programmi
il problema, i problemi

But some are invariable: il clima, i clima.

Some can be masculine or feminine:
il collega, i colleghi
la collega, le colleghe

iii) Nouns ending in -ista

Most can be masculine or feminine:
il turista, i turisti
la turista, le turiste

There are many nouns ending in **-ista**. Masculine versions tend to be more common, especially with male-dominated professions:
il barista, i baristi
il dentista, i dentisti
l'autista, gli autisti (*chauffeur/driver*)

An important irregular noun

l'uomo, gli uomini (*man, men*)

4 Adjectives ending in -ista:

ottimista, pessimista, socialista, comunista

There is one singular form, but two plural forms
un ragazzo ottimista, dei ragazzi ottimisti
una ragazza ottimista, delle ragazze ottimiste

Reinforcement 5

A To and at

Use the correct preposition in each sentence.

1 Da or a?

a È divertente andare . . . mercato perché c'è sempre tanta gente.

b È comodo fare la spesa . . . fruttivendolo perché è vicino a casa mia.

c Oggi devo andare . . . supermercato e dopo voglio andare . . . Carlo.

d Domani preferisco rimanere . . . mia zia perché stasera andiamo . . . ristorante.

2 In or a?

a La sera vado spesso . . . pizzeria, ma ogni tanto mangio . . . trattoria.

b La mattina, di solito prendo un caffè . . . bar e poi vado . . . tabaccheria per comprare le sigarette.

3 Da or a?

a C'è molto . . . fare oggi.

b Cosa c'è . . . bere?

B Nouns and adjectives

1 Make the following phrases plural:

a il turista straniero   b la città famosa

c il computer caro   d l'uomo pessimista

2 Now make these singular:

a gli autisti italiani   b i problemi importanti

c gli sport divertenti   d i partiti socialisti

3 Complete the sentences by translating the English.

a [The English socialist party] si chiama il partito laburista.

b [The Italian communist party] si chiama adesso il Partito Democratico della Sinistra.

C Can you come?

Which of the phrases below can be used with **potere**?

e.g. [Venire – noi] soltanto dopo le cinque:
   Possiamo venire soltanto dopo le cinque.
   [Vedere – io] l'autobus, ma [non vedere – io] il numero:
   Vedo l'autobus ma non vedo il numero.

1 È molto difficile, mi [aiutare – Lei]?

2 [Prendere – io] un opuscolo, per piacere?

3 [Sentire – io] il telefono, [rispondere – tu]?

4 [Non sentire – io] bene, [ripetere – Lei] per favore?

D Using the present tense

Match up the rules for the use of the present tense with each of the sentences below by writing the correct letter in the box. Then write the infinitive of the irregular verbs used in the second box.

The present tense is used for:

a a habitual action or permanent state;

b an action or state of affairs happening now;

c an action linked to the immediate future;

d saying how long something has been going on.

	Rule	Infinitive
e.g. Sono qui da mezzogiorno.	d	essere
1 Vado sempre in ufficio alle otto.		
2 Cosa bevi la mattina?		
3 Domani viene Carlo, vero?		
4 Da quanto tempo producete vino?		
5 Scusa, cosa dice Maria? – Non capisco.		
6 Rimango in Italia per quindici giorni.		
7 Il nostro vino non contiene mai zucchero.		
8 Lei sta a Roma da molto tempo?		
9 Cosa fate qui? Non potete tornare domani?		
10 Esce subito o vuole aspettare un po'?		

Now check you know the verbs in your completed list.

E Read, listen and speak

Read the questions below, then listen to Interaction 4. Answer in Italian using complete sentences:

1 Chi è il responsabile del progetto nel Parco dei Cedri?

2 Andrea Sivelli lavora anche lui per il WWF?

3 Fausto e Andrea lavorano tutti i giorni nel parco?

4 Lavorano tutto l'anno anche quando il tempo è brutto?

5 Da quando esiste il progetto?

6 Fausto e Andrea cosa vogliono studiare?

F Reading: what's on?

Below are four entries from the diary section of an ecological magazine. Try and do the following without looking anything up.

1 Skim through the text to find out what main activities each entry is publicising.
2 Which one appeals to you most?
3 Scan your favourite entry for any useful times or dates.

AGENDA
CHI? DOVE? QUANDO?

■ Anche quest'anno prende il via il **'Cammina-natura'**, una serie di itinerari guidati nella natura, a cura della Lega Protezione Uccelli e la Lega per l'Ambiente. Per cominciare, una serie di facili escursioni: l'11 marzo e il 15 marzo. Il 1 aprile è previsto un **birdwatching nell'oasi di Serre Presano**. Per ulteriori informazioni rivolgersi a: Davide Tufano, tel. (0832) 534324.

■ Lo studio fotografico 'Il fotogramma' di Salerno organizza il **V corso di fotografia naturalistica**. Il corso, tenuto da fotografi esperti, inizia il 6 marzo e si articola in dodici lezioni (due a settimana). Per ulteriori informazioni: 'Il fotogramma', (089) 121657.

■ **Università verde, Voghera**
Il primo corso è dedicato ai principi base di ecologia ed alle problematiche ambientali ed è organizzato in collaborazione con la Coop Lombardia. Le lezioni si tengono ogni martedì e sono aperte a tutti i cittadini. Ad aprile, il secondo corso ('Le immagini della natura nella filosofia occidentale'). Informazioni presso la Coop Lombardia. tel. 215602 o la Civica Biblioteca.

■ La Lega antivivisezione organizza una **manifestazione nazionale contro le pellicce** sabato 10 marzo a Pavia, sede della famigerata Pellicceria Annabella. L'appuntamento è alle 2.30. Per informazioni: tel. (06) 8356768 (Walter Gambini).

Review I

How well am I doing?

This section is designed to help you assess your progress and see how well you're doing. To do this effectively it is worth pausing to review what you set out to achieve.

Review your objectives

1 Which Track did you choose to follow and which skills did you prioritise? – Speaking? Listening? Reading? Writing?

2 What was your main concern? Fluency? Accuracy? Both? If you had not previously thought about this, think about it now and tick the chart below:

	Vital	*Important*	*Quite important*	*Unimportant*
Accuracy:				
Fluency:				

You may have found both equally important. Some **Track 2** learners may have focused on both from the beginning, but many **Track 1** learners are likely to prioritise fluency. On the other hand, those mainly interested in reading and understanding Italian may feel no need to be especially fluent.

3 In achieving your goals, how important have the following been to you?

	Vital	*Important*	*Quite important*	*Unimportant*
Grammar:				
Vocabulary learning:				

4 Which aspect of language learning has proved hardest and which has been the easiest and most enjoyable?

Conclusions. When you assess yourself, it is important to bear in mind your *goals* – the needs and priorities you've analysed. For a realistic assessment you should also take into account the *means* – in other words the amount of time you have had, as well as the degree of help and guidance you received.

Checklists   Now review your progress, using the checklists which follow. The first one is not exhaustive: it covers the main things you should be able to say, whatever track you are on.

A Speaking

I can	Yes	No	Check
1 say hello and goodbye in various ways			Unità 1
2 ask for a drink or an ice-cream			
3 say who I am, spell my name, give my phone number, address and nationality			
4 ask someone's name and tell them mine			Unità 2
5 ask what something is, what it's called and where it is			
6 find out what's available and answer the same question			
7 introduce myself and others, respond when I'm introduced, and ask who someone is			
8 ask how someone is and answer the same question			Unità 3
9 ask someone where they're from and say where I'm from			
10 ask personal questions about someone's family, age, marital status etc., and give the same information			
11 say how long I've been studying Italian and ask the same question			
12 offer someone a drink or a snack			
13 say what I prefer doing and what's nice or enjoyable to do			
14 say what job I do, where I work and how I get there, and ask others the same questions			Unità 4
15 ask what someone's job/day is like and answer those questions myself			
16 tell the time, say when I do things and use the days of the week			
17 talk about how often I do things, how many times/hours per day/week I do them, and ask others the same questions			
18 ask for what I want in a shop, whether a particular item is available, and say I'll have something			Unità 5
19 ask the price and understand numbers – spoken slowly up to 100			
20 ask someone to repeat something			
21 ask what time places open and close			
22 ask permission to do something			
23 find out what it's possible to do			
24 say what I want to do, what I need to do and what needs to be done			

Review I

B Fluency

At this stage it is probably more important to assess your fluency rather than your accuracy. Although you have been working alone you should have been practising, using the cassette/CD exercises and talking to yourself as much as possible! Work through the following checklist and say which statement you identify with at present:

* I need to construct each sentence in my head first.
* I construct sentences in my head first if they aren't stock phrases.
* I often have to pause and think about what I'm going to say, but I don't work it out exactly beforehand.
* I do/don't worry about making mistakes.
* I can only put together a sentence at a time.
* I can sometimes speak several sentences together in a connected way. I find it: Very hard   Difficult   Not too hard   Easy

If you are on Track 1 it would be unusual if you could easily use the language in new or unexpected situations, or be able to use several sentences at a time in a connected way. However, you should be able to recall a range of simple vocabulary and phrases and construct simple questions and answers.

Those on Track 2 should find it possible to put two or three short sentences together and begin to progress beyond the use of stock phrases by adapting them to their needs.

C Listening

You should be able to:
* Understand the familiar stock questions listed in the speaking checklist above, if spoken clearly and not too fast, and make sense of variations.
* Understand the gist of the Course Book conversations on cassette/CD without a transcript, playing them several times if necessary.
* Grasp the basic gist of very short conversations you've never heard before but which are on familiar topics.

If you are on Track 1 it would be unusual if you could follow the thread of conversations of over one or two minutes, especially if you don't know what they're about beforehand and if the sentences are long. This may be possible for a few Track 2 learners.

You can test yourself on unprepared conversations by listening to the Profile section of the cassette/CD – without reading the transcript.

D Reading

At this stage you are likely to read slowly and there will be few authentic texts where you will understand every word.

You should, however, be able to:
* Understand the Course Book dialogues without too much difficulty.
* Follow the poems and information given in the Culture section.

Whether on Track 1 or Track 2, you are unlikely to find the poems and biographies easy, and you will probably have to look up several words.

E Writing

At this stage you are not expected to write much unless you find it helpful to write the exercises or use writing as a memory aid to learning vocabulary. You should, however, be able to write extremely basic messages or simple descriptions of your daily life in very short sentences, using familiar language. Those on Track 2 should be able to do this without meeting spelling difficulties except perhaps with double consonants.

F Grammar

The checklist below uses grammatical terminology and is aimed primarily at those using Track 2. Nevertheless, it covers the language from both tracks. If you are using Track 1 and are familiar with the grammatical terms used (explained in the **Basics** section on pp. 237–8), you will find this list useful.

In assessing your grammar, be critical: grammar is a tool, not a straitjacket. The importance you place on particular points depends very much on what you are learning for. You may find it helpful to differentiate between understanding the grammar and producing it correctly. If your main aim in learning Italian is getting the basic message across – then the accuracy of your noun and adjective agreements is less important than knowing which preposition or possessive adjective to use, since misusing the latter could actually change the sense of what you are saying.

Checklist

		Yes	No	Check
1	I understand the singular and plural forms of regular nouns and adjectives (the **-o, -a** and **-e** endings)			Unità 1 & 2
2	I understand the definite and indefinite articles			Unità 1–3
3	I know when to use **tu** and when **Lei**			Unità 2
4	I can make a statement and ask a question			Unità 1
5	I can make a sentence negative			Unità 1
6	I can ask rhetorical questions (isn't it? aren't you? didn't you? etc.)			Unità 3
7	I can use possessive adjectives, pronouns			Unità 2 & 3
8	I understand when to use **a** and when to use **in**			Unità 1 & 4
9	I know how to join definite articles and prepositions			Unità 4
10	I know the present tense of most regular verbs including reflexive verbs			Unità 2–4
11	I can use **da**			Unità 3 & 5
12	I know most of the following irregular present tenses: **andare, avere, bere, dare, dire, dovere, essere, fare, potere, produrre, rimanere, sapere, tenere, uscire, venire, volere**			Unità 1–5
13	I can deal with basic irregular nouns			Unità 5
14	Pronouns: I know the direct object pronouns **lo, la, li, le**			Unità 5

The above list is not exhaustive: for a thorough grammatical review go through the **Systems** exercises and check the answers in the back. On Track 2 you should aim to achieve a minimum 50% accuracy.

G Vocabulary

The range of your vocabulary crucially affects what you can say and understand. By now you should be trying to consolidate a working vocabulary of everyday objects and topics, plus anything relating to your special needs. Units 1–5 have introduced about 800 words. You should aim to understand about half of these and use a quarter in conversation. Assess yourself by using the Vocabulary and Patterns sections and covering up the English. If you have been making your own vocabulary notebook use this too.

Working on your own I

Diagnosing difficulties

The ability to diagnose your weak spots and to devise ways of overcoming them is a crucial aspect of language learning. The 'menu' of language-learning activities below is designed to help you build up a useful repertoire of practice activities. In Units 1–5 the focus is on listening, speaking and acquiring vocabulary. Reading and grammar learning strategies are discussed on pp. 219–20.

General advice

1 Keep a systematic record of your main difficulties, how you dealt with them and the extent to which you were satisfied.
2 Decide on the specific aim of each practice activity before you begin, e.g. *to improve speaking skills, especially pronunciation; to sort out my grammar, in particular the use of* **da**.
3 Set aside a regular time for practice. The best approach is 'little and often' rather than sporadic mammoth sessions which tire you out.
4 Don't get too bogged down if you encounter difficulties. Note them down and come back to them later with a fresh mind.

A Listening strategies

All learners need to spend time listening and absorbing the language: it helps enormously with speaking and is as necessary, if not more so, than speaking practice itself. If you practise regularly, your ear will become attuned to the language and you will rapidly learn to pick out key words and phrases. Without this skill you may become dependent on the visual word and find it hard to communicate orally. If your previous experience of language learning was based on reading and writing, allow yourself more time to develop your listening skills.

Reasons for listening include:
1 To practise guessing the meanings of words from the topic and follow the gist of what is said.
2 To identify sounds accurately and distinguish between one word and the next.
3 To improve your memory and concentration and extend your listening stamina, i.e. the length of time you can take things in.
4 To improve pronunciation, intonation and stress.

To improve your understanding of the gist, you could:

* Use prediction. Prepare the topic from the title or explanations accompanying the recording. Try and predict three or four words which might come up; look them up if you don't know them in Italian and then listen out for them.
* Break the language into manageable chunks by using the pause button and allowing your brain time to think through what's been said.
* Use grammatical clues. You will find, for example, that recognising the sounds of the verb endings gives you vital clues as to the meaning.
* Take notes. As you listen jot down key words you recognise. Use guesswork and try to piece together what's been said. Listen several times, noting down more words each time. Then refer to the transcript when you can't go any further.

It is important to realise that you don't need to understand every word in order to grasp the message. This is true in your native language as well, for example when you hear someone with an unfamiliar regional accent.

To practise identifying sounds and distinguishing between words, you could:

* Listen to a familiar recording without the transcript. Stop the cassette/CD and try to visualise the previous word by writing it down and checking it against the transcript.
* Read the transcript as you listen to the recording.
* Photocopy the transcript and delete every nth word (e.g. every 5th or 10th word). Listen again later and try to fill in the blanks.

To improve your memory and concentration you could:

* Stop the recording and repeat the last few words. Then try to repeat the last phrase.

To improve pronunciation, intonation and stress, you could:

* Shadow read. Turn the volume low on a familiar recording and read the transcript along with it.
* Record yourself on a cassette.

B Speaking strategies

Your speaking will be helped by listening practice (see above), and by trying to communicate with native speakers. However, even if you cannot go to Italy or communicate with native speakers in the community, there is a lot you can do to improve on your own.

Reasons for speaking practice include:
1 To consolidate new language.
2 To improve fluency and confidence.
3 To improve pronunciation.

To improve your fluency and confidence, you could:

* Practise saying difficult phrases out loud.
* Act out imaginary dialogues – with yourself or another learner – recording yourself on cassette when you can.

To improve pronunciation, intonation and stress you could:

* Shadow-read [see listening section]
* Read a short course dialogue aloud, recording it on cassette, and then compare it with the original.

C Vocabulary learning strategies
Selecting what to learn
1 Be discriminating. Learn words for a purpose, *because you feel they are relevant to your needs.* Don't attempt to learn long lists of words which you might not use.
2 Set yourself some concrete situations, then target five to ten words which you feel are useful for the situation chosen. Use the Vocabulary sections of the Course, but consult a dictionary if the word you want isn't there.

To reinforce your vocabulary you could:

* Organise words into categories which are useful to you, such as travel, the home, etc.
* Pin up short lists to refer to.
* Record words – with a gap for the translation and listen in the car or on public transport.
* Test yourself regularly, from Italian to English and vice versa.

To widen your vocabulary you could:

* Regularly try to name objects around you: look up what you need in the dictionary – but not too much at a time.
* Find the opposites of words you know, especially adjectives, e.g. *grande – piccolo.* [See Ref. p. 244.]
* Learn words related to the ones you know, e.g. **lavoro – lavorare** or, **pranzo – pranzare**.

La famiglia Chiappini

The Chiappinis live in the old part of Ferrara and have chosen an unusual way of keeping the family together. When you've heard the profile, you can see how much you've understood by completing the true or false checklist.

☐CC☐ ◎ 20

Presenter Anna Chiappini ha trentadue anni, e lavora come insegnante.

Anna La nostra famiglia ha, dunque, ha venti persone. Ci sono i miei genitori, mamma e papà; noi cinque, siamo tutte sorelle, tutte donne, e che abbiamo sposato naturalmente cinque ragazzi. In totale, abbiamo adesso ... un attimo ... eh ... quanti bimbi? ... dieci bambini più due in arrivo. Ecco qua quindi, questa è la famiglia:

Io sono qua, sulla sinistra. Vicino ad Antonio, ecco questo che vedi, vicino a me, è mio marito che ha in braccio Francesco, il primo figlio nostro. Noi, viviamo tutti nella stessa casa. È un palazzo molto grande con diversi appartamenti - sono sei. E quindi, sono sei famiglie, ci stiamo tutti per fortuna.

(*Di fronte alla porta*) Questo è l'appartamento di mia sorella, Laura, e di suo marito Mario ... (*chiama Laura*) Laura, ecco, stiamo arrivando ... Ciao, ciao ... Questa è Laura.

Laura Piacere.

Presenter Laura è in cucina. Sta preparando un risotto molto grande ...

Laura Io mi chiamo Laura Chiappini. Abito a Ferrara, in Via Madama numero 31, in una casa dove abitano anche le famiglie delle mie sorelle e dei miei genitori. Io sono medico e lavoro in un ospedale. Questa sera abbiamo con noi a cena tre nipoti. Infatti i loro genitori sono fuori dalla città per una settimana e quindi noi zie e nonni li chiamiamo spesso a mangiare con noi.

Presenter	Il marito di Laura si chiama Mario ...
Mario	Io mi chiamo Mario Bonatti. Sono insegnante. Insegno in una scuola professionale di Ferrara. Abbiamo due bambine, di nome Elena e Maria. La più grande, Maria, ha dodici anni, Elena ne ha otto. E ce n'è un terzo in arrivo. Non so, io ancora non so se è maschio o femmina ma Laura, sì. Ma non lo voglio sapere, voglio la sorpresa.
Presenter	E Laura sa?
Mario	Laura sa, sì, tutti in casa sanno. Io no.
Presenter	**Quali sono i vantaggi e gli svantaggi della vita insieme?**
Anna	È molto bello stare tutti insieme perché si parla, si chiacchiera, i bambini possono giocare assieme, e tutto è più facile. A volte gli adulti discutono per le macchine. Per esempio, in giardino ci sono uno, due, tre, quattro posti per le macchine ma le macchine sono cinque ... e quindi una deve rimanere fuori dal garage.
Nicola	(*Nipote di Anna*) Sì, sì, penso che sia una grande fortuna vivere tutti insieme, tutti i parenti, ci aiutiamo molto, stiamo insieme.
Antonio	È molto divertente. Confusionario, ma molto divertente ... Come vedi qui è sempre un asilo con bambini che corrono, cani che abbaiano, zii che riparano le biciclette ... È veramente uno zoo.

	VERO O FALSO	V	F
1	Tutte le sorelle sono sposate.		
2	Il marito di Anna si chiama Francesco		
3	Laura è medico.		
4	Mario non vuole sapere se il figlio in arrivo è un maschio o una femmina.		
5	Non ci sono animali in casa.		
6	Gli abitanti di ogni appartamento hanno una macchina.		
7	È una vita molto tranquilla.		

Ambrogio Lorenzetti (c. 1285–1348)

'Effetti del Buon Governo in città'. (*The effects of good Government on the Town*) Palazzo Pubblico, Siena

Questo affresco fa parte di uno dei più importanti cicli pittorici profani del medioevo. Si trova nel Palazzo Pubblico *[Town hall]* di Siena, sede del governo senese a partire dall'inizio del Trecento. Rappresenta i benefici della pace, della giustizia e della sapienza nella città di Siena a quell'epoca.

Cercate di descrivere le persone, gli animali, le case e gli oggetti che vedete.

Gianni Rodari (1920–80)

Nato a Omegna sul lago d'Orta in Piemonte, Gianni Rodari è autore di oltre venti libri per bambini ed è apprezzato e letto anche dagli adulti. Nel 1970 riceve il premio Andersen, il "Nobel della letteratura infantile". Rodari comincia la sua carriera come maestro e come giornalista per *l'Unità* di Milano, e ottiene il primo successo letterario scrivendo una rubrica per bambini. Nel 1950 pubblica la sua prima raccolta di canzonette, *Il libro delle filastrocche.* In seguito scrive molti racconti, e nel 1973 pubblica *La grammatica della fantasia,* un' interessante introduzione all'arte di inventare storie. L'opera di Rodari è spesso comica ma anche se la fantasia e l'assurdo ne costituiscono gli elementi principali, le sue storie rimangono legate in qualche modo al mondo reale. *Promemoria ['Memo']* è una delle poesie 'serie', di Rodari, pubblicata dopo la sua morte in *Il secondo libro delle filastrocche [1985].*

PROMEMORIA

Ci sono cose da fare ogni giorno:
    lavarsi, studiare, giocare
      preparare la tavola,
        a mezzogiorno.
  Ci sono cose da fare di notte:
  chiudere gli occhi, dormire,
    avere sogni da sognare,
    orecchie per non sentire.
Ci sono cose da non fare mai,
  né di giorno né di notte,
  né per mare né per terra:
  per esempio, la guerra.

né . . . né	*neither . . . nor*

Primo Levi (1919–87)

Nato a Torino e laureato in chimica, nel 1943 Levi diventa partigiano e combatte nella Resistenza. Nel 1944 viene catturato e deportato ad Auschwitz ma sopravvive fino al gennaio 1945, quando le truppe sovietiche liberano il campo. Tornato in Italia, dopo lunghi viaggi, Levi riprende il suo mestiere di chimico e comincia a scrivere. La fama letteraria giunge con il primo libro, *Se questo è un uomo,* [1947]. Oltre ai libri che nascono dall'esperienza della prigionia, Levi scrive della narrativa d'invenzione, come *Il sistema periodico* [1975] e *Se non ora quando?* [1982], ed è autore di scritti, *L'altrui mestiere* [1985], di traduzioni, e anche di poesie pubblicate nella raccolta *Ad ora incerta* [1984]. I temi trattati da Levi sono spesso legati all'esperienza dei campi di concentramento, ma vanno al di là del personale, come per esempio nel grande libro di saggi intitolato *I sommersi e i salvati* [1986]. Poco dopo, nell'aprile 1987 Primo Levi si suicida a Torino: con la sua morte scompare uno dei più grandi scrittori e umanisti del secolo. La poesia 'Lunedì' viene scritta poco dopo il ritorno di Levi in Italia nel 1946.

LUNEDÌ

Che cosa è più triste di un treno?
Che parte quando deve,
Che non ha che una voce,
Che non ha che una strada.
Niente è più triste di un treno.

O forse un cavallo da tiro.
È chiuso fra due stanghe,
Non può neppure guardarsi a lato.
La sua vita è camminare.

E un uomo? Non è triste un uomo?
Se vive a lungo in solitudine
Se crede che il tempo è concluso
Anche un uomo è una cosa triste.

un cavallo da tiro	*cart horse*
stanghe	*shafts*
a lato	*sideways*
neppure	*not even*

Unità 6

Il mondo della musica
Arts and entertainment

La Scala, Milano

Part 1 (Interactions 1–3, Patterns 1, Practice 1)	Part 2 (Interactions 4–7, Patterns 2, Practice 2)
Learn how to: Talk on the phone Suggest a meeting Talk about what you have done	*Learn how to:* Say what you like and dislike Say what you like doing best Arrange where to meet Talk about where you have been

Grammar	
Object pronouns – *me, you, him, her*, etc. **quale, quali?** – *which?* **piacere**	The **passato prossimo** – past tense Some irregular past participles

Want to take it further?
Grammar: see Systems 6, pp. 193–5 *More practice:* do Reinforcement 6, pp. 195–6

Interactions

 2

Anna has written to a young violinist, Rita Jacobelli, who is studying music at the Bari Conservatorio. She wants to arrange an interview and is following up her letter with a phone call.

First time round

il prefisso	*code*
parlare	*to speak*
richiamare	*to call back*
prima di	*before*

Rita's sister Laura answers the phone.

a Is Rita at home?
b When would be a good time to ring back?

Anna	Allora, il prefisso zero otto zero (080). Ah! il numero di Rita, qual'è? Ah, cinque uno due cinque tre zero.
Laura	**Pronto, chi parla?**
Anna	Buonasera. **Sono** Anna Mazzotti, **posso parlare con** Rita per piacere?
Laura	Mi dispiace, Rita **non c'è** in questo momento. È uscita. È andata in Conservatorio per una prova.
Anna	Ah! Ho capito. [. . .] E Lei **mi sa dire** quando torna?
Laura	Ma torna tardi, credo. Vuole lasciare un messaggio?

Anna	Sì. **Le può dire che** ha chiamato Anna Mazzotti per la questione dell'intervista e che la richiamo domani, se va bene.
Laura	Certo. Ma è meglio chiamare la mattina presto.
Anna	Verso che ora? Prima delle otto?
Laura	Anche dopo le otto va bene. Ma prima delle otto e mezzo.
Anna	D'accordo, La ringrazio. Buonasera.
Laura	Buonasera.

è uscita	*she's gone out*
ho capito	*I see [lit. I have understood]*
ha chiamato	*(she) called, phoned*
per la questione dell'intervista	*about the interview*
è meglio chiamare la mattina presto	*it's best to ring early in the morning*
d'accordo, La ringrazio	*all right, thank you*

Key phrases

pronto, chi parla?	*hello, who's speaking?*
sono . . .	*it's . . .*
posso parlare con . . .	*can I speak to . . .*
non c'è	*she's not in*
mi sa dire . . .	*do you know/can you tell me . . .*
le può dire che . . .	*can you tell her that . . .*

Ansaphone 2

See if you can leave a message on the Ansaphone.

2 🔲 ◎ 3

The next morning Anna is more·successful.

First time round

ieri sera	*yesterday evening*
La chiamo	*I'm calling you*
ha ricevuto?	*did you receive?*

This time Rita answers the phone.

a Did she get Anna's letter?
b When do they agree to meet?

Rita Pronto.
Anna Pronto? Sono Anna Mazzotti. **Ho chiamato** ieri sera. **Ho lasciato** un messaggio per Rita.
Rita Sì, **sono io** Rita. Buongiorno.
Anna Ah! Buongiorno. La chiamo a proposito dell'intervista. Ha ricevuto la mia lettera?
Rita Sì, sì. Va bene. Ho organizzato tutto.
Anna D'accordo. **Quando ci possiamo vedere** allora?
Rita **Perché non ci vediamo** a casa mia, domani alle undici?
Anna Sì.

a proposito di   *about*

Key phrases

ho chiamato	*I called*
ho lasciato	*I left*
sono io	*it's me*
quando ci possiamo vedere?	*when can we see each other?*
perché non ci vediamo?	*why don't we meet?*

3 🔲 ◎ 4

The next day, as arranged, Anna and Rita meet up. Anna finds out about Rita's week and how she began her musical career.

First time round

studiando	*studying*
lo strumento	*instrument*
suonare per gioco	*to play for fun*
la sigla	*signature tune*

a How old is Rita now?
b How old was she when she began playing music?

Rita Il mio nome è Rita, ho diciannove anni e studio musica al Conservatorio Niccolò Piccinni di Bari dove frequento il settimo anno di violino.
Anna **Cos' hai fatto** questa settimana?
Rita Questa settimana, come tutte le mie settimane, l'ho trascorsa studiando in Conservatorio: musica da camera, storia della musica, armonia, orchestra, dove stiamo facendo una sinfonia di Mozart. E chiaramente, la mia lezione di violino, che è il mio strumento principale.
Anna **Come hai cominciato** a studiare la musica?
Rita Ho cominciato a suonare per gioco, all'età di nove anni. La prima musica che ho suonato al pianoforte è stata la sigla di un cartone animato che ho visto in televisione.

questa settimana . . . l'ho trascorsa	*I spent this week*
stiamo facendo	*we are doing*
un cartone animato che ho visto	*a cartoon I saw*

Key phrases

cos'hai fatto?	*what did you do?*
come hai cominciato?	*how did you begin?*

Patterns I

i) Getting in touch by phone

Identifying the speaker
Pronto, chi parla?   *Hello, who's speaking?*

Saying who you are

Sono	Rita	*It's/this is*	*Rita*
	il dottor Baldini		*Doctor Baldini*
	la signora Manzi		*Mrs Manzi*
	io		*me*

Asking to speak to someone

Posso parlare con	Anna?	*Can I speak to*	*Anna?*
	il signor Guerci?		*Mr Guerci?*
	la dottoressa Neri?		*Doctor Neri?*

Saying someone isn't in
Mi dispiace, non c'è   *I'm sorry, he/she isn't in*

Requesting information

Mi sa dire	quando torna?	*Can you tell me*	*when he/she will be back?*
	quando tornano?		*when they will be back?*

The phrase **mi sa dire** literally means *do you know how to tell me?* There's more on **sapere** *(to know)* in Systems 7, note 6, p. 198, Systems 8, note 4, p. 201 and Systems 9, note 6, p. 207.

Asking about leaving a message

Vuole/vuoi	lasciare un messaggio?	*Do you want to*	*leave a message?*
Posso		*Can I*	

Leaving a message
Le può dire che **la** richiamo domani?   *Can you tell her I'll call her tomorrow?*
Gli può dire che **lo** richiamo domani?   *Can you tell him I'll call him tomorrow?*
See Troubleshooting, p. 126 and Systems, note 1, p. 193 for **le, la, gli** and **lo**.

Ringing off: polite thanks
La ringrazio   *Thank you [lit. I thank you]*

Use **La** for both men and women.

ii) Making suggestions

To make a suggestion you can use **perché non**, plus the verb:

Perché non	ci vediamo a casa mia?	*Why don't we*	*see each other at my house?*
	andiamo al cinema?		*go to the cinema?*
	ceniamo insieme?		*have dinner together?*

You can also make a suggestion simply by using the **noi** form of the verb on its own:

Andiamo a teatro   *Let's go to the theatre*

Patterns I

iii) Accepting and agreeing

volentieri	*I'd like to*	va bene	*fine, all right*
mi fa piacere	*with pleasure*	d'accordo	*all right, agreed*

iv) Arranging when to meet

Use the verb **potere** *(to be able to)* with either **vedersi** *(to see each other)* or **incontrarsi** *(to meet)*:

Quando ci possiamo	vedere?	*When can we*	*see each other?*
	incontrare?		*meet?*

Perché non ci vediamo	stamattina	*Why don't we see*	*this morning*
ci incontriamo	oggi pomeriggio	*each other/meet*	*afternoon*
andiamo	stasera	*go*	*evening*
	questa settimana		*week*
	domani mattina		*tomorrow morning*
	dopodomani		*the day after tomorrow*
	la settimana prossima		*next week*
	sabato prossimo		*next Saturday*

v) Specifying times

A che ora? or Verso che ora? *At [about] what time?*

The answer can vary:

Ci vediamo	verso le undici	*See you*	*at about 11.00*
	alle cinque		*at 5.00*
	prima delle otto e mezzo		*before 8.30*
	dopo le otto		*after 8.00*
	fra le due e le tre		*between 2 and 3*

vi) Talking about the past (1)

To ask what someone has done, you need the past tense of **fare**. This is formed with the present tense of the verb **avere** and the past participle **fatto** *(done)*.

Che cosa	hai/ha	fatto?	*What*	*have you done/did you do?*
	avete			
Che cosa	ha	fatto?	*What*	*has he, she done/did he, she do?*
	hanno			*have they done/did they do?*

To reply, use part of the verb **avere** in the present tense plus the past participles of the verb describing the action. See Systems, notes 3 and 4 p. 194.

Most **–are** and **–ire** verbs have regular past participles ending in **–ato** and **–ito**:

[chiamare]	ho/abbiamo	chiam**ato** ieri sera	*I/we called*	*yesterday evening*
[lasciare]	ho/abbiamo	lasci**ato** un messaggio	*I/we left a*	*message*
[capire]	ho	cap**ito** tutto	*I (have)*	*understood everything*
[pulire]	ho	pul**ito** la macchina	*I (have)*	*cleaned the car*

> If the verb ends in **-ere** the regular pattern is:
>
> [ricevere]   ho | rice**vuto** la lettera   *I (have)* | received the letter
>
> But many **-ere** verbs have irregular past tense endings which have to be memorised individually as you need them:
>
> [vedere]   ho | visto un programma   *I* | *saw a programme*
> [leggere]   ho | letto un articolo   *I* | *read an article*
> [prendere]   ho | preso il treno   *I* | *took the train*
>
> There's more on the past tense in Patterns 2, p. 122 and Systems, notes 3, 4 and 5, p. 194.

Practice I

Can I speak to . . .?

Here is the transcript of a telephone conversation but it's in the wrong sequence. Read it through and put it in the right order, beginning with **a**:

Speaker 1	*Speaker 2*
a Pronto, chi parla?	**1** Posso lasciare un messaggio?
b Sì, certo.	**2** Buonasera. Sono Ettore, posso parlare con Valerio?
c Torna tardi, credo.	**3** Gli può dire che lo richiamo domani?
d Mi dispiace, non c'è. È uscito.	**4** Mi sa dire quando torna?
e Chiama domani? Va bene.	**5** La ringrazio, buonasera.

Refresh your memory   5

Listen again to Anna's phone conversation with Rita, without looking back at the text, and answer the questions on the cassette/CD.

Overbooking   5

Giovanni Casanova arrives home to find three messages on his Ansaphone. Work out who called, why and what problem he is going to have.

Stop the cassette/CD as often as you like and have paper and pencil handy to jot down the messages.

Appointments

It's Monday morning. You're going through your appointments with a colleague who's in a muddle. Consult your diary and tell him the time of day you are seeing or ringing each person mentioned.

e.g. La dottoressa Muratori viene oggi pomeriggio, vero?
No, la vedo stamattina.

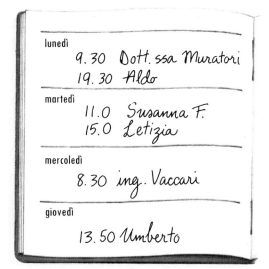

These are his other questions:
1 Aldo Carfagnini viene oggi pomeriggio, vero?
2 Devi chiamare Susanna Fallaci dopodomani?
3 Allora, quando vedi Letizia – mercoledì pomeriggio?
4 E chiami l'ingegner Vaccari giovedì mattina, vero?

Alibi

A Stradivarius violin was stolen on Tuesday evening. The Inspector – **il commissario** – has narrowed the suspects to two people. After he's heard the statements below, he is sure he's found the culprit. Can you spot him or her by reading the statements and checking the facts, using the radio and TV programmes?

Il com.	Signorina Agostini, dopo le sette, martedì sera, che cos'ha fatto?
Sig.na A.	Beh, non ho fatto molto. Ho letto il giornale, ho preparato la cena e ho ascoltato la radio.
Il com.	E che cos' ha sentito?
Sig.na A.	Ma . . . ho sentito un po' di musica al IV canale: il programma musicale delle otto.
Il com.	E quali cantanti ha sentito?
Sig.na A.	Mah, molti – Claudio Baglioni, Gianna Nannini, Venditti, Tozzi . . .
Il com.	La ringrazio, signorina.
Il com.	Allora, Signor Petronio, martedì sera, dopo le sette, che cos'ha fatto?
Sig. P.	Mah . . . ho fatto una telefonata, ho letto un po' e ho cenato. Dopo ho guardato la televisione. Ho visto *Blob* su Raitre.
Il com.	E che altro ha visto?
Sig. P.	Subito dopo, su Raidue, ho visto un film giallo, *Delitto sotto il Sole*.
Il com.	Signor Petronio, La ringrazio.

FILODIF

IV CANALE | **Musica leggera**

6/BUONGIORNO IN MUSICA
8/CONCERTO DEL MATTINO
9/CANTANDO IN ITALIANO
10/MUSICA DALLO SCHERMO
11/CANTAUTORI
12/ROCK & POP
13/JAZZ VARIETÀ
14/FOLKLORE DA TUTTO IL MONDO
15/PARATA DI STELLE
16/FACILE ASCOLTO
18/DISCOTECA
20/CONCERTO: Claudio Baglioni - Antonello Venditti - Gianna Nannini - Pino Daniele - Umberto Tozzi - New Patetic «Elastic» - Gilbert Bécaud - Jair Rodrigues - Maria Bethania - Toquinho - Harry Belafonte - Jorge Ben - Count Basie - B. B. King - Mel Lewis - Duke Ellington - Benny Goodman - Woody Herman - Sonny Rollins - Stan Kenton - Buddy De Franco - Pee Wee Russell - Louis Armstrong
22-23,30/MUSICA NELLA SERA

di Margherita Lo...

RAITRE

11 Mountain Bike.
11,30 Pallavolo femminile.
12 Tennis.
14,45 La scuola si aggiorna.
17 Vita col nonno, telefilm.
17,45 La rassegna - Giornali e Tv estere.
18 Bodymatters, telefilm.
19,30 Rai regione.
19,45 Cartoni animati.
20 Blob. Di tutto di più.
20,25 Una cartolina spedita da Andrea Barbato.
20,30 Un giorno in pretura.
21,45 Allarme in città.
23,50 Le mura di sabbia. Texas: ricordi di guerra e di prigionia.
0,45 Tg3 Nuovo giorno.
1,10 Fuori orario.

1,20 Mezzanotte e dintorni.

RAIDUE

10 Questa volta ti faccio ricco, film comm. con Antonio Sabato (1974).
11,55 I fatti vostri.
13,50 Quando si ama, telefilm.
14,20 Santa Barbara, telefilm.
15,30 Sale e pepe super spie hippy, film comm. con Sammy Davis Jr (1968).
17,20 Hill Street giorno e notte, telefilm.
18,10 Rock Cafè.
18,35 Il commissario Köster.
20,30 Senza limiti - Due casi per Sam Dietz, film poliz. con Leo Rossi, 2° epis.
22,15 Hunter, telefilm.
23,10 Tg2 Pegaso.
0,20 Delitto sotto il sole, film giallo con Peter Ustinov, James Mason.

RAITRE

Now you say what *you* did yesterday evening after seven o'clock. Did you . . . watch TV? prepare the supper? listen to the radio? read a book? write a letter? make a phone call? see a friend? have a bath?

Practise what you want to say, making notes if necessary. See if you can eventually do it from memory, perhaps into a cassette. Finally, write a brief report for the Inspector!

Cultura e parole

Italy's longstanding musical tradition, particularly in the field of popular song, is alive and well in the shape of her **cantautori** – singer songwriters. Some have achieved the stature of poets rather like the troubadours of old, and the best of them attract a wide following. Their songs are constantly in the charts alongside rock and pop stars. They vary in style from the philosophical and nostalgic to the humorous and irreverent, including biting satire and social and political comment. The music blends different influences: Dylan, rock music and blues as well as the French *chansonniers* Brel and Bécaud. What the songs have in common is the importance of the words as well as the music and the fact that the themes concern ordinary people. Much of the 'old guard' of cantautori from the golden era of the 1970s is still going strong: Lucio Dalla, Franco Battiati, Lucio Battisti, Eduardo Bennato, Fabio Concato, Paolo Conte, Claudio Baglioni, Fabrizio De Andrè, Francesco De Gregori and Giorgio Gaber. The tradition still continues with new talent such as Alex Britti, Luca Carboni, Luciano Ligabue, Mango, and Eros Ramazzotti.

I Conservatori. These state music schools, found in most major towns, are where Italy cultivates much of her musical talent. Entry is by exam, usually at 11 and courses last 7 to 10 years, depending on the instrument and speciality chosen. Until the age of 14 all students study other subjects. Once they have obtained the basic diploma, they take other exams if they want to progress to **corsi specialistici** which will give them a qualification equivalent to a **laurea** – a university degree.

Italy's cultivation of musical talent in the conservatori has produced rebels like the rock singer Gianna Nannini and, of course, world-class musicians and performers – not just Luciano Pavarotti but the conductors Claudio Abbado and Riccardo Muti, the pianist Maurizio Pollini and the contemporary composers Berio, Nono, Maderna and Togni.

The language of music

Be it **allegro** or **adagio**, **forte** or **piano**, the vast majority of expressive musical terms are in Italian. The practice of including indications of force and speed started in Italy in the seventeenth century and the enormous popularity of Italian music helped to spread these expressions. Many are familiar in colloquial Italian: you may know that **forte** means 'loud', **adagio** is 'slow', **piano** is 'soft', **vivace** is 'lively' and **presto** can mean 'quick'. But not all the terms coincide exactly with everyday Italian. In spoken Italian **piano** can also mean 'slow', whereas **presto** is also 'soon'. In music, **allegro** signifies 'lively and rather fast' while in spoken Italian it's 'happy' or 'jolly'. And if you take the diminutives of **allegro** or **andante** ('at a moderate pace'), there is room for confusion: **allegretto** instructs the musician to play a little more slowly, but if it's **andantino**, then he must play faster, not slower than **andante**. How fast, or slow, then, is **andante ma non troppo**?

Interactions

4   6

In the course of the conversation with Rita, Anna finds out about her musical tastes.

First time round

ti piace?	*do you like?*
il frastuono	*racket*
la batteria	*drums*

What sort of music does she like and what sort does she dislike?

Anna **Quale** musica **ti piace?**

Rita **Mi piace** principalmente la musica classica. Poi mi piace anche il jazz, sia nello stile moderno che classico. E poi anche la musica leggera.

Anna E **quale** musica **non ti piace?**

Rita La musica che non mi piace e che dà tanto fastidio alle mie orecchie è il frastuono che fanno le chitarre elettriche, il basso, la batteria. Una musica odiosa, terribile.

sia nello stile moderno che classico	*both in the modern and the classic style*
che dà fastidio alle mie orecchie	*which bothers (offends) my ears*

Key phrases

quale . . . ti piace?	*which . . . do you like?*
mi piace	*I like*
quale . . . non ti piace?	*which . . . don't you like?*
non mi piace . . .	*I don't like*

5   7

Anna pays a visit to the Conservatorio where she meets several students. Marcello is a guitarist and Luciano is a violinist.

First time round

il compositore	*composer*

Who is Marcello's favourite composer?

Anna Marcello, **quale** compositore **ti piace di più?**

Marcello Io sono un musicista classico, suono la chitarra e quindi preferisco Mauro Giuliani.

Anna Quale strumento ti piace di più?

Luciano Lo strumento che **mi piace di più** è il violino, perché permette di esprimere meglio i propri sentimenti.

[Anna E quando non suoni il violino, **che cosa ti piace fare?**

Luciano Quando non suono il violino a me piace leggere e piacciono tante altre cose, come la fotografia.]

esprimere	*to express*
a me piace	*I like [more emphatic than* mi piace*]*

Key phrases

quale . . . ti piace di più?	*which . . . do you like most?*
mi piace di più	*I like most*
che cosa ti piace fare?	*what do you like doing?*

6 8

Rita invites Anna to attend a chamber-music concert to be given on the seafront by a quartet she has formed with friends.

First time round

sul lungomare	on the seafront
dietro	behind

a Where do they agree to meet?
b What time do they decide on?

Rita	Allora vuoi venire domani?
Anna	Sì. Volentieri. **Dove ci incontriamo?**
Rita	Direttamente al Barion. È un club in centro, sul lungomare. Dietro il teatro Margherita.
Anna	E quando? Verso che ora? Alle due?
Rita	No. Prima delle due. Verso l'una e mezzo.
Anna	D'accordo. Ci vediamo domani, allora.
Rita	Va bene. Ciao.
Anna	Ciao.

Key phrase

dove ci incontriamo? *where shall we meet?*

Rendez-vous 8

Listen to the cassette/CD and say you'll meet at the places associated with the sounds you hear.

7 9

Anna attends a rehearsal in the magnificent hall – **Aula Magna** – of the Conservatorio and talks to two more students about where they were yesterday.

First time round

ieri	*yesterday*
la musica d'insieme	*ensemble music*
il violoncello	*cello*

Pick out one thing each of them did.

Anna	Mara, **dove sei stata** ieri?
Mara	Ieri sono stata in Conservatorio a fare lezione di musica d'insieme. Poi **sono ritornata** a casa. Ho studiato violoncello e **sono uscita** con gli amici.
Anna	Ciao, Pietro.
Pietro	Ciao.
Anna	Pietro, dove sei stato ieri?
Pietro	**Sono stato** al Conservatorio a fare lezione di violoncello. Poi **sono andato** a casa. Ho cenato e poi sono andato a giocare a biliardo.

Key phrases

dove sei stato/a?	*where were you/have you been?*
sono ritornato/a	*I returned*
sono uscito/a	*I went out*
sono stato/a	*I was/have been*
sono andato/a	*I went*

Patterns 2

i) Saying what you like

To say what you like, you use the verb **piacere** *(to like)*, which literally means *to be pleasing to.* The verb is used differently from most other verbs.

If you like one thing, you use the same form – **piace** – with a different pronoun for each person:

Mi piace	Pavarotti	*I like*	*Pavarotti*
Ci piace	il rock	*We like*	*rock*

If you like more than one thing, use the form **piacciono**:

Mi piacciono	i gialli	*I like*	*detective stories*
Ci piacciono	i western	*We like*	*westerns*

Saying you like it, her or them

Ti piace	Lucio Dalla?	Sì, mi piace	*Do you like*	*Lucio Dalla?*	*Yes, I like him*
Le piace	il jazz?	Sì, mi piace		*jazz?*	*Yes, I like it*
Vi piace	la professoressa di disegno?	Sì, ci piace		*the art teacher?*	*Yes, we like her*

Ti piacciono	i film dell'orrore?	Sì, mi piacciono	*Do you like*	*horror films?*	*Yes, I like them*
Le piacciono	i romanzi?	Sì, mi piacciono		*novels?*	*Yes, I like them*
Vi piacciono	i documentari?	Sì, ci piacciono		*documentaries?*	*Yes, we like them*

There is no need to use the words for *it, him, her* or *them* in your reply [see Troubleshooting, p. 174]. For more on **piacere** see Systems, note 2, p. 193.

Saying what you don't like

Put **non** in front of the verb and the pronoun:

Non mi piace la fantascienza   *I don't like science fiction*

Asking and saying which things you like best

The key phrases are **quale/i?** *(which?)* **che tipo di?** *(what sort of?)* and **di più** *(best)*:

Quale strumento	ti/Le vi	piace di più? *Which instrument do you like best?*
Quali cantanti	ti/Le vi	piacciono di più? *Which singers do you like best?*
Che tipo di film	ti/Le vi	piacciono di più? *What sort of films do you like best?*

ii) Saying what you like doing

To say what you and others like doing you always use **piace** (with **mi, ci,** etc.) followed by the infinitive of the verb you want:

Cosa	ti Le vi	piace fare? *What do you like doing?*	Mi piace suonare la chitarra	*I like playing the guitar*
			Ci piace giocare a biliardo	*We like playing billiards*

Saying what others like doing

Gli	piace ballare in discoteca	He	likes dancing at the disco
Le	piace cantare nel coro	She	likes singing in the choir
Gli	piace suonare nell'orchestra	They	like playing in the orchestra

Gli piace means both *he likes* and *they like.*

iii) Talking about the past (2)

To talk about where you and others have been, you normally need verbs which form their past tense with **essere** rather than **avere**. For example, to form the past tense of **essere** itself, you use the present tense of **essere** with the past participle **stato/a** *(been)*.

Piero, dove	sei stato?	*Where have you been/were you?*
Maria,	sei stata?	

Sono stato/a	a lezione	*I've been/I was*	in class
Sono stato/a	in ufficio		in the office

Ragazze, dove siete state?	*Girls, where have you been/were you?*
Ragazzi, dove siete stati?	*Boys, where have you been/were you?*

Siamo stati/e in Inghilterra   *We've been to England*

In talking about where you've been, you're also likely to need other verbs which form their past tense with **essere**:

Sei andato/a	a casa	*You went/have gone*	home
È tornato/a		*You, he, she came back*	

Siamo usciti/e	presto	*We went out/have gone out*	early
Siete partiti/e		*You left/have left*	
Sono arrivati/e		*They arrived/have arrived*	

Some of these verbs are irregular, for example **rimanere** and **venire**:

Sono rimasto/a	a casa ieri	*I stayed at home yesterday*
Sono venuto/a	subito	*I came at once*

The endings of past participles used with the verb **essere** change according to the subject of the verb:

Posso parlare con	Rita? – È uscita	Can I speak to	Rita? She's gone out
	Piero? – È uscito		Piero? He's gone out
	Anna e Renzo? – Sono usciti		Anna and Renzo? They've gone out

See Systems, notes 3 i and iii and 4 ii, p. 194 for further explanations.

Patterns 2

iv) Arranging where to meet

To discuss venues, use the verb **incontrarsi** *(to meet)*:

Dove ci incontriamo?   *Where shall we meet?*

Ci possiamo incontrare	dietro	il teatro	*We can meet behind*	*the theatre*
		la posta		*the post office*
	davanti	al cinema	*outside*	*the cinema*
		alla stazione		*the station*
	di fronte	al bar	*opposite*	*the bar*
		alla trattoria		*the trattoria*
	accanto	all'albergo	*next to*	*the hotel*
		al ristorante		*the restaurant*

Davanti a literally means *in front of*.

Some expressions of place need **in** or **a**:

| Ci incontriamo | in centro/in piazza | *We'll meet* | *in town/in the square* |
| | a casa mia/tua/sua | | *at my/your/his/her house* |

And there are many expressions which need **a** combined with the definite article:

all'entrata del cinema	*at the entrance to the cinema*
all'uscita del teatro	*at the exit of the theatre*
all'angolo di via Manin	*on the corner of via Manin*

If you're meeting at someone's house, you need to use **da**, which, when followed by a person, means *at* or *to*. See Unit 5, Systems, note 2 i, p. 97.

Ci incontriamo	da Rita	*We'll meet*	*at Rita's*
	da mio fratello		*my brother's*
	dal mio amico		*my friend's*
	dalla mia amica		*my friend's*
	dai miei amici		*my friends'*
	dalle mie amiche		*my friends'*

Practice 2

Look at the map

You are arranging to meet a friend in a bar car park. He'll be arriving by bus and, as you show him your detailed plan of the town centre, you point out the exact location of the following landmarks:

1 the car park in relation to the bar
2 the bar in relation to the hotel
3 the bar in relation to the church
4 and the bus stop in relation to the hotel

Use the following phrases: **accanto a, dietro, davanti a, di fronte a**.

Now try to describe your local town square or similar location.

What do you like?

You are hoping to arrange an outing to a concert or the cinema for your colleagues at work. But what would they like to go to? You start by asking them whether they like a) music and b) films.

e.g. Giulia, ti piace la musica?

1 Your friend Giulia
2 Signora Pacini
3 Anita and Miriam

Now you want them to be more specific. What kind of films or music do they like best?

e.g. Giulia, quali film ti piacciono di più?
or Che tipo di film ti piacciono di più?

Personal tastes

1 Say which you like in each of these three groups:
   a Poetry, novels, biographies
   b Documentaries, horror films, the news (TV/radio)
   c Going to the cinema, to the theatre, to concerts
2 Now say which you like best.
3 Which, if any, of the above do you dislike?
If you are learning in a group, ask each other what you like and dislike. [See Vocabulary, p. 125.]

An invitation   10

Answer the phone and speak to your friend Aldo who's just finished work.

You	[Say hello and ask who's speaking.]
Aldo	Ciao, sono io, Aldo.
You	[Say hello and ask him how he is.]
Aldo	Benissimo. Ho finito di lavorare per oggi. Senti, andiamo a cena stasera?
You	[Say yes, you'd like to.]
Aldo	Bene. Che cosa ti piace di più: la cucina italiana o la cucina francese?
You	[Say you like Italian food.]
Aldo	D'accordo. Andiamo al Cavallo Bianco, allora?
You	[Say fine and ask him where you can meet.]
Aldo	Ci possiamo incontrare in piazza alle 9.30 davanti al bar. Va bene?
You	[You didn't get that. Ask, which bar?]
Aldo	Il bar di fronte alla banca. Hai capito dove?
You	[Ah, outside the bar opposite the bank . . . Say yes I see.]
Aldo	D'accordo, a più tardi, allora. Ciao.

Now practise saying where you went yesterday.

Matchmaking

Rosanna and Susanna are looking for an Italian pen-friend. They've had some letters sent to them through a pen-friend agency and have narrowed the choice to Dino and Lino. Susanna is a bit of a wine buff and she likes cooking and listening to music into the early hours. Rosanna is a sporty type. She is a health freak but enjoys life in the fast lane. Who do they each choose?

Dino

Mi piace molto la musica rock e anche il jazz: suono il pianoforte e la chitarra. Quando ho tempo mi piace cucinare e invitare gli amici a cena. Lo trovo molto rilassante, e stiamo insieme fino a tardi. Qualchevolta gioco a tennis la domenica, ma gli unici sport che mi piacciono veramente sono il calcio e l'automobilismo... in televisione!

Lino

Mi piacciono i cantanti rock e vado spesso ai concerti. Mi piace soprattutto lo sport e stare all'aria aperta. Mi tengo sempre in forma: vado in palestra due volte alla settimana. Sono vegetariano e anche astemio, ma mi piace andare al ristorante! Mi piacciono tanto le macchine veloci e ho una Ferrari bellissima, un regalo di mio padre.

Vocabulary

Music

la musica classica	classical music
la musica leggera	light music
la musica pop	pop music
il jazz	jazz
la lirica	opera
il canto	singing, song
la canzone	song
il concerto	concert
la prova	rehearsal
la danza	dance, dancing
un ballo	a dance
il balletto	ballet
il complesso	group, band
il coro	choir
l'orchestra	orchestra
la sinfonia	symphony

il violino

Instruments

l'arpa	harp
la batteria	drums
la chitarra	guitar
il clarinetto	clarinet
il corno	horn
il contrabbasso	double bass
il fagotto	bassoon
il flauto	flute
l'oboe (m)	oboe
l'organo	organ
il pianoforte	piano
il sassofono	saxophone
la tromba	trumpet
il trombone	trombone
la viola	viola
il violino	violin
il violoncello	cello

Arts and mass media

l'arte (f)	art
la mostra	exhibition
lo spettacolo	show,
il teatro	theatre
la commedia	play, comedy
la tragedia	tragedy
la trama	plot
il cinema	cinema
il film giallo	detective film
il film ...	
comico	comedy
poliziesco	thriller
dell'orrore	horror film
il cartone animato	[film] cartoon
la televisione	television
il canale	channel
il programma	programme
il documentario	documentary
il telegiornale	TV news
il telefilm	TV film
la telenovela	'soap'
lo sceneggiato	TV serial
la puntata	episode
la radio	radio
il giornale radio	radio news
la letteratura	literature
l'articolo	article
la biografia	biography
la fantascienza	science fiction
il romanzo	novel
il fotoromanzo	photoromance
il fumetto	cartoon comic
il giallo	detective story
la poesia	poetry
la rivista	magazine

lo scultore	

People

l'artista	artist
l'attore	actor
l'attrice	actress
l'autore	author
il/la cantante	singer
il cantautore	singer composer
il compositore	composer
il conduttore	TV presenter (m)
la conduttrice	TV presenter (f)
il direttore/	conductor (m)
la direttrice d'orchestra	conductor (f)
il/la musicista	musician
il/la pianista	pianist
il/la regista	producer
la star	star (m or f)
il soprano	soprano
lo scrittore	writer
la scrittrice	writer (f)
lo scultore	sculptor (m)
la scultrice	sculptor (f)
il/la violinista	violinist

Verbs

ballare	to dance
cantare	to sing
recitare	to act
suonare	to play [music]

Idioms

dare fastidio a	to bother, to be a nuisance to
dare una mano a	to give a hand, to help
dare un passaggio a	to give a lift to
fare una telefonata	to make a phone call
fare il numero	to dial

Troubleshooting

La: you   Le: to you

By now you will know that the subject pronoun **Lei** is used for the formal *you* as well as for *she*. Similarly the object pronouns **La** and **Le** mean *you* and *to you* as well as *her*. When **la** and **le** mean *you*, they are often written with a capital letter.

You	To you
La ringrazio *Thank you [lit. I thank you]*	**Le** presento mio marito *Let me introduce my husband to you*
La disturbo? *Am I interrupting? [lit. do I interrupt you?]*	**Le** posso offrire qualcosa? *Can I offer you anything? [lit. offer to you]*
La chiamo domani *I'll call you tomorrow*	**Le** telefono domani *I'll telephone [to] you tomorrow*

Le is used with verbs which require the preposition **a** before a person. Try and learn some of the following:

chiedere a	*to ask*	dare a	*to give*
dire a	*to tell, to say to*	mandare a	*to send to*
offrire a	*to offer (to)*	parlare a	*to speak to*
portare a	*to bring (to)*	presentare a	*to introduce to*
prestare a	*to lend (to)*	regalare a	*to give [as a present]*
restituire a	*to give back (to)*	rispondere a	*to reply (to)*
spiegare a	*to explain to*	telefonare a	*to telephone (to)*

Lo strumento   Il mio strumento

Remember that the article you use also depends on the initial spelling of the following word, not just on its gender and number. If an adjective precedes the noun this may change the article:

il treno	**il** ragazzo	**lo** specchio	**l'**apparta-mento
l'ultimo treno	**lo** stesso ragazzo	**il** tuo specchio	**il** nuovo appartamento
l'idea	**i** ragazzi	**gli** amici	
la buona idea	**gli** altri ragazzi	**i** miei amici	

The changes also apply to the indefinite article:

un'idea	**un** ragazzo	**uno** specchio
una buona idea	**uno** stupido ragazzo	**un** vecchio specchio

Unità 7

A casa nostra
Invitations and hospitality

Casale tipico, Val d'Orcia

Part 1 (Interactions 1–4, Patterns 1, Practice 1)	**Part 2** (Interactions 5–6, Patterns 2, Practice 2)
Learn how to: Talk on the phone (2) Invite someone to visit, using dates Agree and accept Check and confirm arrangements Make apologies and excuses Find out how something works	*Learn how to:* Find out what places of interest there are Talk about places you know Request information

Grammar	
Position of object pronouns Stressed pronouns The impersonal **si**	Uses of **ci** **dispiacere** **sapere** and **conoscere**

Want to take it further?
Grammar: see Systems 7, pp. 197–8   *More practice:* do Reinforcement 7, pp. 199–200

Interactions

1   📼 ◎ 12

Anna lives and works in Rome. Her friends Peppe and Lucia Leone want her to spend a few days at Rionero, in one of Italy's least known regions, the Basilicata.

First time round

un attimo	*hold on*
ce l'ha?	*have you got [it]?*
l'interno	*extension*

Peppe tries to ring Anna at her home.

Where has Anna gone, and what's her number?

Rudy   Pronto, chi parla?
Peppe   Buongiorno, sono Peppe. Chiamo da Rionero. **C'è Anna per caso?**
Rudy   No, Anna non c'è. Io sono il fratello. È uscita molto presto, questa mattina, per andare in ufficio. Se vuole, Le do il suo numero.
Peppe   Sì. Grazie. Molto gentile.
Rudy   Un attimo. Il prefisso di Roma, ce l'ha?
Peppe   Sì, sì. Zero sei, vero?
Rudy   Esatto: il numero è: tre tre quattro otto, **interno quattro tre due.**
Peppe   Allora, ha detto: **trentatré, quarantotto,** interno quattro tre due. Grazie, buongiorno.
Rudy   Buongiorno. Prego.

molto gentile	*that's very kind of you*
esatto	*that's right*
ha detto	*you said*
prego	*that's all right, don't mention it*

Key phrases

c'è Anna per caso?	*is Anna in by any chance?*
interno 432	*extension four three two*
trentatré, quarantotto	*three three four eight*

2   📼 ◎ 13

Peppe next has a go at contacting Anna at work.

First time round

rimanere in linea	*to hold the line*
abbiamo comprato	*we've bought*
c'è posto	*there's room*

He talks first to the operator.

a Has Anna ever been to the Basilicata?
b What date does she say she can go?

Peppe   (to operator) Ah, l'interno **è occupato?** Sì, preferisco rimanere in linea.
Anna   Pronto, chi parla?
Peppe   Ciao Anna, sono Peppe. Come stai?
Anna   Ciao Peppe. Mah! insomma . . . non c'è male. E tu?
Peppe   Io sto benissimo e anche Lucia. Sai, abbiamo trovato un bellissimo appartamento in Basilicata e lo abbiamo comprato.
Anna   Che bello! Non conosco la Basilicata. Non ci sono mai stata.
Peppe   Allora, **perché non vieni a trovarci?** C'è posto nell'appartamento.
Anna   Eh, **mi dispiace, ma non posso.** Ho troppo lavoro.
Peppe   Ma dai, lavori troppo. Perché non vieni a trovarci per un paio di giorni?
Anna   Posso venire **verso il venti aprile.**
Peppe   Il venti aprile. Ma certo. Ti veniamo a prendere alla stazione di Rionero.
Anna   D'accordo. **Ci vediamo il** venti sera allora?
Peppe   OK, **a presto.** Ciao.
Anna   Ciao, Peppe.

non ci sono mai stata	*I've never been there*
ma dai	*go on/come off it*

Key phrases

è occupato?	*is it engaged?*
perché non vieni a trovarci?	*why don't you come and visit us?*
mi dispiace ma non posso	*I'm sorry, I can't*
verso il venti aprile	*about 20 April*
ci vediamo il . . .	*see you on . . .*
a presto	*see you soon*

Months of the year 🔲 ◎ 13

Listen to the months and repeat them after the speaker.

3 🔲 ◎ 14

On the evening of 20 April Anna arrives in Rionero.

First time round

i cassetti	*drawers*
sistemare	*to put, arrange*
la roba	*things, stuff*

She is shown to her room by Lucia.

a How do you turn on the television?
b What time are they having supper?

Lucia Allora Anna, questa è la tua camera.
Anna Ah, simpatica! Posso usare i cassetti?
Lucia Certo! Puoi sistemare qui la tua roba. C'è la televisione.
Anna E **come si accende?**
Lucia È semplice. C'è il telecomando.
Anna Ah, ecco il telecomando. Bene. Ah . . . che bella camera luminosa!
Lucia Sono contenta. Senti, noi ceniamo alle nove stasera. **Ti va bene?**
Anna Va benissimo! Grazie.
Lucia **D'accordo. Ci vediamo dopo.**
Anna **A più tardi.** Ciao.

ah, simpatica!   *oh, it's lovely! [lit. friendly]*

Key phrases

come si accende?	*how do you turn it on?*
ti va bene?	*does that suit you?*
d'accordo	*agreed, all right*
ci vediamo dopo	*see you in a while [lit. after-wards]*
a più tardi	*see you later*

4 🔲 ◎ 15

Later, in the well-equipped, modern kitchen, Lucia shows Anna the various appliances and how some of them work.

First time round

i fornelli	*gas burners*
girare	*to turn*
schiacciare	*to press*
il frigorifero	*fridge*

a How do you light the cooker?
b Can Anna help herself to what's in the fridge?

Lucia Vieni, Anna. **Ti faccio vedere** il resto della casa.
Anna Eh, sì, è molto utile se domani non ci siete.
Lucia Certo. Questo è il piano di cottura, con quattro fornelli.
Anna E come funzionano, i fornelli?
Lucia Molto semplice, guarda. **Basta** girare, e schiacciare.
Anna Ah, ecco!
Lucia Questa, invece, è la lavastoviglie . . . Così, puoi aprire l'acqua.
Anna E il frigorifero?
Lucia Da questa parte. Vieni. Ecco. Se hai bisogno di qualcosa, serviti pure.
Anna Grazie. Ma . . . la lavatrice, non c'è in cucina?
Lucia No. La lavatrice è nel bagno di servizio. Adesso, Anna, io preparo un buon caffè. Peppe intanto ti fa vedere il bagno. Bene?
Anna D'accordo. Torno subito. Ciao!

la lavastoviglie	*dishwasher*
la lavatrice	*washing machine*
se domani non ci siete	*if you're not there tomorrow*
il piano di cottura	*the hob*
da questa parte	*this way*
serviti pure	*do help yourself*
il bagno di servizio	*utility room*

Key phrases

| **ti faccio vedere . . .** | *I'll show you* |
| **basta . . .** | *all you have to do is . . .* |

Patterns I

i) Making a phone call

Asking if someone is in

Use **c'è?** [lit. *Is there?*]

C'è	Anna	per caso?	Is	Anna	in by any chance?
	la Signora Parisi			Signora Parisi	
	il dottor Rossi			.Doctor Rossi	

Asking if the line is engaged

The word for *engaged* is **occupato**:

È occupato?	*Is it engaged?*
La linea è occupata?	*Is the line engaged?*

Asking someone to hold on

Just use the word for *moment*:

un attimo   *hold on, one moment*

To ask whether someone wants to hold on you say:

Preferisce	rimanere in linea?	*Do you prefer*	*to hold the line?*
Vuole		*Do you want*	

Giving a phone number

The code – **prefisso** – and extension – **interno** – are generally said digit by digit, as in English:

Il prefisso	di Roma è zero sei
	per l'Inghilterra è zero zero quattro quattro

L'interno è quattro tre due

But when you give the actual phone number you group the digits in pairs:

Qual è il suo numero di telefono?   *What's your phone number?*
Il mio numero è trentatré quarantotto uno   *My number is 33481*

If the number is three digits you generally say it as one number:

Per i vigili del fuoco, chiama il centoquindici   *For the fire service, call 115*

Patterns I

ii) Making plans and arrangements

Inviting someone to come and visit you

The verb to use is **venire a trovare** (**visitare** is only for places). The pronouns, **mi** *(me)* **ci** *(us)*, etc. go in front or on the end. See Systems, note 2 iii, p. 197.

Perché non	vieni/e a trovarmi?		*Why don't*	*you come and visit me?*
	mi vieni/e a trovare?			
	venite a trovarci?			*you come and visit us?*
	ci venite a trovare?			

Sì, va bene	*Yes, fine*		D'accordo	*All right*			
vengo	a trovarti	presto	ti	vengo a trovare	presto	*I'll come and visit you soon*
	a trovarLa		La			
	a trovarvi		vi			

Checking suitability and inclination

For making arrangements and giving invitations the following phrases may be useful:

Ti	va bene	cenare	fuori?	*Does it suit you to*	*have supper/eat/have lunch*	*out?*
Le		mangiare				
Vi		pranzare				

Ti	va di	andare	domani?	*Do you feel like*	*going/coming/leaving*	*tomorrow?*
Le		venire				
Vi		partire				

Agreeing and accepting

If you're emphasising that an arrangement suits you, you can say:

per me va bene	*that's fine by me*
mi va bene	*that suits me*

And if you are agreeing, you can say:

d'accordo	*agreed, all right*
va bene	*fine, all right*

See also Unit 6 Patterns 1 iii, p. 115.

Setting a date

Italians use cardinal numbers for the date except for the first of the month:

Quando puoi/può venire?		*When can you come?*	
Posso venire	il primo gennaio	*I can come*	*on the first of January*
	il cinque febbraio		*on the fifth of February*
	l'otto marzo		*on the eighth of March*
	l'undici aprile		*on the eleventh of April*

The months are listed in Reference p. 241 and you have heard them on the cassette/CD.

Confirming an arrangement

If you're confirming or summing up an arrangement, use **ci vediamo** or simply **a**:

Allora, ci vediamo	sabato sera il venti aprile la settimana prossima		*Right, see you*	*on Saturday evening* *on 20 April* *next week*	
A Al Alla	sabato sera venti aprile settimana prossima	allora	*See you*	*on Saturday evening* *on 20 April* *next week*	*then*

Declining an invitation

The key phrase is **mi dispiace**, from the verb **dispiacere** *(to mind, to be sorry)* [see Systems, note 4, p. 198].

Mi dispiace, non posso	*I'm sorry, I can't*
Ci dispiace, non possiamo	*We're sorry, we can't*

If you want to give a reason you could say:

Ho da fare	*I've got a lot to do*
Sono impegnato/a	*I'm busy*
Ho un altro impegno	*I've got another engagement*

iii) Being hospitable: showing people round

Use the verb **far vedere a** *(to show)*. [See Systems, note 3 ii, p. 198.]

Ti Le Vi	faccio vedere	la camera la cucina il soggiorno	*I'll show you*	*the bedroom* *kitchen* *living-room*

iv) Asking and saying how things work

You need the verb **funzionare** *(to work)*.

Come funziona	il riscaldamento il ferro da stiro la lavatrice	*How does*	*the heating* *the iron* *the washing machine*	*work?*

The simplest explanation involves the verb **bastare** *(to be enough)*. Literally you say, *it is enough to.*

Basta	girare schiacciare/premere attaccare/staccare spingere/tirare	*All you have to do is*	*turn* *press* *plug in/unplug* *push/pull*

Another way to find out how things work is to use the impersonal **si** *(one)* with a verb:

Come si	accende la luce? spegne lo scaldabagno? apre il rubinetto? apre il portone? chiude la porta a chiave?	*How does one/do you*	*turn on the light* *turn off the water heater?* *turn on the tap?* *open the front door?* *lock the door?*

Practice 1

Servizi telefonici

Here are some of Telecom Italia's services explained on the web. Try to understand the general meaning and only consult the Lexis in the back if you have to.

1

412 (o 892.412 da cellulare)

Un solo numero per consultare in modo automatico o con operatore tanti servizi utili e informazioni sempre aggiornate, dalle ricerche evolute sull'elenco abbonati, alle notizie su oroscopo, borsa, meteo, taxi e altro ancora, alla programmazione dei cinema ed ai turni delle farmacie a te più vicine.

12 – ELENCO ABBONATI

Il primo e più conosciuto servizio di ricerca elenco abbonati. Una guida vocale automatica ti assisterà nella ricerca di numeri telefonici e indirizzi di abbonati Telecom Italia.

4114 – SVEGLIA AUTOMATICA

La sveglia telefonica da programmare al numero di telefono da te indicato.

4161– L'ORA ESATTA

L'infallibile servizio che ti dà l'ora esatta al minuto secondo.

ZEROEVIA

Zeroevia ti permette di chiamare direttamente i numeri trovati con il servizio 12 o 412 (o 892.412 dai cellulari), senza riagganciare, semplicemente premendo il tasto zero.

4197 – CHIAMATA URGENTE SU OCCUPATA

Libera in fretta un numero occupato inviando un messaggio di sollecito.

www.187.it

premendo — *by pressing*
inviando — *by sending*

a Which two numbers can you call for directory enquiries? Which one has operator facilities?
b You've been given a number by directory enquiries and you want to call it without hanging up. What do you do?
c If a line is engaged how do you let them know you are calling?
d Pick out a few of the other services on offer.

2

CHAT SMS
PACCHETTO CHAT SMS

Tutti gli SMS ed i Messaggi Vocali che vuoi in un'offerta straordinaria!

Scrivi molti SMS? Allora l'offerta CHAT SMS è l'offerta per te per inviare tutti gli SMS che vuoi senza limiti. E da oggi puoi registrare un messaggio vocale con la tua voce ed inviarlo ad un telefono fisso di Telecom Italia. Basta digitare **4** e *****, dire **INVIA** e seguire le istruzioni vocali. Con CHAT SMS è gratis.

COSA OFFRE?

SMS e Messaggi Vocali ai telefoni fissi senza fine

L'offerta Chat SMS permette di:
*   Inviare SMS in modo illimitato e senza pagare alcun costo per l'invio **da un telefono fisso a un altro telefono fisso**
*   Inviare Messaggi Vocali in modo illimitato e senza pagare alcun costo per l'invio **da un telefono fisso a un altro telefono fisso**
*   Inviare un SMS **da un telefono fisso a un cellulare** con una **riduzione** del **10%** rispetto al prezzo base

Sfrutta questa nuova offerta che arricchisce il tuo telefono di casa, aggiungendo tutta la convenienza di un abbonamento al divertimento di una 'chat' via SMS.

senza pagare alcun — *without paying any*
aggiungendo — *by adding*

a What do you have to do to send voice mail or a text message for free?
b Can you send them free to mobiles?
c What mobile service is offered?

Festivities   16

Listen to the recording and give the date of the following festivities in Italian.

1 Il giorno di Natale – Christmas Day.
2 L'Epifania – Twelfth Night.
3 La Festa dei Lavoratori – May Day.
4 Il pesce d'aprile – April Fool's Day.
5 Ferragosto – the Assumption of the Virgin Mary, – equivalent to our midsummer bank holiday.
6 Il tuo compleanno – when is your birthday?

Refresh your memory

Listen again to Interaction 2. Answer the questions in Italian. Don't refer to the written text but replay as often as you need to.

1 How does Peppe ask if the extension's engaged?
2 How does Anna say she doesn't know the Basilicata?
3 How does she say she's never been there?
4 How does Peppe say, 'Why don't you come and visit us?'
5 How many words and phrases conveying agreement can you pick out?

Hotel de luxe

You've booked into an expensive hotel but unfortunately nothing seems to work. You've called the manager to your room to sort things out.

Ask how the following work:

a the TV
b the iron
c the phone
d the heating

It's all a bit confusing! Here in the wrong order are the replies. Can you match them up with the right question?

1 Basta alzare il ricevitore e fare lo zero.
2 Basta aprire il rubinetto del termosifone!
3 Basta premere qui. C'è un pulsante rosso sulla destra dello schermo.
4 Basta attaccare qui: c'è una presa accanto al letto.

Party time   16

It's Maurizio's birthday and he has left you an invitation on the Ansaphone.

Jot down the occasion, the date and the extension number you are given.

R.S.V.P.   16

Unfortunately you can't come so you ring Maurizio back at work. Can you take part in the conversation?

Centralinista	Pronto . . .
You	*[Say hello and ask for the extension number he gave you – 359.]*
Centralinista	Un attimo . . . È occupato. Vuole rimanere in linea?
You	*[Say yes.]*
Maurizio	Pronto . . .
You	*[Say hello to Maurizio and give him your name.]*
Maurizio	Ciao! Puoi venire alla festa, allora?
You	*[Say you're sorry but you can't.]*
Maurizio	Ah! Mi dispiace . . . Ma quando vieni a trovarci, allora? Senti, ho un'idea. Il mese prossimo facciamo un'escursione nel Parco Nazionale del Pollino. Ti va di venire?
You	*[Hmm, an excursion in the Pollino National Park: tell him yes, it suits you.]*
Maurizio	Ti va bene partire il dieci marzo?
You	*[Say yes, fine, see you on the tenth then.]*
Maurizio	Benissimo! Ciao, a presto.

Cultura e parole

The saying 'An Englishman's home is his castle' has no direct equivalent in Italian, but the home is just as important to Italians: **'Casa mia, casa mia, per piccina che tu sia, tu mi sembri una badia'** – 'Home, sweet home' or, more literally, 'However small my home is, to me it seems like an abbey'. Despite rapid social change, the home remains the centre of the family: it is estimated that at least half of all 20- to 35-year-olds live at home. In part this is due to the difficulty and expense of finding accommodation – **un alloggio in affitto**, but it is also a question of choice. In today's society it is considered possible to live at home and enjoy personal freedom and independence – **l'autonomia**.

Despite a marked decrease in savings – **i risparmi**, largely due to a growing lack of trust in big business and the financial institutions, many Italians still invest in the housing market – **il mercato immobiliare**. On average 68 per cent of Italians are home owners and in some regions this is as high as 76 per cent. Buying a home can involve a deposit – **un deposito** – of up to a third of the price, and a mortgage – **un mutuo**. Maintaining the home – **la mantenuzione della casa** – is a major preoccupation and absorbs increasing amounts of disposable income – **il reddito disponibile**. The cost of maintenance often involves service charges – **le spese di condominio** – since the majority of Italians live in blocks of flats – **i palazzi** – which operate under a system of joint ownership – **il condominio**. In addition, Italians spend large amounts on furniture and furnishings – **mobili e arredamento** – and on hi-fi or new domestic appliances – **elettrodomestici**.

Buying and selling property in Italy involves a bewildering variety of terms, which can vary slightly according to the region. **Una villa**, **un villino** or **una villetta** usually refers to a detached house, but **a schiera** means terraced. Nowadays **un rustico** is much favoured to describe what might be called a cottage, although it is frequently modern, whereas **un casale** or **una cascina** refers to an older, traditional farmhouse. Flats – **appartmenti** – are advertised according to the number of **locali** or **vani** – rooms, not bedrooms:

I Sassi di Matera

a bedsit is a **monolocale** while a one-bedroom flat is **2 locali**. Beware of confusing terms: **box** means garage, and if you see the word **attico** don't expect an attic. It's a penthouse, which usually comes complete with alarm system – **impianto antifurto**, and roof garden – **terrazzo**.

The **Sassi** of Matera in the Basilicata region are some of the oldest houses in the world. They were originally primitive cave-like dwellings lining the two ravines between which Matera was built, and their name derives from the word **sasso** – rock or stone. For centuries the **Sassi** were notorious for extreme poverty and were abandoned in the 1950s. Times have now changed: they are being restored and have become a world heritage site protected by UNESCO. In the neighbouring and more prosperous region of Puglia, in the Murgia area, the strange single-storey conical houses known as **Trulli** are still built and lived in today. They are constructed of limestone, without any mortar, and the older ones are topped by traditional, often obscure symbols, some of them believed to be pre-Christian.

Interactions

5   17

The next morning, at breakfast, plans are laid for the day. There's a great deal to see, both in Basilicata and in the neighbouring region of Puglia.

First time round

una gita	*an outing*
scegliere	*to choose*
i castelli . . . i laghi	*castles . . . lakes*
un giro per	*a tour round*

a What do they decide to do that day?
b What about the following day?

Anna Ciao.
Lucia Buongiorno.
Peppe Dormito bene?
Anna Sì. Bene, grazie.
Peppe Allora, cosa facciamo oggi?
Lucia Eh, perché non facciamo una gita?

Anna E dove? Eh, Peppe, sei tu l'esperto, Lucia mi ha detto che **conosci** tutta **la Basilicata. Ma che cosa c'è di bello da vedere?**
Peppe Tanto. Basta scegliere. Ci sono i laghi di Monticchio. C'è Matera con i Sassi. Ci sono i castelli di Federico.
Anna Mmm . . .
Lucia Io ho una proposta da fare. Oggi perché non facciamo un giro per la Basilicata. Domani, poi, andiamo in Puglia.
Anna In Puglia?
Lucia Sì. Ad Alberobello. Hai sentito nominare i Trulli, tu? Alberobello è famosa per i Trulli. Perché non andiamo lì?
Anna Ma, interessante.
Peppe **Non è una brutta idea.** Passiamo una giornata in Puglia e oggi ti facciamo vedere la zona qui intorno.
Anna Ah, beh, per me va bene. Ho sentito nominare il castello di Melfi, ma **non ci sono mai stata.**
Lucia Eh, allora, cosa aspettiamo? Andiamo?
Peppe Perfetto.

hai sentito nominare . . .? *have you heard of . . .?*

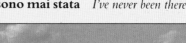
Key phrases

conosci la Basilicata	*you know the Basilicata*
che cosa c'è di bello da vedere?	*what is there worth seeing*
non è una brutta idea	*it's not a bad idea*
non ci sono mai stata	*I've never been there*

6   🔲   ⊙   18

After a day spent in the Basilicata, as planned, Lucia and Peppe take Anna to Alberobello where she visits a genuine Trullo. Afterwards she's keen to find out how much it would cost to rent one.

First time round

		She visits
affittare	*to rent*	an estate
da due posti letto	*which sleeps two*	agent and
la biancheria	*linen*	talks to
migliore	*best*	Maria
		Gargano.

a How much does a Trullo for four cost per week?
b Which season is the best, according to Maria Gargano?

Anna	Buongiorno.
Maria G.	Buongiorno.
Anna	Signora, **mi può dire** quanto costa affittare un Trullo?
Maria G.	Certo. Un Trullo, da due posti letto, costa cinquecento euro. Da quattro posti letto, invece, ottocento euro.
Anna	Alla settimana?
Maria G.	Alla settimana.
Anna	Ma, nel prezzo **è tutto compreso**?

Maria G.	Certo. È tutto compreso. È compresa la biancheria, è compreso il riscaldamento, è compresa la luce. È compreso tutto quello di cui uno ha bisogno per il soggiorno.
Anna	Bisogna pagare un anticipo?
Maria G.	Certo. Si dà un anticipo e poi, alla fine del soggiorno si dà il saldo.
Anna	E qual è la stagione migliore per venire qui?
Maria G.	Beh, tutte le stagioni sono buone perché d'inverno, per esempio, ci trova i Trulli con la neve. Qua di solito nevica ed è molto bello. D'estate, poi, è favoloso.
Anna	Grazie.

tutto quello di cui uno ha bisogno	*everything you need*
si dà un anticipo	*you pay an advance*
si dà il saldo	*you settle up/pay the difference*
alla fine del soggiorno	*at the end of the stay*

Key phrases

mi può dire . . .	*can you tell me . . .?*
è tutto compreso?	*is everything included?*

Troubleshooting

Ci

Ci is used a lot in Italian. Here is a summary of its uses:

1 *there*

C'è, ci sono	*There is, there are*
Ci sei stato?	*Did you go there?*
Non **ci** sono mai stato	*I've never been there*

Its use is wider than in English: it is often needed when talking about an activity:
Sei andato a ballare ieri? – Sì, **ci** sono andato *Did you go dancing yesterday? Yes, I went (there)*

2 *Reflexive: ourselves, each other*

ci incontriamo *we meet (each other)* **ci** divertiamo *we enjoy ourselves* **ci** vediamo *we see each other*

3 *Direct object: us*

Ci chiami domani? *Will you call us tomorrow?*
Perché non vieni a trovar**ci** domani? *Why don't you come and visit/see us tomorrow?*

4 *Indirect object: to us*

Ci può dire quanto costa? *Will/can you tell us how much it costs? [lit. can you say to us]*
Ci piace la Basilicata *We like Basilicata [lit. Basilicata is pleasing to us]*

5 *Pleonastic* ci

Ce l'hai il prefisso? *Have you got the code? [lit. have you got it, the code?]*

Ci has become **ce** because it precedes another pronoun, **lo** [and **lo** has become **l'** in front of **hai**].
Ci here has no specific meaning. It is used for reasons of pronunciation:
Hai il mio indirizzo? Sì **ce** l'ho *Have you got my address? Yes,*

Unità 8

Che giornata!
Accidents and emergencies

Un ingorgo del traffico in via del Corso, Roma

Part 1 (Interactions 1–5, Patterns 1, Practice 1)	**Part 2** (Interactions 6–8, Patterns 2, Practice 2)
Learn how to: Make polite requests Say you're mistaken and apologise Ask and explain the way Express regret, relief, resignation	*Learn how to:* Ask what's happened Talk about what's gone wrong Say you know and don't know Say what's not allowed Express dismay

Grammar	
Uses of **ne** Prepositions with question words **piacere** with **a** More on **sapere**	Double object verbs Negatives – **non...niente**, **non...più**, etc. More irregular past participles

Want to take it further?
Grammar: see Systems 8, pp. 201–2   *More practice:* do Reinforcement 8, pp. 203–4

Interactions

Anna is all set for more time off in the south, this time with her friend Alberto. Arranging the trip to the beautiful baroque town of Lecce, in Puglia, is more difficult than she expects.

First time round

linea disturbata	*bad line*

She dials Alberto's number.

a Who does Anna get through to?
b What number was she trying to dial?

Anna   Cinque sette, sette due, sei uno. Pronto, Alberto? **Con chi parlo, scusi?** Con chi, scusi? La linea è disturbata. – Con Angelo! Ma che numero ho chiamato? Ah, ho capito! Cinque sette, sette due, sette uno. **Mi dispiace! Ho sbagliato numero.** Buonasera.

Key phrases

con chi parlo, scusi?	*excuse me, who am I speaking to?*
mi dispiace	*sorry*
ho sbagliato numero	*I've got the wrong number*

Wrong one   ⌨ ◉ 21

Listen to the cassette/CD and say you've got it wrong.

Anna gets through next time and suggests a date.

First time round

ancora	*yet*
tra una settimana	*in a week*
fra poco	*soon*
l'agenda	*diary*

a Has Alberto definitely decided to come?
b What dates does Anna suggest?

Anna   Pronto? Alberto, **sei tu?**
Alberto   Sì, sono io. Ciao Anna.
Anna   Ciao Alberto. Allora hai deciso? Puoi venire?
Alberto   Ma non lo so ancora. **Quando pensi di partire** esattamente?
Anna   Mah! Veramente non ho ancora deciso. Probabilmente la settimana prossima, fra il due e il cinque maggio. Come vuoi tu, insomma. Non ho deciso niente ancora.
Alberto   Ma, per me è lo stesso. Non ho molti impegni in quel periodo.
Anna   Ah, perfetto! Allora perché non partiamo tra una settimana? Il tre maggio, per esempio.
Alberto   Benissimo. Ma **ti dispiace se** ti richiamo fra poco per confermare? Sai, preferisco controllare la data sulla mia agenda e non ce l'ho qui con me.
Anna   Va bene. A presto allora.
Alberto   Sì, **ci sentiamo dopo.** Ciao.

per me è lo stesso	*it's all the same to me*
controllare la data	*to check the date*
non ce l'ho qui	*I haven't got it here*

Key phrases

Alberto, sei tu?	*Alberto, is that you?*
quando pensi di partire?	*when are you thinking of leaving?*
ti dispiace se . . .?	*do you mind if . . .?*
ci sentiamo dopo	*speak to you later*

Quando, quando, quando 22

Listen to the cassette/CD and say when you are thinking of leaving.

3 23

Alberto calls back having checked his dates.

First time round

la partenza	*departure*

He is unusually decisive . . .

a Where in Lecce does he suggest they meet?
b What time does he suggest?

Anna	Pronto?
Alberto	Ciao Anna, sono Alberto.
Anna	Ciao Alberto.
Alberto	Ti chiamo velocemente per confermare la partenza il tre maggio.
Anna	**Meno male.** E dove ci incontriamo?
Alberto	Davanti al Teatro dell'Opera di Lecce.
Anna	Davanti al Teatro dell'Opera di Lecce. A che ora?
Alberto	Verso le dodici.
Anna	A mezzogiorno, davanti al Teatro dell'Opera di Lecce. Ci rivediamo il tre. Ciao.

Key phrase

meno male   *good, thank goodness*

4 24

On 3 May Anna arrives in Lecce to meet Alberto. The plan is to go on to Gallipoli near the southern tip of Italy to meet their friend Cioto.

First time round

per questa strada	*along this road*
ti accompagno io	*I'll take you*
figurati	*it's no bother*

Anna finds a theatre but Alberto isn't there, so she checks things out with a passer-by.
a Has Anna gone to the right place?
b What route is she told to take?

[*Anna*	Scusa, mi puoi dire se questo è il Teatro dell'Opera?]
Signorina	No, hai sbagliato teatro. Devi **continuare per questa strada**, devi **prendere la seconda a destra**, all'angolo c'è una bella chiesa barocca, devi continuare per quella strada.
Anna	Allora: prendere questa strada, la seconda a destra, alla chiesa barocca **sempre dritto**.
Signorina	Se vuoi ti accompagno io.
Anna	Ah, non voglio darti troppo fastidio.
Signorina	Figurati! Facciamo la strada insieme.
Anna	Grazie. **Mi fa piacere.** Sei gentile.
Signorina	Andiamo.
Anna	Sì.

non voglio darti troppo fastidio
I don't want to give you too much bother

Key phrases

continuare per questa strada	*carry on along this street*
prendere la seconda a destra	*take the second on the right*
sempre dritto	*straight on*
mi fa piacere	*it's a pleasure*

Il teatro romano, Lecce

5 [cc] [◎] 25

Anna eventually meets up with Alberto, who's been chatting to the local doctor while waiting for her. The doctor takes them to taste **arancini**, a local cheese and rice savoury.

First time round

macchiata	*stained*
la gonna	*skirt*

But it's not Anna's day . . .

How does Anna react to the accident?

Dott. N. Allora vi piacciono gli arancini?
Alberto Sì! Sono buonissimi!
Anna Mm! **Anche a me piacciono** tanto. Dopo **ne prendo un altro**. E tu, Alberto?
Alberto No, io no. Basta così. Io non ho più fame.

[In her eagerness to take another arancino Anna drops one]

Anna Ah! Oh no! Mi si è macchiata la gonna!
Alberto **Come mi dispiace!**
Anna Ah, uff, **pazienza! Non importa.** Mah, **non è niente.** Tanto non è nuova.

Alberto Ragazzi, è ora di partire se vogliamo arrivare all'appuntamento con Cioto.
Anna È vero. Andiamo.

non ho più fame   *I'm not hungry any more*
tanto non è nuova   *anyway it's not new*

Key phrases

anche a me piacciono	*I like them too*
ne prendo un altro	*I'll have another one*
come mi dispiace!	*I am sorry!*
pazienza!	*never mind!*
non importa	*it doesn't matter*
non è niente	*it's nothing*

Santa Chiara, Lecce

8

Patterns I

i) On the phone
Checking who you're speaking to

Con chi parlo, scusi? *Excuse me, who am I speaking to?*

If you think you know who it is, you say:

Sei tu, Alberto? *Is that you, Alberto?*
È Lei, signor Abruzzi? *Is that you, Mr Abruzzi?*

Setting a date

To find out what day someone has got in mind, use **pensare di**:

Quando pensi di | partire? *When are you thinking of* | *leaving?*
pensa | venire? | *coming?*

The answer can vary in precision:

domenica/il 3 maggio *on Sunday/on 3 May*
fra il 2 e il 5 maggio *between 2 and 5 May*
fra una settimana/fra poco *in a week/soon*

To say when you will next speak to someone, use **sentirsi** (lit. *to hear each other*):

Ci sentiamo | presto/dopo *Speak to you* | *soon/later*
| il 18 luglio | *on 18 July*
| sabato | *on Saturday*

There is no article with a specific weekday but you always use the article with the date.
See Ref. II, 1, 3, p. 241. **Fra** or **tra** must be used to say *in* when you're referring to the future: you cannot use the Italian word **in**.

ii) A polite request

To ask whether someone minds if you do something:

Ti dispiace se ti | chiamo più tardi? *Do you mind* | *if I call you later?*
Le dispiace se La |

Ti dispiace | venire più tardi? *Do you mind* | *coming later?*
Le dispiace | darmi una mano? | *giving me a hand?*

iii) Excusing yourself and apologising

Scusi, ho sbagliato | numero *Excuse me, I've got the wrong* | *number*
| strada | *street*
| porta | *door*

Ho sbagliato strada often means *I've gone the wrong way.*

Mi dispiace, | abbiamo bucato *I'm sorry,* | *we've got a puncture*
| abbiamo finito la benzina | *we've run out of petrol*
| il telefono è guasto | *the phone is out of order*
| è (tutto) esaurito | *it's booked up, sold out, out of print*

iv) Expressing your feelings

Come mi dispiace!	*I am so sorry!/Bad luck!*	Non è niente	*It's nothing*
Che peccato!	*What a shame!*	Davvero?	*Really?*
Accidenti!	*Bother! Damn!*	Meno male!	*Good! Thank goodness!*
Pazienza!	*Ah well/Too bad/Never mind*		*(lit. less bad)*
Non importa	*It doesn't matter*	Mi fa piacere	*That's nice, I'd love to*

v) Saying you like it too

Gli arancini piacciono anche | a te?   *Do you like arancini too?*
| a Lei?
| a voi?

Piacciono anche | a me   *I like them too*   [See Systems, note 3, p. 201.]
| a noi   *We like them too*

vi) Talking about quantities

The key word is **ne** (*of it, of them*), often not expressed in English:

Quanto/a ne ha?   *How much (of it) have you got?*
Quanti/e ne vuole?   *How many (of them) do you want?*

Ne ho	uno, due, tre	*I've got*	*one, two, three*
Ne voglio	alcuni, alcune	*I want*	*some, a few*
Ne prendo	un po', un altro po'	*I'll have*	*a bit, a bit more*
	una fetta, un pezzo		*a slice, a piece*

See Systems, note 1, p. 201.

vii) Asking and explaining the way

One simple way of asking for directions is to say *'Excuse me'* and name the place:

Scusa | il Teatro dell'Opera?
Scusi | viale Marconi?

The more complete question includes the phrase **come faccio?**

Scusi, per il Teatro dell'Opera, come faccio?   *Excuse me, how do I get to the Teatro dell'Opera?*

Deve/devi	seguire questa/quella strada	You have to	*follow this/that road*
	continuare per questa strada		*carry on along this road*
	fino al semaforo		*up to the lights*
	fino all'incrocio		*up to the crossroads*
	andare sempre diritto/dritto		*go straight on*
	andare in fondo alla strada		*go to the end of the road*
	girare a destra/a sinistra		*turn right/left*
	prendere la prima strada/traversa		*take the first road/turning*
	la seconda a destra/sinistra		*the second on the right/left*

viii) Negative expressions

Non ho **più** fame   *I'm no longer hungry*
Non ho **ancora** deciso   *I haven't yet decided*
Non vado **mai** al mare   *I never go to the seaside*

8

Practice I

When are you off?

You're being quizzed about when you're going to take a holiday. At first you hedge a bit – you haven't worked it out. Tell your friend you're thinking of leaving:

> soon
> in two weeks
> in a month
> between 8 June and 16 June

Finally you settle on a date:

> Thursday 15 June

When are you thinking of taking your next holiday?

Bad Blood 26

Anna and Michela are tucking into some exotic specialities in Lecce and you're their guest. Included on the menu are **lampasciumi** – cooked wild onions and **sanguinaccio** – a pork-based blood sausage, actually more delicious than it sounds (the name literally means 'bad blood'). Anna and Michela like everything: what about you?

Anna	Mmm, Michela, mi piacciono questi lampasciumi.
Michela	Mmm, che buoni! Sì, piacciono anche a me. A te piacciono?
You	*[You don't actually like onions. Be polite, though, and say you don't like them very much.]*
Anna	Ah, peccato, sono buoni, sai – io ne prendo un altro, allora. E dopo c'è il sanguinaccio.
You	*[You're a bit doubtful about this. Ask if it's good.]*
Anna	Ma sì! Il sanguinaccio è squisito, è buonissimo! È una specialità di Lecce. Non ne vuoi?
You	*[You'll have to try some. Say yes thanks, you'll have a bit.]*
Michela	Ah, ne prendo anch'io, Anna. A me piace il sanguinaccio! E a te, piace allora?
You	*[Surprisingly, it's wonderful! Say you like it a lot and you'll have a bit more.]*
Anna	Bene, un altro po' per te . . . e un altro po' per me.
Michela	Eh, scusa, un altro po' anche per me!

Help!

You live in Italy and you have to go to England suddenly to visit a sick relative. At the airport you realise you've forgotten to do a few vital things. Luckily your elderly neighbour has a key. Ring her up and ask her if she minds helping you out. You've jotted down what you need to ask her:

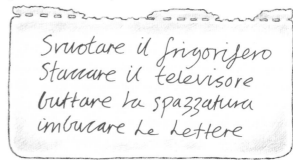

> Svuotare il frigorifero
> Staccare il televisore
> buttare la spazzatura
> imbucare le lettere

Here's how the first part of the conversation should go: can you carry on?

> Signora, Le dispiace svuotare il frigorifero?

You   *Vicina*

> Ma no, sono sempre contenta di aiutare.

You	*[Ask her if she minds unplugging the TV in the sitting room?]*
Vicina	Staccare la TV? Ma non c'è problema! Ha dimenticato altro?
You	*[Yes! Does she mind emptying the rubbish? It's behind the door.]*
Vicina	Buttare la spazzatura? Ma certo!
You	*[Oh, and does she mind posting the letters? They are on the table.]*
Vicina	Imbucare le lettere? Ma sì, vado subito. Buon viaggio!

Accident prone

Alberto is supposed to be coming to see you this morning but he's having his usual run of bad luck! Can you express how you feel when he rings up to tell you?

1 Mi dispiace, non posso venire stamattina.
2 La macchina è guasta.
3 Ho perso il treno delle undici . . .
4 Ma posso prendere un treno oggi pomeriggio.

Mystery tour 🅒🅒 🄲🄳 26

You've been sightseeing on your own in the centre of Lecce and you're in your car outside the church of Santa Croce waiting for your Italian friend. He has promised to guide you to a mystery spot. Listen to his instructions and follow the route on the map. Where do you end up?

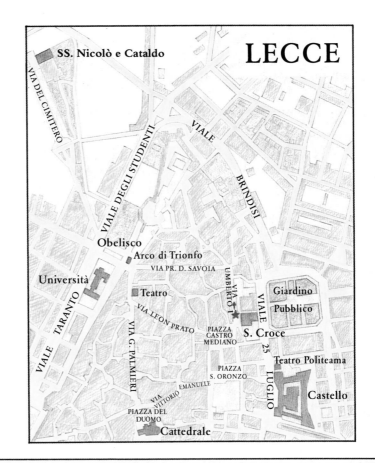

Which way please?

Now it's your turn to do some guiding. You've been in Gallipoli some time and people often ask you the way. Can you tell the following people how to get to their destination?

1 You are at the information office.

Ragazza Dov'è la posta, per favore?

2 You are outside the church of San Francesco.

Sig. anziano Scusi, per la cattedrale come faccio, per favore?

3 You are at the station.

Coppia Come facciamo per andare alla fontana ellenistica?

Back at home, can you now try to explain to a friend how to get to your nearest bus stop, post-office or chemist's?

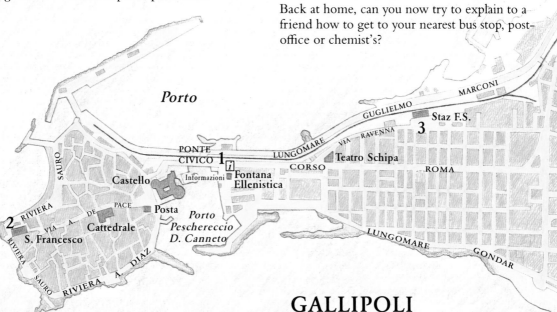

GALLIPOLI

Cultura e parole

In Italy **l'ordine pubblico** – law and order – is the province of two bodies: the blue-uniformed **Arma dei Carabinieri** and the grey-uniformed **PS, la Polizia di Stato** – State Police. They both originated in the kingdom of Piedmont before the unification of Italy. The carabinieri were originally the royal guard, the **Corpo dei Carabinieri Reali**, while the police were originally a civilian militia, the **Guardia Nazionale**. Nowadays the carabinieri are a special corps of the Italian army and are in part controlled by the **Ministero della Difesa** – the Ministry of Defence – and in part by the **Ministero degli Interni** – the Interior Ministry. The PS have always been under the Interior Ministry. The tasks of these two forces are not always easy to separate, since both deal with civilian crime: you can report a theft, for example, to either the **polizia** or the **carabineri**. There are numerous carabinieri jokes which portray them as very stupid: in fact they are the more prestigious force and they have maintained their traditional right to provide the presidential guard of honour and to be on duty in the law courts. Surveys consistently show that the carabinieri are the institution most trusted by Italians – just ahead of the Church – and they have even become the subject of a TV series which features a **carabiniera** with the rank of Maresciallo! Women carabinieri – often known as **donne carabiniere** – have existed since 2000 when it finally became possible for a woman to join the army. There have been women in the police force since 1980. A policewoman is **una donna poliziotto** or **una poliziotta** and a traffic policewoman is **una vigilessa** or **una donna vigile**.

La sicurezza stradale – road safety – is taken seriously in Italy. Getting a licence – **prendere la patente** – involved a theory exam long before this was compulsory in Britain. An Italian driving licence is only issued with a medical certificate. It is valid for ten years and then has to be renewed following a medical; the over-50's have to re-apply every five years, the over-70's every three years. Infringing the highway code – **il codice della strada** – and committing an offence – **una infrazione** – such as speeding – **superare il limite** – involves heavy fines, while illegal parking may get you clamped – **bloccato con le ganasce**. Most drivers belong to **l'ACI, l'Automobile Club d'Italia**. With the right insurance – **l'assicurazione** – it takes care of everything if you have a breakdown – **un guasto**.

Interactions

6 [cc] [CD] 27

Driving to the fishing port of Gallipoli, Anna and Alberto are relieved to be getting there in good time, because neither of them knows the place.

First time round

il cartello	*signpost*
mi sono dimenticata di	*I forgot to*

a How long have they got before they are due to meet Cioto?
b Has either of them got a map of Gallipoli?

Alberto Siamo quasi arrivati. Hai visto il cartello per Gallipoli sulla destra?
Anna Ah! Meno male. E che ore sono?
Alberto Sono le tre e mezza. A che ora abbiamo appuntamento con Cioto?
Anna Alle quattro, vicino alla fontana greca.
Alberto E tu **conosci la strada**, Anna?
Anna No, io non la conosco. Ah, e mi sono dimenticata di portare la pianta della città. Tu **ne hai una**, Alberto?
Alberto Eh, non l'ho portata neanch'io.
Anna Ah, pazienza. Quando arriviamo in città **chiediamo la strada** in centro.

Key phrases

conosci la strada?	*do you know the way?*
ne hai una?	*have you got one?*
chiediamo la strada	*we'll ask the way*

7 [cc] [CD] 28

So near and yet so far: the car grinds to a halt.

First time round

controllo	*I'll check*

Why have they stopped?

Anna Alberto, perché ci fermiamo?
Alberto **C'è qualcosa che non va.**
Anna Oddio! Che cosa abbiamo combinato adesso?
Alberto **Non lo so** Anna. Adesso controllo.
Anna Stiamo qui un attimo, allora?
Alberto Sì.
[Alberto gets out to see]
Anna Allora, mi puoi dire che **cos'è successo?**
Alberto **Che guaio**! Abbiamo bucato.

che cos'abbiamo combinato?	*what have we done?*
abbiamo bucato	*we've got a puncture*

Key phrases

c'è qualcosa che non va	*there is something wrong*
non lo so	*I don't know*
cos'è successo?	*what's happened?*
che guaio!	*what a pain!*

8 `⎡cc⎤` `◔` 29

They fix the puncture and arrive at Gallipoli. They park the car on the seafront and meet up with Cioto. But their troubles are not quite over . . .

First time round

la multa	*fine*
il vigile	*traffic policeman*

Why are they being fined?

Cioto   Ciao.
Alberto   Ciao.
Anna   Ciao.
Cioto   Ragazzi, vi stanno facendo la multa. **Non si può** parcheggiare sul lungomare.
Anna   Oh no!

Alberto   Ma tu conosci il vigile. Puoi fare qualcosa?
Cioto   Credo . . . non si può fare niente.
Alberto   Ah, ma allora è proprio vero. Non c'è due senza tre. Che giornata!

vi stanno facendo la multa	*they're giving you a fine*
non c'è due senza tre	*it never rains but it pours* [lit. *there isn't two without three*]

Key phrase

non si può . . .   *you can't, it's not allowed*

Patterns 2

i) Asking about what happened

The verb *to happen* is **succedere**. In the past tense it takes **essere**:

Cos'è successo?   *What happened? What has happened?*

If you think there is something wrong, you can use the verb **andare**:

C'è qualcosa che non va?   *Is there something wrong?*

ii) Talking about what's gone wrong

Ho	rotto la torcia		I've	broken the torch
	perso la patente			lost my driving licence
	perso il treno			missed the train
	dimenticato l'apriscatole			forgotten the tin-opener
	lasciato il cavatappi a casa			left the corkscrew at home

It could be something that's happened to you: in this case you say literally *they have stolen/given*:

Mi hanno rubato	il portafoglio	I've had my	wallet	stolen
	la valigia		suitcase	
	la cartella		briefcase	

Mi hanno dato la camera sbagliata   *I've been given the wrong room*
Ci hanno dato il piatto sbagliato   *We've been given the wrong dish/order*

See Systems, note 5, p. 202.

It could be that something important is missing: use **mancare** (*to be lacking*):

Manca il sapone   *There's no soap*
Mancano le lenzuola   *There aren't any sheets*

See Unit 9, Systems, note 7, p. 207 and Ref. I, 8, p. 240.

iii) Being sure and unsure

Lo so . . .	*I know* [lit. *I know it*]	Penso di sì	*I think so*
Non lo so	*I don't know (it)*	Non ho idea	*I don't have a clue*

See also Unit 5, Systems, note 1 ii, p. 97 and Unit 7, note 6, p. 198.

iv) Expressing dismay

Che guaio!   *What a pain!*
Che disastro!   *What a disaster!*
Che pasticcio!   *What a mess/mix up/muddle!*

v) What is not allowed

Non	è permesso	guidare a sinistra	It's not allowed to	drive on the left
	si può	sorpassare sulla destra	You can't	overtake on the right

You can also use the word **vietato**, from the verb **vietare** (*to forbid*): **È vietato fumare.**

Practice 2

Odd one out

1 Which of these phrases wouldn't you use to express regret or dismay?
che pasticcio   che peccato   che bello   che guaio

2 Which of these couldn't you have lost from your briefcase?
un'agenda   un'agenzia   una carta di credito   una patente

3 Which one of the following could you do without?
un cavatappi   un apriscatole   un rompiscatole   una torcia

4 Which one of the following can't be used to give directions?
diritto   destra   davvero   dietro

5 Which of these wouldn't you eat?
cannelloni   carabinieri   sanguinaccio   arancini

Fawlty towers

The hard-pressed manager of a hotel is faced with a spate of disasters and complaints: would you give him a job? To make up your mind match up the complaints and his answers and see how he copes.

1 Ci hanno dato la stessa camera!
2 Ho perso la chiave!
3 Manca il sapone!
4 Mancano le lenzuola!
5 Il gabinetto/water è intasato!
6 Manca l'acqua calda!

a Ah! Non siete sposati? Che pasticcio. La camera è grande, però.
b Ah, che guaio! Ma scusi, perché non chiama l'idraulico? Le do subito il numero.
c Mi dispiace, non ne abbiamo altre. Basta entrare per la finestra.
d Davvero? Ma Lei non ne ha portato?
e Non c'è problema. Abbiamo anche l'acqua fredda.
f Che peccato! Ma oggi per fortuna non fa freddo.

Chapter of accidents   30

You've hired an idyllic **rustico** with a friend and are all set for a blissful week. You're nearing your destination and are looking forward to supper and a nice drink.

Amico   Ah! che bello! Siamo quasi arrivati.
You   [*Say thank goodness, you're tired.*]
Amico   Quando arriviamo, assaggiamo quel vino pugliese. A me piace tanto.
You   [*Say you like it too.*]
You   [*. . . Car splutters. Ask if there's something wrong.*]
Amico   Ma non lo so . . . Eh, penso di sì . . . Oh, no!
You   [*Ask what's happened.*]
Amico   Abbiamo finito la benzina!
You   [*Say really? – what a pain!*]

But in the end you make it to the cottage. Now for that wonderful Pugliese wine . . .

Amico   Ah, eccoci finalmente! Prendiamo il vino?
You   [*Oh no . . . where can it be? Own up, say you've forgotten the corkscrew.*]
Amico   No! che disastro!

What people forget   30

Listen to the hotelier describing the things people leave behind. What are they?

Missing!

You have gone to the Pensione Millerose where your friend Jane Mitchell is supposed to be staying. But she isn't there. You start by asking the owner if he knows her and then try to find out what else he knows. Here are his answers: what were the questions you asked?

1 . . .? Sì, sì, la conosco. Ma è partita una settimana fa.
2 . . .? No, mi dispiace, non so dov'è andata.
3 . . .? Eh no. Non ha lasciato l'indirizzo.
4 . . .? Mi dispiace, non so neanche il numero di telefono.
5 . . .? Eh, no. Non so perché è partita. Non ho idea, mi dispiace.

Road sense

Can you match up the road signs with the descriptions given?

1 Doppia curva, la prima a destra
2 Animali domestici vaganti
3 Pericolo di incendio
4 Passaggio a livello senza barriere
5 Animali selvatici
6 Transito vietato ai pedoni

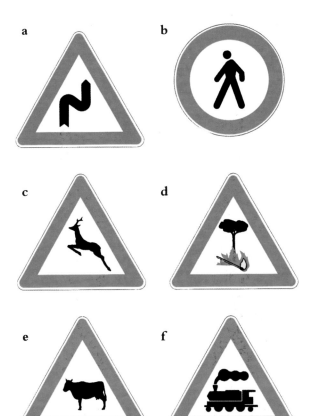

a   b

c   d

e   f

Before and after

Someone's broken into your house and items have been stolen. To find out what they are, compare the two pictures. Make an inventory, tell your flatmate what's missing (using **manca, mancano**), then tell the police what's been stolen (using **mi hanno rubato**).

Vocabulary

Documents

l'agenda	*diary*
il calendario	*calendar*
la carta assegni	*cheque card*
la carta di credito	*credit card*
la carta d'identità	*identity card*
il documento	*document*
il libretto degli assegni	*cheque book*
il modulo	*form*
il passaporto	*passport*
la patente	*driving licence*
la rubrica	*address book*
la tessera	*card*
i travellers cheques	*travellers' cheques*

People

il delinquente	*criminal*
il giudice	*judge*
il ladro	*thief*
la polizia	*police*
. . . doganale	*border/customs police*
. . . stradale	*road police*
il vigile, la vigilessa	*traffic police*

Adjectives

giusto	*right*
sbagliato	*wrong*
bucato	*punctured*
esaurito	*out of print, booked up*
guasto	*out of order*
intasato	*blocked up*
permesso	*allowed*
rotto	*broken*
scarico	*flat [battery]*
scaduto	*expired, run out*
vietato	*forbidden*

Crime, accidents and the law

la contravvenzione	*fine [formal]*
il danno	*damage*
il disguido	*mix-up*
la disgrazia	*disaster*
la fuga	*[gas] leak*
il furto	*theft*
l'incendio	*fire*
l'incidente	*[car] accident*
l'infortunio	*[industrial] accident*
l'infrazione	*offence*
la multa	*fine*
la questura	*police station*
la rapina	*armed robbery*
il reato	*crime*
il ritardo	*delay*
lo scippo	*[handbag] snatching*
il verbale	*statement*
divieto	
di sosta	*no waiting*
di transito	*no thoroughfare*

Personal property

la cartella	*briefcase*
la cinepresa	*cine-camera*
il compact disc	*compact disc*
la macchina fotografica	*camera*
il personal computer	*word processor*
lo stereo	*stereo*
il televisore	*television set*
la valigia	*suitcase*
il videoregistratore	*video recorder*

Verbs

bruciare	*to burn*
confermare	*to confirm*
controllare	*to check*
fissare un appuntamento	*to make an appointment*
fare un errore	*to make a mistake*
dimenticare	*to forget*
disdire	*to cancel*
firmare	*to sign*
guidare	*to drive*
lasciare cadere	*to drop*
mancare	*to be missing, lacking*
perdere	*to lose; miss; leak*
ricordare	*to remember*
riempire	*to fill in [form]*
rimandare/rinviare	*to postpone*
riparare	*to mend*
rompere	*to break*
rovesciare	*to spill*
rubare	*to steal*
sbagliare	*to make a mistake; get it wrong*
sorpassare	*to overtake*

Troubleshooting

Non mi piace   *Mi dispiace*
Non mi dispiace

The above phrases have quite distinct meanings.
Non mi piace is the opposite of **mi piace**. It means *I don't like, I dislike*:

> Non mi piace questa città

Mi dispiace is used to express regret and sympathy.
It means *I'm sorry* [*lit. it is displeasing to me*].

> Mi dispiace, non posso venire
> Hai perso il passaporto? – Mi dispiace

Non mi dispiace means *I quite like, don't mind something*:

> Non mi dispiace cucinare

Mi dispiace   *Scusi   Scusa*

Scusi [formal] and **scusa** [informal] mean *excuse me, sorry, forgive me.*
They are used both to interrupt or attract attention and also to apologise for what you've done:

> Scusi, può ripetere?
> Scusa, mi puoi dire se c'è Maria?
> Scusi se La disturbo
> Scusi, ho rovesciato il caffè!

Mi dispiace is also used to say sorry, but for something which is not directly your fault:

> È tutto esaurito. – Mi dispiace!

It is possible to use both expressions together:

> Ho rotto il piatto! Scusi! Mi dispiace!
> *I've broken the plate! Forgive me! I'm sorry!*

Unità 9

A caccia di funghi
The countryside and food

Bosco fiorito, Val d'Orcia

Part 1
(Interactions 1–4, Patterns 1, Practice 1)

Learn how to:
Say what you want or hope to do
Talk about your plans and intentions
Ask for clarification
Talk about quantity
Point out where things are
Say you're sure or unsure

Part 2
(Interactions 7–8, Patterns 2, Practice 2)

Learn how to:
Say what you're doing
Say who likes what
Say what you love and what you hate
Take part in mealtime conversation

Grammar

More possessives – **un mio amico**, etc.
ce n'è, ce ne sono
quello – *that*
The present progressive
Past participle agreement with **avere** verbs

conoscere/sapere summary
Impersonal verbs and expressions
More on negatives

Want to take it further?
Grammar: see Systems 9, pp. 205–7   *More practice:* do Reinforcement 9, pp. 208–9

Interactions

I 〔cc〕 〔CD〕 2

Anna is staying in Borgotaro, the 'mushroom capital' of Emilia Romagna in the mountains of the Val Taro region, about 65 km from Parma. She's discovered a good place for finding the prized **porcino** mushroom and rings up her friend Michela Alberti to see if she feels like mushroom-picking.

First time round

		Anna is in
a caccia di funghi	*mushroom-picking*	a phone
proprio stufa	*really fed up*	box in a
posto segreto	*secret place*	noisy street.

Michela agrees to come. Why?

Michela Pronto, casa Alberti.
Anna Ciao Michela. Sono Anna. Come stai?
Michela Ciao! Benissimo, e tu?
Anna Anch'io, grazie. Senti, ti ho telefonato per sapere **se hai voglia di** andare a caccia di funghi.
Michela **Dove hai intenzione di** andare?
Anna **Come hai detto? Non ti sento bene.**
Michela Ho detto: dove hai intenzione di andare?
Anna Beh, conosco un posto segreto, molto bello. La settimana scorsa ci ho trovato moltissimi funghi porcini.

Michela L'idea mi piace e sono proprio stufa di studiare. E poi mi piacciono tanto i porcini.
Anna Bene. Allora vieni?
Michela Volentieri. **Posso portare un mio amico?** È simpaticissimo. L'ho conosciuto a Roma dagli zii.
Anna Certo. Perché no! Viene anche un altro mio amico, Paolo. Lo conosci?
Michela Sì, sì. L'ho conosciuto a casa tua, l'anno scorso.
Anna Ah! già, è vero. Bene, allora, ci troviamo tutti a casa mia sabato mattina.

casa Alberti — *one way of identifying the house when answering the phone: you never say your number*

l'ho conosciuto — *I met him*
già, è vero — *that's right, it's true*

Key phrases

se hai voglia di . . .	*if you feel like . . .*
dove hai intenzione di . . .?	*where do you intend to . . .?*
come hai detto?	*what did you say?*
non ti sento bene	*I can't hear you properly*
posso portare un mio amico?	*can I bring a friend of mine?*

2 📼 💿 3

Anna, Paolo, Michela and her friend Totò have met up early; it's damp and misty but Anna makes light of Michela's ironic comment about the weather.

First time round

speriamo	*let's hope*
senz'altro	*definitely*

a Is Anna confident about finding mushrooms? Why?
b What is Paolo's particular interest in them?

Michela	Che bella giornata per andare a funghi!
Anna	Sì, siamo proprio fortunati.
Michela	**Speriamo di trovare** funghi, almeno.
Anna	Ne troviamo senz'altro. Ne ho visti tanti l'altro giorno.
Paolo	Meno male! Stasera li mangiamo tutti.
Totò	Ma li sai preparare, Paolo?
Paolo	Certo. Sono un esperto, io!
Totò	Benissimo! Allora Anna, dove li hai visti questi funghi? **Da che parte andiamo** per trovarli?
Anna	Bisogna andare **di qua**. Sempre dritto. Andiamo!

andare a/per funghi	*to go mushroom-picking*
siamo proprio fortunati	*we're really lucky*
almeno	*at least*
ne ho visti tanti	*I saw lots*
li sai preparare?	*do you know how to prepare them?*
dove li hai visti?	*where did you see them?*

> ### Key phrases
>
> | | |
> |---|---|
> | **speriamo di trovare** | *let's hope we find* |
> | **da che parte andiamo?** | *which way do we go?* |
> | **di qua** | *this way* |

3 📼 💿 4

The boys are fairly hopeless, but Anna turns out to be quite an expert at finding mushrooms.

First time round

guardare	*to look*
il cestino pieno	*full basket*
quell'albero	*that tree*

a What advice does Michela give the boys?
b Where does Anna go off to?

Anna	Che bello! Ne ho trovati tanti!
Paolo	Ma dove? Io non ne ho visti.
Totò	Neanch'io. **Non ho visto niente.**
Michela	Ma voi ragazzi non sapete come fare. Bisogna avere pazienza per trovarli. I funghi ci sono. Basta guardare bene.
Totò	Ho guardato. **Non ce ne sono.**
Michela	Ci sono. **Ce ne sono tantissimi.** Guarda, ho il cestino pieno.
Totò	Forza Paolo, ne dobbiamo trovare anche noi. Perché non provi? Non si sa mai!
Paolo	Ma non trovo mai niente io. A me piace soprattutto mangiare i funghi. Ma Anna dov'è?
Michela	È andata **un po' più avanti, lì in fondo** a sinistra, dietro a quell'albero. Non la vedi? Lei conosce i posti migliori.
Totò	E noi i posti peggiori!

non sapete come fare	*you don't know how to do it*
forza	*come on!*
non si sa mai	*you never know*
non trovo mai niente	*I never find anything*
migliori/peggiori	*best/worst*

> ### Key phrases
>
> | | |
> |---|---|
> | **non ho visto niente** | *I haven't seen anything* |
> | **non ce ne sono** | *there aren't any* |
> | **ce ne sono tantissimi** | *there are lots* |
> | **un po' più avanti** | *a bit further on* |
> | **lì in fondo** | *right over/down there* |

4   5

Anna is rejoined by the others. She's found plenty of mushrooms – and a few of the prized **porcini.** They're so enormous you only need a few to make a meal.

First time round

in tutto	*in total*
solo	*only*
altri	*more*

a How many **porcini** has Anna found?
b Does Paolo manage to find any?

Anna	Avete visto quanti funghi si trovano nel bosco? Io ho anche trovato alcuni porcini.
Michela	Ma dove?
Anna	Là, a sinistra sotto l'albero.
Totò	**E già!** Sono porcini! belli, grossi! Sei fortunata, Anna.

Michela	Quanti ne hai trovati in tutto?
Anna	**Non lo so.** Il cestino è pieno. Però ho trovato solo tre porcini. **Forse** ne troviamo altri fra poco.
Paolo	Ragazzi! Porcini! Ne ho trovati altri tre!
Michela	Altri porcini? **Sei sicuro?**
Paolo	**Certo**, è facile riconoscerli. Anche se non è facile trovarli. Sono enormi! Giganteschi! E stasera li mangiamo tutti!

ne ho trovati altri tre	*I've found three more*
è facile riconoscerli	*it's easy to recognise them*

Key phrases

e già!	*that's right!*
non lo so	*I don't know*
forse	*maybe*
sei sicuro?	*are you sure?*
certo	*of course*

Patterns I

i) Asking for clarification

If you can't hear what someone has said, you can say:

Come hai detto?/Cos'hai detto, scusa? *What did you say?*
Come ha detto?/Cos'ha detto, scusi?
Non ti/La sento bene *I can't hear you properly*
Puoi/può ripetere, per piacere? *Can you please repeat?*

ii) Wishes and intentions

To find out what someone feels like doing, use **avere voglia di** (*lit. to have desire to*):

Hai voglia di	andare per funghi?	*Do you feel like*	going mushroom picking?
	prendere qualcosa?		having something?
	uscire stasera?		going out tonight?

To say you plan to do something use **avere intenzione di** (*lit. to have intention to*):

Dove hai intenzione di andare? *Where do you plan to go?*
Cosa ha intenzione di fare? *What do you intend to do?*

To say what you're thinking or hoping of doing use **pensare di** or **sperare di**:

| Penso di | andare in montagna | *I think I'll* | go to the mountains |
| Speriamo di | fare una scampagnata | *We hope to* | go on a picnic, country outing |

iii) Bringing a friend of yours

The verb **portare** has various meanings including *to bring*.

Posso portare	un mio amico?	*Can I bring a friend of mine?* (*lit. a my friend*)
	una mia amica?	
	un altro mio amico?	*Can I bring another friend of mine?*
	un'altra mia amica?	

See Systems, note 2, p. 205.

iv) Talking about place

Da che parte andiamo? *Which way do we go?*   Di qua/da questa parte   *Over here/this way*

Andiamo	avanti	*Let's go*	on, forward
	lì in fondo		over, down there
	lassù, laggiù		up there, down there
Torniamo indietro		*Let's turn back, round*	

v) Nothing and no-one

In Italian you say: *I haven't seen nothing/no-one.*

Non ho visto	niente	*I haven't seen*	anything
	nessuno		anyone
Non hai trovato	niente?	*Didn't you find*	anything?
	nessuno?		anyone?

vi) Talking about quantity

Some of it

To say 'there is some', you combine **c'è** with **ne,** which becomes **ce n'è**:

C'è dell'acqua qui?	*Is there any water here?*	No, non ce n'è *No, there isn't any*

Sì,	ce n'è	Yes,	*there is (some)*
	ce n'è molta, un po'		*there's lots, a little*
	ce n'è poca		*there isn't much*

C'è	un rifugio qui?	*Is there*	*a hut here?*	No, non ce ne sono *No, there aren't any [i.e.*
	una locanda qui?		*an inn*	*isn't one]*

Sì,	ce n'è uno	*Yes, there is one*
	ce n'è una	

Some of them

You combine **ci sono** with **ne,** which becomes **ce ne sono**:

Ci sono animali selvatici qui?	*Are there wild animals here?*	No, non ce ne sono	*There aren't*
Sì, ce ne sono	*Yes,* *there are*		*any*
ce ne sono molti/alcuni	*there are many/a few*		
ce ne sono pochi	*there aren't many*		

See Systems, note 1, p. 205.

More

To talk about another, or more of something, you use **altro**.

un altro tartufo   *another truffle*   altre castagne   *more chestnuts*

To specify how much more, you can use the following with **altro**:

Ho visto	tantissime	altre bacche	*I've seen*	*lots*	*more berries*
	molte			*many*	
	alcune			*a few*	

With numbers or **un po'**, the quantity comes last:

Ne prendo un altro po'   *I'll have a bit more*

Ho trovato	un altro po' di	mirtilli	*I've found*	*a few more*	*bilberries*
	altri due	lamponi		*two more*	*raspberries*
	altre cinque	more		*five more*	*blackberries*

vii) Being sure and unsure

Sei sicuro?	*Are you sure?*	Forse	*Maybe, perhaps*
Certo	*Of course*	Dipende	*It depends*
Senz'altro	*Definitely*	Non lo so	*I don't know*
Penso di sì	*I think so*		

If you're acknowledging something is true you can say:

Già	*[That's] right*	*Note:* you are familiar with **già** meaning *already*.
È vero	*It's, that's true*	

Practice I

Hold up   [cc] [CD] 6

How effective are you when it comes to holding up the proceedings? Listen to the cassette/CD and find out.

NB Some of the expressions you'll need have come in previous units. Can you remember them?

1 You're on the phone: ask someone to hold on.
2 How do you tell someone it's a bad line and you can't hear them properly?
3 You didn't catch what someone's just said: ask what did you say?
4 And what if you've heard, but haven't understood? How do you say: Sorry I haven't understood.
5 Ask someone if he minds repeating.

Wrong spot   [cc] [CD] 6

It's a lovely day and you're taking some Italian guests on a picnic. You're carrying the food and looking for a picnic spot. Play the host or hostess and take part in the conversation.

You	*[Say what a lovely day it is.]*
Patrizia	Sì, siamo proprio fortunati!
Carlo	Senti, dove andiamo adesso? Di qua o di là?
You	*[Tell him, this way.]*
Carlo	D'accordo, andiamo.
Patrizia	È pesante questa roba! Siamo quasi arrivati?
You	*[The stuff **is** heavy: tell her you're nearly there.]*
Patrizia	Meno male!
You	*[The picnic spot is at the end of the path: say it's down there.]*
Carlo	Ah, che bello! Io ho fame.
You	*[Oh dear, he'll have to wait a bit. This isn't the right place: tell them you're sorry, you've gone the wrong way, you'll have to turn back.]*
Patrizia	Ah, che pasticcio!

Point it out

Look at the picture below. Using the words given to help, point out where things are.

accanto a   lì in fondo   lassù   laggiù   avanti   indietro

1 A wants to get to the church. Point out where it is.
2 B is there already and wants to get back to the river. Point out where it is.
3 C wants to know where D is. You tell her exactly.
4 On the way to the tree, C wants to stop at the inn. Tell her she must keep going.
5 When she gets there, D tells C she wants something to eat. Tell C she must go back.

A friend of mine

You're having a party to welcome the Italian couple who've come to stay. Introduce them to your friends:

e.g. Allora, vi presento Charles, un mio amico.

Now here's who the others are:
1 Margaret, a colleague of yours.
2 Francesca, a neighbour of yours.
3 Andrew, a cousin of yours.
4 John, another colleague of yours.
5 Simon, another friend of yours.

Making tracks

You're leading a group on a hike and are collecting the equipment and provisions at your place. One of the participants calls in to check everything first: he's the anxious type.
First tell him about the equipment so far:

e.g. Quante tende ci sono?   *[5]*
Ce ne sono cinque.

1 Quanti zaini ci   2 E quanti sacchi a pelo
sono? *[8]*   ci sono? *[9]*

Now he asks you about the provisions you've packed. Can you answer his questions?
e.g. La cioccolata c'è? *[molto]*
Ma sì, ce n'è molta.

3 Le mele ci sono?   *[abbastanza]*
4 I biscotti ci sono? *[tanto]*

Finally, reassure him that if all else fails there is shelter at the end of the road:

5 C'è un rifugio se il tempo è brutto? *[uno]*
6 C'è anche una locanda? *[uno]*

Inquisition

You're notoriously vague and your friends are trying to check up on your plans. Try to answer their questions, using phrases in Italian such as:

> *I don't know   of course   maybe   definitely*
> *it depends   I think so   I hope so*

1 Hai intenzione di andare alla festa?
2 Hai deciso di invitare gli Alberti?
3 Hai intenzione di prenotare i biglietti?
4 Pensi di venire con noi?
5 Hai intenzione di lavorare domani?
6 Pensi di partire presto?

Mushrooms and the Law

Collecting mushrooms is subject to strict regional regulations. Can you answer the questions on the regulations below in Italian?

Disciplina della raccolta dei funghi

Art. 12 – *Nel territorio della regione è consentita la raccolta dei funghi spontanei soltanto per le specie commestibili e per una quantità giornaliera non superiore a due chilogrammi per persona.*

commestibili

velenosi

È altresì consentita, per scopi didattici e scientifici, la raccolta giornaliera di due esemplari per persona di ciascuna specie dei funghi non commestibili.

1 Di solito è permesso raccogliere i funghi velenosi?
2 Qual è la quantità di funghi permessa per persona?
3 Se qualcuno vuole studiare i funghi non commestibili, quanti ne può raccogliere?

Cultura e parole

Emilia e Romagna. If you were to ask people from Emilia Romagna where they come from, some would be likely to say, '**sono emiliano**', while others might reply, '**sono romagnolo**'. This reflects the fact that until 1947 Emilia and Romagna were two regions, with separate histories and distinct culinary traditions.

La cucina regionale. It is difficult and frequently impossible to translate different foods from one language to another, hence the existence in English of many Italian words, from pasta and spaghetti to ravioli or radicchio. The problem of translating food, however, also exists within Italy itself. It is not uncommon in a restaurant to hear a customer from another region asking for a dish to be explained. 'Italian' food, in fact, still remains to a large extent regional. Even basic items such as bread come in a huge variety of forms: **la biova** comes from Piedmont, **la michetta** and **il miccone** from Lombardy, Ferrara is known for its **coppia** bread and Rome for **ciriole** rolls. Romagna has **la piadina** and Sardinia the paper-thin **carasau**, also known as **la carta da musica**. Pasta dishes are also very local in origin: the famous **tortellini** from Bologna, known as early as the 15th century, gave rise to variants throughout Emilia Romagna such as **tortelli, cappelletti** – little hats – and **cappellacci** – 'ugly big hats'.

This regional diversity is coming under threat from the impact of **il fast food** served in **i self service** which have sprung up everywhere. Concern to halt this trend and fight food standardisation has led to a movement called **lo Slow Food** with its logo of **una chiocciola** – a snail. Founded in Piedmont by an Italian, the members of this international movement are committed to preserving their heritage of regional foods. With their website, their publications and the courses that they run, they aim to promote an awareness of good food and wine and to educate the public in the importance of biodiversity – **la biodiversità**. They also campaign against genetically modified food – **i cibi transgenetici**.

The countryside and the culinary use of its natural resources have always been an important element in Italy's cuisine, from wild herbs and salads to mushrooms. Nowadays mushrooms, fresh or dried, are expensive to buy, particularly the **porcini**, so for many, going mushroom picking is a favourite autumn pastime. The danger of being poisoned is very real – some porcini are lethal – and most local authorities have trained personnel (sometimes the local vigili!) to check pickers' findings and the market produce. The countryside is also the source of edible wildlife, for example snails, whose nutritional virtues are nowadays extolled in cooking magazines. The rearing of snails has been an agricultural activity recognised by law since 1986, but eating them goes back at least as far as Roman times.

Popular food festivals and celebrations – **sagre** – have long been associated with much of Italy's countryside produce and wildlife, from the chestnut or wild boar festivals – **sagre della castagna** or **del cinghiale** – to the festival of the humble snail itself.

 Slow Food

Interactions

5 [cc] [CD] 7

Mushrooms are vital to the economy of Borgotaro and the surrounding valley. Anna visits a factory where dried mushrooms are selected and packaged. She finds out what some of the workers are doing.

First time round

scegliere	to choose, select
pesare	to weigh
la scatola	box, packet

How much must each box weigh?

Anna   Signora, **cosa sta facendo?**
Rina   **Sto scegliendo** i funghi per poter confezionare il cestino.
[...]
Anna   E Lei, signora, cosa sta facendo?
Silvana   Devo pesare queste scatole, perché devono avere il peso di cento grammi. Un etto.

per poter confezionare   *to be able to make up*

Key phrases

cosa sta facendo?   *what are you doing?*
sto scegliendo   *I'm selecting*

6 [cc] [CD] 8

The mayor of Borgotaro, Pier Luigi Ferrari, is something of an expert on mushrooms. Anna watches him prepare some.

First time round

tagliare	to cut	velenosi	*poisonous*
far cuocere	to cook	commestibili	*edible*

What does Anna want to know?

Anna   **A tutti piacciono i funghi.** È difficile prepararli?
Sig. Ferrari   No. C'è una ricetta semplice. Trifolati. Bisogna tagliarli a pezzi e farli cuocere in padella.
[*Anna*   È difficile riconoscere i funghi velenosi?
Sig. Ferrari   Sì. Può essere difficile distinguerli dai funghi commestibili. L'importante è chiedere l'aiuto di un esperto.
Anna   Ecco. Chiedere l'aiuto di un esperto.]

trifolati	*cooked with oil, garlic and parsley*
distinguerli	*to distinguish them*
in padella	*in a pan*
l'importante è	*what's important is*

Key phrase

a tutti piacciono i funghi   *everyone likes mushrooms*

7 [cc] [CD] 8

Paolo, that other mushroom expert, prepares a dish of **tagliatelle ai funghi**.

First time round

Did Paolo produce a good meal?

Paolo   Ecco le tagliatelle.
Anna   Allora, **buon appetito!**
Tutti   Buon appetito!
Michela   Uhm! Che buone!
Paolo   Ti piacciono, Totò?
Totò   Sì mi piacciono moltissimo. Ma **le hai cucinate proprio tu?**
Paolo   Certo! Sono un esperto io!
Anna   **Mi passi un po' di vino ...?**

Key phrases

buon appetito!	*good appetite!*
le hai cucinate proprio tu?	*did you really cook them yourself?*
mi passi un po' di vino?	*can you pass me some wine?*

Patterns 2

i) Saying what you are doing

To say what you are in the process of doing right now use the present tense of the verb **stare**, plus the '-ing' form of the verb.

Cosa	stai sta state	facendo?	*What are you doing?*

Sto Stiamo	parlando al telefono scegliendo un regalo pulendo la casa	*I am / we are*	*talking on the phone* *choosing a present* *cleaning the house*

See Systems, note 4, p. 206.

ii) Saying who likes what

A tutti A nessuno A Giacomo A mia madre Ai miei amici	piacciono	i funghi le castagne le nocciole le noci i pinoli	*Everyone* *No-one* *Giacomo* *My mother* *My friends*	*likes*	*mushrooms* *chestnuts* *hazelnuts* *walnuts* *pine-nuts*

See Unit 6, Systems, note 2 iii, p. 193.

iii) Talking about your loves, hates and fears

La campagna La montagna	mi piace	parecchio tanto	*I like*	*the countryside* *the mountains*	*a lot* *a great deal*

Le farfalle I gufi I daini Gli scoiattoli	mi piacciono	da morire da impazzire tantissimo moltissimo	*I'm crazy about* *I'm mad about* *I adore* *I love*	*butterflies* *owls* *deer* *squirrels*

This is how you express your dislike of something:

Non mi piace per niente	l'anguilla il buio la pioggia	*I don't like*	*eel* *the dark* *rain*	*at all*

Non mi piacciono per niente	le mosche le formiche	*I don't like*	*flies* *ants*	*at all*

If you hate or dislike something intensely, use the verb **odiare** *(to hate)*:

Odio	il freddo il caldo	*I hate*	*the cold* *the heat*

You might hear the expression **fare schifo** *(to be disgusting, revolting)*:

Mi fanno schifo	i lumaconi i rospi	*I find*	*slugs* *toads*	*revolting*

See Systems, note 7, p. 207.

To say you're frightened of something use **avere paura di**:

| Ho paura | del fuoco/del lampo | *I'm frightened of* | *fire/lightning* |
| | delle vespe/dei ragni | | *wasps/spiders* |

If something really scares you, use the phrase **avere il terrore di**:

| Ho il terrore | dei topi/dei pipistrelli | *I'm terrified of* | *mice/bats* |
| | degli scorpioni/delle vipere | | *scorpions/vipers* |

iv) Saying you did it, etc.

Hai preparato tu	il dolce?	Sì, l'ho preparato io	*Yes I prepared it*
	l'insalata?	Sì, l'ho preparata io	
Ha cucinato Lei	i fusilli?	Sì, li ho cucinati io	*Yes I cooked them*
	le tagliatelle?	Sì, le ho cucinate io	

Notice how the ending of the past participle changes after **lo, la, li, le**.

v) Saying you tasted some, visited some, etc.

Hai assaggiato	del vino?	Sì, ne ho assaggiato	*Yes, I tasted some*
preso	della grappa?	Sì, ne ho presa	*Yes, I had some*
Ha visitato	dei castelli?	Sì, ne ho visitati	*Yes, I visited some*
visto	delle chiese?	Sì, ne ho viste	*Yes, I saw some*

Notice how the ending of the past participle changes after **ne**. See Systems, note 5, p. 206.

vi) Mealtime conversation

In Italy you always begin your meal with a greeting:
Buon appetito!   *Good appetite!*
The standard reply is:
Grazie, altrettanto   *Thank you and you too*

You can also say **Buon appetito** back.

You frequently need to compliment the host:
Che buono, buoni, buona, buone!   *How nice!*
È ottimo/a   *It's excellent!*   Sono squisiti/e!   *They are delicious!*

You need to ask for things:

Mi passi	il vino?	*Will you pass me*	*the wine? [informal]*
Mi passa	l'acqua?		*the water? [formal]*
Ti/Le dispiace passarmi	il pane?	*Do you mind passing me*	*the bread?*
	il sale?		*the salt?*

And you need to offer things:

| Ne vuole | ancora? | *Do you want* | *some more?* |
| Ne prende | un altro po'? | *Are you having* | *a bit more?* |

Practice 2

Legenda

vino

chiesa

castello

abbazia

acquedotto
ponte

museo

isole

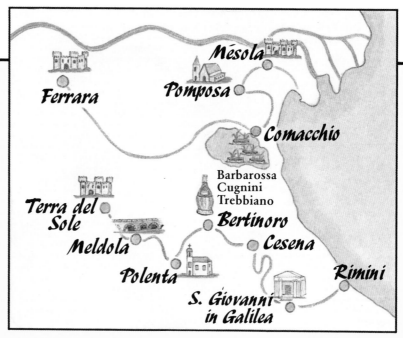

Ferrara

Mésola

Pomposa

Comacchio

Barbarossa
Cugnini
Trebbiano

Terra del
Sole

Meldola

Bertinoro

Cesena

Polenta

Rimini

S. Giovanni
in Galilea

Emilia and Romagna:

You've been visiting parts of Emilia Romagna, stopping mostly at lesser-known places (shown on the map). On the way back to Ferrara you meet an elderly couple on the train (he's from Emilia and she's from Romagna) who ask you about your trip.

Signore emiliano

1 Ha visitato Comacchio? – la chiamano 'la Venezia dei poveri'.   *[Sí, . . .]*
2 Ha visto tutte le isolette – le piccole isole – a Comacchio?   *[Sì, . . .]*
3 Ha mangiata dell'anguilla?   *[Sì, . . . tanta!]*
4 Ha visto l'abbazia di Pomposa?   *[Sì, . . .]*
5 E ha visitato tutti i monumenti di Ferrara?   *[Sì, . . . tutti]*

Signora romagnola

6 A Bertinoro ha bevuto dei vini romagnoli?   *[Sì, . . . alcuni]*
7 Ha assaggiato la piadina – il pane romagnolo?   *[Sì, . . .]*
8 Ha visitato i castelli di Terra del Sole?   *[No, . . .]*
9 Ha visto l'acquedotto e il ponte di Meldola?   *[Sì, . . .]*

Now use the map to answer their general questions:

10 Ha visitato alcuni musei?   *[Sì, . . . uno]*
11 Ha visto alcune belle chiese?   *[Sì, . . . una]*

Imagine you are talking to a friend who has just had an interesting trip. Work out the questions you would ask, and see if you can answer them.

Fads and fancies

It's Ferragosto and you're helping your Italian friend sort out what to get for the festive picnic. Here's who's coming:

Giovanni, i gemelli, la zia, lo zio, gli amici di Giovanni.

And here are their fads and fancies:

Giovanni:

Mi piace parecchio la pasta al forno

1 *I gemelli:* La ricotta ci piace da morire!
2 *La zia:* Non mi piace per niente l'insalata di riso.
3 *Lo zio:* Mi piace tantissimo il vino Trebbiano!
4 *Gli amici:* Ci piacciono molto le patatine!

Now you go through everyone's likes and dislikes with your friend – you've already begun with Giovanni:

A Giovanni piace parecchio la pasta al forno.

Can you talk about the likes and dislikes of people you know? Use the Vocabulary to help.

Strong reactions   9

Listen to the sounds and say how you feel about what you hear. [See Patterns 2 iii, p. 171]

Table talk

Can you sort out who's talking to who?

1 Buone queste tagliatelle!
2 Buon appetito!
3 Le dispiace passarmi il sale?
4 Ti verso un altro po' di vino?
5 Ottimi questi funghi, mi dà la ricetta?

a) Grazie, altrettanto.
b) Ma no, eccolo qua.
c) Ne vuoi ancora?
d) Ma certo, è semplice.
e) No, grazie, basta così.

Better luck next time   9

Here's the sequel to your blunder earlier on. You've found the picnic spot and have settled down to eating.

You	[Wish everyone a good meal.]
Carlo	Grazie, altrettanto.
Patrizia	Mm, ottima quest'insalata di riso. L'hai preparata tu?
You	[Tell her yes, and ask her if she wants a bit more.]
Patrizia	Va bene, sì, grazie.
You	[You'd like some ham: ask Carlo to pass you the ham.]
Carlo	Va bene, eccolo . . . Oh no!
Patrizia	Che c'è? – C'è qualcosa che non va?
Carlo	Ma ci sono formiche dappertutto . . .
You	[Ugh: say you're scared of ants.]
Patrizia	Andiamo! Troviamo un altro posto!
Carlo	Ragazzi, non c'è due senza tre!

Early bird   9

Listen and answer the questions about this mushroom expert, Mario Ugolini.

In Defiance of Death!

Read this passage from a magazine about one of Italy's greatest mushroom experts. Remember, you don't need to understand every word.

PER AMORE DEI FUNGHI A TAVOLA SFIDO LA MORTE

San Paolo di Morsano (Pordenone), ottobre

" Ho sessantasei anni e da quasi trenta rischio, se non la vita, almeno grandi sofferenze tutti i giorni per provare su di me le reazioni dei funghi velenosi. Ma non ho paura perché questa è molto più di una passione, è una vera e propria missione: andando incontro a pericoli non indifferenti, infatti, permetto agli specialisti di fare gli studi sull'avvelenamento da funghi e così, in futuro, potranno salvare molte vite umane".

Chi parla è Umberto Nonis: quelli che si intendono di funghi e che in questo periodo dell'anno vagano per i boschi alla ricerca di porcini, sanno che non c'è esperto più esperto di lui. Ne ha assaggiate, cucinate e mangiate millecinquecento specie. Buone e cattive, tossiche e non, commestibili e perfino mortali.

È talmente bravo che è in grado di riconoscere un porcino o un ovulo soltanto dall'odore. Così i suoi amici giocano spesso con lui nelle sere di autunno, lo bendano ben bene e gli mettono sotto il naso un'infinità di tipi di funghi. E non ne sbaglia uno.

Can you answer these questions?

1 How long has Umberto Nonis been eating poisonous mushrooms?
2 How does he explain the fact that he isn't afraid of eating them?
3 How many types of mushrooms has he tasted, cooked and eaten?
4 Does he have to see a mushroom to tell what type it is?

sfido   *I defy;* potranno   *they will be able to;* chi   *he who;* quelli che   *those who;* vagare per *to wander through;* bendare   *to blindfold*

Vocabulary

Countryside

il bosco	wood
il campo	field
la cascata	waterfall
la collina, il colle	hill
il fiume	river
il lago	lake
la montagna	mountain
la palude	marsh, bog
il panorama [inv.]	view
la pianura	plain
il sentiero	path, track
il ruscello	stream
la valle/ vallata	valley
la caccia	hunting
il cacciatore	hunter
la pesca	fishing
il pescatore	fisherman

Equipment

il binocolo	binoculars
la bussola	compass
il campeggio	camping; campsite
la giacca a vento	wind-cheater
la tenda	tent
il sacco a pelo	sleeping-bag
lo zaino	rucksack

Trees and plants

la pianta	plant
l'erba	grass
il prato	meadow

l'albero	tree
il tronco	trunk
il ramo	branch
il ramoscello	twig
la foglia	leaf
l'abete (m)	fir
il castagno	chestnut
il cipresso	cyprus
il faggio	beech
il pino	pine
il pioppo	poplar
il platano	plane
la quercia	oak
il fiore selvatico	wild flower

Animals

l'animale (m)	animal
l'agnello	lamb
l'asino	donkey
il bue (pl. buoi)	ox
la capra	goat
il cavallo	horse
il cervo	stag
il cinghiale	wild boar
il coniglio	rabbit
il daino	deer
la lepre	hare
la lumaca	snail
il lumacone	slug
il lupo	wolf
la mucca, vacca	cow
la pecora	sheep
il pipistrello	bat
il porco, maiale	pig
la rana	frog
il ratto	rat
il rospo	toad
lo scoiattolo	squirrel
il serpente	snake
il topo, topolino	mouse
il toro	bull
la vipera	adder
la volpe	fox

Birds

l'uccello	bird
l'anatra	duck
l'aquila	eagle
il gufo	owl
l'usignolo	nightingale

Insects

l'ape (f)	bee
la farfalla	butterfly
la formica	ant
la mosca	fly
il ragno	spider
lo scorpione	scorpion
la vespa	wasp
la zanzara	mosquito

Feelings

ridere	to laugh
piangere	to cry
sorridere	to smile
gridare	to shout
litigare	to quarrel
arrabbiarsi	to be angry
annoiarsi	to get bored
stufarsi	to be fed up
seccarsi	to be annoyed
arrabbiato	angry
contento	happy, pleased
scontento	displeased
felice	happy
triste	sad
stufo	fed up
aver paura di	to be afraid of
aver il terrore di	to be terrified of

Troubleshooting

else another more other

The word **altro** is used in a variety of contexts.

1 Adding to what you've got

> Vuole altro?   *Do you want anything else?*
> Sì, mi dà . . .   *Yes, give me . . .*
>   altre due arance   *two more oranges*
>   un altro po' di formaggio   *a bit more cheese*

Another way of expressing more of the same is to use **ancora** (which literally means *again*):

> Ne vuole ancora?   *Do you want some more?*

2 Referring to something which is different

> Preferisco vedere un altro colore – un colore diverso
> *I prefer to see another colour – a different colour*

piace piacciono

1

> mi piacciono i porcini   *I like porcini*
> mi piace mangiare i porcini   *I like eating porcini*

Piacciono is used if you're naming several items you like.
Piace is used if it's one item you like or if you're saying what you like doing, whether this is more than one thing or not.

2 *It* and *them* with **piacere**. Compare **piacere** with **preferire**:

> Mi piace la pasta – mi   Preferisco la pasta – la
>   piace   preferisco
> *I like pasta – I like it*   *I prefer pasta – I prefer it*
> Mi piacciono i funghi   Preferisco i funghi
>   – mi piacciono   – li preferisco
> *I like mushrooms*   *I prefer mushrooms*
>   *– I like them*   *– I prefer them*

You may wonder why there seems to be no word for *it* and *them* when **piacere** is used. This is because:

> **piace** on its own means *it is pleasing*
> **piacciono** on its own means *they are pleasing*

Unità 10

La moda

The world of Italian fashion

Pubblicità Armani a Milano

Part 1	Part 2
(Interactions 1–4, Patterns 1, Practice 1)	(Interactions 5–8, Patterns 2, Practice 2)
Learn how to:	*Learn how to:*
Compare one thing with another	Point out what you want
Say what's best and worst	Make polite requests
Talk about price	Ask if something suits you
Talk about colours and materials	Ask about availability in your size
Say what year something happened	

Grammar	
Comparative and superlative forms	Verbs used with indirect object pronouns
Using **che** or **di** in comparisons	Verbs needing **a** and verbs needing **di**
bello, buono, grande	Review of **per, da, fra**
che and other relative pronouns	More irregular past participles

Want to take it further?
Grammar: see Systems 10, pp. 210–12   *More practice:* do Reinforcement 10, pp. 213–14

Interactions

I 🔲 💿 11

The Fashion Designer's Guild – **La Camera Nazionale della Moda Italiana** – has its headquarters in Rome. Anna Mazzotti talked to its coordinator, the designer Renato Balestra, who, like many famous fashion designers, began his career in another field, in his case engineering.

First time round

l'artigianato	*craftsmanship*
le mani d'angelo	*angel's hands*
i sarti	*tailors*
i tessuti	*textiles*
le case di confezione	*clothing manufacturers*

Balestra thinks that Italian fashion is more dynamic than its French rivals.
What do you think he means when he talks about the importance of 'angel's hands'?

[Anna   La moda italiana è diventata un fatto economico importante. A tutti piacciono gli stilisti italiani. **Secondo Lei,** come sono riusciti ad avere tanto successo?]

Balestra   La moda italiana forse è **più fresca della moda francese**, io trovo. La moda francese ha una lunga tradizione, è un po' incamerata in certi canoni, forse. La moda italiana è più viva, è più colorata, è più giovane, forse, è più vivace e forse anche gli stessi stilisti sono, sono … provengono da vari settori. Non tutti hanno cominciato con la moda o col disegno.

Anna   **Secondo Lei,** l'artigianato italiano è un fattore fondamentale?

Balestra   Certamente è un fattore molto importante. Noi abbiamo in Italia quello che chiamiamo 'le mani d'angelo'. Cioè, **le mani** più … **più brave**, più … più artigianali forse **del mondo**. Tant'è vero che anche i sarti stranieri, per esempio, i sarti francesi, vengono a iniziare e a collaborare con le case italiane di tessuti, di confezione, italiane perché ci sono queste mani favolose.

cioè	*that is to say*
un po' incamerata in certi canoni	*a little hidebound by certain rules*
gli stessi stilisti	*the designers themselves*
quello che	*what [lit. that which]*
tant'è vero che	*so much so that*

Key phrases

più fresca della moda francese	*fresher than French fashion*
secondo Lei	*in your opinion [lit. according to you]*
le mani più brave del mondo	*the cleverest hands in the world*

2   [cc]   (CD)   12

Out in the elegant via Condotti, in Rome's main fashion district, Giorgio finds out what sort of clothes people actually buy and how much they pay for them.

First time round

Here are two of the women he speaks to.
What has each of them bought and how much have they paid? The prices are higher than you might think.

Giorgio	Signora, che cosa ha comprato?
Signora	Ho comprato una giacca da MaxMara.
Giorgio	E . . . si può dire **quanto l'ha pagata?**
Signora	L'ho pagata trecentottantasette euro.

Giorgio	Che cosa hai comprato?
Ragazza	Ho comprato un pantaloncino, un bermuda.
Giorgio	E **di che colore?**
Ragazza	Grigio.
Giorgio	E . . . quanto l'hai pagato?
Ragazza	L'ho pagato centotrenta euro.

si può dire?   *is it possible to say?*

Key phrases

quanto l'ha pagato/a?	*how much did you pay for it?*
di che colore?	*what colour?*

Price is right   [cc]   (CD)   12

Listen to the cassette/CD and try and make the prices fit the items.

3 📼 💿 13

Francesco Maria Bandini is a young and much-sought-after designer of haute couture who lives in the artistic quarter of Rome a stone's throw away from his smart salon in via Condotti.

First time round

la carriera	*career*
prima di	*before*
cominciare	*beginning*

Anna arrives to interview him at his home.

a When did Bandini start his career as a fashion designer?

b What did he do before?

Anna	Signor Bandini, Lei è uno dei designers più conosciuti in Italia e senz'altro quello più giovane. Quando esattamente ha cominciato la Sua carriera di designer?
Bandini	Ho cominciato **nel millenovecentottantaquattro.**
Anna	E che cosa ha fatto prima di cominciare a disegnare i vestiti?
Bandini	Ho fatto molte cose, per esempio architettura.
Anna	Ho capito. E dove lavora? Qui nel Suo appartamento?
Bandini	Sì, qui sopra. Andiamo, Le faccio vedere.

qui sopra   *here upstairs*

Key phrase

nel millenovecentottantaquattro   *in 1984*

Year in question 📼 💿 13

Listen to the cassette/CD. Can you give in Italian the years of the important events mentioned?

4 📼 💿 14

Bandini takes Anna up to his studio.

First time round

finora	*so far*
ho realizzato	*I've created*

Apart from clothes, what else has he designed?

Bandini	Ecco, questo è il mio studio. E qui è dove disegno.
Anna	E quante ore lavora al giorno?
Bandini	Cinque ore.
Anna	E **che cos'altro** ha fatto nel campo del design?
Bandini	Mah, finora ho realizzato un orologio e questa casa.
Anna	Tra le cose che ha disegnato, quale preferisce, quale Le piace di più?
Bandini	Mah, tutte e nessuna.

Key phrase

che cos'altro?   *what else?*

Patterns 1

i) Expressing opinions

Use **Secondo** (lit. *according to*):

| Secondo | te/Lei | gli stilisti italiani sono bravi? | *In your opinion, are Italian designers good?* |
| | voi | | |

| Sì, secondo | me | sono molto bravi | *Yes, in* | *my* | *opinion they're very good* |
| | noi | | | *our* | |

ii) Making judgements and comparisons

The most and the least

Use the definite article, plus **più** or **meno**:

| Quel vestito è | il più | elegante di tutti | *That dress is* | *the smartest* | *of all* |
| | il meno | | | *the least smart* | |

| Quei sandali sono | i più comodi | di tutti | *Those sandals are* | *the most comfortable* | *of all* |
| | i meno comodi | | | *the least comfortable* | |

The article is often separated from **più** or **meno**:

| È la giacca | più bella | di tutte | *It's* | *the nicest* | *jacket of all* |
| | meno bella | | | *least nice* | |

The best and the worst

Use the definite article plus **migliore** (*best*) or **peggiore** (*worst*):

| Il vino francese è | il migliore | del mondo | *French wine is* | *the best* | *in the world* |
| | il peggiore | | | *the worst* | |

| La cucina italiana è | la migliore | del mondo | *Italian food is* | *the best* | *in the world* |
| | la peggiore | | | *the worst* | |

Notice that in these examples **di** is used to mean *in*.

See Systems, note 3, p. 211.

More and less

When you compare things, you need the words **più** and **meno** without the article:

Le scarpe nere sono	più care	delle scarpe marrone
	meno care	
The black shoes are	*more expensive*	*than the brown shoes*
	less expensive	

| Quei pantaloncini sono | più belli | degli altri | *Those shorts are* | *nicer* | *than the other ones* |
| | meno belli | | | *not as nice* | *as* |

Better and worse

Use **migliore** and **peggiore** without the articles:

| La cucina italiana è | migliore | della cucina francese | Italian food is | better | than French food |
| | peggiore | | | worse | |

Note that in these examples **di** means *than*. It is used when directly comparing two things.

But if you compare two activities use **che**:

È meglio risparmiare soldi che spendere troppo   *It's better to save money rather than spend too much*

See Systems, note 2, p. 210; note 3, p. 211.

iii) Talking about price

What you paid

The verb **pagare** means *to pay for*.

Che bella camicetta, l'hai pagata molto?   *What a lovely blouse, did you pay a lot for it?*
Che begli occhiali, li hai pagati molto?   *What lovely glasses, did you pay a lot for them?*

See Systems, note 4, p. 211 for the spelling changes of **bello**.

Quanto	l'hai pagato?	*How much did you*	pay for it?
	l'hai pagata?		
	li hai pagati?		pay for them?
	le hai pagate?		
L'ho pagato/a	centotrenta	*I paid*	130	*for it*
Li/le abbiamo pagati/e	trecentottanta	*we paid*	380	*for them*

The word **cento** for talking about the hundreds is often left out, along with the word **euro**.

How much you've spent

Use **spendere** which has an irregular past participle:

Quanto ha speso in tutto?   *How much did you spend altogether?*

iv) Colours and materials

If you want to know what colour or material something is, you say, literally, *of which colour, material?*

| Di che colore | è l'abito da sera? | *What colour* | is the evening dress? |
| | sono i cappotti? | | are the coats? |

| L'abito da sera è | rosa | *The evening dress is* | pink |
| | viola | | purple |

| I cappotti sono | marrone | *The coats are* | brown |
| | blu scuro | | dark blue |

Some adjectives of colour, such as the ones above, are invariable.

Patterns I

Di che stoffa	è l'abito da sera? sono i cappotti?	*What*	*is the evening dress* *are the coats*	*made of?*
Gli abiti da sera sono	di seta di raso	*The evening dresses are made*		*of silk* *of satin*
I cappotti sono	di lana di cachemire	*The coats are made*		*of wool* *of cashmere*

v) Finding out more

The key word is **altro**:

Che cos' altro	ha fatto? ha comprato? ha scelto?	*What else*	*did you*	*do?* *buy?* *choose?*
Chi altro	hai visto? hai incontrato? sei andato a trovare?	*Who else*	*did you*	*see?* *meet?* *visit?*

vi) Saying the year

In Italian, the year is always accompanied by the definite article. You literally say *the 1993*, etc.

Il milleottocentosessantuno (1861) è una data importante   *1861 is an important date*
Il millenovecentoquarantasei (1946) è una data importante   *1946 is an important date*

To say *in 1861, 1946* etc., join **in** to the article:

Nel 1861 il regno d'Italia è stato creato   *In 1861 the Kingdom of Italy was created*
Nel 1946 gli italiani hanno votato per la Repubblica   *In 1946 the Italians voted for a Republic*

For more on dates, see Ref. II, 3, p. 241.

Practice I

Good advice?

You've arrived in a new place and want to know which are the best clothes shops. You ask the hotel receptionist for her opinion:

> Mah, il migliore è La Capanna, secondo me. Hanno dei bellissimi vestiti d'alta moda – un po' cari, forse.

> Secondo Lei, quali sono i migliori negozi di abbigliamento qui vicino?

But maybe it would be too expensive. Can you put the same question to a couple in the hotel and then to their teenage daughter? What do you think they would say?

When did it happen?

Quando sono successi questi avvenimenti?
When did these events take place? Choose from these years:

1776   1492   1861   1957   1939   1989

1 Cristoforo Colombo ha scoperto l'America.
2 Il Belgio, La Francia, la Germania, l'Italia, il Lussemburgo e l'Olanda hanno firmato il trattato di Roma per fondare la Comunità Economica Europea.
3 L'America ha dichiarato la sua indipendenza.
4 È scoppiata la seconda guerra mondiale.
5 È caduto il muro di Berlino.
6 Il Conte Camillo di Cavour è diventato il primo Primo Ministro dell'Italia unita.

Figure conscious   [cc] [CD] 15

Buying anything involves some rapid thinking when it comes to figures. How quick off the mark are you? Listen and write down the prices mentioned.

Shopping spree   [cc] [CD] 15

You're entertaining an Italian acquaintance. She's come back laden from a shopping spree. Listen and join in the conversation.

Sig.ra P.   Sono proprio stanca! Ho comprato tante cose.
You   [*Express interest and ask her what she's bought.*]
Sig.ra P.   Beh, sono riuscita a trovare due golf di cachemire, e un cappotto di lana pura.
You   [*Ask her to show you the sweaters*].
Sig.ra P.   Ma certo . . . Eccoli. Belli, vero?
You   [*They're lovely. You've always wanted a cashmere sweater. Ask if she paid a lot for them.*]
Sig.ra P.   Mah . . . non tanto. Mi hanno fatto un piccolo sconto. Adesso Le faccio vedere il mio cappotto.
You   [*Mm, it's a lovely coat, is it black or navy blue? Ask her what colour it is.*]
Sig.ra P.   È blu marino.
You   [*See if she'll tell you what she paid for it.*]
Sig.ra P.   Ah, questa è stata una vera occasione. L'ho pagato soltanto 765 euro!
You   [*Well, for some people it's a bargain: ask her what else she's bought.*]
Sig.ra P.   Ah, ho comprato un bellissimo foulard di seta, un paio di stivali, delle camicette di puro cotone, due gonne scozzesi favolose . . .

Can you remember?   [cc] [CD] 15

You are being asked to do certain things. What are they? Listen to the cassette/CD and try to remember what they are.

Home truths

Think about the places you know. Can you tell your Italian guests which is:
1 the best restaurant
2 the most friendly pub
3 the most interesting market
4 the least expensive clothes shop.
Now give some further advice. Tell them:
5 It's more fun to go by bus than by tube.
6 It's better to shop at the supermarket than in small shops.
7 It's cheaper and easier to travel after nine than before.

10

A whiff of astrology

Read the descriptions of the designer perfumes below. Choose one for a man and one for a woman. Can you say what it is about that person which made you choose the perfume?

eg. Ho scelto … perché … Tony è un uomo sensibile.

Now answer the following questions:

1 Secondo Lei, si può veramente scegliere il profumo secondo il segno dello zodiaco?
2 Lei crede nell'astrologia?
3 Lei sa di che segno è?
4 Lei ha mai regalato un profumo? A chi?
5 Le piace ricevere un profumo per regalo?
6 Qual è il profumo che Le piace di più?

VERGINE'

Intelligente e razionale, non è facile agli innamoramenti, ma quando incontra l'uomo giusto...

Il suo profumo è...

Ferrè by Ferrè: un bouquet ricco e persistente, pensato per la donna anni '90. Il flacone è unico: sferico, avvolto in una preziosa rete di seta (da €55).

PESCI

È un uomo sensibile, sempre pronto ad aiutare chi si trova in difficoltà. S'innamora difficilmente.

Il suo profumo è...

Ungaro Pour l'Homme, dove primeggiano i freschi aromi della lavanda, dell'abete e del bergamotto, dando vita a una fragranza che evoca mille emozioni. (da €58).

CANCRO

È difficile prevedere le sue mosse. Ma è proprio questo a renderlo straordinariamente affascinante.

Il suo profumo è...
Romeo Gigli: un bouquet complesso che fa riscoprire il fascino di aromi esotici, addolciti delle fresche fragranze del bosco, (da €58).

BILANCIA

Non è soltanto la più bella dello zodiaco, ma anche la più raffinata. Vive attorniata da molti ammiratori.

Il suo profumo è...

Via Spiga: un sapiente mix di note fiorite, tra cui la rosa e il neroli, che sfumano nelle note calde della vaniglia (da €56).

183

Cultura e parole

The language of fashion

In comparison with French fashion, which was established at the turn of the century, Italian fashion is very young. Yet over the past thirty years it has established itself as a leader in haute couture – **l'alta moda** – and has conquered the mass market of **il prêt à porter** – ready-to-wear.

Despite Italy's leading international position, French and English dominate the language of fashion: it is the language of exclusivity and snob appeal, and uses words rarely found in everyday conversation. Colours are a case in point: **foncé** is often preferred to **scuro** – dark, while **rouge** [rosso], **jaune** [giallo], **marron** [marrone], **orange** [arancione], and **gris** [grigio] are just a few of the unnecessarily gallicised words. If you are well off you wear **bijoux** not **gioielli** – jewels, and amongst the garments you might wear are **tailleurs, gilets, chemisiers,** and **blousons. Lo chic** and **l'aplomb** are what every modern woman hopes to have, along with **il glamour** and **il sex-appeal**, which comes from having the right **look** as well as clothes carefully chosen to suit **il mood** of the day, be it casual or not! **Il t-shirt, il top, il blazer, il cardigan** and even **il bomber** have

all become stylish creations in Italian hands, worn by **le top model** on the catwalk – **la passerella**. And then, of course, there are **i blue jeans**… The name, however, is Italian in origin! It comes from **blu di Genova**, the name used to describe the heavy-duty material produced since the 13th century in Genoa and commonly worn by Ligurian peasantry in the 18th and 19th centuries. The export of the cloth to the USA eventually paved the way to its mass production by the famous Levi Strauss.

Interactions

5   [cc]   🔘 16

Bandini shows Anna the busy workshop in via Condotti where his designs are made up by skilled women seamstresses.

First time round

misurare	*to measure*
le maniche	*sleeves*
tagliare	*to cut*

a What is Antonietta doing?
b Has she ever made a mistake?

Bandini	Prego, **si accomodi**. Questa è la sartoria. Loro sono le persone che lavorano con me. Lei è Antonietta che sta preparando un vestito.
Anna	Buongiorno, signora Antonietta.
Antonietta	Buongiorno.
Anna	**Le dispiace spiegarmi** cosa sta facendo?
Antonietta	Sto misurando il tessuto per tagliare delle maniche.
Anna	Ho capito. Quindi prima di tagliare, di cominciare a cucire l'abito, Lei ha molto da fare, eh?
Antonietta	Eh, abbastanza.
Anna	Ma Lei ha mai sbagliato?
Antonietta	Sì, e gli errori costano cari!

la sartoria	*workshop*
cucire	*to sew*

Key phrases

si accomodi	*come this way; make yourself at home*
Le dispiace spiegarmi?	*do you mind explaining?*

6   [cc]   🔘 17

Bandini's mother, Alba Bandini, directs the business and runs the salon where clients come for fittings.

First time round

A client rings up to check up on a dress.
a Is it ready?
b Why is the client going to ring back in a week?

Sig.ra Alba	Pronto, sartoria Bandini. Buongiorno, sono la signora Alba. Sì, il Suo vestito è già pronto. Però un attimo che controllo in sartoria . . .
She speaks through the intercom.
Antonietta, è pronto l'abito della contessa Pecci?
Now she speaks to the client
Sì, signora, l'abbiamo qui. Vuol passarlo a prendere o vuole che lo mandiamo noi? Scusi, non La sento bene. Può ripetere? Ah, ho capito, Lei non può prenderlo oggi perché è rimasta a Milano. Eh, se Lei non è sicura quando può tornare a Roma, perché non ci richiama? Fra una settimana? **Ce l'ha, il nostro numero?** Grazie, molto gentile, buongiorno.

vuol passarlo a prendere . . .?	*do you want to drop by and collect it?*

Key phrase

ce l'ha il nostro numero?	*have you got our number?*

7   🔲   ◎ 18

Anna asks Signora Alba about their clients.

First time round

trattare con	*to deal with*
consigliare	*to advise*

a Who are the Bandini's clients?
b What does Anna ask permission to see?

Anna	Signora Alba, Lei è la direttrice della sartoria Bandini?
Sig.ra Alba	Sì, io sono la direttrice e mio figlio è lo stilista.
Anna	Vedo che riesce ad accontentare le Sue clienti. Chi sono?
Sig.ra Alba	Sono delle clienti italiane e abbiamo anche delle clienti straniere importanti.
Anna	E vengono sempre qui, in via Condotti, per scegliere?
Sig.ra Alba	Sì, riescono anche a stare tutto il giorno da noi.
Anna	Ah, beate loro! Signora, è difficile trattare con le Sue clienti?
Sig.ra Alba	No, debbo dire che le nostre clienti diventano sempre amiche, perché sappiamo consigliarle bene.
Anna	**Mi permette di** vedere i vostri nuovi vestiti?
Sig.ra Alba	Cosa preferisce vedere?
Anna	Degli abiti da sera.
Sig.ra Alba	Prego, si accomodi.
Anna	Grazie.

debbo	*an alternative for* devo, *I must*
beate loro!	*lucky them!*
accontentare	*to keep happy*

Key phrase

mi permette di . . .?   *would you let me . . .?*

8   🔲   ◎ 19

Anna sits down with Bandini to watch a mini fashion show and then takes part herself.

First time round

a Does she like both dresses equally?
b What do Bandini and the model think of the suit Anna models?

Anna	*[looking at a bright red, purple and yellow dress]* Mm . . ., **quello lì mi piace molto!**
Bandini	Davvero? Le piace?
Anna	Sì, **è proprio bello!** *[Looking at a chiffon dress with a grey skirt and purple bodice]* Quel vestito . . . **mi piace un po' meno**.
Bandini	Non Le piace il colore?
Anna	Sì, mi piace, ma preferisco l'altro. *Now Anna has a go at modelling a bright blue and red suit. She's watched by Bandini and the model.*
Modella	Che bel modello! **Le sta proprio bene!**
Bandini	Eh, sì. Effettivamente le sta proprio bene.

effettivamente le sta proprio bene   *it really does suit her*

Key phrases

quello lì mi piace molto	*I like that one a lot*
è proprio bello	*it's really lovely*
mi piace un po' meno	*I like it a bit less*
le sta proprio bene	*it really suits her*

Patterns 2

i) Asking if someone has got something

Ce l'	hai ha avete	il numero? il prefisso? l'indirizzo?	*Have you got the*	*number?* *code?* *address?*

Sì, ce l'ho   *Yes, I've got it*
No, non ce l'abbiamo *No, we haven't got it*

The literal translation is: *the number/code/address, have you got it?* In speech it is much more common to use this expression than simply **'hai il nostro numero?'**

Ce l'hai un abito da sera?   *Have you got an evening dress?*
Ce l'ha una giacca di pelle?   *Have you got a suede-leather jacket?*
Ce l'avete una cintura di cuoio? *Have you got a leather belt?*

See Troubleshooting, Unit 7, p. 142.

ii) Making polite requests [see also Unit 8, Patterns ii, p. 154.]

Le dispiace	spiegarmi dirmi farmi vedere	cosa sta facendo?	*Do you mind*	*explaining to me* *telling me* *showing me*	*what you are* *doing?*

To ask permission to do something, say:

Mi permette di	vedere provare	quel vestito?	*Would you let me*	*see* *try on*	*that dress?*

iii) In the clothes department

Pointing out what you want

Quale vestito?	– Quello lì	*Which dress?*	*– That one*
Quale giacca?	– Quella lì	*Which jacket?*	*– That one*
Quali pantaloni?	– Quelli lì	*Which trousers?*	*– Those ones*
Quali scarpe?	– Quelle lì	*Which shoes?*	*– Those ones*

The word **proprio** (*really*) is handy for emphasis:

Quella borsa lì è proprio bella	*That bag*	*is really nice*
Quelle cinture lì sono proprio belle	*Those belts*	*are really nice*

What suits you?

Come mi sta? *How does it suit me?*
Quel vestito ti sta proprio bene *That dress really suits you*
Quelle scarpe Le stanno proprio bene *Those shoes really suit you*

To suit is **stare bene a**. See Systems, note 6, p. 211.

What you like best

| Quell' impermeabile mi piace | (di) meno
di più | *I like that raincoat* | *less*
more |
| Quelle camicie mi piacciono | (di) meno
di più | *I like those shirts* | *less*
more |

Saying what size you take

Che numero porta?	*What size [shoe, shirt] do you take?*
[Porto] il 38	*I take a 38*
Che taglia ha?	*What size [coat, trousers, jacket etc.] do you take?*
[Porto] la 40	*I take a 40*
La mia taglia è 38	*My size is 38*

General clothes sizes (including chest/hip measurements)

GB	USA	Europe	ins	cms
8	6	36	30/32	76/81
10	8	38	32/34	81/86
12	10	40	34/36	86/91
14	12	42	36/38	91/97
16	14	44	38/40	97/102
18	16	46	40/42	102/107
20	18	48	42/44	107/112
22	20	50	44/46	112/117

iv) Being hospitable

The following are much-used all-purpose phrases deriving from the verb **accomodarsi** (*to settle oneself, make oneself comfortable*). They can mean, *do come in; do sit down; this way please.*

Accomodati	*[tu]*
Si accomodi	*[Lei]*
Accomodatevi	*[voi]*

Practice 2

Lucky you!

Here's some things you might love to have:

Ce l'hai un forno a microonde?

Beato te!

Ma certo!

Choose three and ask the following people whether they have one. If so, can you tell them each time how lucky they are using **beato te, Lei** or **voi**?

1 a female friend
2 the couple next door
3 a male acquaintance

Sales talk

You are trying on a jacket but it's definitely too large! Which of the following remarks by the sales assistant would be inappropriate in the circumstances?

1 Le sta molto bene.
2 Quel modello lì è proprio bello.
3 Il colore Le sta bene.
4 È proprio la Sua taglia.
5 Ma possiamo accorciare le maniche.
6 Le giacche larghe vanno di moda quest'anno.
7 No, non è troppo stretta.

Footloose   20

You've just spied a lovely pair of shoes in the shop window – **in vetrina**. They're not cheap, but you want to try them on. Listen to the cassette/CD and take part in the conversation.

Commesso	Buongiorno, desidera?
You	*[Say hello and ask if you can see the black shoes in the window.]*
Commesso	Ma certo. Mi fa vedere quali?
You	*[Say of course and point out the shoes you want.]*
Commesso	Ho capito. Va bene. Che numero porta?
You	*[Tell him you take size 38.]*
Commesso	*[He comes back but with a different black pair]* Mi dispiace, ma nel 38 abbiamo solo queste. Le vuole provare?
You	*[Bother, you'd rather have the others. Still these are nice too: say yes, that's fine.]*
Commesso	Ah, è proprio un bel modello. Le stanno proprio bene . . .
You	*[Actually, they're too tight: tell him.]*
Commesso	Troppo strette? È sicura?
You	*[You're quite sure – they're killing you: ask if he's got a bigger size.]*
Commesso	In questo modello, no, mi dispiace.
You	*[Say what a pity, then thank him and say goodbye.]*

Getting what you want   20

Can you remember the various ways you've come across so far for getting what you want? Listen to the cassette/CD to find out.

1 You want the man in the information office to tell you what time the museum opens.
2 You ask the woman at the bus stop if she can tell you when the next bus is due.
3 You ask the man on the train if he minds opening the window.
4 You ask the sales-assistant to show you another style.
5 You ask the greengrocer to give you a few more apples.
6 You ask your host if he will let you see the house.

Comparing styles

Read the extract below from an article on language. Style, it seems, is not only a question of how things look. It's reflected in your speech and it's a gender issue. Do you agree?

Se dici 'fantastico' sei donna.

Lui è volgare e rispetta poco la grammatica, lei usa molto i superlativi ed è pignola; c'è una differenza di linguaggio fra i due sessi. Lo provano alcune indagini scientifiche.

Lo stile della donna

- Dice le cose in maniera indiretta, fa cioè dei giri di parole prima di arrivare alla conclusione.

- Parla molto correttamente usando parecchi aggettivi e eufemismi.

- Usa i superlativi 'bellissimo', 'fantastico', 'delizioso', 'adorabile' in molte situazioni, anche poco entusiasmanti.

- Usa espressioni neutre come 'forse' 'non è vero?' 'ma chissà' per prendere tempo e organizzare le frasi successive.

Lo stile dell'uomo

- Quando parla è molto obiettivo e va direttamente al nocciolo del discorso e non si perde in mille particolari.

- Rispetta poco la grammatica

- Usa i superlativi come 'bellissimo' e 'facilissimo' soltanto nelle situazioni di minore importanza; per esempio riesce a lanciare un 'bellissima' a qualsiasi donna che passa per strada e a essere imbarazzato se deve dirlo a una che lo interessa davvero ...

- Mentre parla fa delle pause per organizzare ciò che dirà in seguito

---

Secondo me è assurdo!
Non sono d'accordo!
Sono d'accordo! È giusto!

Using some of the adjectives given below, express your views on each of the eight statements you've just read.

assurdo   falso/vero   giusto/sbagliato   ridicolo   buffo

Gender games

How many comparisons between men and women can you make? Use the text above and the words below to help, but you don't need to restrict yourself to this. Be as outrageous as you like!

---

obiettivo   *objective;* equilibrato   *balanced*
razionale   *rational;* irrazionale   *irrational*
sensibile   *sensitive;* insensibile   *insensitive*
sicuro di sè   *confident;* timido   *shy*
spendaccione   *extravagant*
tirchio   *mean;* generoso   *generous*
aver buon senso   *to have common sense*
esprimersi   *to express oneself*

---

e.g. Gli uomini sono più obiettivi delle donne!
    Le donne sanno esprimersi meglio degli uomini!

---

pignola   *particular, precise*
l'indagine [f]   *survey*
il nocciolo del discorso   *the heart of the matter*
qualsiasi   *any;* chissà   *who knows*
ciò che dirà   *what he'll say*

Vocabulary

Clothes and accessories

l'abbiglia-mento	clothing
l'abito	man's suit, dress
l'abito da sera	evening dress
i blue jeans	jeans
la calzamaglia	tights
le calze	stockings
i calzini	socks
la camicia da notte	nightdress
la canottiera	vest
il cappello	hat
il cappotto	coat
il cardigan	cardigan
il costume da bagno	bathing-costume
la cravatta	tie
il fazzoletto	handkerchief
il foulard	headscarf
il gilè	waistcoat
il golf	jumper
i guanti	gloves
l'imperme-abile	raincoat
il maglione	sweater
le mutande	underpants
le mutandine	panties
la pelliccia	fur coat
il pigiama	pyjamas
il reggiseno	bra
lo slip	briefs
il tailleur	woman's suit
la vestaglia	dressing-gown
la taglia	size [clothes]
il numero	shoe/shirt size
il bottone	button
la chiusura lampo, la zip	zip
il colletto	collar
la manica	sleeve
l'orlo	hem
la tasca	pocket
il sandalo	sandal
lo scarpone	ski, walking-boot
lo stivale	boot
lo zoccolo	clog
il tacco	heel
la stringa	shoe-lace

Jewellery and other accessories

la gioielleria	jewellery
l'anello	ring
il bracciale, braccialetto	bracelet
la collana	necklace
l'orecchino	earring
la spilla	brooch
il diamante	diamond
l'argento	silver
l'oro	gold
gli occhiali da sole	sunglasses
la pelletteria	leather goods
il borsellino	purse
la borsetta a tracolla	shoulder-bag
la cintura	belt
la profumeria	perfumery
il profumo	perfume
il trucco	make-up
la cipria	face-powder
il rossetto	lipstick

Materials

la stoffa	material
il tessuto	textile, fabric
il cachemire	cashmere
il cotone	cotton
il feltro	felt
la lana	wool
il lino	linen
il nailon	nylon
la paglia	straw
il pizzo	lace
il raso	satin
la seta	silk
il velluto	velvet, corderoy
il camoscio	suede
il cuoio	leather
la pelle	soft leather, suede
a maglia	knitted
il metallo	metal
l'acciaio	steel
l'ottone	brass
il rame	copper
la carta	paper
il legno	wood

Colours and patterns

blu	blue
blu marino	navy blue
turchino	dark blue
turchese	turquoise
rosa	pink
viola	purple
chiaro	light
scuro	dark
a righe	striped
a quadretti	checked
a fiori	flowered

Adjectives

corto	short
lungo	long
largo	loose
stretto	tight
bravo	good [at s.thing]
assurdo	absurd
buffo	funny
falso	false, untrue
giusto	right, fair
ridicolo	ridiculous
sbagliato	wrong, mistaken
strano	strange

Verbs

accorciare	to shorten
allungare	to lengthen
restringere	to take in
provare	to try on

Troubleshooting

meglio migliore peggio peggiore

Learn to distinguish between the use of **meglio** (adverb) and **migliore** (adjective). Both words can mean *better* and *best*.

Rita conosce Bari **meglio** di me	*Rita knows Bari better than me*
È **meglio** chiamare la mattina presto	*It's best to call early in the morning*
Questa pasta è **migliore** dell'altra	*This pasta is better than the other*
Lei conosce i posti **migliori**	*She knows the best places*

Similarly, **peggio** is an adverb and **peggiore** is an adjective. Both words can mean *worse* and *worst*:

Lui parla inglese **peggio** di me	*He speaks English worse than me, than I do*
Lui parla **peggio** di tutti	*He speaks worst of all*
La situazione è **peggiore** del previsto	*The situation is worse than expected*
Tu conosci i posti **peggiori**	*You know the worst places*

bravo buono bene

These words can all mean *good*.

Bravo implies good at something, clever:
    È un designer molto bravo.
    Lui è bravo in matematica.

It can be used to express praise and say 'well done':
    Hai finito? – Bravo!

Buono refers to the quality of something:
    Il film è molto buono

If it is used with reference to a person it tends to imply kindness:
    È una persona molto buona

Bene is an adverb meaning *well*, but it is also used for expressing approval and saying 'good':
    Hai finito? – Bene

Systems 6

1 Object pronouns

> **La** richiamo
> **Le** può dire?

i) Direct and indirect

Object pronouns are so called because they stand in for the noun objects of verbs. Indirect object pronouns are used with verbs which normally require the preposition **a** before a person. In Italian, some direct and indirect object pronoun forms are different:

Direct object		Indirect object	
mi	me	mi	to me
ti	you	ti	to you
lo	him, it	**gli**	to him
la	her, it	**le**	to her
La	you	**Le**	to you
ci	us	ci	to us
vi	you	vi	to you
li/le	them	**gli**	to them
		loro	to them★

★ **Loro** is not common in speech and comes after the verb: Do loro un libro

Compare direct and indirect forms:

Direct him, her, it:	Indirect
lo vedo stasera **la** vedo stasera	**gli** telefono stasera **le** telefono stasera
them: **li** vedo stasera (m) **le** vedo stasera (f)	**gli** telefono stasera (m & f)
Formal you: **La** vedo stasera	**Le** telefono stasera

ii) Position of pronouns

These generally come before the verb. If a verb is used with **potere, volere** and **dovere**, the pronoun can precede the whole phrase:

> le può dire che . . .
> la voglio invitare

In some cases pronouns go after the verb. See Unit 7, note 2 ii and iii, p. 197 for further information.

2 Piacere (to like)

> **mi piace** la musica
> **mi piacciono** i concerti
> **mi piace** andare ai concerti

Piacere is a difficult verb. One way to get it right is to remember what it means literally:

> mi piace la musica   *music is pleasing to me*
> mi piacciono i concerti   *concerts are pleasing to me*
> mi piace andare ai concerti   *going to concerts is*
> *pleasing to me*

i) Form

There are only two basic present-tense forms: **piace** if you like (doing) one thing, and **piacciono** if you like several things.

ii) Use of pronouns

Piacere doesn't use the usual subject pronouns. The indirect object pronouns are used instead. Here's how the present tense of **piacere** looks in full:

mi piace/piacciono	*I like*
ti piace/piacciono	*you like*
gli piace/piacciono	*he likes*
le piace/piacciono	*she likes*
Le piace/piacciono	*you like*
ci piace/piacciono	*we like*
vi piace/piacciono	*you like*
gli piace/piacciono	*they like*
piace/piacciono loro	*they like* [mostly written form]

iii) Using piacere:

If the object is a noun, (*i.e.* the person doing the liking), then **a** must go in front, combined with the article if there is one:

> A Maria piace la letteratura   *Mary likes literature*
> *[lit. literature is pleasing to Mary]*
> Al signor Porrino piacciono i gialli
> Alla gente piace guardare la televisione
> Ai miei amici piace uscire la sera

With pronouns such as **tutti, nessuno, molti** and **tanti, a** is also needed:

> A tutti piace ascoltare la musica
> A nessuno piace il rumore

Take care using **piacere** with the following:

> mi piacciono gli spaghetti   *[spaghetti is plural]*
> mi piace l'uva   *[grapes are singular]*

See also Unit 8, Systems, note 3, p. 201.

3 The past: il passato prossimo

ho lasciato un messaggio
sono andata in Conservatorio

auxiliary → ho / sono
past participle → lasciato / andata

The **passato prossimo** expresses simple past actions. It is made up of an auxiliary verb in the present – **avere** or **essere** – plus the past participle of the verb you are using. Some verbs take **avere** while others require **essere**.

i) Which auxiliary?

There is no simple answer. Many more verbs require **avere** than **essere**. It may be helpful to learn that many verbs of movement require **essere**, but there are exceptions. It is best to learn the main verbs which require **essere**. [See the list in Ref. p. 250]. You can then assume the rest take **avere**.

ii) The regular past participle

To form the regular past participle you drop the **-are**, **-ere** and **-ire** infinitive ending and substitute **-ato**, **-uto**, **-ito**. To form the complete verb, use part of the present tense of **avere** or **essere**, whichever is appropriate, in front of the past participle.

iii) Using the passato prossimo

This tense corresponds to three English tenses:
Ho chiamato   *I have called / I called / I did call*
Sono andato   *I have gone / I went / I did go*
The way it is translated depends on the context.

4 Verbs with regular past participles

i) Verbs with avere

	lasciare *to leave*	ricevere *to receive*	capire *to understand*
ho	lasciato	ricevuto	capito
hai	lasciato	ricevuto	capito
ha	lasciato	ricevuto	capito
abbiamo	lasciato	ricevuto	capito
avete	lasciato	ricevuto	capito
hanno	lasciato	ricevuto	capito

The verb **avere** is regular in the past and takes the auxiliary **avere**:

ho avuto	abbiamo avuto
hai avuto	avete avuto
ha avuto	hanno avuto

ii) Verbs with essere

	andare *to go*	cadere *to fall*	uscire *to go out*
sono	andato/a	caduto/a	uscito/a
sei	andato/a	caduto/a	uscito/a
è	andato/a	caduto/a	uscito/a
siamo	andati/e	caduti/e	usciti/e
siete	andati/e	caduti/e	usciti/e
sono	andati/e	caduti/e	usciti/e

Verbs which have no direct object [intransitive verbs], tend to require **essere**:
e.g. arrivare, tornare, partire
But there are some exceptions which require **avere**:
e.g. camminare, cenare, pranzare, dormire
See list in Reference, p. 251.

Past participle agreement

If a verb uses **essere** as the auxiliary, the participle agrees with the subject of the verb:
Rita è uscita
Le ragazze sono riuscite a prendere il treno

5 Verbs with irregular past participles

i) Verbs with avere

Many common verbs have irregular past participles. Here are 12 key ones:

bere	bevuto	leggere	letto
chiedere	chiesto	mettere	messo
dare	dato	prendere	preso
decidere	deciso	rispondere	risposto
dire	detto	scrivere	scritto
fare	fatto	vedere	visto

See list in Reference, pp. 251–2.

ii) Verbs with essere

The verb **essere** itself is irregular in the past and takes the auxiliary **essere**:

sono stato/a	siamo stati/e
sei stato/a	siete stati/e
è stato/a	sono stati/e

The verb **stare** *(to be, to stay)* takes the auxiliary **essere** and has the same past participle as **essere**:
sono stato/a da mia zia per due giorni

6

194

Reinforcement 6

Here are four more key irregular verbs requiring **essere**:

nascere	nato	morire	morto
rimanere	rimasto	venire	venuto

And here are three which can take **essere** but also **avere**:

correre	corso	scendere	sceso
vivere	vissuto		

For a full explanation see Reference p. 250.

6 Interrogatives: which? what?

i) Quale? Quali?

Quale musica preferisce?
Quali strumenti preferisce?

Quale means *which? what?* Like all adjectives ending in **-e** it has only one singular and one plural form:
Quale rivista ti piace?   Quali riviste ti piacciono?
Quale libro ti piace?   Quali libri ti piacciono?

Quale can also be used as a pronoun:
Quale libro vuole? – Quale?   *Which one?*
Quali libri vuoi? – Quali?   *Which ones?*

In front of **è** the final **-e** is dropped:
Il numero di Rita, qual è?

ii) Che

The word **che** is sometimes used as an interrogative adjective, meaning *what?* It is quite colloquial:
Che libri vuoi?   *What (which) books do you want?*

Unlike **quale**, **che** cannot be used as a pronoun.

7 A note on ordinal numbers

il mio **primo** strumento
frequento il **settimo** anno

Ordinal numbers are used for numbering things in order: first, second, third, etc. There is a list of these in Reference, p. 239.

A Piace *or* piacciono?
Fill in the correct form.
1 Ti . . . il teatro?
2 Le . . . le commedie di Dario Fo?
3 Vi . . . andare a teatro?
4 Ti . . . l'uva?
5 Le . . . gli spaghetti?
6 Vi . . . mangiare gli spaghetti?

B What do they like?
You ask a friend about the tastes of members of his family and friends.
e.g. Tuo fratello: la lirica?
  Gli piace la lirica?

1 Tua sorella: il balletto?
2 Le tue amiche: la chitarra?
3 Antonio: i documentari?
4 Norma: le telenovele?
5 I tuoi figli: i cartoni animati?
6 Il professore: i fumetti?

C They don't like anything!
Your friend answers in the negative each time.
e.g. La lirica: tuo fratello?
  No, la lirica non piace a mio fratello.

1 Il balletto: tua sorella?
2 La chitarra: le tue amiche?
3 I documentari: Antonio?
4 Le telenovele: Norma?
5 Cartoni animati: i tuoi figli?
6 Fumetti: il professore?

D Check your pronouns
Say whether the pronoun in each of the sentences below is a direct object or an indirect object.
1 Signor Petrucci, *La* ringrazio.
2 Dov'è la mia borsa? Non *la* vedo qui.
3 Hai visto Angela? *La* devo vedere subito.
4 Hai visto Maria? *Le* devo parlare subito.
5 Dottor Alberoni, *Le* presento mia moglie.
6 Dove sono le riviste? Non *le* trovo qui.
7 Mario, dov'è? *Gli* voglio parlare.
8 I tuoi cugini dove sono? *Gli* devo dire una cosa.
9 Edda *ci* chiede di venire presto domani.
10 Aldo *ci* richiama dopodomani.

E I'll phone you tomorrow

Complete the following sentences using the appropriate direct object pronoun.

e.g. Carla, . . . chiamo domani, se vuoi. *[you]*
Carla, ti chiamo domani, se vuoi.

1 Non ho visto il film. . . . vedo domani. *[it]*
2 Non ho letto la rivista. . . . leggo più tardi. *[it]*
3 Va bene, dottore, . . . richiamo martedì. *[you]*
4 Gemma e Lucio sono simpatici. . . . invito per domani. *[them]*
5 Le chiavi dove sono? Non . . . vedo. *[them]*
6 Devo scappare, ragazzi. . . . saluto. *[you]*
7 Non abbiamo capito. . . . puoi aiutare? *[us]*

F I'll give him the book back

Substitute the phrase in brackets with an appropriate indirect object pronoun. Check it is in the right place.

e.g. Domani restituisco il libro *[a mio fratello]*.
Domani gli restituisco il libro.

1 Posso offrire *[a Lei]* qualcosa da bere?
2 Devo chiedere *[a Monica]* di venire più tardi.
3 Dobbiamo rispondere *[a Alberto]*.
4 Perché non dai una mano *[a Marta e a Susanna]*?
5 Per favore, Alessio, non vedi che dai fastidio *[a me]*?
6 Se volete, do un passaggio *[a voi]*.
7 Perché non spiegate *[a noi]* il problema?
8 Perché non mando un'email *[a te]*? È più rapido.

G Use the past tense

Complete the questions below, choosing an appropriate verb from this list.

ricevere, uscire, vendere, suonare, capire, cantare, dormire, arrivare, cadere.

e.g. Hai suonato il flauto?

1 Hai . . .	la canzone?
2 Sei . . .	in ritardo?
3 Ha . . .	una lettera?
4 Ha . . .	la macchina?
5 È . . .	per strada?
6 Avete . . .	la trama?
7 Avete . . .	tutta la mattina?
8 Siete . . .	con gli amici?

H Daily routine

Here is an account of someone else's daily routine. Can you adapt it to your own routine and say what you have done today?

> Di solito . . .
> faccio colazione alle sette. Esco di casa alle sette e mezzo. Prendo il treno e arrivo in ufficio alle nove. Verso le undici bevo il caffè, poi lavoro fino all'una, e pranzo con i colleghi. Rimango in ufficio fino alle sei, perché vedo molti clienti. Poi viene il mio amico: mi dà un passaggio fino alla stazione. Torno a casa verso le sei e mezzo.

Start: Oggi . . .

I Viva Verdi

A class is doing a project on Giuseppe Verdi's life. They've been asked to read through the biographical notes below and prepare questions for a quiz. Can you make up 5–10 questions for the quiz, using the *passato prossimo*?

e.g. Quando è nato Giuseppe Verdi?

Giuseppe Verdi nasce nel 1813, a Roncole vicino a Busseto, in Emilia Romagna. Impara a suonare l'organo a 11 anni, ma non riesce ad entrare nel Conservatorio di Milano. Diventa ben presto comunque uno dei compositori più famosi nella storia della musica lirica italiana. La prima delle 22 opere di Verdi è *Oberto*, [1839], scritta a appena 26 anni. Il successo internazionale arriva nel 1842 con la sua terza opera, il *Nabucco*. Giuseppe Verdi ha una vita triste e difficile. Sua moglie muore giovane nel 1840. Soltanto due mesi dopo, muoiono anche i due figli e Verdi è sul punto di abbandonare la musica. Continua però per il resto della sua vita a comporre altre opere che sono destinate a diventare grandi successi. L'ultima, dopo oltre 50 anni dalla prima, è *Falstaff*, [1893]. Muore a Milano nel 1901 all'età di 87 anni.

Biographies, historical events and stories often make use of the 'historic present'.

Systems 7

1 Stressed pronouns

> per me va bene
> vengo **con te**

These pronouns are used after prepositions. They are exactly the same as the subject pronouns, except for **me** and **te**.

me	*me*
te	*you*
lui, lei	*him, her*
Lei	*you*
noi	*us*
voi	*you*
loro	*them*

Carlo ha parlato **di** te
Gina è venuta **da** me

Stressed pronouns are also used to replace direct or indirect object pronouns when two of them are contrasted:

> lo vedo domani   *But:*
> vedo **lui**, non **lei**   *I'm seeing him, not her*
> gli telefono domani   *But:*
> telefono a **lui**, non a **lei**   *I'm phoning him, not her*

For all personal pronouns, see Ref. IV, p. 243.

2 Position of pronouns

i) Pronouns before the verb

> **lo** abbiamo comprato
> **ci** sono stato

Pronouns generally precede the verb. In the case of the past tense, this means they go in front of the auxiliary:

> gli hai telefonato?
> Ci sei andato?

In front of the auxiliary **avere**, the direct object pronouns **lo** and **la** are frequently shortened to **l'**:

> Tu l'hai visto?

These are the only pronouns elided in this way:

> L'ha vista (Maria) *but* Le ha parlato (a Maria).

ii) Pronouns after the verb

> **eccolo**
> preferisco telefonar**gli** dopo

Pronouns used with **ecco** are always joined on the end, to form one word:

Dove sono i ragazzi? Eccoli.   *Here they are [lit. behold them].*

With expressions using the infinitive, the final **-e** is dropped and the pronouns are attached to form one word:

preferisco far**lo** subito	*[direct object]*
è meglio spiegar**gli** la situazione	*[indirect obj.]*
sono qui per divertir**mi**	*[reflexive]*
basta andar**ci** una volta	*[ci]*★

There are other cases when pronouns follow the verb: you will come across them in Book 2.

★ Strictly speaking, in the examples used here, **ci** is an adverb, but it is used like a pronoun.

iii) Optional position of pronouns

> posso telefonar**gli**?
> **gli** posso telefonare?
> sai far**lo**
> **lo** sai fare?

With modal verbs such as **volere, potere, dovere**, and with **sapere**, the position of the pronoun is optional: it can precede the verb or be attached to the infinitive:

Modal verbs

ti voglio vedere	*or* voglio vederti
la posso aiutare	*or* posso aiutarla
le devo telefonare	*or* devo telefonarle

Sapere

Lo sai spiegare?   *or* sai spiegarlo?

The pronoun position is also optional with some **compound verbs**:

andare a trovare	*to go and visit*
venire a trovare	*to come and visit*
andare a prendere	*to go and collect*
venire a prendere	*to come and collect*

perché non vieni a trovar**ci**?
or perché non **ci** vieni a trovare?
domani andiamo a trovar**lo**
or domani **lo** andiamo a trovare.
vengo a prender**ti** subito
or **ti** vengo a prendere subito.

3 Choosing object pronouns

La vengo a trovare?
Le va bene

It is important to learn which verbs require direct object pronouns and which need indirect object pronouns.

i) Direct object pronouns
These are used with the compound verbs listed in 2 ii) on p. 197.
> I figli tornano domani, li vado a prendere alla stazione.
> Claudia è tornata, la vado a trovare domani

ii) Indirect object pronouns
These are used with many common verbs requiring **a** before the person:

andar bene a qlcu.	to suit, be fine
andare a qlcu. di	to feel like
far vedere a	to show

> Le va bene venire con noi?
> Gli va di partire domani?
> Le faccio vedere l'ufficio domani.

Look back at the list in Unit 6 Troubleshooting, p. 126.

4 Dispiacere

mi dispiace, non posso
Le dispiace se vengo?

Dispiacere *(to be sorry, to mind)* is formed exactly like **piacere**. It is used to express regret or sympathy:
> Mi dispiace, non posso venire   *I'm sorry . . .*
> Stai male? Mi dispiace!

It is also used to make a request:
> Le dispiace se porto un amico?   *Do you mind if . . .?*

In the negative – **non dispiacere** – the verb means *I don't mind, I quite like . . .*:
> Non mi dispiace uscire stasera, ho poca voglia di studiare.
> Non gli dispiace aiutare, ha molto tempo libero.

Dispiacere is only used in the singular **dispiace**. See also Unit 8 Troubleshooting, p. 158.

5 Impersonal si

si dà un anticipo
come **si**
accende?

Si is a pronoun used in a general sense, meaning *one, you, people*. It is used a lot in Italian:
> qui si parla italiano   *here one speaks Italian [i.e., Italian is spoken]*

If **si** is used with plural objects, the verb must be plural:
> Questo libro si vende solo in Italia
> Questi libri si vendono solo in Italia
> Come si accende il gas?
> Come si accendono i fornelli?

6 Conoscere and sapere

non **conosco** la Basilicata
sai, ho comprato una casa

Conoscere and **sapere** both mean *to know* but they are not interchangeable. **Conoscere** is used to say you know a place:
> Conosce la zona? Conoscete l'Italia?

or a person:
> Conosci mio cugino? Conoscete Daniela?

Sapere is used for knowing a fact:
> Lei sa se lui conosce Alberobello?   *Do you know if he knows Alberobello?*

or for saying what you know how to do:
> So nuotare   *I can swim*

There's more on these verbs in Units 8 and 9.

7 Irregular present

Continue to learn the irregular present tense of useful verbs. In Practice 2 p. 140 the exercise 'Home improvements' includes the verb **possedere**:

possiedo	possediamo
possiedi	possedete
possiede	possiedono

A verb like **possedere** is **sedersi** *(to sit)*:

mi siedo	ci sediamo
ti siedi	vi sedete
si siede	si siedono

Reinforcement 7

A Partners

You want to find out if it's all right for you to join up with the following people:
Can you reconstruct the sentences to make sense.

1 Beppe, ti   va bene se gioco | con Lei?
2 Signor Bruni, Le   va bene se vengo | con voi?
3 Carlo e Anna, vi   va bene se pranzo | con te?

B One not the other!

Try and put your friend right. He needs to know who you have in mind:

e.g. Mi aiuti domani? Li aiuti domani?
    Aiuto te domani, non loro!

1 Lo inviti a cena? La inviti a cena?
2 Gli *[pl.]* telefoni stasera? Mi telefoni stasera?
3 Le fai un regalo? Gli fai un regalo?
4 Gli dai una mano? Ci dai una mano?

C Pronoun practice

Use the right Italian word for the formal *you* (**Lei, le, la**).

1 Ma signore, . . . ho mandato una lettera espresso!
2 Per . . . va bene, professore?
3 D'accordo signora, . . . vengo a trovare giovedì prossimo.

Now use the right word for *them* (**li, gli, loro**).
4 I Bianchi sono esperti: perché non ha parlato con . . . prima di decidere?
5 I signori·Valenti sono tornati: . . . chiamo dopo il telegiornale.
6 Gli studenti non lo sanno: . . . avete spiegato il problema?

Use the correct words for *her* (**la, le, lei**).
7 Ma, no, ho prestato il libro a . . . non a Roberto.
8 Per il suo compleanno . . . abbiamo regalato un telefonino!
9 Monica ha comprato una villetta in campagna. . . . vado a trovare il sedici giugno.

Finally, fill in the correct words for *him* (**lo, gli, lui**).
10 Il compleanno di Angelo è domani: . . . hai comprato un regalo?
11 C'è posto nell'appartamento di Antonio – perché non rimani da . . . domani sera?
12 Il marito di Carlotta è simpatico, . . . conosco da anni.

D Your advice, please

Read each pair of sentences then rewrite the last one, beginning with the word given.
e.g. Ho rovesciato il caffè sul divano!
    L'hai pulito con un po' d'acqua? *[Bisogna]*
    Bisogna pulirlo con un po' d'acqua.

1 Non trovo il numero di Paolo.
    L' hai cercato sull'elenco telefonico? *[Basta]*
2 Non ho voglia di accettare l'invito.
    L'hai rifiutato, allora? *[Basta]*
3 Luca mi ha invitato al matrimonio.
    Gli hai risposto subito? *[Bisogna]*
4 Giovanna non mi ha spiegato come funziona la lavatrice.
    Le hai chiesto come funziona? *[Bisogna]*

E Quite contrary

Say you haven't done any of the following:
e.g. Hai studiato la lezione? – No, non ho cominciato a . . .
    No, non ho cominciato a studiarla.

1 Hai letto l'articolo? – No, non ho finito di . . .
2 Hai fatto i compiti? – No, non sono riuscito a . . .
3 Hai parlato al professore? – No, non mi piace . . .
4 Hai scritto a Maria? – No, non ho bisogno di . . .
5 Hai pulito la moquette? – No, preferisco . . . domani.

F Both are right

There's more than one way of saying the same thing. Rewrite the sentences below, putting the pronouns in the alternative position.
e.g. Mi può dire come funziona lo scaldabagno?
    Può dirmi come funziona lo scaldabagno?

1 La biancheria è sporca, la devo lavare.
2 È un bellissimo castello, lo voglio visitare.
3 Mia cugina è simpatica, la vado a trovare domani.
4 Mi sa dire se la mostra è aperta domenica?
5 Giovanni arriva il dieci marzo: lo vado a prendere alla stazione.
6 Non ho la macchina, mi puoi dare un passaggio?

7

G Coming and going

Answer these questions using **ci** in two alternative positions:

e.g. Volete andare a ballare? – Sì, . . .
Sì, ci vogliamo andare.
Sì vogliamo andarci.

1 Potete andare al cinema? – Sì, . . .
2 Dovete andare a fare la spesa? – Sì, . . .
3 Volete venire con noi in piscina? – Sì, . . .

H Preferences

You're checking out your guests' preferences. Can you use one phrase from each part to make meaningful sentences?

Ti va di	partire presto	o preferite mangiare dopo?
Le dispiace	cenare adesso	o preferisci andare a teatro?
Vi va bene	andare al cinema	o preferisce partire più tardi?

I Houseproud

You're delighted with your new home and possessions and lose no opportunity to show them off.

e.g. nuovo divano – molto comodo.
Ti faccio vedere il nuovo divano – è molto comodo. Ti piace?

Show your best friend the following:
1 nuove tende – molto belle
2 nuova cucina – molto pratica

Show your new neighbour the following:
3 nuovi tappeti – molto raffinati
4 nuovo specchio – molto antico

And get your in-laws to look at the following:
5 nuovi scaffali – molto belli
6 nuovo quadro – molto originale.

J Excuses excuses

No one really wants to come to the party. As the diplomat you've got the task of making the excuses. Using **dispiacere**, pass on your friends' regrets, choosing a plausible reason why they can't come.

e.g. Annalisa non può venire.
[avere: molto da fare/molti impegni/molta fame]
Annalisa non può venire. Le dispiace, ma ha molti impegni.

1 Alessia non può venire.
[essere: molto impegnata/molto stanca/molto in gamba]
2 Beppe non può venire.
[avere: un altro appuntamento/un'altra ragazza/un altro impegno]
3 Elisa e Franco non possono venire.
[avere: l'influenza/fretta/ospiti in casa]

K Is it all right if . . .?

You tend to put things off but you know how to get round others! Try it on with these people.

e.g. Signora Monetti – se vengo più tardi?
Signora Monetti, Le va bene se vengo più tardi? Le dispiace?

1 Ragazzi – se lo faccio la settimana prossima?
2 Signor Arbasino – se La chiamo domani?
3 Giorgio – se arrivo in ritardo?

L Do you know?

Can you remember when to use **conoscere** and when to use **sapere**?

1 Non *[conosco/so]* dove ci incontriamo.
2 La Basilicata è molto interessante, è una zona che *[conosco/so]* bene.
3 Scusi, Lei *[conosce/sa]* a che ora parte il treno?
4 Scusa, tu *[conosci/sai]* il marito di Elena?

M False friends, double meanings

Can you give the correct meaning of each of the following words, and give the Italian for the English word which it sounds like:
1 attico; 2 pavimento; 3 box

The following Italian words all have more than one meaning. How many can you give?
4 Il soggiorno *(×2)*; 5 il palazzo *(×2)*; 6 il posto *(×3)*

Systems 8

I The pronoun ne

ne hai una?
ne prendo un altro

Ne is a pronoun meaning *of it, of them*. It can replace singular and plural, masculine and feminine nouns. You use it with expressions of quantity:

Quanto/a **ne** prende?
How much [of it] will you have?
Ne prendo un chilo/una fetta
I'll have a kilo/a slice [of it]
Quanti/e **ne** prende?
How many [of them] will you have?
Ne prendo dieci/una ventina
I'll have 10/about 20 [of them]

Although **ne** may not appear in the question, it is required in the answer:

Quanto pane mangi al giorno?
Ne mangio molto/un po'/poco

The position of ne
Ne comes before the verb unless it is used with **ecco** or an infinitive [See Unit 7, Systems, note 2 ii, p. 197.]
For more on **ne** see Unit 9, Systems, note 1, p. 205 and Ref. I, 8v)c), p. 240.

2 Prepositions in questions

con chi parlo?
con cosa li fanno?

Prepositions precede the question words **chi? (che) cosa? dove? che?/quale?**:
A chi scrivi?
Per che cosa lo fai?
Da dove parte il treno?
Di che colore è?
In quale città sei nato?

Note the following useful expressions:
Di chi è?   *Whose [of whom] is it?*
Di chi sono?   *Whose [of whom] are they?*

3 Piacere with a

piacciono anche **a me**
piacciono anche **a lui**

In Unit 6, you learned that **piacere** is used with the indirect object pronouns: **mi, ti, gli**, etc.

However, it is sometimes used with **a**, plus the stressed pronouns, **me, te, lui, lei, noi, voi, loro** [See Unit 7, Systems, note 1 i, p. 197.].

When to use a + stressed pronoun
a) With **anche**:
   Piace anche a te? Piace anche a Lei?
   Do you like it too?

b) For contrast and comparison:
   A me piace la carne, ma a lui piace il pesce.
   A te piace il mare, ma a me non piace.

c) When emphasising the subject:
   A Lei piace la cucina italiana?

You could equally well say, less emphatically:
   Le piace la cucina italiana?

In colloquial speech it is common to hear both pronouns used together with **piacere**, but, strictly speaking, this is incorrect:
   A me mi piace la cucina italiana.

4 Sapere

lo sai che non è permesso?
sì, **lo so**

Common uses include

a) Knowing a fact:
   Lo so   *I know [lit. I know it]*
   Non lo so   *I don't know*

Although not strictly necessary, **lo** is often used for emphasis:
   Lo sai che è vietato fumare?

b) Finding out a fact:
   Ti chiamo per sapere se puoi venire

c) Knowing how to do something:
   So scrivere a macchina   *I can type*
   Mi sa dire dov'è la posta   *Can you tell me . . .?*
Mi sa dire is used in preference to **mi può dire** when you are not sure the person has the information.
There is more on **sapere** in Unit 9.

5 Double object verbs

> **mi** hanno rubato **la macchina**
> **gli** hanno rubato **lo stereo**

Many verbs can be used with two objects: direct and indirect.
Verbs of this type include:

comprare	*to buy something for someone*
mandare	*to send something to someone*
portare	*to bring something to someone*
regalare	*to give something to someone*
rubare	*to steal something from someone*

> Gli hanno rubato la macchina
> *He had his car stolen [lit. they stole the car from him]*

Note that in expressions of this type, you use the indirect object pronoun for the person.

For a list of similar verbs, see Ref. VII, 4ii, p. 247.

6 Double negatives

> **non** è **niente**
> **non** ho **più** fame

A simple negative is made by putting **non** in front of the verb:

> Non vengo

A double negative contains **non** plus a second negative word.
Here are the main ones:

non ... nessuno	*no-one*
non ... niente/nulla	*nothing*
non ... ancora	*not yet*
non ... mai	*never*
non ... più	*no longer, not any more*
non ... affatto	*not at all*
non ... neanche/ nemmeno/ neppure	*not even*
non ... mica	*not really*

> Non vedo nessuno
> Non capisco niente

Word order

Non always precedes the verb.

a) Present tense. The verb goes between **non** and the second part of the negative:

> Non studia mai
> Non mi diverto affatto

If the verb is part of a phrase, e.g. **aver fame, avere voglia di, essere in ritardo**, the second negative word tends to come between the verb and the rest of the verbal phrase.

> Non ho più fame
> Non ho affatto voglia di venire
> Non sono mai in ritardo

However, **niente** and **nessuno** are exceptions:

> Non ho voglia di fare niente
> Non ho voglia di vedere nessuno

b) Past tense. If the verb is in the **passato prossimo** tense, the second negative word tends to come after the auxiliary:

> Non ho ancora deciso
> Non ho mica capito
> Non mi ha neanche salutato

But, again, the exceptions are **niente** and **nessuno:**

> Non ho deciso niente
> Non ha visto nessuno

The word order can vary with double negatives, but for the learner it is helpful to grasp a basic pattern.
For more on negatives see Systems 9, note 8, p. 207.

7 Irregular verbs

The following new verbs with irregular past participles have been used in this unit:

decidere	deciso	*to decide*
perdere	perso	*to lose, miss*
permettere	permesso	*to allow*
rompere	rotto	*to break*
succedere	successo	*to happen*

Reinforcement 8

A Escalation

Your friends and acquaintances have twice as much as you have. Can you complete the mini dialogues?

e.g. Ho una figlia. E Lei ...?
    E Lei, quante ne ha? – Ne ho due.

1 Bevo cinque caffè al giorno. E tu ...?
2 Prendo due vacanze all'anno. E voi ...?
3 Fumo tre sigari alla settimana. E Lei?
4 Leggo quattro riviste al mese. E tu?

B Nosey parker

You're curious about your glamorous new neighbour, so you ask your home help about her. Below is what she told you. What were your questions?

e.g. ...? *[chi?]*
    Lavora per una grande società straniera.
    Per chi lavora?

1 ...? *[chi?]*
    È sposata con un avvocato molto ricco.
2 ...? *[che cosa?]*
    Con suo marito parla di soldi e di affari.
3 ...? *[quali?]*
    Ha vissuto in vari paesi, in Giappone, negli Stati Uniti.
4 ...? *[dove?]*
    Il suo cane strano viene dalla Cina.
5 ...? *[che]*
    Dorme nella stanza che dà sul giardino.
6 ...? *[che]*
    La sua biancheria è tutta rosa.
7 ...? *[chi?]*
    La Lamborghini rossa è sua.

C Soul mates

Here are some like-minded people, who enjoy the same things. Bring them closer together by making a single sentence out of each pair.

e.g. Gli piace andare al mare. Le piace andare al mare.
    A lui piace andare al mare e piace anche a lei.

1 Ci piace viaggiare. Gli *(he)* piace viaggiare.
2 Mi piacciono le orecchiette. Le piacciono le orecchiette.
3 Vi piacciono lunghe passeggiate sulla spiaggia. Gli *(they)* piacciono lunghe passeggiate sulla spiaggia.
4 Ti piace leggere poesie. Mi piace leggere poesie.

D Incompatible

Now here are some pretty incompatible people. They just don't like the same things. Sum up the sorry situation each time:

e.g. *Girl:* Mi piace la lirica!
    Boy: Non mi piace la lirica!
    A lei piace la lirica ma a lui no.
1 *Class:* Ci piacciono i fumetti!
    Male teacher: Non mi piacciono i fumetti!
2 *Wife:* Mi piacciono le macchine veloci.
    Husband: Non mi piacciono le macchine veloci.
3 *Parents:* Ci piace visitare i musei.
    Daughter: Non mi piace visitare i musei!

E Do you know it?

Have you got to grips with **sapere**?
How well can you cope in the following situations?

1 You tell Enrico that you've called to find out if he can come. What do you say?
2 Your son wants an expensive computer game. You tell him you need to know how much it costs.
3 You're wondering whether this passer-by can tell what time the banks close.
4 You want to explain that you can't type but you can drive.

F Nice or nasty?

Match up the two parts of the sentences below to discover which are the pleasant experiences and which not so pleasant. Link each part with the pronoun **mi, le/Le, gli** or **ci** as appropriate.

1	Davvero, signore,	**mi**	ho regalato un computer.
2	Lisa è malata,	**le**	hanno rubato l'orologio?
3	È il compleanno di Angelo,	**gli**	hanno mandato dei fiori.
4	Sono disperata,	**ci**	ho portato un po' di frutta.
5	I Fortunato sono così gentili,	**Le**	hanno rubato la collana.

G What next?

Complete the sequel by translating the second part into Italian.

e.g. Mario la conosce da anni.
  But he doesn't love her any more.
  Ma non la ama più.

1 Devo invitare anche Norma.
  But I haven't written to her yet.
2 Non gli piace andare al mare.
  He never goes.
3 Sono molto stanco.
  I don't want to see anyone.
4 Ma non importa.
  It's nothing.
5 Le sue feste sono sempre noiose.
  I don't feel at all like going.
6 Renata è veramente antipatica.
  She doesn't even say hello to me. [*Use* salutare]
7 Ho mangiato troppo.
  I'm not really hungry.

H Making sense

Can you reorder these sentences to make sense?

1 Deciso non ancora ho.
2 Non mai sono stato ci.
3 Più venuto sono non.
4 Niente non preso ho.
5 Non nessuno arrivato è.

I Chalk and cheese

These two are total opposites. They always contradict each other.

e.g. Vado sempre al cinema – Non vado mai al cinema.

1 Ho già mangiato.
2 Ho visto arrivare qualcuno.
3 Ho fatto qualcosa oggi.
4 Ho ancora fame.

J Irregular past participles

Below are parts of irregular verbs which have appeared in this unit. Match up the two parts of the past participle and give the infinitive and meaning of each verb.

VISS SUC PER AP CHI R P

erto erso uso otto cesso uto messo

K Pardon me

Complete the sentences using the phrases given.

scusa scusi
mi dispiace non mi piace
non mi dispiace

1 . . ., signora, per il Teatro dell'Opera come faccio?
2 No Carlo, . . . è impossibile uscire domani.
3 L'idea . . ., il tempo è ideale per fare una gita.
4 Oh, . . . Laura! Colpa mia! Ti ho macchiato la gonna?
5 La proposta . . ., sono già stato/a a Gallipoli.

L Word perfect

How well do you know the irregular past tense? Can you give the past participle of the verbs listed here? They have all appeared in the course so far.

bere	morire
chiedere	nascere
correre	prendere
dare	rispondere
decidere	scendere
dire	stare
fare	scrivere
leggere	vedere
mettere	venire

M Fra o Fa?

Do you remember which is which?

e.g. Quando hai incontrato Delio? *[20 anni]*
  Ho incontrato Delio 20 anni fa.
  Quando vi vedete? *[10 giorni]*
  Ci vediamo fra 10 giorni.

1 Quando pensate di venire? *[15 giorni]*
2 Quando sei venuto a Bari per la prima volta? *[15 anni]*
3 Quando ha cominciato a studiare l'italiano? *[6 mesi]*
4 Quando vengono i tuoi genitori? *[un paio di giorni]*
5 Quando siete venuti per l'ultima volta? *[molto tempo]*

Systems 9

1 Pronouns: combining ci and ne

ce n'è uno qui
ce ne sono alcuni qui

The expressions **c'è [ci è]** (*there is*) and **ci sono** (*there are*) are often used in conjunction with **ne**. **Ci** always precedes **ne**, and both pronouns must come before the verb: **ci** becomes **ce** in front of **ne**.

Ce n'è derives from:	**ci + ne + è**
This becomes:	**ce + ne + è**
And finally:	**ce n'è**

(**Ne** elides with the verb **è** to make the expression pronounceable.)
The expression **ce ne sono** derives from:

ci + ne + sono

This becomes: **ce ne sono**

Using ce n'è, ce ne sono
Ce n'è, ce ne sono must be used with expressions of quantity:

Quanto/a ce n'è?
Ce n'è molto/a, un chilo, un litro
Quanti/e ce ne sono?
Ce ne sono molti/e, 2 chili, 3 litri

2 Possessives

i) Possessive adjectives with indefinite articles

è un mio amico: sono amici **miei**
è un tuo amico: sono amici **tuoi**

È		
un mio, una mia	amico/a	*He, she is a friend of mine*
un tuo, una tua		*of yours*
un suo, una sua		*of his, hers*
un Suo, una Sua		*of yours*
un nostro, una nostra		*of ours*
un vostro, una vostra		*of yours*
un loro, una loro		*of theirs*
Sono amici, amiche miei, mie tuoi, tue ecc.		*They are friends of mine of yours, etc.*

ii) Position of the possessives
In singular expressions they tend to come before the noun and in plural expressions they often come after it. However, the position depends to some extent on emphasis and region.

iii) Possessive adjectives with other quantifiers

ho visto **degli** amici **tuoi**
ho visto **alcuni** amici **suoi**
ho visto **molti** colleghi **vostri**

You can use many other quantifiers with possessive adjectives:

Sono venuti pochi amici miei
Ho parlato con due amici tuoi

3 Demonstratives

quel cespuglio
quell'albero
quella pianta

i) Quello as an adjective
Quello always precedes the noun. Like the definite article, its form varies according to the initial spelling of the noun as well as its number and gender.

	sing.	*plu.*
masc.	quel ragazzo	quei ragazzi
	quello studente	quegli studenti
	quell'uomo	quegli uomini
fem.	quella ragazza	quelle ragazze
	quell'arancia	quelle arance

ii) Quello as a pronoun
The forms are simpler:

masc. sing. quello	*masc. pl.* quelli
fem. sing. quella	*fem. pl.* quelle

Quale ragazzo/uomo/studente? – Quello lì
Quali ragazzi/uomini/studenti – Quelli lì
Quale ragazza/arancia? – Quella lì
Quali ragazze/arance? – Quelle lì

4 Present progressive

sto scegliendo i funghi
stiamo lavorando molto

This is formed from the present tense of the verb
stare and the gerund of the verb required.
There are only two gerund endings: **–ando** for **–are**
verbs and **–endo** for the rest. These are added to
the stem of the infinitive.

i) Regular gerunds

stare	*gerund*	*infinitive*
sto		
stai	parl**ando**	*(parlare)*
sta	legg**endo**	*(leggere)*
stiamo	part**endo**	*(partire)*
state	fin**endo**	*(finire)*
stanno		

ii) Irregular gerunds

A few verbs with 'contracted' infinitives have
irregular gerunds. Most of them use the **–endo** form
of the gerund added to an 'expanded' stem of the
verb:

infinitive	*gerund*
bere	**bev**endo
dire	**dic**endo
fare	**fac**endo
attrarre	**attra**endo
produrre	**produc**endo
proporre	**propon**endo

★ All verbs ending in **–arre**, **–urre** or **–orre** form
the gerund in the same way:
  estrarre (*to extract*) **estra**endo;
  tradurre (*to translate*) **traduc**endo;
  supporre (*to suppose*) **suppon**endo.

★ **Dare** and **stare** use the **–are** form of the gerund:
  dando stando

iii) Uses of the present progressive

In Italian the present progressive has a far more
restricted use than in English and is only used to
focus on an activity taking place at the time of
speaking. In the following examples, the English
'What are you doing?' is not **'Cosa sta facendo?'**,
though it would be possible in the third example.
  Cosa fai domani? Vado a Roma
  What are you doing tomorrow? I'm going to Rome
  Cosa fai qui? Sono qui in vacanza
  What are you doing here? I'm here on holiday
  Cosa fai con i funghi? Li sto tagliando
  *What are you doing with the mushrooms? I'm cutting
  them up*

5 Passato prossimo with avere

le hai cucinate tu?
ne ho visti tanti

Past participle agreement

Verbs which use **avere** as the auxiliary in the **passato
prossimo** past tense normally require no changes
in the past participle:
  Ho visto tanti porcini

However, if the verb is preceded by a direct object
pronoun, **lo, la, li, le** or **ne**, the participle must
agree with it:
  Ne ho visti tanti   Li ho visti tutti
  Ho conosciuto Maria.   L'ho conosciuta
  Ho conosciuto le ragazze. Le ho conosciute

With **ne** the form of the agreement depends on
what **ne** stands for:
  Hai mangiato un po' di pizza?
  Sì, ne ho mangiata molta
  Hai mangiato delle mele?
  Sì, ne ho mangiate due

Note: There are occasions when **ne** is not a direct
object and no agreement of the past participle is
made. See Book 2.

Agreements with the direct object pronouns **mi, ti,
ci, vi** and **La** are less consistently made:
  Quando ci ha visto? is very common instead of:
  Quando ci ha visti?

With the formal direct object **La** (*you*) the
agreement, if made, must be feminine even if you
are formally addressing a man:
  L'ho vista ieri, signor Marini.

Systems 9

Beware: never make past participles agree with a preceding *indirect* object pronoun. Compare:

Ho visto Marina. L'ho vista   *[direct]*

Ho telefonato a Marina. Le ho   *[indirect]*
telefonato

6 Conoscere and sapere

Here is a summary of the uses of each verb:

i) Conoscere

Knowing a place:	Conosce Bari
	Conosce i posti migliori
Knowing a person:	Conosce il signor Fanfani?
Knowing a work –	Conosce *La Primavera* di
a painting or book:	Botticelli?
In the past: meeting	L'ho conosciuto a Roma.
somebody:	

ii) Sapere

Knowing a fact:	So che viene domani
	So il suo numero
Knowing a language:	So quattro lingue
Knowing by heart:	Lo so a memoria
Finding out:	Ho telefonato per sapere ...
Knowing how to do	Li so preparare
something:	So parlare italiano

iii) Comparing conoscere and sapere

Conoscere implies being acquainted with, while **sapere** implies complete knowledge of something. Sometimes the same phrase can be used with either **sapere** or **conoscere**, but with a different meaning:

La sai quella poesia di Carducci?

[i.e. have you studied the poem, learned it?]

Conosci quella poesia di Carducci?

[i.e. have you heard of the poem?]

The use of **sapere** and **conoscere** can be subject to individual and regional differences. Both verbs are used for knowing the way:

Conosci la strada? *or* La strada la sai?

The learner should nevertheless follow the basic guidelines.

7 Impersonal verbs and expressions

mi fa paura il fuoco
gli fanno paura le vipere

There are many common verbs other than **piacere** which can be used impersonally, i.e. with the third person of the verb:

fare piacere (a)	*to give pleasure*
fare schifo (a)	*to disgust*
fare paura (a)	*to frighten*
bastare (a)	*to be enough*
mancare (a)	*to be missing*

As with **piacere**, indirect object pronouns are used:

Le manca qualcosa?   *Is anything missing (for you)?*

Le bastano due chili?   *Are 2 kilos enough (for you)?*

For similar verbs see Ref. VIIIB, l ii and iii, p. 250.

8 Negatives

non trovo **mai niente**
non vedo **più nessuno**

When negative expressions such as **non ... mai**, **non ... più**, **non ... ancora** are combined with **niente** or **nessuno**, the order of negatives can vary, but there are some basic rules. [See also Unit 8, Systems, note 6, p. 202.]

a) **Non** always comes before the verb.

b) In the present tense the two negatives come together:

Non c'è **ancora nessuno**

c) In the past tense, **niente** and **nessuno** tend to come after the participle:

Non ha **mai** trovato **niente**

Non abbiamo **più** visto **nessuno**

9 Irregular verbs

Continue to learn irregular verbs:

scegliere *to choose*	**togliere** *to remove*	**salire** *to go up*
scelgo	tolgo	salgo
scegli	togli	sali
sceglie	toglie	sale
scegliamo	togliamo	saliamo
scegliete	togliete	salite
scelgono	tolgono	salgono

Scegliere and **togliere** have irregular past participles:

scegliere: scelto   togliere: tolto

Reinforcement 9

A Down your way

You're being asked what amenities you have in your area. Give the answers, following the guidelines below and using **per fortuna** (*luckily*) if the answer is yes and **purtroppo** (*unfortunately*) if the answer is no.

e.g. C'è un buon ristorante vicino a casa Sua? *[Sì – molti]*

Sì, per fortuna ce ne sono molti.

1 C'è un parco nel tuo quartiere? *[Sì – 1]*
2 Ci sono dei cinema nella Sua città? *[Sì – alcuni]*
3 C'è una macelleria nel tuo quartiere? *[No]*
4 C'è una banca vicino a casa Sua? *[Sì – 1]*
5 C'è una piscina nella tua città? *[Sì – 2]*
6 Ci sono scuole nel tuo quartiere? *[No]*

B Who's that?

You're showing your holiday snapshots and are explaining who everyone is in relation to you. You need to rewrite the sentences below:

e.g. Giacomo è un collega. Giacomo è un mio collega.

1 Susanna è un'amica.
2 I Moro sono amici.
3 Lidia e Marta sono colleghe.
4 Gianni è un cugino.

C Who's who?

You've gone through a round of introductions but you're still a little unsure about who Sandro and Giovanna are. You ask Pino, signor Bruni and a couple of friends about them.

e.g. Pino, Sandro . . . parente?

Pino, Sandro è un tuo parente?

1 Signor Bruni, Sandro . . . collega?
2 Ragazzi, Sandro . . . amico?
3 Pino, Giovanna . . . sorella?
4 Signor Bruni, Giovanna . . . cugina?
5 Ragazzi, Giovanna . . . collega?

D Who came?

You and your partner are explaining who came to the barbecue last night.

e.g. tanti amici

Ieri sera sono venuti tanti amici nostri.

Continue using the following:
1 molti colleghi   4 una zia
2 alcuni cugini   5 un vicino
3 pochi parenti   6 quattro amiche

E Point it out

Last night you had guests and cleared up in a hurry, putting things in odd places. No-one can find anything, so point out where you put things, using the correct form of **quello**.

e.g. Le matite? – nella tazza

Ho messo le matite in quella tazza.

1 Il giornale? – sotto il cuscino.
2 Le foto? – dietro lo specchio.
3 I vestiti? – nei cassetti.
4 Le scarpe? – nell'armadio.
5 Le riviste? – sugli scaffali.
6 I giocattoli? – nelle borse.

F Spell it out

Which do you prefer? You're being asked to pick out the item you want. The one you want is always different:

e.g. Quale pasta vuole?   Questa?

No, quella lì.

1 Quali panini preferisce?   Questi?
2 Quale salame prende?   Questo?
3 Quali caramelle vuole?   Queste?
4 Quale arancia preferisce?   Questa?

G Otherwise engaged

All the following invitations and requests are turned down. The reasons are given in English. Put these into Italian: all but two of them are to do with what's going on right now.

e.g. Possiamo vederci fra poco?

No, I'm sorry, I'm preparing the supper.

No, mi dispiace, sto preparando la cena.

1 Avete voglia di venire a prendere un caffè?
We're sorry, we can't, we're studying.
2 Senti, vuoi venire a cena con noi?
No, I can't, I'm waiting for my friends.
3 Carlo e Pietro possono venire da noi stasera?
I'm sorry, they can't, they're going to their grandmother's.
4 Pronto, posso parlare con Francesca?
I'm sorry, but she's sleeping.
5 Posso parlarti adesso?
I'm sorry, but I'm going out right now.
6 Venite al cinema con noi?
We can't, we're going out tonight.

Reinforcement 9

H The first time

Where and when did you first meet these people?

e.g. I miei vicini – a una festa 3 anni fa.
   Li ho conosciuti a una festa 3 anni fa.

1 La suocera – a casa sua 5 anni fa.
2 La moglie – in casa di parenti 20 anni fa.
3 Gina e Franco – in casa di amici l'altro giorno.
4 Il nuovo collega – in ufficio l'anno scorso.

I Killjoy

You're at a loose end: here's what your various friends suggest you do. Say you've done it all already. There's one sentence which doesn't fit the pattern below: which is it?

e.g. Andiamo a vedere la mostra?
   No, mi dispiace, l'ho già vista.

1 Vuoi visitare l'abbazia di Pomposa?
2 Perché non leggi quelle nuove riviste?
3 Ti va di visitare i musei?
4 Non hai voglia di scrivere alla tua ragazza?
5 Perché non senti questi dischi nuovi?

J Not yet

You have joined a group of friends on holiday. When you ask what they've been up to so far, it doesn't amount to much!

e.g. Giovanni, hai fatto alcune gite?
   No, non ne ho ancora fatte.

1 Anita e Paolo, avete fatto delle passeggiate?
2 Emilio, hai assaggiato i vini locali?
3 Franca, hai mandato delle cartoline?
4 Rosaria e Carmelo, avete visto alcuni monumenti?
5 Riccardo, hai comprato delle specialità del paese?

K What do you know?

Using **conoscere** and **sapere** can be tricky. Try and complete the sentences using the words below:

*sa   conosce   sappiamo   conosci
sapete   so   sanno   ho conosciuto*

1 Tu . . . Lucio? – Certo, l' . . . a Parma.
2 Lei . . . quella poesia? – Certo la . . . anche a memoria.
3 Scusi, . . . se è permessa la caccia?
4 Noi . . . riconoscere tutti i funghi velenosi.
5 I miei figli . . . due lingue.
6 Ragazzi, lo . . . il mio indirizzo e il telefono?

L Black list

These people are all on the black list. Why? Match up the sentences to find out.

e.g. Perché non chiedi a Antonella di dare una mano?
   Ma lei non aiuta mai nessuno!

1 Perché non dici a Giorgio di fare la spesa oggi?
2 Perché non chiedi a Giulio di spiegare la lezione?
3 Perché non dici a Stefania di stare a casa?
4 Perché non chiedi a Francesca di preparare la cena?

a Ma lui non fa mai niente!
b Ma lei non cucina mai niente!
c Ma lei non aiuta mai nessuno!
d Ma lui non capisce mai niente!
e Ma lei non ascolta mai nessuno!

M Nobody loves me

Nothing ever goes right. Can you reorder the sentences to explain?

e.g. Quando telefono in ufficio *[c'è non mai nessuno]*
   Non c'è mai nessuno

1 Quando telefono in Inghilterra *[risponde nessuno non mai]*
2 Quando telefono a casa tua *[non nessuno mai trovo]*
Things have even got worse. Can you explain?
3 Quando vado in ufficio *[più nessuno mi parla non]*
4 Quando ho bisogno di aiuto *[nessuno più non mi aiuta]*

Systems 10

1 Comparative and superlative adjectives

è **più bravo**
è **meno bravo**
i designer **meno bravi**
le mani **più brave**

Superlatives (*most, -est, least*) generally differ from comparatives (*more, less*) only in the use of the article with **più** and **meno**.

Regular adjectives

Adj.	Comparative	Superlative
bello	più bello meno bello	il/la/i/le più bello/a/i/e meno bello/a/i/e
facile	più facile meno facile	il/la/i/le più facile meno facile

Irregular adjectives

buono	migliore/i	il/la/i/le migliore/i
cattivo	peggiore/i	il/la/i/le peggiore/i

Note: **più/meno buono/cattivo** can be used instead of **migliore/peggiore**, e.g. in relation to food:

> Questi spaghetti sono più buoni   (*nicer*)
> Queste tagliatelle sono le più buone   (*the nicest*)

Here are some examples of superlatives:

> Roma è la città più grande d'Italia
> Carlo è il ragazzo meno bravo della classe
> È il risultato peggiore della stagione

The article can also go next to **più**, **migliore** and **peggiore**:

> Roma è la più grande città d'Italia
> È il peggiore risultato della stagione

Examples of comparatives:

> Sandro è più bravo di lui
> Giorgio è meno simpatico di Susanna

2 Comparative and superlative adverbs

Regular comparative and superlative forms differ only in the use of the article:

Regular adverbs

Adverb	Comparative	Superlative
rapidamente	più rapida- mente meno rapida- mente	il più rapida- mente il meno rapida- mente
forte	più forte meno forte	il più forte il meno forte

Here are some examples of superlatives:

> Gaetano parla il più forte possibile
> Vittorio lavora il meno rapidamente possibile

Examples of comparatives:

> Anita legge più rapidamente di Edda
> Patrizio parla meno forte di Mario

Irregular adverbs

With irregular adverbs the comparative and superlative forms are often the same, but the context will tell you whether the adverb is comparative or superlative:

Adverb		Comparative		Superlative	
molto	(*very*)	di più	(*more*)	di più	(*most*)
poco	(*not very*)	di meno	(*less*)	di meno	(*least*)
bene	(*well*)	meglio	(*better*)	meglio	(*best*)
male	(*badly*)	peggio	(*worse*)	peggio	(*worst*)

Examples of superlatives:

> Mario mangia più di/meno di tutti   (*most/least of all*)
> Venezia è la città che mi piace di più/di meno   (*most/least*)

Comparatives:

> Mario mangia più/meno di me   (*more/less*)
> Mi piace Roma, ma Venezia mi piace di più   (*more*)

3 Making comparisons

> è più vivace **della** moda francese
> è più bello vivere qui **che** a Parigi

When making a comparison of inequality you need to know how to translate *than*:

Di is used to express *than* if you are directly comparing people or objects:

> Piero è più alto di te
> Elisabetta è meno intelligente di Mina
> Questa casa è più bella dell'altra
> Gianna fuma meno di me.

Di is also used where numbers are involved:

> Abbiamo più di tre milioni da spendere
> Sara ha meno di cinque anni

Che is used

When two activities are compared:

> È meno divertente andare da Marco che rimanere qui
> È più bello vivere a Berlino che a Atene
> Bero più tè che caffè

When two items are related to a single person or thing:

> A Roma ci sono più chiese che parchi
> Pino ha più nemici che amici

When there is a comparison between two adjectives:

> Quel vestito è più elegante che comodo
> Paola è più intelligente che simpatica

4 A note on bello, buono and grande

Bello follows the spelling changes of **quello** when it is used before a noun [See Unit 9, Systems, note 3, p. 205.]

un bel modello	bei modelli
un bello specchio	begli specchi
un bell'appartamento	begli appartamenti
una bell'estate	belle estati

Buono becomes **buon** before a noun whose indefinite article is **un**:

> un buon caffè   un buon amico
> *but:* un buono stipendio

Grande can optionally become **gran** with a noun whose indefinite article is **un**, unless it begins with a vowel where **grand'** can be used:

> un gran romanzo *or* un grande romanzo
> un grand'amico *or* un grande amico

5 Relative pronouns

> il designer **che** mi piace
> il modello **che** ho visto
> **quello che** io chiamo …

The pronoun **che** means *who, whom, which/that*:

> È l'amico che mi piace di più
> L'amico che ho visto si chiama Andrea
> È il film che mi piace di meno
> Il film che ho visto si chiama 'Novecento'.

It is possible to omit relative pronouns in English but never in Italian.

Quello che, or **ciò che** mean *what*:

> Ho capito quello che vuoi dire
> Quello che Lei dice è interessante.

For more on relative pronouns, see Book 2.

6 Verbs used with indirect object pronouns

> **le** sta bene
> **gli** permette di vedere?

Stare bene a (*to suit*) requires an indirect object pronoun:

> Quelle scarpe Le stanno bene, signore.

Permettere a qualcuno di (*to allow someone to*) is also used with an indirect object pronoun:

> Gli permette di uscire?

There are several similar verbs, such as **proibire a qualcuno di** (*to prohibit someone to*), **vietare a qlcu. di** (*to forbid s.one to*).

See the list in Ref. VII, 5, pp. 247–8.

7 Verbs and prepositions

> cominciare **a** disegnare
> finire **di** lavorare
> quanto l'ha pagato?

Many common verbs require either **a** or **di** after them. Often the English equivalent is *to*:

Sono riuscito a studiare   *I managed to*
Ho deciso di venire   *I decided to*

It is worth gradually learning which prepositions accompany the common verbs. See Ref. VII, pp. 246–8.

Some common Italian verbs require no prepositions, unlike their English equivalents:

Quanto l'avete pagato?   *How much did you pay for it?*

Similar verbs include:

ascoltare	*to listen to*	cercare	*to look for*
aspettare	*to wait for*	guardare	*to look at*

See Ref. VII,1, p. 246.

8 Review of prepositions

i) Per

Its various meanings include:

for:	Sono qui per tre giorni	[time]
	Lo preparo per domani	[time]
	L'ho comprato per poco	[cost]
	Lo faccio per te	[purpose]
	È partito per Roma	[place]
to:	Sono qui per divertirmi	[purpose]
in:	L'ho incontrato per strada	[place]
through:	Ho camminato per i campi	[place]
around:	Hanno camminato per la città	[place]
along:	Continuiamo per questa strada	[place]
by:	L'hanno mandato per posta	[means]
because of:	Non sono venuto per la neve	[cause]
	È famoso per la sua importanza economica	[reason]

ii) Da

Apart from the meanings listed in Unit 5, **da** can describe the purpose of an object:

Una sala da pranzo, una stanza da letto
Un abito da sera, un ferro da stiro

It can also be used to describe the quality of something:

La ragazza dai capelli rossi.
Una fame da lupo

iii) Fra/tra

between:	Arrivo fra l'una e le due	[time]
	È seduto fra Pino e Carlo	[place]
amongst:	Fra le cose che ha disegnato	[relations]
in:	Arrivo fra due giorni	[future time]

9 Irregular nouns

i) Invariable nouns

Apart from the ones mentioned in Unit 5, the following are also invariable:

a) Nouns ending in **–isi** [they are always feminine].
   la crisi, le crisi   l'analisi, le analisi   la tesi, le tesi
b) Nouns ending in **–ie**.
   la specie, le specie   la serie, le serie
   But: la moglie, le mogli

ii) Nouns which change gender

These include:

l'uovo, le uova	*egg, eggs*
il lenzuolo, le lenzuola	*sheet, sheets*
il paio, le paia	*pair, pairs*
il braccio, le braccia	*arm, arms*
il dito, le dita	*finger, fingers*
il ciglio, le ciglia	*eyelash, eyelashes*
il labbro, le labbra	*lip, lips*
il ginocchio, le ginocchia	*knee, knees*

iii) Also irregular are:

la mano, le mani	*hand, hands*
il bue, i buoi	*ox, oxen*
il dio, gli dei	*god, gods*

10 Irregular verbs

Spendere (*to spend*) has an irregular past participle: **speso**.
Costare (*to cost*) and **diventare** (*to become*) take the auxiliary **essere**.

Mi è costato tanto
La moda italiana è diventata famosa

11 A note on numbers

The definite article is required with:

the year:	il 1999
percentages:	il 20 per cento
half:	la metà

See Ref. I, 3, 4, p. 239 and Ref. II, 3, p. 241.

Reinforcement 10

A Pros and cons

Make your own comparisons using the adjective indicated, with either **più** or **meno**, depending on your view. Can you use **di** and **che** correctly?

e.g. Il nuoto   il tennis   *[rilassante]*

   Il nuoto è più rilassante del tennis

1 L'alpinismo   il parapendismo   *[pericoloso]*
2 gli inglesi   gli scozzesi   *[simpatico]*
3 Fare la spesa   fare il bucato   *[noioso]*
4 Vivere in città   vivere in campagna   *[sano]*

B How are you feeling?

Specify which of the two possibilities is most relevant by rewriting the sentences.

e.g. Ma, sei contento o scontento?

   Sono più contento che scontento.

1 I bambini sono stufi o stanchi?
2 Gaetano è nervoso o irritato?
3 Sei triste o arrabbiato?
4 Avete fame o avete sete?

C Appraisal

Two of you are comparing the merits of your colleagues and you don't agree with each other. Complete your friend's part of the dialogue using **di** or **che**, and then say what *you* think, using one of the following adjectives:

   simpatico   cortese   coscienziosa
   intelligente   nevrotica

e.g. Valerio è più pigro *[di]* Carlo.

   Certo, ma Valerio è più *[cortese!]*

1 Sara è meno intelligente . . . Anna.
   Sì, forse, però Sara è meno . . .
2 Adalgisa ha più esperienza . . . Maria.
   Lo so, ma Maria è più . . .
3 Lisa sbaglia più spesso . . . Rita.
   È vero, però Lisa è più . . .
4 Franco lavora meno . . . Enzo.
   Sì, ma Franco è più . . .

D Recommendations

Advise your friend on the items below by saying they are the best – or worst, and repeat what you've said for emphasis.

e.g. Quegli stivali sono senz'altro   *[comodo]*

   Quegli stivali sono senz'altro i più comodi. Sono gli stivali più comodi.

1 Quella giacca è indubbiamente   *[bello]*
2 Quei pantaloni sono sicuramente   *[elegante]*
3 Quelle scarpe sono senz'altro   *[caro]*
4 Quelle camicette sono probabilmente   *[brutto]*
5 Quel prezzo è sicuramente   *[buono]*
6 Quel modello è sicuramente   *[cattivo]*

E For better or worse

Things have turned out differently from what you expected. Complete the sentences, using **meglio, migliore, peggio** or **peggiore**.

1 Il tempo è stato *[worse]* del previsto.
2 La riunione è andata *[better]* del previsto.
3 Lo spettacolo è stato *[better]* del previsto.
4 Ha recitato *[worse]* del previsto.

F Relating

Rewrite the pairs of sentences as one, using a relative pronoun.

e.g. Il tailleur di lana è troppo caro.

   Ho provato il tailleur di lana.

   Il tailleur di lana che ho provato è troppo caro.

1 L'appartamento è molto spazioso.
   L'appartamento è al quinto piano.
2 L'amica è molto simpatica.
   L'amica mi ha accompagnato al cinema.
3 Il collega è un tipo allegro.
   Ho incontrato il collega.
4 I pantaloni di velluto sono un po' stretti.
   Hai voluto comprare i pantaloni di velluto.

G What? or What

See if you can distinguish between the interrogative *what?* and the relative *what*. Complete the sentences, using **che cosa** or **quello che**.

1 Non capisco . . . vogliono fare.
2 . . . vogliono fare?
3 . . . dicono?
4 . . . dicono è assurdo.
5 Mi fai vedere . . . hai comprato?
6 . . . hai comprato?

H Good

Can you fill in the right word for *good* in each case?

1 È un ragazzo molto .... Aiuta sempre gli altri.
2 È una ragazza molto .... Sa quattro lingue.
3 Possiamo finire presto oggi. ...!
4 Ho preso il voto più alto in matematica. ...!
5 Angela è ... in inglese.

I Saying 'to'

Can you decide which prepositions, if any, are needed to translate *to*? Choose between **a** or **di**, but note that not all the sentences require a preposition.

1 Abbiamo cominciato ... lavorare presto stamattina.
2 Mi piace ... dormire dopo pranzo.
3 È necessario ... partire presto.
4 Siete riusciti ... finire in tempo?
5 Sono molto contento ... aiutare.
6 Mi dispiace ... disturbarLa.
7 L'importante è ... analizzare il problema.
8 Sono andato ... trovarli ieri.

J Per/fra

Use **per** or **fra**, as appropriate to complete the sentences.

1 Vengo a trovarti ... un'ora
2 Passa a prenderci ... le due e le tre
3 Il bar si trova ... l'albergo e il ristorante
4 Sono qui ... una settimana
5 Arrivo ... una settimana
6 L'ho incontrato ... strada
7 Siete venuti ... la festa?
8 Pisa è famosa ... la sua torre pendente.
9 Bologna è ... le città che mi piacciono di più.
10 Ho trovato la lettera ... le mie cose.

K Irregular noun practice

What's the singular of the following nouns?
le crisi   le analisi   le mogli   le mani
le paia   le ginocchia

What's the plural of the following?
il dio   il bue   il braccio   l'uovo

Now say:
1 My hands are dirty (*sporco*).
2 I need six fresh (*fresco*) eggs.
3 I want to buy two pairs of shoes.

L Procrastination

You haven't got round to doing anything. Let your friend know, using the verbs given here:
decidere   comprare   scegliere   scrivere   leggere

Scusa, ma non ho ancora deciso niente

Review 2

Refine and review your objectives

Before assessing your progress and performance, review your objectives: have they remained the same? Are you satisfied with the Track you have chosen? If not, do you need to review the way you are using the course? Use the chart below to focus your thoughts.

	Important:			Enjoyable:			Making progress:		
	Yes	No	why?	Yes	No	why?	Yes	No	why?
Speaking									
Listening									
Reading									
Writing									
Vocabulary learning									
Grammar									

Try and answer the 'why?' question each time, as this will help you analyse your methods as well as your aims. Being aware of *how* you learn best is as important as knowing *what* to learn.

Learning styles: what kind of a learner am I?

Are *you* a successful learner? By and large the most successful learners are curious and motivated, build on what they know and relate what they learn to their own needs and experience. 'Good' learners, therefore, can vary enormously in their methods, but what they have in common is self-awareness: they think about how and why they learn and experiment to find language learning strategies which work for them.

How much do *you* think about language learning? What do you think it entails? Below are some common views regarding language learning. They express one of two opposing assumptions: language is something you learn through analysis and conscious effort [A]; language is acquired naturally through immersion, by some kind of osmosis. [O]. What's your reaction?

1 You can only really learn a language by living in the country.   *I agree . . . I disagree . . . Not sure . . . [O]*
2 You can only really learn a language if you learn all the grammar. *I agree . . . I disagree . . . Not sure . . . [A]*
3 If you're over 11 there's no hope of learning a foreign language properly.   *I agree . . . I disagree . . . Not sure . . . [O]*
4 It's embarrassing to make mistakes.   *I agree . . . I disagree . . . Not sure . . . [A]*
5 There's no point in guessing what something means.   *I agree . . . I disagree . . . Not sure . . . [A]*
6 It's fun trying to get the message across even if you make the odd 'howler'.   *I agree . . . I disagree . . . Not sure . . . [O]*
7 It's boring learning by heart.   *I agree . . . I disagree . . . Not sure . . . [O]*
8 It's vital to have someone to correct all your mistakes.   *I agree . . . I disagree . . . Not sure . . . [A]*

Is your learning 'profile': *a*) mainly analytical? *b*) mainly 'osmosis'? *c*) a mixture? Whichever it is, does it reflect your learning methods so far? If not, are you inclined to reconsider your views, or do you think you should modify your methods instead? You might in any case consider modifying your approach, especially if your profile was either entirely 'analytical' or entirely 'osmosis'. If you are predominantly 'analytical' you could benefit by relaxing a little and allowing yourself to make mistakes, while if you believe in 'picking up' a language, you would probably improve by paying more attention to detail! If you were consistently unsure, try to think more carefully about how you are learning.

Conclusion

It is important to think about *how* you are learning – and *why,* not only about *what* you are learning. If you can, discuss your views, exchange ideas and relate this to your personal learning strategies.

A Speaking Checklist

I can	Yes	No	Check
1 say hello on the phone, ask to speak to someone, ask when he/she'll be back and leave a message			Unità 6
2 suggest doing something in two ways and accept in two ways			
3 ask at what time to meet, and where, and answer the same questions			
4 ask someone what he/she has done recently and say what I've done			
5 say what I like/dislike and ask others what they like			
6 ask someone to visit, find out if an arrangement suits, say what suits me and turn down an invitation			Unità 7
7 ask if someone is in, get someone to hold on, ask who I'm speaking to on the phone and say when we'll speak next			Unità 7 & 8
8 use dates when making an arrangement and confirm when I'm seeing someone			Unità 7–10
9 ask someone to show me something and say I'll do the same			Unità 7
10 ask how something works and explain it simply myself			
11 ask what's worth doing or seeing			
12 ask someone if he/she knows a place, has ever been there and answer these questions myself			
13 ask someone if he/she minds if I do something, or minds doing something for me			Unità 8
14 ask what's happened and what's wrong, and answer these questions – say I've gone the wrong way, lost something or had it stolen, missed a bus or train			

Review 2

15 apologise, express sympathy, dismay, displeasure as well as pleasure and relief			
16 say how much or how many I require and ask the same question			
17 ask and explain the way and point out where things are			Unità 8–9
18 ask people what they feel like doing and what they intend to do and answer the same questions			Unità 9
19 ask for more of something, and how much of something there is and answer the same questions			Unità 9
20 Talk about what others like and what I love or hate			
21 Talk about my fears and phobias and ask others about theirs			
22 say what I think and ask others for their opinions			Unità 10
23 compare things and say what's best			
24 ask to see and try on clothes, point out which items I require, and talk about what suits me and others			

B Fluency

Look at the **Review 1** section on p. 101 to help you assess your progress. For those on Track 1 it should now be easier to use more than one sentence at a time in fairly stock situations and you should be beginning to try to express yourself more independently.

You will probably still find it difficult to talk in new situations, but on Track 2 you should be capable of this, albeit with some hesitation.

C Listening

You should be able to:
* Understand the stock questions from Checklist A if spoken clearly and at a reasonably normal speed.
* Follow the Course Book conversations on cassette/CD or video without a transcript, if necessary playing them several times.
* Grasp the basic gist of short conversations on familiar topics you haven't heard before, and find it easier to guess the meaning of words.
* Find it easier to concentrate and understand for longer periods.

D Reading

Reading becomes increasingly important as you progress.
You should be able to:
* Follow the Course Book dialogues with ease.
* Extract basic information from menus and simple leaflets or posters.
* Follow the gist of the transcript in the **Profile** section on p. 221, and the material in the **Culture** section on p. 223.

If you are on Track 2 you should be finding it possible to follow the gist of some short articles on familiar topics in mass market magazines, such as *Oggi* or *Gente,* even though they will contain a lot of language you haven't covered. You will not find it easy to read a newspaper, but it is worth scanning them for items of news or entertainment you recognise.

E Writing

It should be possible for you at this stage to write a simple postcard or message and give an account of what you have done in fairly short sentences.

On Track 1 you may be finding it difficult to analyse or express your views. On Track 2 you should find it possible to express simple views with relative ease.

F Grammar Checklist

If you are on Track 1 you might wish to use this list selectively.

		Yes	No	Check
1	I can recognise and use direct object pronouns			Unità 6
2	I can recognise and use indirect object pronouns			Unità 6–7
3	I am familiar with the position of pronouns, can use them with **venire/ andare a trovare, dovere, potere, volere, sapere**			Unità 7 & Systems 6–7
4	I can use **ci** and **ne** and **ce n'e/ce ne sono**			Unità 7–8 Unità 9
5	I can recognise and use stressed pronouns and relative pronouns			Unità 7 & 10
6	I know the present tense of **piacere**			Unità 6
7	I know the present tense of **possedere, sedersi, scegliere, togliere** and **salire**			Systems 7 & 9
8	I can use **conoscere** and **sapere**			Unità 7–9
9	I can form and use the present progressive tense			Unità 9
10	I can form the **passato prossimo** and use the correct auxiliary			Unità 6
11	I know the rules for the agreement of past participles with **essere** and **avere**			Unità 6 & Systems 9
12	I have learnt the important irregular past participles			Unità 6–8
13	I can use the impersonal **si**			Systems 7
14	I can use double negatives			Unità 8–9
15	I can form and use **quello** and I know the changes of **bello, buono, grande**			Systems 9–10
16	I know how to make adjectives and adverbs superlative			Unità 10
17	I can make adjectives and adverbs comparative and know when to use **di** or **che** to express *than*			Unità 10
18	I know the meanings of **per, fra, da**			Systems 10
19	I have begun to learn which key verbs take **di** and which **a**			Systems 10
20	I have learnt some invariable nouns plus those which change gender in the plural			Systems 10

G Vocabulary

The number of words introduced has approximately doubled. By now you should have acquired an active vocabulary of approximately 500 words, and a passive vocabulary roughly twice as large.

Working on your own 2

At this stage the language-learning strategies you use should be influenced by your ability to diagnose not just your objectives, but the reasons for your success or failure.

Analysing success and failure

Try and review the areas in which you feel most confident. Can you find reasons for your success? Bear these in mind when organising your practice. Now review your least successful areas. Try and pinpoint the reasons for your difficulties: *e.g., I find listening to speech at normal speed hard because:*
1 *I still sometimes have difficulty hearing each word distinctly.*
2 *I cannot concentrate for long.*
3 *I lack vocabulary.*
Action. Decide what to do next, for example:
1 *Learn five new words per day.*
2 *Spend half an hour, Monday, Wednesday, Friday on improving ability to distinguish sounds.*
3 *Practise building up concentration for 20 mins, Tuesday and Sunday.*

A few more learning strategies

At this stage you will probably still be trying out some of the suggestions in **Working on your own 1**, pp 105–6, but here are a few more to add to your repertoire.

A Listening strategies

To develop your ability to understand the gist, you could:
* Stop the recording and try to predict what the speaker will say or talk about next. [You'll need a transcript to be able to check: the **Profile** on p.221 is suitable material].
* Try to take notes and write a short summary in English, again checking it against the transcript.
* Listen in stages. If a dialogue is long, concentrate on one speaker first, then replay for the next speaker and finally play again and listen to both.
* Exploit every opportunity to hear Italian: you can use video films, especially if they have subtitles. Play short sequences, with the subtitles in view and then after an interval – of 10 minutes, say – cover them up and see what you can grasp. As you improve, extend the interval.

To develop your concentration and memory, you could:
* Listen for about a minute, stop the recording and summarise the points – in English. Extend the length of time and see how you get on.

B Speaking strategies

Remember you can make progress even without the opportunity to speak to native Italians.

To improve your confidence, you could:
* Read aloud.

To develop fluency, you should:
* Avoid translating in your head from English to Italian. This can be demoralising and frustrating and will certainly slow you down. It is best to express yourself simply, using what you know.

C Vocabulary learning strategies

To reinforce your vocabulary, you could:
* Build up a word-file of small cards you can carry around: put the translation on the other side, with a short sentence in which the word is used.
* Associate words. You often learn words best in groups which have something in common. The links can be phonetic or grammatical as well as semantic. Make your own associations, e.g. **lezione** can be linked to **stazione** and **televisione** or to **classe, imparare, studiare,** etc.

To extend your vocabulary:
* Associate along the lines mentioned above.

D Grammar strategies
Reasons for grammar practice include:
1 Difficulties with understanding the rules
2 Problems in memorising details
3 Difficulties in applying the grammar in new contexts

To improve your understanding of a difficult point, you could:
* Look up the point in **Systems** if you need more help:
* Do the **Reinforcement** exercises first, with the aid of the answers. Look at the completed, correct exercise and see if you can discover a pattern which makes sense to you. Now try and say what the rule is, in your own words, then go back to the explanations and see if they make more sense.

To improve your capacity to memorise detail, such as agreements or verb endings, you could:
* Do plenty of exercises, checking the answers carefully.
* Try out the structures frequently in short sentences.
Don't divorce grammar from meaning. Never do an exercise mechanically — make sure you know what it's testing and what it means.

To improve your ability to apply the grammar learned you could:
* Take a couple of examples which interest you from a Patterns section in the course and write them down. A day later, come back to them and see how many similar examples of your own you can create.

E Reading strategies
What to read
* When selecting material, focus on familiar topics or on subjects of interest to you: the former is good for your confidence and the latter sustains motivation.
  Some learners also find parallel texts motivating and useful.

Reading for meaning
* At this stage, particularly if you are on Track 1, you need to focus on basic comprehension and build up your speed.
You should:
* Use the dictionary sparingly, rely as much as possible on guesswork using the layout, pictures, headlines or titles as clues.
* Avoid details. Focus on the beginning of paragraphs and on words you recognise to help piece together the gist.

Reading for language
You can use reading for vocabulary and grammar consolidation. If you are on Track 1 this should not be your priority. If you are on Track 2 you could begin to read familiar texts for language [e.g. to look at pronoun position], but at this stage your focus should still be on the general meaning.

Giordano Mazzolini

Giordano Mazzolini is an officer in the Corpo Forestale dello Stato: The Italian Forestry Service. He lives in Abetone, a Tuscan ski resort high in the Appenines, and his work involves both protecting forest habitats and educating people in ways of enjoying them. He gives talks and classes, runs guided tours of the protected Nature Reserves, is in charge of Abetone's 'Orto Botanico' and has written books about the local flora and fauna as well as guides to the footpaths of Abetone. Giordano took Mick Webb on one of his forest trails, and their journey began in the car.

[CC] [CD]   21

Giordano	Allora Mick, come vedi, ci sono i torrenti, che sono ricchi di acqua perché ha piovuto tantissimo. Però bisogna dire che negli ultimi dieci anni, è piovuto poco all'Abetone, è piovuto poco. Oggi, quattordici giugno, c'è ancora neve sulle montagne. È una stazione dove nevica tanto e piove anche tanto. Oggi è una bella giornata. Oggi ho guidato, questa mattina, un gruppo di escursionisti di Firenze. Le mie gite sono indirizzate a far capire alle persone i problemi della montagna, del bosco, e della natura. Parlo dei fiori, parlo degli animali della zona, parlo dell'ambiente. Parlo a queste persone come ci si deve comportare nell'ambiente in montagna, nell'ambiente naturale. Ora andiamo, su, e ci fermiamo e poi andiamo a fare anche una camminata nel bosco. Mettiamo la macchina all'ombra e possiamo anche scendere.
Presenter	Scendono dalla macchina, davanti a un cartello:
Giordano	Ecco qui, Mick, vedi un cartello con scritto 'La natura è un patrimonio. Non distruggetela.' È stata fatta una campagna per l'ambiente nel milleottocento, nel mille, . . . scusate, nel millenovecentottantanove. È buona l'aria, è buona anche l'acqua che troviamo in questa zona. Questa è la viola biflora. È una bellissima viola, questa qui, che, sì sì che non è viola. Perché le viole non sono solo viola. Ma possono essere gialle e possono essere anche un colore più bianco, ecco.

Presenter	Giordano ha scritto diversi libri.

Giordano Nel 1990 ho scritto un libro sui fiori dell'Abetone. Quest'anno, a Firenze, proprio il 3 giugno, ho presentato un libro – sempre sul trekking – che s'intitola *Abetone trekking* che sono ventotto itinerari naturalistici che la gente può percorrere quando viene all'Abetone. Guarda . . . ti faccio vedere una pianta velenosa o mortale. Questa qui, si chiama . . . si chiama Mezzereo o Fior di Stecco. Il nome scientifico è Dafne Mezzereum e le bacche sono velenose . . . sono rosse, rosse, molto rosse . . . sì.

Vogliamo continuare per questo sentiero . . . Ah, guarda. Poi ci sono anche le orchidee. Attenzione . . . le vedi? Stanno per fiorire. Ecco, sono orchidee selvatiche, chiaramente, e protette dalla legge. I funghi si trovano da tutte le parti. A cominciare da marzo i primi funghi, che si chiamano dormienti. Il fungo più ricercato è il porcino, quello che abbiamo mangiato oggi noi . . . Boletus Edulis. Edulis vuol dire . . . buono da mangiare. Qui fra qualche giorno cominciamo a trovare i porcini eh . . . ma ci sono anche i funghi velenosi e i funghi velenosi . . . quelli . . . bisogna fare attenzione!

Presenter **Per la gente che va in montagna, Giordano offre questi consigli:**

Giordano Bisogna mettere nello zaino, prima di tutto, energetici: cioccolata, marmellata, zucchero. Bisogna portarsi dietro dello zucchero in montagna. Non salame o salsicce eh? Perché salame e salsicce non si digeriscono – viene mal di stomaco. Poi nello zaino metterei senz'altro un binocolo per osservare gli animali, acqua sempre, giacca a vento, perché è utile. Poi, può anche piovere . . .

come ci si deve . . .	*how you should . . .*
stanno per . . .	*they are about to . . .*
metterei . . .	*I would put . . .*

The following statements are based on what Giordano Mazzolini said. Are they true or false?

	Vero o Falso?	V	F
1	A Giordano piace molto la natura.		
2	C'è sempre sole ad Abetone.		
3	Si possono mangiare le bacche del Fior di Stecco.		
4	Si possono mangiare i porcini.		
5	Giordano e Mick trovano qualche porcino.		
6	Bisogna portare salsicce in montagna.		

Vittore Carpaccio (1460–c. 1526)

'Storie di S. Orsola: Arrivo dei Pellegrini a Colonia' (*Arrival of the Pilgrims in Cologne*)
Accademia, Venezia

Questo quadro fa parte di un ciclo di nove dipinti che rappresentano la triste storia di sant'Orsola, massacrata a Colonia dagli Unni, con il fidanzato e il papa, durante il ritorno da un pellegrinaggio a Roma. L'arrivo a Colonia è il preludio al martirio: a sinistra si vedono Orsola e il papa nella prima nave, e a destra ci sono gli Unni che assediano la città. Cercate di descrivere il quadro e di dire che cosa stanno facendo i vari personaggi.
Vi piace il quadro? Perché?

Giuseppe Ungaretti (1888–1970)

Nato a Alessandria d'Egitto da genitori toscani (di Lucca), Giuseppe Ungaretti si afferma rapidamente come uno dei poeti più importanti del Novecento. Nella sua lunga carriera di poeta scrive centinaia di poesie e traduce anche sonetti di Shakespeare, *Phèdre* di Racine e poesie di Góngora e William Blake. La conoscenza di varie lingue deriva da • un'esistenza cosmopolita: dopo l'infanzia e la gioventù passate in Egitto studia per due anni a Parigi. Negli anni Trenta viaggia molto in Europa e in Africa, e per alcuni anni insegna letteratura italiana all'università di San Paolo in Brasile. Nel 1942 torna in Italia dove insegna all'università di Roma fino al 1958. L'opera poetica di Ungaretti è priva di retorica, e il linguaggio, a prima vista, è semplice, perché sembra avvicinarsi alla lingua di tutti i giorni. Nelle poesie, spesso brevissime, il fascino delle immagine poetiche sta nella loro sorprendente semplicità: Ungaretti è il maestro della concentrazione della lingua poetica e attraverso questa riesce a condensare i sentimenti ed a esprimersi con un'intensità a volte straziante. La vita del poeta è segnata da due tragedie: la prima guerra mondiale e la morte del figlio di nove anni. La prima lo porta a scrivere il diario poetico che lo rende famoso: *l'Allegria* [1914–19] e la seconda ispira la terza raccolta di poesie, *Il Dolore* [1937–46].

Le poesie 'Veglia' e 'Sono una creatura' vengono da *l'Allegria*: raccontano la sua esperienza di soldato al fronte. Ungaretti scrive queste poesie sul monte San Michele del Carso, una regione nel nord-est d'Italia, luogo di feroci battaglie al fronte. Nella prima poesia racconta una notte passata accanto a un compagno morto, e nella seconda il poeta diventa il simbolo dell'umanità, sconvolta dal dolore.

VEGLIA

Cima Quattro il 23 dicembre 1915

Un'intera nottata
buttato vicino
a un compagno
massacrato
con la sua bocca
digrignata
volta al plenilunio
con la congestione
delle sue mani
penetrata
nel mio silenzio
ho scritto
lettere piene d'amore

Non sono mai stato
tanto
attaccato alla vita

Giuseppe Ungaretti

digrignata	*grinning, grimacing*
volta al plenilunio	*turned to the full moon*

SONO UNA CREATURA

Valloncello di Cima Quattro il 5 agosto 1916

Come questa pietra
del S. Michele
così fredda
così dura
così prosciugata
così refrattaria
così totalmente
disanimata

Come questa pietra
è il mio pianto
che non si vede

La morte
si sconta
vivendo*

Giuseppe Ungaretti

* *You pay for death by living*

Reference Section

Answers

Units 1–5 PRACTICE

Unit 1 – Practice 1

Odd one out (p. 7)
1 cin cin. **2** Olivetti. **3** vermicelli. **4** dolcevita.

Places (p. 8)
Irlanda.

Spot the city (p. 8)
1 Roma. **2** Firenze. **3** Napoli. **4** Venezia. **5** Torino.

Hello or goodbye? (p. 8)
1 hello. **2** goodbye. **3** goodbye. **4** hello. **5** goodbye.

Buying breakfast (p. 8)
Buongiorno./Una pasta, per favore./Sì./Due euro e venti. Grazie, arrivederci [*or* Buongiorno].

How many? (p. 8)
1 quattro. **2** cinque. **3** sette. **4** otto. **5** nove (o sette, in Italia). **6** tre. **7** dieci.

Ordering drinks (p. 8)
Buonasera./Un caffè e tre birre, per favore./Grazie – e due cappuccini, per favore.

Unit 1 – Practice 2

Where? (p. 14)
Sono . . . **1** in bagno. **2** in cucina. **3** a casa. **4** in biblioteca. **5** a scuola.

What's this? (p. 14)
1 Questa è una macchina. **2** Questo è un quadro. **3** Questa è una pasta. **4** Questo è un ragazzo.

What are these? (p. 14)
1 Queste sono macchine. **2** Questi sono quadri. **3** Queste sono paste. **4** Questi sono ragazzi.

Buying an ice-cream (p. 14)
Buonasera, un gelato, per favore./Sì grazie. Questo è caffè?/ Questo è pistacchio?/Pistacchio e caffè, per favore./Grazie, arrivederci [or Grazie, buonasera].

What's in a name? (p. 14)
1 Guglielmo Marconi/Benito Mussolini/Luciano Pavarotti/Enzo Ferrari. **2 a)** la lirica – Pavarotti. **b)** la radio – Marconi. **c)** la macchina – Ferrari. **d)** il fascismo – Mussolini. **3** They all come from the region of Emilia Romagna.

Unit 2 – Practice 1

What's your name (p. 22)
1 Ciao, come ti chiami? **2** Buongiorno, come si chiama? **3** Come vi chiamate?

What about you? (p. 22)
Io mi chiamo . . . **1** E Lei? **2** E tu? **3** E voi?

Who is it? (p. 22)
Giancarlo.

Spot the relations (p. 22)
Suocera, zia. e.g., *Susanna:* 'Giovanni è mio suocero'. *Lucia:* 'Maria è mia zia'.

Guess who? (p. 22)
1 Bianca. **2** Maria. **3** Patrizio. **4** Giovanni.

What's in it? (p. 23)
Ci sono pomodori./C'è mozzarella./Sì, c'è basilico.

House with all amenities (p. 23)
e.g., **1** Sì, c'è un parco grande. **2** Sì, c'è una bella piscina. **3** Sì, c'è una vecchia chiesa. **4** Sì, c'è una piccola trattoria.

What's on today? (p. 23)
Buongiorno. Oggi, che cosa c'è?/La stracciatella che cos'è?/Gli spaghetti all'amatriciana che cosa sono?/Gli spaghetti, per favore.

Home cooking (p. 23)
1 Grandmother. **2** Here is your vol. on free trial. **3** 103. **4** 320. **5** 505.

Unit 2 – Practice 2

What's this? (p. 28)
1 È un orologio. Si chiama 'Orbis'. **2** Sono caffettiere. Si chiamano 'La Cupola'.

Odd one out (p. 29)
1 elefante. **2** pomeriggio. **3** pesce. **4** giallo. **5** acciaio.

Where is everyone? (p. 29)
1 Mia madre è a scuola. Studia lingue. **2** Mio padre è in cucina. Prepara la cena. **3** Mio figlio è in camera. Ascolta la musica. **4** Mio nonno è in salotto. Guarda la televisione.

Friends and neighbours (p. 29)
1 Questa è la mia amica Gina e questo è suo fratello Paolo. **2** Questa è la mia vicina Sandra e questa è la sua amica Susanna. **3** Questo è il mio amico Giuseppe e questo è suo fratello Enrico. **4** Questo è il mio vicino Manlio e questa è sua cugina Cristina.

I too . . . (p. 29)
1 Anch'io abito in Gran Bretagna. **2** Anch'io lavoro molto. **3** Anch'io sono di nazionalità britannica.

You too? (p. 29)
1 Anche Lei abita a Bologna? **2** Anche Lei lavora in via Cavour? **3** Anche Lei studia lingue? *For the couple, your questions should be:* **1** Anche voi abitate a Bologna? **2** Anche voi lavorate in via Cavour? **3** Anche voi studiate lingue?

Colour associations (p. 30)
1 La bandiera italiana è rossa, bianca e verde. **2** azzurro: un azzurro *is an Italian international sportsman.* **3** giallo: *the early detective novels, published by Mondadori, had yellow covers, hence the name.* **4 a)** rosso [essere in rosso]. **b)** nero [essere in nero]. **c)** bianco. **d)** verde.

Unit 3 – Practice 1

How are you all? (p. 38)
Ciao, Roberto. Come stai?/Bene, grazie. E tu?/Sto bene anch'io.
E tua moglie?/Sta bene anche lei./E i figli?/Stanno bene anche
loro./Allora, voi state tutti bene!/Sì, stiamo tutti bene.

Getting to know you (p. 38)
Buonasera. Come sta?/Sto bene anch'io./Sono di . . . Lei, di
dov'è?/È sposato?/Sua moglie, di dov'è?/Ha figli?/Quanti anni
ha Sua figlia?/E i Suoi figli?

Kindred spirits (p. 39)
Ah, davvero? . . .   **1** Non ho fratelli neanch'io!   **2** Non sono
sposato neanch'io!   **3** Non ho figli neanch'io!   **4** Non gioco
a golf neanch'io!

Tea or coffee? (p. 39)
1 Andrea, cosa preferisci . . .?   **2** Signor Fante, cosa preferisce
. . .?   **3** Signori, cosa preferite . . .?

What you'd rather do (p. 39)
1 Andrea, cosa preferisci fare . . .?   **2** Signor Fante, cosa
preferisce fare . . .?   **3** Signori, cosa preferite fare . . .?

Choosing a holiday (p. 40)
piacevole   divertente

Golf in Italy (p. 40)
1954: 1.200 giocatori e 18 campi. 1960: 2.500; 25 campi. 1970:
7.000; 30 campi. 1980: 13.000 giocatori; 1985. 25.000 giocatori.
Nowadays: 40.000 e 137 campi.

Unit 3 – Practice 2

May I introduce . . .? (p. 45)
Ti presento . . .   **1** mia madre.   **2** mio fratello.   **3** le mie
sorelle.   **4** il mio vicino/la mia vicina. Le presento . . .   **5** i
miei genitori.   **6** mia zia.   **7** la mia amica.   **8** i miei nonni.

How lovely! (p. 45)
1 Che bella macchina! È Sua?   **2** Che bel bambino! È
Suo?   **3** Che belle scarpe! Sono Sue?   **4** Che bel cane! È Suo?

It's on me (p. 45)
Signor Giustini, cosa prende da bere?/Cosa prende da
mangiare?/Sandra, cosa prendi?/Prendi qualcosa da mangiare?/
Anch'io. E prendo un Cinzano.

How long for? (p. 46)
1 Gioco a carte . . .   **2** Nuoto . . .   **3** Canto . . .   **4** Gioco a
tennis . . . *e.g.* da un'ora; da tre settimane; da diciotto mesi; da
sette anni.

Give your reasons (p. 46)
Choose from the following: Ho bisogno di/È bello/È importante/È
necessario/È essenziale . . .   **1** imparare una lingua straniera.
2 stare con la famiglia.
È divertente/È interessante . . .   **3** lavorare in un paese
straniero.   **4** essere socio di un circolo.   **5** giocare a scacchi.

Questionnaire (p. 46)
Speaker 1: read novels, watch TV or video, listen to classical
music, be with friends, play chess, belong to a club.
Speaker 2: play tennis, do yoga, belong to a gym, do gardening,
cooking.

Unit 4 – Practice 1

Excuses! Excuses! (p. 55)
1 Ogni martedì vado in piscina.   **2** Ogni mercoledì vado al
supermercato.   **3** Ogni giovedì vado in ufficio.   **4** Ogni
venerdì vado all'istituto.   **5** Ogni sabato vado allo stadio.
6 *e.g.* Ogni domenica vado a messa/vado in campagna.

Refresh your memory (p. 55)
1 Esco di casa.   **2** Prendo la macchina.   **3** Arrivo a
Bologna.   **4** Prendo un autobus.   **5** Vado a lavorare.

Getting to work (p. 55)
1 Vado in aereo. Sì, prendo l'aereo.   **2** Vado in autobus. Sì,
prendo l'autobus.   **3** Vado in bicicletta. Sì, prendo la
bicicletta.   **4** Vado in macchina. Sì, prendo la macchina.

How do you get there? (p. 55)
Esco di casa e vado alla fermata dell'autobus./No, non devo
aspettare molto./Quando arrivo a Manchester vado in ufficio a
piedi./Sì, è vicino alla stazione.

Where's everybody? (p. 56)
1 . . . vanno al parco.   **2** . . . va al mercato.   **3** . . . andiamo al
bar.   **4** . . . va alla fermata.   **5** . . . vanno al cinema.   **6** Tutti
vanno allo stadio.

Memory test (p. 56)
1 venerdì.   **2** mercoledì.   **3** lunedì.   **4** domenica.
5 sabato.   **6** giovedì.   **7** martedì.

What's it like? (p. 56)
La sua vita è veramente   **1** . . . poco divertente.   **2** . . . molto
noiosa.   **3** . . . tanto interessante.

Unit 4 – Practice 2

I work for the state (p. 62)
Lei, che lavoro fa?/Dove lavora esattamente?/Lei fa il postino?/
Lei, signora, che lavoro fa?/Lei è insegnante?/Io sono . . . *or,*
faccio il/la . . .

What do you have? (p. 62)
1 Il martedì mattina faccio colazione a casa.   **2** Il mercoledì
pranzo a mezzogiorno.   **3** Il giovedì faccio uno spuntino alle
4,30.   **4** Il venerdì sera prendo un aperitivo con i suoceri.   **5** Il
sabato sera ceno a casa.   **6** La domenica alle 5 prendo il tè con
amici inglesi. [*To say how often you do the above, choose from:* sempre
(*always*); spesso (*often*); di solito (*usually*); qualche volta
(*sometimes*); ogni tanto (*occasionally*); raramente (*rarely*). *e.g.* Il
martedì mattina faccio sempre colazione a casa.]

Timetables (p. 62)
a Partenza   **b** Arrivo   **c** journey duration   **d** il treno delle
nove e quarantadue (l'Eurostar).

What time? (p. 62)
1 Si alza alle sei e cinquantacinque.   **2** Fa colazione alle sette e
un quarto/e quindici.   **3** Prende il treno alle sette e
cinquantatrè.   **4** Va a letto a mezzanotte.

Unit 5 - Practice 1

The buildings of Bologna (p. 70)
1 Che cosa si può vedere a Bologna? **2** la chiesa di San Petronio; la chiesa di Santo Stefano; il santuario di San Luca; l'università; le due torri; i palazzi e i monumenti in Piazza Maggiore; la fontana di Nettuno.

Information seeking (p. 70)
Avete/Ha ... dei poster della città?/dei dépliant sugli alberghi?/degli opuscoli sui musei?/delle informazioni sugli autobus?/delle piante di Bologna?

When is it open? (p. 70)
A che ora apre la posta? A che ora chiude la posta?/A che ora aprono le banche? A che ora chiudono la banche?/A che ora aprono i musei? A che ora chiudono i musei?

How much? (p. 70)
1 €4,50 all'etto. **2** €0,77 al chilo. **3** €2,68 all'etto. **4** €2,25 all'etto.

Il fruttivendolo (p. 71)
Ha delle pesche?/Quanto costano?/Due e trentacinque al chilo. Mi dà un chilo, per favore?/ Sì. Mi dà due chili di spinaci per favore./Sì. Ha dell'uva?/Due euro e sessanta. Mi dà mezzo, chilo, per favore./Sì, basta così.
Quant'è?/Nove euro e cinquantacinque centesimi. Ecco a Lei.

I'll have it (p. 71)
Va bene ... **1** li prendo. Sì, prendo i pantaloni grigi. **2** la prendo. Sì, prendo la camicia azzurra. **3** le prendo. Sì, prendo le scarpe nere. **4** la prendo. Sì, prendo la giacca verde. **5** lo prendo. Sì, prendo il vestito arancione. **6** lo prendo. Sì, prendo il cappotto marrone.

Aguapark (p. 71)
1 Sì, l'Aguapark è aperto tutto l'anno. **2** Sì. Da giugno a settembre è aperto tutti i giorni. **3** No, non è aperto tutto il giorno. È chiuso dalle 18,30 alle 20,30. **4** La mattina apre alle 9,30. **5** La sera chiude alle 01,00. **6** Per un adulto l'ingresso costa quindici euro. **7** Per un bambino di dieci anni costa lo stesso prezzo, quindici euro. **8** Ci sono tre tipi di abbonamenti: settimanale, mensile e stagionale.

Unit 5 - Practice 2

A better world! (p. 75)
1 Per un mondo migliore bisogna ... rispettare gli altri! ... condannare la guerra! ... lavorare per la pace! ... essere tolleranti!

New Year resolutions (p. 76)
1 Voglio perdere 5 chili. Devo mangiare pochissimo. **2** Voglio fare più esercizio. Devo praticare uno sport. **3** Voglio imparare il tedesco. Devo andare a un corso serale. **4** Voglio risparmiare soldi. Devo spendere di meno. **5** Voglio essere più tollerante. Devo ascoltare gli altri. *e.g., for family:* Mia madre vuole dimagrire. Deve mangiare di meno.

At the tobacconist's (p. 76)
1 No. Lavora a Bologna da 40 anni.
2 No. Il negozio è aperto tutto il giorno dalle 6,30 alle 7,30 di sera.
3 No. Viene in bicicletta. D'inverno prende l'autobus.
4 Sì. Il quartiere è abbastanza silenzioso perché non ci sono molte macchine.

Unit 1

A Your sitting room (p. 81)
1 Ecco ... la finestra, la sedia, la poltrona, la lampada, la tazza, il tavolo, il piatto, il divano, il vaso, il quadro, il tappeto, il camino. **2** Ecco ... le finestre, le sedie, le piante, le tazze, i piatti, i quadri.

B Apples or pears? (p. 81)
1 È una penna. È una matita. **2** È un portafoglio. È una borsa. **3** È un libro. È un quaderno. **4** È un pomodoro. È una cipolla. **5** È un ragazzo. È una ragazza.
1 No, non è una matita, è una penna. **2** No, non è un portafoglio, è una borsa. **3** No, non è un quaderno, è un libro. **4** No, non è un pomodoro, è una cipolla. **5** No, non è un ragazzo, è una ragazza.

C The cathedral is famous (p. 82)
1 La frutta è fresca. **2** Il cappuccino è caldo. **3** La birra è fredda. **4** Il ragazzo è stanco. **5** I giardini sono belli. **6** Le paste sono buone. **7** I caffè sono pronti. **8** Le città sono antiche.

D This is a car! (p. 82)
1 Questa è una casa vecchia. **2** Questo è un telefono rosso. **3** Questa è una guida nuova. **4** Questi sono gelati buoni. **5** Queste sono birre fredde. **6** Questi sono biglietti vecchi.

E Check out your spelling (p. 82)
1 Le basiliche sono antiche. **2** I libri sono lunghi. **3** Le strade sono lunghe. **4** Le signore sono stanche. **5** I ragazzi sono stanchi. **6** Le pesche sono fresche. **7** I pomodori sono freschi.

F I or they? (p. 82)
1 Io. **2** Io. **3** Loro. **4** Loro.

G Do you know your prepositions? (p. 82)
1 a ... in. **2** a ... in. **3** di ... in ... a. **4** di ... a. **5** di ... in. **6** di ... a ... in.

Unit 2

A Memory game (1) (p. 86)
1 l'amica, le amiche; l'autostrada, le autostrade; l'attrice, le attrici; l'autorità, le autorità. **2** l'edicola, le edicole; l'entrata, le entrate; l'emigrazione, le emigrazioni; l'età, le età. **3** l'isola, le isole; l'idea, le idee; l'immigrazione, le immigrazioni; l'indennità, le indennità. **4** l'offerta, le offerte; l'opinione, le opinioni; l'occasione, le occasioni; l'opportunità, le opportunità. **5** l'utopia, le utopie; l'uscita, le uscite; l'unione, le unioni; l'università, le università.

B About Italy (p. 86)
(1) La popolazione *(a)* simile *(1)* popolazione *(2)* 58 milioni *(3)* abitanti *(4)* la capitale *(2)* 3 milioni *(3)* abitanti *(b)* grande *(5)* 20 regioni *(6)* i fiumi *(c)* principali *(b)* grandi *(d)* importanti

C My brother (p. 86)
1 la mia famiglia. **2** la mia amica. **3** mio fratello. **4** mia cugina. **5** il mio fratellino.

D It's all yours (p. 86)
1 la tua amica. **2** il tuo giornale. **3** la Sua penna. **4** la Sua borsa. **5** la Sua chiave. **6** il Suo dolce.

E Get it right (p. 86)
1 studia. **2** legge. **3** abitano. **4** scrivono. **5** beve, bevono. **6** produce, producono.

F Using reflexives (p. 86)
1 Si chiama . . . si alza . . . si corica. **2** Ci chiamiamo . . . mi sveglio . . . mi alzo, mi lavo, mi pettino . . . si riposa . . . si alza.
3 Si chiamano . . . si riposano . . . si addormentano . . . si svegliano.

G Multiple choice (p. 86)
1 Dov'è la pasta? È qui. **2** C'è molto lavoro oggi? **3** Ci sono molti bambini qui? **4** Cosa c'è qui? Ci sono gelati e torte.

Unit 3

A Which pattern? (p. 90)
1 offrire: offro. **2** capire: capisco. **3** preferire: preferisco. **4** aprire: apro. **5** seguire: seguo. **6** finire: finisco. **7** pulire: pulisco. **8** dormire: dormo. **9** partire: parto. **10** servire: servo. **11** bollire: bollo. **12** sentire: sento.

B Reflexives (p. 90)
1 Mio figlio si diverte in piscina. **2** Mio nonno si riposa in giardino. **3** Le mie figlie si divertono a scuola. **4** I miei genitori si riposano in montagna. **5** Noi ci vestiamo rapidamente perché abbiamo fretta.

C Can you supply the question? (p. 90)
1 Rimanete in Italia per un anno? **2** Appartieni/e a un circolo? **3** Tieni/e animali domestici in casa? **4** Ti tieni in forma?/Si tiene in forma?

D Basic needs (p. 91)
N.B. Some phrases suit more than one sentence.
1 Abbiamo caldo – abbiamo voglia di prendere un succo di frutta. **2** Avete sete? – Avete bisogno di prendere un'acqua minerale? **3** Hai fame? – Hai voglia di prendere un toast? **4** Ho fretta – non ho tempo di fare colazione.
5 Non abbiamo fretta – abbiamo tempo di fare uno spuntino.

E How long for? (p. 91)
1 Stai a Sanremo da 15 giorni? **2** State in montagna da 3 settimane? **3** Stanno al mare da 2 mesi? **4** Sta in campagna da molto tempo? *Personal examples:* Sono in salotto da un'ora./ Abito a Winchester da 12 anni. etc.

F What do you do and why? (p. 91)
1 Mia moglie nuota per rilassarsi/perché ha bisogno di rilassarsi. **2** I miei parenti giocano a bridge per divertirsi/perché hanno bisogno di divertirsi. **3** Ascolto la musica per riposarmi/perché ho bisogno di riposarmi. **4** Giocate a squash per tenervi in forma?/perché avete bisogno di tenervi in forma? **5** Prendi il sole per abbronzarti?/perché hai bisogno di abbronzarti?

G Using the definite article (p. 91)
1 l'Egitto l'Iran l'Iraq gli Stati Uniti la Spagna lo Zaire lo Zimbabwe la Zambia la Svezia la Svizzera lo Sri Lanka il Sudafrica l'Afghanistan. **2** lo straniero, gli stranieri; la straniera, le straniere; lo svago, gli svaghi; la spiaggia, le spiagge; il suocero, i suoceri; lo spumante, gli spumanti; lo zabaglione, gli zabaglioni; la zia, le zie; lo zio, gli zii; lo psicologo, gli psicologi; l'hobby, gli hobby; l'animale, gli animali; l'isola, le isole; l'uccello, gli uccelli; l'esercizio, gli esercizi; l'origine, le origini; l'ordine, gli ordini; l'aperitivo, gli aperitivi; lo stato, gli stati.

H There's only one! (p. 91)
1 Quanti esercizi ci sono? C'è un esercizio soltanto. **2** Quanti stranieri ci sono? C'è uno straniero soltanto. **3** Quante ragazze ci sono? C'è una ragazza soltanto. **4** Quanti ragazzi ci sono? C'è un ragazzo soltanto. **5** Quante isole ci sono? C'è un'isola soltanto.

I My friend Fabrizio (p. 91)
Il mio amico Fabrizio ha **gli** occhi azzurri e **i** capelli biondi. [. . .] L'Italia è un paese molto bello, con tante montagne, **le** Alpi, **gli** Appennini e **le** Dolomiti. Il lago più grande d'Italia è **il** lago di Garda. [. . .] **La** Liguria è una regione che confina con **la** Francia. **La** famiglia di Fabrizio non è grande. [. . .] **Le** sue sorelle studiano **[l']** inglese, ma Fabrizio studia **[la]** matematica. [. . .] Fabrizio ama moltissimo **lo** sport e anche **la** musica.

J Say it's yours (p. 92)
1 tuo. **2** Suoi. **3** vostro. **4** nostro. **5** loro. *Reading down, the extra possessive is* tuo *and the colour* rosso. *e.g.* Dov'è il tuo vestito rosso?/È bello il tuo cappotto rosso.

K It and the (p. 92)
1 pronoun. **2** article; pronoun. **3** article; pronoun.
4 pronoun.

Unit 4

A Which verb makes sense? (p. 95)
1 vai vado. **2** viene vengono. **3** esco. **4** parte.
5 andiamo. **6** va. **7** fa.

B Do you come here often? (p. 95)
1 Vieni a Bologna ogni mese? **2** Andate alla partita ogni sabato? **3** Andate al mercato ogni venerdì? **4** Va al ristorante ogni sera?

C I must go! (p. 95)
1 dobbiamo uscire. **2** devo andare. **3** deve andare. **4** devo andare. **5** devo fare. **6** devo trovare. **7** devo andare a letto. **8** devo alzarmi.

D Do you have to? (p. 95)
1 No, di solito faccio il bucato la mattina. **2** No, faccio sempre il bagno dopo cena. **3** No, non facciamo mai colazione.

E Think of a reason (p. 96)
1 . . . perché usciamo spesso. **2** . . . perché fa i compiti.

F The engineer's wife (p. 96)
1 in + la = **nella**. **2** in + la = **nella**; su + il = **sul**. **3** da + il = **dal**; a + il = **al**. **4** di + l' = **dell'**. **5** di + le = **delle**.
6 di + i = **dei**.

G From dawn to dusk (p. 96)
1 dalla alla. **2** degli. **3** del. **4** dalle alle. **5** nello sullo.

H Where do you live and work? (p. 96)
1 in a in. **2** in a in in. **3** in a in in. **4** a in.

I The house in Garibaldi street (p. 96)
1 in in nel. **2** in nella in. **3** in in a.
4 nell' a a al ai. **5** da dalla a.
6 in dall'. **7** dall' allo in al.

Unit 5

A To and at (p. 99)
1 a al mercato. **b** dal fruttivendolo. **c** al supermercato
da Carlo. **d** da mia zia al ristorante. **2 a** in pizzeria
in trattoria. **b** al bar in tabaccheria. **3 a** da fare.
b da bere.

B Nouns and adjectives (p. 99)
1 a i turisti stranieri. **b** le città famose. **c** i computer
cari. **d** gli uomini pessimisti. **2 a** l'autista italiano. **b** il
problema importante. **c** lo sport divertente. **d** il partito
socialista. **3 a** il partito socialista inglese. **b** il partito
comunista italiano.

C Can you come? (p. 99)
1 mi può aiutare? **2** Posso prendere un opuscolo . . .?
3 Sento il telefono, puoi rispondere? **4** Non sento bene, può
ripetere . . .?

D Using the present tense (p. 99)
1 a andare. **2 a** bere. **3 c** venire. **4 d** produrre.
5 b dire. **6 c** rimanere. **7 a** contenere. **8 d** stare.
9 b fare; potere. **10 c; b** uscire; volere.

E Read, listen and speak (p. 99)
1 Il responsabile del progetto nel Parco dei Cedri è Fausto
Bonafede. **2** Sì, anche Andrea Sivelli lavora per il WWF.
3 No, non lavorano tutti i giorni nel parco, ma molto spesso.
4 Sí, lavorano tutto l'anno, anche d'inverno e anche quando
piove. **5** Il progetto esiste dal novembre del 1989.
6 Vogliono studiare la natura abbandonata a sé stessa – la flora
e anche la fauna.

F Reading: what's on? (p. 100)
1 The activities are: **a** Nature rambles, including
birdwatching. **b** A nature photography course. **c** Two
Green university courses: basic ecology and environmental
problems; nature in Western philosophy. **d** An antivivisection demonstration outide a well-known fur shop.

Profile I

La famiglia Chiappini (p. 107)
1 vero. **2** falso. **3** vero. **4** vero. **5** falso. **6** vero.
7 falso.

UNITS 6–10 PRACTICE

Unit 6 – Practice I

Can I speak to . . .? (p. 116)
a 2, **d** 4, **c** 1, **b** 3, **e** 5.

Refresh your memory (p. 116)
1 Sono io. **2** La chiamo a proposito dell'intervista.
3 Quando ci possiamo vedere?

Overbooking (p. 116)
Mirella called to invite him to a jazz concert; Letizia asked him
to come to the cinema and Marinella called to suggest dinner.
His problem is that they all suggest the same day: next Saturday
evening.

Appointments (p. 116)
1 No, lo vedo stasera. **2** No, la chiamo domani mattina.
3 No, la vedo domani pomeriggio. **4** No, lo chiamo
mercoledì mattina.

Alibi (p. 117)
The culprit is Signor Petronio. *Delitto sotto il sole* was not shown
immediately after *Blob*.

Unit 6 – Practice 2

Look at the map (p. 123)
1 Il parcheggio è dietro il bar. **2** Il bar è accanto
all'albergo. **3** Il bar è di fronte alla chiesa. **4** La fermata è
davanti all'albergo.

What do you like? (p. 124)
1 Giulia, ti piace la musica?/ti piacciono i film? **2** Signora
Pacini, Le piace la musica?/Le piacciono i film? **3** Anita e
Miriam, vi piace la musica?/vi piacciono i film? **1** Quale
musica/che tipo di musica ti piace di più? Quali film/che tipo
di film ti piacciono di più? **2** Quale musica/che tipo di musica
Le piace di più? Quali film/che tipo di film Le piacciono di
più? **3** Quale musìca/che tipo di musica vi piace di più? Quali
film/che tipo di film vi piacciono di più?

Personal tastes (p. 124)
1 a Mi piace la poesia. Mi piacciono i romanzi/le biografie.
b Mi piacciono i documentari/i film dell'orrore. Mi piace il
telegiornale/il giornale radio. **c** Mi piace . . . andare al
cinema/a teatro/ai concerti. **2** *Your preferences will be personal.*
Here are examples: Mi piace di più . . . la poesia; Mi piacciono di
più i romanzi; Mi piace di più andare a teatro. **3** *Examples of*
dislikes: Non mi piace la poesia; Non mi piacciono i
documentari.

An invitation (p. 124)
Pronto. Chi parla?/Ciao, come stai?/Sì, volentieri/Mi piace la
cucina italiana/Va bene. Dove ci possiamo incontrare?
allora?/Non ho capito. Quale bar?/Davanti al bar di fronte alla
banca. Sì, ho capito.
   To practise saying where you went yesterday, begin: Ieri . . . *You could*
use some of the following phrases: Sono andato/a da mia sorella/dagli
amici; sono rimasto/a a casa; sono stato/a in piscina/a scuola;
sono uscito/a con gli amici/i figli; sono tornato/a presto/tardi.

Matchmaking (p. 124)
Rosanna chooses Dino and Susanna chooses Lino.

Unit 7 – Practice 1

Servizi telefonici (p. 133)
1 a 412 and 12. 412 has operator facilities. **b** Press the zero key. **c** Dial 4197. **d** On **412**: information on horoscopes, the stock exchange, weather, taxis, cinema, chemists open; **4114** early morning calls; **4161** gives you the right time. **2a** Dial 4 then ★, then say 'invia' and follow the instructions. **b** No. The service is free only between landline phones. **c** You can send voice mail or texts from a normal phone to a mobile phone for a 10% reduction.

Festivities (p. 134)
1 il venticinque dicembre. **2** il sei gennaio. **3** il primo maggio. **4** il primo aprile. **5** il quindici agosto. **6** *To check on your birthday look at the date section in Ref. II, 3, p. 241.*

Refresh your memory (p. 134)
1 L'interno è occupato? **2** Non conosco la Basilicata. **3** Non ci sono mai stata. **4** Perché non vieni a trovarci? **5** Certo; d'accordo; OK.

Hotel de luxe (p. 134)
Come funziona … **a** la TV? **b** il ferro da stiro? **c** il telefono? **d** il riscaldamento?
1 d. 2 e. 3 a. 4 c.

Party time (p. 134)
The occasion is a party on 18 February and the number given is his extension at work: 359.

R.S.V.P. (p. 134)
Pronto, interno 359 per favore./Sì./Ciao, sono …/Mi dispiace ma non posso./Sì, va benissimo./Sì, va bene. Ci vediamo il dieci allora.

Unit 7 – Practice 2

Odd one out (p. 139)
1 il telegramma. **2** fare la spesa. **3** un tavolo da biliardo. **4** la lavagna.

D'accordo (p. 139)
Allora, cosa facciamo oggi?/Cosa c'è da vedere a Castellana?/Non ho mai visitato una grotta./Perché non andiamo a Castellana stamattina e poi stasera andiamo al mare?/Andiamo allora.

Have you ever been to …? (p. 139)
1 Sì, ci sono stato/a due anni fa. **2** Sì, sì, ci sono stato/a la settimana scorsa. **3** Sì, ci sono stato/a l'anno scorso. **4** Sì, ci sono stato/a due settimane fa. **5** No, non ci sono mai stato/a.

Home improvements (p. 140)
a The couple is writing to get advice on how to plan their second home. **b** The house is for themselves, their six-year-old and a few friends now and again. **c** There is water and electricity. **d** They hope to invite the magazine editors to visit their home the following year.

Identikit (p. 140)
To a friend your description will be a personal one, e.g. Al pianterreno c'è la cucina, il soggiorno e uno studio. La cucina è un po' buia, ma mi piace perché è abbastanza grande e ci possiamo mangiare. In cucina c'è … *[say where everything is, using* accanto a, davanti a, *etc.].* Il soggiorno è in fondo al corridoio: è molto disordinato. C'è … *[describe position of objects].* Accanto al soggiorno c'è lo studio. È piccolissimo con scaffali pieni di libri. Al primo piano ci sono due camere da letto e il bagno. Il bagno è spesso sporco ma è abbastanza luminoso … *[describe position of contents].*

To a potential buyer the picture will look rosier, e.g., Questa è una casa d'epoca. Al pianterreno abbiamo la cucina, il soggiorno e lo studio. La cucina è spaziosa e molto carina: è anche attrezzata molto bene … Abbiamo un soggiorno elegante …, *etc.*

Grand tour (p. 140)
Caro … *[give a name]* Siamo partiti da Venosa e siamo arrivati a Rapolla verso le undici – siamo andati a vedere il duomo. Siamo rimasti a pranzare in una trattoria molto simpatica. Poi siamo partiti per Melfi dove abbiamo visitato il castello. Abbiamo fatto il giro della città e abbiamo visto della bella terracotta. Dopo siamo andati ai laghi di Monticchio e abbiamo noleggiato una barca. Abbiamo salito il monte Vulture in funivia. Al ritorno siamo passati per Rionero e abbiamo bevuto dell'ottimo vino.

Unit 8 – Practice 1

When are you off? (p. 149)
Penso di partire … presto/fra poco; fra due settimane; fra un mese; fra l'otto e il sedici giugno. Parto giovedì quindici giugno. Penso di andare in vacanza il …

Bad Blood (p. 149)
A me non piacciono molto./È buono?/Sì, grazie, ne prendo un po'./Mi piace molto, ne prendo un altro po'.

Help (p. 149)
Le dispiace staccare la televisione in salotto?/Le dispiace buttare la spazzatura? È dietro la porta./Le dispiace imbucare le lettere? Stanno sul tavolo.

Accident prone (p. 149)
There are various possible reactions: **1** Davvero?/Che peccato. **2** Mi dispiace. **3** Che peccato/pazienza/non importa. **4** Meno male.

Mystery tour (p. 150)
Follow *Via Umberto 1* – take second left – go as far as *l'Arco di Trionfo* then straight on towards *l'obelisco*. Then turn right into *Viale degli Studenti* and immediately left. Go right to the end of the street and there you are! You end up at the church of *SS Nicolò e Cataldo*, one of the most interesting churches in Lecce.

Which way please? (p. 150)
1 Bisogna andare sempre diritto fino al castello, poi prendere la prima a sinistra. La posta si trova sulla destra. **2** Bisogna andare sempre diritto. La cattedrale si trova dopo la quarta traversa a destra. **3** Bisogna seguire questa strada e andare sempre diritto fino a corso Roma. Poi deve girare a destra, andare avanti fino all'ufficio informazioni e girare a sinistra. La fontana ellenistica si trova vicino, sul lungomare.

Unit 8 – Practice 2

Odd one out (p. 155)
1 che bello.   2 un'agenzia.   3 un rompiscatole.   4 davvero.
5 carabinieri.

Fawlty towers (p. 155)
1 a.   2 c.   3 d.   4 f.   5 b.   6 e.

Chapter of accidents (p. 155)
1 Meno male, sono stanco/a. Piace anche a me./C'è qualcosa
che non va?/Cos'è successo?/Davvero? Che disastro! or Che
guaio!/Ho dimenticato il cavatappi.

What people forget (p. 155)
i costumi da bagno, i documenti, le cose più strane, più personali.

Missing (p. 155)
1 Conosce Jane Mitchell?   2 Sa dov'è andata?   3 [Sa se] ha
lasciato l'indirizzo?   4 Sa il suo numero di telefono?   5 Sa
perché è partita?

Road sense (p. 156)
1 a.   2 e.   3 d.   4 f.   5 c.   6 b.

Before and after (p. 156)
Manca la macchina fotografica, la televisione, il vaso, il video [*or*
il televisore] e la mia cartella. Mancano i due quadri e i due
orologi. Mi hanno rubato ...

Unit 9 – Practice 1

Hold up (p. 165)
1 Un attimo.   2 La linea è disturbata, non La/ti sento
bene.   3 Scusi, Come ha detto? *or, informally,* Scusa, Come hai
detto? *You can also say,* Cosa ha/hai detto?   4 Scusi/scusa, non
ho capito.   5 Le/ti dispiace ripetere?/Può ripetere per favore?

Wrong spot (p. 165)
Che bella giornata!/Di qua/Siamo quasi arrivati/È lì in
fondo/Mi dispiace, ho sbagliato strada. Dobbiamo tornare
indietro.

Point it out (p. 165)
1 La chiesa è lassù.   2 Il fiume è laggiù.   3 È lì in fondo,
accanto all'albero.   4 Devi/bisogna andare avanti.
5 Devi/bisogna tornare indietro.

A friend of mine (p. 166)
Allora vi presento ...   1 Margaret, una mia collega.
2 Francesca, una mia vicina.   3 Andrew, un mio cugino.
4 John, un altro mio collega.   5 Simon, un altro mio amico.

Making tracks (p. 166)
1 Ce ne sono otto.   2 Ce ne sono nove.   3 Ma sì, ce ne sono
abbastanza.   4 Ma sì, ce ne sono tanti.   5 Ma sì, ce n'è uno.
6 Ma sì, ce n'è una.

Inquisition (p. 166)
The phrases in Italian to choose from are: non lo so; certo; forse;
senz'altro; dipende; penso/credo di sì; spero di sì.

Mushrooms and the Law (p. 166)
1 No, di solito non è permesso.   2 Ogni persona può
raccogliere due chili di funghi commestibili al giorno.   3 È
permesso raccogliere soltanto due esemplari di ciascuna specie.

Unit 9 – Practice 2

Emilia and Romagna (p. 171)
1 Sì, l'ho visitata.   2 Sì, le ho viste.   3 Sì, ne ho mangiata
tanta.   4 Sì, l'ho vista.   5 Sì, li ho visitati tutti.   6 Sì, ne ho
bevuti alcuni.   7 Sì, l'ho assaggiata.   8 No, non li ho
visitati.   9 Sì, li ho visti.   10 Sì, ne ho visitato uno.   11 Sì,
ne ho vista una.

Fads and fancies (p. 171)
1 Ai gemelli piace da morire la ricotta.   2 Alla zia non piace
per niente l'insalata di riso.   3 Allo zio piace tantissimo il vino
Trebbiano.   4 Agli amici piacciono molto le patatine. [*It is
possible to change the order and say, e.g.* Ai gemelli la ricotta piace
da morire, *etc.*]

Strong reactions (p. 172)
1 Mi fanno schifo le zanzare (*or* non mi piacciono per niente, *or*
mi fanno paura).   2 Mi piacciono gli uccelli.   3 Mi piacciono
tantissimo gli usignoli.   4 Mi fa paura il tuono.   5 Mi
piacciono i gatti (*or* mi fanno paura).

Table talk (p. 172)
1 to c.   2 to a.   3 to b.   4 to e.   5 to d.

Better luck next time (p. 172)
Buon appetito/Sì. Ne vuoi un altro po'? [*You could also say:* ne
vuoi ancora?]/Mi passi il prosciutto?/Le formiche mi fanno paura
or Ho paura delle formiche.

Early bird (p. 172)
1 Mario Ugolini is a waiter.   2 The mushroom season is from
June to October.   3 He gets up early to avoid walking too far
in the heat of the day.

In Defiance of Death! (p. 172)
1 For almost 30 years.   2 He says he has a mission to help
studies on poisonous mushrooms and hence save lives.
3 1,500.   4 No, he can tell by the smell, and even blindfold.

Unit 10 – Practice 1

Good Advice! (p. 181)
Secondo voi, quali sono i migliori negozi di abbigliamento qui
vicino? Secondo te ...

When did it happen? (p. 182)
1 nel 1492.   2 nel 1957.   3 nel 1776.   4 nel 1939.   5 nel
1989.   6 1861.

Figure conscious (p. 182)
1 silk scarf: 115 euro.   2 sunglasses: 98 euro.
3 cashmere sweater: 265 euro.   4 wool coat: 670 euro.
5 boots: 116 euro.

Shopping spree (p. 182)
Ah, davvero? Che cos'ha comprato?/Mi fa vedere i golf?/Li hai
pagati molto?/Di che colore è?/Quanto l'ha pagato?/Che
cos'altro ha comprato?

Home truths (p. 182)

The specific answers depend on you, but here's how they should begin: **1** Il ristorante migliore è . . . **2** Il pub più simpatico è . . . **3** Il mercato più interessante è . . . **4** Il negozio di abbigliamento meno caro è . . . **5** È più divertente andare in autobus che andare in metropolitana. **6** È più economico/meno caro e più semplice/facile viaggiare dopo le nove che prima.

A whiff of astrology (p. 183)

The answers you give depend on your own tastes. Here are some possibilities: **1** Secondo me non si può scegliere il profumo secondo il segno dello zodiaco. **2** Qualchevolta sì, credo nello zodiaco/No, non ci credo. **3** Sì, sono del segno del Pesce. **4** Sì, ho regalato un profumo a mia madre, alla zia e alle mie sorelle. **5** Mi piace tantissimo ricevere il profumo. **6** Il profumo che mi piace di più è . . .

Unit 10 – Practice 2

Lucky you! (p. 189)

1 Ce l'hai . . . un cavallo/un pianoforte/una spider/un forno a microonde/un personal computer/un orologio d'oro? Beata te! **2** Ce l'avete . . .? Beati/e voi! **3** Ce l'ha . . . ? Beato Lei!

Sales talk (p. 189)

1 It really suits you. **4** It's exactly your size.

Footloose (p. 189)

Buongiorno, posso vedere (*or* mi fa vedere) le scarpe nere in vetrina?/Certo, sono quelle lì/Porto il 38/Sì, va bene/Sono troppo strette/Sì. Ha un numero più grande?/Che peccato. Grazie, buongiorno.

Getting what you want (p. 189)

1 Mi può dire a che ora apre il museo? **2** Mi sa dire quando arriva il prossimo autobus? **3** Le dispiace aprire la finestra? **4** Mi fa vedere un altro modello? **5** Mi dà un altro po' di mele? **6** Mi permette di vedere la casa?

Comparing styles (p. 190)

The answers depend on your views. Here are some possibilities: È assurdo/ridicolo/falso/giusto dire . . . che gli uomini sono più obiettivi delle donne./ . . . che le donne non sanno arrivare ad una conclusione/ . . . che gli uomini non si perdono in particolari/ . . . che le donne parlano molto correttamente e che gli uomini rispettano poco la grammatica/ . . . che le donne esagerano e che usano molti superlativi/ . . . che gli uomini usano i superlativi soltanto quando non gli interessa una donna, *etc.*

UNITS 6–10 REINFORCEMENT

Unit 6

A Piace or piacciono? (p. 195)

1 ti piace. **2** Le piacciono. **3** vi piace. **4** ti piace. **5** Le piacciono. **6** vi piace.

B What do they like? (p. 195)

1 le piace il balletto? **2** gli piace la chitarra [piace loro]? **3** gli piacciono? **4** le piacciono? **5** gli piacciono [piacciono loro]? **6** gli piacciono?

C They don't like anything! (p. 195)

1 No, il balletto non piace a mia sorella. **2** No, la chitarra non piace alle mie amiche. **3** No, i documentari non piacciono ad Antonio. **4** No, le telenovele non piacciono a Norma. **5** No, i cartoni animati non piacciono ai miei figli. **6** No, i fumetti non piacciono al professore.

D Check your pronouns (p. 195)

1 direct. **2** direct. **3** direct. **4** indirect. **5** indirect. **6** direct. **7** indirect. **8** indirect. **9** indirect. **10** direct.

E I'll phone you tomorrow (p. 196)

1 lo. **2** la. **3** La. **4** li. **5** le. **6** vi. **7** ci.

F I'll give him the book back (p. 196)

1 Le posso offrire. **2** le devo chiedere. **3** gli dobbiamo rispondere. **4** gli dai una mano. **5** mi dai fastidio. **6** vi do un passaggio. **7** ci spiegate. **8** ti mando un'email.

G Use the past tense (p. 196)

1 Hai cantato. **2** Sei arrivato. **3** Ha ricevuto. **4** Ha venduto. **5** È caduto/a. **6** Avete capito. **7** Avete dormito. **8** Siete usciti.

H Daily routine (p. 196)

Oggi ho fatto colazione alle sette. Sono uscito/a di casa alle sette e mezzo. Ho preso il treno e sono arrivato/a in ufficio alle nove. Verso le undici ho bevuto il caffè, poi ho lavorato fino all'una, e ho pranzato con i colleghi. Sono rimasto/a in ufficio fino alle sei, perché ho visto molti clienti. Poi è venuto il mio amico: mi ha dato un passaggio fino alla stazione. Sono tornato/a a casa verso le sei e mezzo.

I Viva Verdi! (p. 196)

Possible 10 questions include: **1** Quando è nato Verdi? **2** Dov'è nato Verdi? **3** Quale strumento ha imparato a suonare? **4** È riuscito a entrare nel Conservatorio di Milano? **5** Qual è stata la prima opera di Verdi? **6** Quando ha ottenuto il successo internazionale – e con quale opera? **7** Quante opere ha scritto Verdi? **8** Ha avuto una vita sempre felice? **9** Verdi ha pensato di abbandonare la musica – quando e perché? **10** Quand'è morto Verdi? – dove?

Unit 7

A Partners (p. 199)

1 Beppe, ti va bene se pranzo con te? **2** Signor Bruni, Le va bene se gioco con Lei? **3** Carlo e Anna, vi va bene se vengo con voi?

B   One not the other! (p. 199)
1 Invito lui a cena, non lei!   **2** Telefono a loro stasera, non a te!   **3** Faccio un regalo a lei, non a lui!   **4** Do una mano a lui, non a voi!

C   Pronoun practice (p. 199)
1 Le.   **2** Lei.   **3** La.   **4** loro.   **5** li.   **6** gli.   **7** lei.
8 le.   **9** la.   **10** gli.   **11** lui.   **12** lo.

D   Your advice, please (p. 199)
1 Basta cercarlo sull'elenco telefonico.   **2** Basta rifiutarlo, allora.   **3** Bisogna rispondergli subito.   **4** Bisogna chiederle come funziona.

E   Quite contrary (p. 199)
1 No, non ho finito di leggerlo.   **2** No, non sono riuscito a farli.   **3** No, non mi piace parlargli.   **4** No, non ho bisogno di scriverle.   **5** No, preferisco pulirla domani.

F   Both are right (p. 199)
1 devo lavarla.   **2** voglio visitarlo.   **3** vado a trovarla.   **4** sa dirmi?   **5** vado a prenderlo.   **6** puoi darmi un passaggio?

G   Coming and going (p. 200)
Sì, ...   **1** ci possiamo andare/possiamo andarci.   **2** ci dobbiamo andare/dobbiamo andarci.   **3** ci vogliamo venire/vogliamo venirci.

H   Preferences (p. 200)
1 Ti va di andare al cinema o preferisci andare a teatro?   **2** Le dispiace partire presto o preferisce partire più tardi?   **3** Vi va bene cenare adesso o preferite mangiare dopo?

I   Houseproud (p. 200)
1 Ti faccio vedere le nuove tende – sono molto belle. Ti piacciono?   **2** Ti faccio vedere la nuova cucina – è molto pratica. Ti piace?   **3** Le faccio vedere i nuovi tappeti – sono molto raffinati. Le piacciono?   **4** Le faccio vedere il nuovo specchio – è molto antico. Le piace?   **5** Vi faccio vedere i nuovi scaffali – sono molto belli. Vi piacciono?   **6** Vi faccio vedere il nuovo quadro – è molto originale. Vi piace?

J   Excuses excuses (p. 200)
1 Le dispiace ma ... è molto impegnata/è molto stanca.   **2** Gli dispiace ma ... ha un altro appuntamento/ha un altro impegno.
3 Gli dispiace ma ... hanno l'influenza/hanno ospiti in casa.

K   Is it all right if ...? (p. 200)
1 Ragazzi, vi va bene se lo faccio la settimana prossima? Vi dispiace?   **2** Signor Arbasino, Le va bene se La chiamo domani? Le dispiace?   **3** Giorgio, ti va bene se arrivo in ritardo? Ti dispiace?

L   Do you know? (p. 200)
1 so.   **2** conosco.   **3** sa.   **4** conosci.

M   False friends, double meanings (p. 200)
1 attico – *penthouse. An attic is* una soffitta.   **2** pavimento – *floor. The pavement is* il marciapiede.   **3** box – *garage. A box is* una scatola.   **4** Soggiorno – *stay, residence; living room.*   **5** il palazzo – *block of flats; palace. [In political terms it can also mean The Establishment].*   **6** Il posto – *place; seat; job.*

A   Escalation (p. 203)
1 Ne bevo dieci.   **2** Ne prendo quattro.   **3** Ne fumo sei.   **4** Ne leggo otto.

B   Nosey parker (p. 203)
1 Con chi è sposata?   **2** Di che cosa parla con suo marito?
3 In quali paesi ha vissuto/è vissuta?   **4** Da dove viene il suo cane strano?   **5** In che stanza dorme?   **6** Di che colore è la sua biancheria?   **7** Di chi è la Lamborghini rossa?

C   Soul mates (p. 203)
1 A noi piace viaggiare e piace anche a lui.   **2** A me piacciono le orecchiette e piacciono anche a lei.   **3** A voi piacciono lunghe passeggiate sulla spiaggia e piacciono anche a loro.   **4** A te piace leggere poesie e piace anche a me.

D   Incompatible (p. 203)
1 A loro piacciono i fumetti ma a lui no.   **2** A lei piacciono le macchine veloci ma a lui no.   **3** A loro piace visitare i musei ma a lei no.

E   Do you know it? (p. 203)
1 Ho chiamato per sapere se puoi venire.   **2** Ho bisogno di sapere quanto costa il gioco.   **3** Mi sa dire a che ora chiudono le banche?   **4** Non so scrivere a macchina ma so guidare.

F   Nice or nasty? (p. 203)
1 Davvero signore, Le hanno rubato l'orologio?   **2** Lisa è malata, le ho portato un po' di frutta.   **3** È il compleanno di Angelo, gli ho regalato un computer.   **4** Sono disperata, mi hanno rubato la collana.   **5** I Fortunato sono così gentili, ci hanno mandato dei fiori.

G   What next? (p. 204)
1 Ma non le ho ancora scritto.   **2** Non ci va mai.   **3** Non voglio vedere nessuno.   **4** Non è niente.   **5** Non ho affatto voglia di andarci.   **6** Non mi saluta nemmeno.   **7** Non ho mica fame.

H   Making sense (p. 204)
1 Non ho ancora deciso.   **2** Non ci sono mai stato.   **3** Non sono più venuto.   **4** Non ho preso niente.   **5** Non è arrivato nessuno.

I   Chalk and cheese (p. 204)
1 Non ho ancora mangiato.   **2** Non ho visto arrivare nessuno.   **3** Non ho fatto niente oggi.   **4** Non ho più fame.

J   Irregular past participles (p. 204)
vissuto [*vivere*], successo [*succedere*], permesso [*permettere*], aperto [*aprire*], chiuso [*chiudere*], rotto [*rompere*], perso [*perdere*]

K   Pardon me (p. 204)
1 scusi.   **2** mi dispiace.   **3** non mi dispiace.   **4** scusa.
5 non mi piace.

L   Word perfect (p. 204)
bevuto   chiesto   corso   dato   deciso   detto   fatto   letto   messo   morto   nato   preso   risposto   sceso   stato   scritto   visto   venuto

M   Fra or fa? (p. 204)
1 fra quindici giorni.   **2** quindici anni fa.   **3** sei mesi fa.
4 fra un paio di giorni.   **5** molto tempo fa.

Unit 9

A   Down your way (p. 208)
1 Sì, ce n'è uno.   **2** Sì, ce ne sono alcuni.   **3** No, non ce n'è.   **4** Sì, ce n'è una.   **5** Sì, ce ne sono due.   **6** No, non ce ne sono.

B   Who's that? (p. 208)
1 Susanna è una mia amica.   **2** I Moro sono amici miei.
3 Lidia e Marta sono colleghe mie.   **4** Gianni è un mio cugino.

C   Who's who? (p. 208)
1 un Suo collega?   **2** un vostro amico?   **3** una tua sorella?   **4** una Sua cugina?   **5** una vostra collega?

D   Who came? (p. 208)
Ieri sera sono venuti . . .   **1** molti colleghi nostri.   **2** alcuni cugini nostri.   **3** pochi parenti nostri.   **4** È venuta una nostra zia.   **5** È venuto un nostro vicino.   **6** Sono venute quattro amiche nostre.

E   Point it out (p. 208)
Ho messo . . .   **1** il giornale sotto quel cuscino.   **2** le foto dietro quello specchio.   **3** i vestiti in quei cassetti.   **4** le scarpe in quell'armadio.   **5** le riviste su quegli scaffali.   **6** i giocattoli in quelle borse.

F   Spell it out (p. 208)
1 No, quelli lì.   **2** No, quello lì.   **3** No, quelle lì.   **4** No, quella lì.

G   Otherwise engaged (p. 208)
Numbers 3 and 6 refer to the immediate future so it is not possible to use the present progressive.
1 Ci dispiace, non possiamo, stiamo studiando.   **2** No, non posso, sto aspettando i miei amici.   **3** Mi dispiace, non possono, vanno dalla nonna.   **4** Mi dispiace, ma sta dormendo.   **5** Mi dispiace ma sto uscendo adesso.   **6** Non possiamo, usciamo stasera.

H   The first time (p. 209)
1 L'ho conosciuta.   **2** L'ho conosciuta.   **3** Li ho conosciuti.
4 L'ho conosciuto.

I   Killjoy (p. 209)
No, mi dispiace . . .   **1** l'ho già visitata.   **2** le ho già lette.   **3** li ho già visitati.   **4** le ho già scritto.   **5** li ho già sentiti. [*Number 4 is the odd one out. In this context* le *is an indirect object, 'to her', and the past participle does not agree.*]

J   Not yet (p. 209)
No, non . . .   **1** ne abbiamo ancora fatte.   **2** ne ho ancora assaggiati.   **3** ne ho ancora mandate.   **4** ne abbiamo ancora visti.   **5** ne ho ancora comprate.

K   What do you know? (p. 209)
1 conosci, l'ho conosciuto.   **2** conosce, so.   **3** sa.
4 sappiamo.   **5** sanno.   **6** sapete.

L   Black list (p. 209)
1 a.   **2** d.   **3** e.   **4** b.

M   Nobody loves me (p. 209)
1 non risponde mai nessuno.   **2** non trovo mai nessuno.
3 non mi parla più nessuno.   **4** non mi aiuta più nessuno.

Unit 10

A   Pros and cons (p. 213)
1 L'alpinismo è meno/più pericoloso del parapendismo.   **2** Gli inglesi sono più/meno simpatici degli scozzesi.   **3** È meno/più noioso fare la spesa che fare il bucato.   **4** Vivere in città è meno/più sano che vivere in campagna.

B   How are you feeling? (p. 213)
1 I bambini sono più stufi che stanchi.   **2** Gaetano è più nervoso che irritato.   **3** Sono più triste che arrabbiato.   **4** Ho più fame che sete.

C   Appraisal (p. 213)
1 di Anna; nevrotica.   **2** di Maria; più coscienziosa/intelligente.
3 di Rita; più intelligente/coscienziosa.
4 di Enzo; simpatico.
[*None of the comparisons here require* che *as in each case two people are being directly compared. Che* would be necessary in the following examples: *Anna è più simpatica che intelligente. Lina ha più esperienza che conoscenza.*]

D   Recommendations (p. 213)
1 la più bella. È la giacca più bella.   **2** i più eleganti. Sono i pantaloni più eleganti.   **3** le più care. Sono le scarpe più care.   **4** le più brutte. Sono le camicette più brutte.   **5** il migliore. È il prezzo migliore.   **6** il peggiore. È il modello peggiore.

E   For better or worse (p. 213)
1 peggiore.   **2** meglio.   **3** migliore.   **4** peggio.

F   Relating (p. 213)
1 L'appartamento che è al quinto piano è molto spazioso.
2 L'amica che mi ha accompagnato al cinema è molto simpatica.
3 Il collega che ho incontrato è un tipo allegro.   **4** I pantaloni di velluto che hai voluto comprare sono un po' stretti.

G   What? or What (p. 213)
1 quello che.   **2** che cosa?   **3** che cosa?   **4** quello che.
5 quello che.   **6** che cosa?

H   Good (p. 214)
1 buono.   **2** brava.   **3** Bene!   **4** Bravo!   **5** brava.

I   Saying 'to' (p. 214)
1 a.   **4** a.   **5** di.   **8** a. *No prepositions are needed with the other questions.*

J   Per/fra (p. 214)
1 fra.   **2** fra.   **3** fra.   **4** per.   **5** fra.   **6** per.   **7** per.
8 per.   **9** fra.   **10** fra.

K   Irregular noun practice (p. 214)
la crisi   l'analisi   la moglie   la mano   il paio   il ginocchio
gli dei   i buoi   le braccia   le uova
1 Ho le mani sporche/le mie mani sono sporche.   **2** Ho bisogno di sei uova fresche.   **3** Voglio comprare due paia di scarpe.

Procrastination (p. 214)
Scusa ma non ho ancora . . . comprato/scelto/scritto/letto . . . niente.

Profile 2

Giordano Mazzolini (p. 222)
1 vero.   **2** falso.   **3** falso.   **4** vero.   **5** falso.   **6** falso.

Basics

These notes are meant as a guide for those learners who have little or no experience of the terminology of grammar.

I Noun

A noun is a word used for naming people, animals, places, objects and concepts, e.g., *Mary; cat; Italy; table; justice.*

Number and gender: the number of a noun refers to whether it is singular or plural. The gender refers to whether it is masculine, feminine or neuter. In English nouns have no gender, but in Italian they are either masculine or feminine. In Italian the gender and number of a noun is shown by the article.

2 Article

Articles are words meaning *the, a, an*. They are used before a noun or its accompanying adjective. *The* is a **definite** article and is used with specific objects, e.g. *the boy, the flowers. A* and *an* are **indefinite** articles and are used with non-specific objects, e.g. *a cat, an idea.*

3 Adjective

Adjectives are words which describe or 'modify' nouns or pronouns. There are four main kinds:

Descriptive: *the happy boy, a black cat, he is sad, it is difficult.*
Possessive: *his book, your cat, my boy, their problems*
Demonstrative: *this book, that cat, these boys, those problems*
Interrogative: *how much bread? how many books? which cat? what sort?*

4 Pronoun

This is a word which replaces a noun. There are different kinds of pronouns.

i) Personal pronouns

These include **subject** pronouns and **object** pronouns.

Subject	Object			
Subject	*Reflexive*	*Disjunctive (stressed)*	*Direct Object*	*Indirect Object*
I	myself	me	me	me
you	yourself	you	you	you
he	himself	him	him	him
she	herself	her	her	her
we	ourselves	us	us	us
you	yourselves	you	you	you
they	themselves	them	them	them

Although in English the forms are frequently identical, it is worth knowing how they are used because in Italian the forms vary far more.

A **subject** pronoun denotes the subject or doer of a verb: *I read, you write, it works.*
A **reflexive** pronoun denotes what you do to yourself: *I wash myself.*
A **disjunctive** pronoun is used with prepositions and for emphasis: *come with me, take him not her.*

An **object** pronoun denotes the object of an action, and there are two types of object, **direct** and **indirect**. A **direct** object pronoun denotes what is directly affected by the action of the verb and it immediately follows the verb: *Mary saw me; Charles invited you. Susan met him; Anna thanked them; the children ate it.* An **indirect** object pronoun is less directly linked to the action of the verb and generally answers the questions of whom? of what? to whom? etc. It follows a preposition linked to the verb: *John spoke to me, Alex wrote to you.*

ii) Other types of pronoun

Relative: words like *who, whom, which, that* and *what: the boy who is here; the man whom I saw; the book which is on the table; what I want is a drink.*
Interrogative: words like *who? whom? what? which [one/ones]? how much/many?.* They introduce questions: *who did you say was coming? What/which one do you want? How many are there?* In English the forms of relative and interrogative are in most cases identical. This is not true of Italian and it is important to distinguish between the two.
Demonstrative: words like *this [one] these [ones] that [one] those [ones].* They refer to nouns which have been pointed out: *I'll take this one; I like that one; these ones are best; I'll have those.*
Possessive: words like *mine, yours, his, hers, ours, theirs.* They replace a phrase containing a possessive adjective: *this is mine [my book]; show me yours [your book].*

5 Preposition

This is a word or words indicating the position of one object in relation to another in space or time: *on, in, from, with, at, of, in front of, next to,* etc.

Prepositions are often differently used in English and Italian, which means that they need to be studied carefully.

6 Verb

This is a word used for denoting a physical or mental action or state: *to eat, to drink, to think, to be* [these are the **infinitive** forms of a verb]. In Italian the infinitive is a single word, not two as in English.

i) Tenses

A verb has different tenses. A tense indicates the time when the action of the verb takes place, e.g. now – the **present**: *I sing, he sings*, etc.; later – the **future**: *I will sing*; in the past – the **perfect**: *I sang, I have sung, I did sing.*

ii) Compound tenses

A tense can be made up of two or more parts: e.g. an **auxiliary** verb and a **past participle**: *I have eaten; he has finished.*

The **auxiliary** is the 'helper' verb which in English is usually *to have.* The **past participle** of English verbs often ends in *-ed* or *-en* and forms part of various tenses: *I have written; he had played; we will have started.* Many English past participles are irregular, e.g. *thought, sung, run.* In Italian the auxiliary can be *to have (avere)* or *to be (essere).* As in English, many past participles are irregular.

iii) The person of a verb

The shorthand way of referring to the form of a verb is to talk about the **first, second** and **third person singular** or **plural**.

	Sing.	Plural
First person: [the speaker]	I	we
Second person: [person spoken to]	you	you
Third person: [person spoken about]	he she it	they

In the verb *to go, I go* and *we go* are the first persons singular and plural; *you go* is the second person singular and plural; *he/she/it goes* is the third person singular and *they go* is the third person plural.

iv) Transitive and intransitive verbs

A **transitive** verb is a verb which can take a direct object [see 4i. above]: *I saw her; they ate pasta; he wrote a letter.* In these examples the direct objects are: *her, pasta, letter.* A verb defined as transitive is not always used with a direct object: *they ate quickly; he wrote to her.* Nevertheless, if a verb can be used with a direct object it is generally defined as transitive.

An **intransitive** verb can never be used with a direct object: *Mary arrived late; I lay down.* In Italian it can be useful to understand these broad distinctions when learning about which auxiliary to use with a verb: *essere* or *avere.*

7 Adverb

This is a word used to give extra information about, or 'modify', verbs, other adverbs or adjectives.

When used with a **verb,** an adverb describes an action: *they eat quickly; he runs fast; Ann sings well.*
When **two adverbs** come together, the degree or intensity of that action is described: *they eat too quickly; he runs very fast; Anne sings extremely well.*
Adverbs can also modify **adjectives**: *Mary is very good; my car is too old; this is extremely difficult.*

Reference

I QUANTITY

I Cardinal numbers: numbers for counting

I numeri da zero a duecento [0–200]

0 zero	31 trentuno, *etc.*
1 uno	40 quaranta
2 due	41 quarantuno, *etc.*
3 tre	50 cinquanta
4 quattro	51 cinquantuno, *etc.*
5 cinque	60 sessanta
6 sei	61 sessantuno, *etc.*
7 sette	70 settanta
8 otto	71 settantuno, *etc.*
9 nove	80 ottanta
10 dieci	81 ottantuno, *etc.*
11 undici	90 novanta
12 dodici	91 novantuno, *etc.*
13 tredici	100 cento
14 quattordici	101 centouno
15 quindici	108 centootto [cento otto]
16 sedici	111 centoundici
17 diciassette	120 centoventi
18 diciotto	121 centoventuno
19 diciannove	128 centoventotto
20 venti	130 centotrenta, *etc.*
21 ventuno	140 centoquaranta, *etc.*
22 ventidue	150 centocinquanta, *etc.*
23 ventitré	160 centosessanta, *etc.*
24 ventiquattro	170 centosettanta, *etc.*
25 venticinque	180 cento ottanta [centottanta]
26 ventisei	190 centonovanta, *etc.*
27 ventisette	200 duecento
28 ventotto	
29 ventinove	
30 trenta	

Notes

a) When **uno** and **otto** are part of numbers above 20, the final vowel of **venti, trenta,** etc. is omitted: **quarantuno** – 41; **sessantotto** – 68; **centoventuno** – 121; **centoventotto** – 128; **duecentotrentuno** – 231; **duecentotrentotto** – 238, etc.

b) When **tre** is part of another number it must be written with an accent: **ventitré** – 23; **trentatré** – 33.

c) Odd and even numbers: 2, 4, 6 sono numeri **pari**; 1, 3, 5 sono numeri **dispari**.

I numeri da duecento a due miliardi [200–2000.000.000]

200 duecento	1001 milleuno
201 duecento uno, *etc.*	1008 milleotto
300 trecento	1528 millecinquecentoventotto
301 trecento uno	2000 duemila
400 quattrocento, *etc.*	2001 duemilauno
500 cinquecento	2008 duemilaotto
600 seicento	10.000 diecimila
700 settecento	15.000 quindicimila
800 ottocento	100.000 centomila
900 novecento	1.000.000 un milione
999 novecentonovantanove	2.000.000 due milioni
1000 mille	1000.000.000 un miliardo
	2000.000.000 due miliardi

Notes

a) **Cento** is invariable but **mille** changes.
The plural of **mille** is **mila**:
   mille lire; duemila lire
The plural of **milione** and **miliardo** is regular: **milioni, miliardi.**

b) **Mille** and **mila** retain the final **–e** and **–a** in front of **uno** and **otto**.

c) **Milione/i, miliardo/i** require **di** before a noun:
   un milione di sterline   tre miliardi di dollari
This is not the case when additional numbers are used:
   un milione [e] duecentomila sterline   tre miliardi [e] cinquecentomila dollari

2 Ordinal numbers: numbers for indicating order

1st	primo	**11th**	undicesimo
2nd	secondo	**12th**	dodicesimo
3rd	terzo	**13th**	tredicesimo
4th	quarto	**14th**	quattordicesimo
5th	quinto	**15th**	quindicesimo
6th	sesto	**16th**	sedicesimo
7th	settimo	**17th**	diciassettesimo
8th	ottavo	**18th**	diciottesimo
9th	nono	**19th**	diciannovesimo
10th	decimo	**20th**	ventesimo

Notes

a) Roman numerals are used to abbreviate ordinal numbers:
   I – 1st   II – 2nd   XX – 20th

b) Alternatively ordinal numbers can be abbreviated thus: 1° 2° 20°, etc.

c) Like adjectives, they agree with the accompanying noun. They generally precede the noun except in the case of monarchs and popes:
   la terza pagina *but* Enrico terzo

3 Fractions (*le frazioni*)

With the exception of *a half*, fractions are expressed by combining cardinal and ordinal numbers, as in English:

un quarto **di**	*a quarter of*
tre quarti **di**	*three quarters of*
un terzo **di**	*a third of*
due terzi **di**	*two thirds of*
un decimo **di**	*a tenth of*
la metà **di**	*half*

Notes

a) **Di** is always required:
la metà del mio stipendio   *half my salary*
tre quarti del mio stipendio   *three quarters of my salary*

b) **Mezzo** (not **metà**) is used for units of measure:
mezzo chilo per favore   *half a kilo please*

c) **Metà** can also mean *mid*:
Arrivo a metà settimana   *I'm coming midweek*
Parto a metà luglio   *I'm leaving in mid July*

4 Percentages (*le percentuali*)

The definite article is always used:
il cinquanta per cento   *fifty per cent*

To indicate a decimal point, a comma (**virgola**) is used in Italian:
1,5 – uno virgola cinque   *1.5 – one point five*
99,9 – novantanove virgola nove   *99.9 – ninety nine point nine*

5 Collective numbers

un paio **di**	*a pair, a couple*
due paia **di**	*two pairs*
una decina **di**	*about ten*
una dozzina **di**	*a dozen*
una trentina **di**	*about thirty*
una quarantina **di**	*about forty*
una cinquantina **di**	*about fifty*
un centinaio **di**	*about a hundred*
centinaia **di**	*hundreds of*
un migliaio **di**	*about a thousand*
migliaia **di**	*thousands of*

6 Basic arithmetic

L'addizione:	3 più/e 2 fa 5	*3 + 2 = 5*
La sottrazione:	10 meno 6 fa 4	*10 − 6 = 4*
La moltiplicazione:	6 per 6 fa 36	*6 × 6 = 36*
La divisione:	10 diviso 2 fa 5	*10 ÷ 2 = 5*

7 Basic measurement

La stanza è **lunga** 4 metri e **larga** 3 metri
   The room is 4 metres by 3
La stanza è **alta** 5 metri   *The room is 5 metres high*
La valigia **pesa** 20 chili   *The suitcase weighs 20 kilos*

Note
The words **lungo** (*long*), **largo** (*wide*), **alto** (*high*) agree with the noun.

8 Useful expressions of quantity

i) *Double, treble:* il doppio di; il triplo di
il doppio/il triplo del mio stipendio

ii) *Twice, 3,4 times, etc:* due, tre, quattro volte
È due volte più grande   *It's twice as big*

iii) *Both:* tutti e due *[m/m & f];* tutte e due *[f]*
Vengono tutti e due i bambini   *Both children are coming*
Sono arrivate tutte e due le ragazze   *Both girls arrived*

iv) *All 3/4/5, etc:* tutti/e e tre/quattro/cinque
Vengono tutti e tre   *All three are coming [m/m & f]*
Sono arrivate tutte e quattro   *All four came [f]*

v) *Some, any* [see Systems 5, 2 iii, p. 98]:

To express *some/any* in Italian it is necessary to distinguish between countable and non-countable nouns. *[Non-countable nouns have no plurals, e.g. substances and some foods.]* The partitive article [**di** + definite article] is used to express unspecific quantity:

Countable nouns	*Non-countable nouns*
dei/degli/delle	**del/dello/della/dell'**
Ci sono dei francobolli	C'è del pane
Ci sono delle buste?	C'è della marmellata?
There are some stamps	*There is some bread*
Are there any envelopes?	*Is there any jam?*

To express the idea of an unspecific quantity more clearly, the following are used:

Countable nouns	*Non-countable nouns*
un po' di + *plu.*	**un po' di**
alcuni/e + *plu.*	
qualche + *sing.*	
Mi dà un po' di/alcune ciliegie?	Mi dà un po' di formaggio?
Mi dà qualche ciliegia?	*Will you give me some/a bit of*
Will you give me some/a few cherries?	*cheese?*

Notes

a) The above are all used only when amount is in focus, otherwise they can be omitted, as in English:
C'è pane e burro da mangiare   *There's bread and butter to eat*
Ci sono riviste e giornali da leggere   *There are magazines and newspapers to read*

b) **Qualche** is followed by a singular verb as well as a singular noun, despite the plural meaning:
Ieri è venuto qualche amico   *Yesterday a few friends came*

c) On its own, as a pronoun, *some/any* is **ne**:
Ne vuoi?   *Do you want some/any?*
Ne ho, grazie   *I've got some, thanks*
[See Systems 8, 1, p. 201.]

vi) *No, Not any:*
In negative expressions the partitive article is dropped. However, with non-countable nouns the definite article is needed:
   La carta non c'è   *There isn't any paper*
but: Non ci sono guide   *There aren't any guides*
Alternatively, **mancare** (*lit. to be lacking*) can be used:
   Manca la carta   *There isn't any paper*
   Mancano guide   *There aren't any guides*

vii) *No, Not a single:*
If the negative is emphatic, **nessun** can be used, with countable nouns only [*i.e. nouns with plurals*].
   Non c'è ... nessun problema/errore
                 nessuno sbaglio
                 nessuna difficoltà
                 nessun'aspirina

Note
The spelling changes of **nessun** follow the rules for the indefinite article.
[See Systems 1, 3, p. 79 and 2, 1, p. 83.]

II TIME

For notes on telling the time see Unit 4, Patterns 2, note 2 ii–iv, p. 60.

1 Days of the week (*i giorni della settimana*)

(il)	lunedì	*Monday*	(il)	venerdì	*Friday*
(il)	martedì	*Tuesday*	(il)	sabato	*Saturday*
(il)	mercoledì	*Wednesday*	(la)	domenica	*Sunday*
(il)	giovedì	*Thursday*			

Notes

a) Weekdays are written without capitals in Italian.

b) The article is only used to express habitual action:

La domenica vado a Roma e il lunedì vado a Napoli   *On Sundays I go to Rome and on Mondays I go to Naples*

c) To say *on* a specific day drop the article:

Domenica vado a Roma e lunedì vado a Napoli   *On Sunday I'm going to Rome and on Monday I'm going to Naples*

d) **Di** is sometimes used to express habitual action:

Siete aperti anche di domenica?   *Are you open on Sundays too?*

2 Months of the year (*i mesi dell'anno*)

gennaio	*January*	luglio	*July*
febbraio	*February*	agosto	*August*
marzo	*March*	settembre	*September*
aprile	*April*	ottobre	*October*
maggio	*May*	novembre	*November*
giugno	*June*	dicembre	*December*

Notes

a) Months are written without capitals in Italian.

b) To express *in*, either **a** or **in** is used:

Arrivo **a** luglio   *I'm arriving in July*

Sono nato **in** luglio   *I was born in July*

c) **In** is more common if habitual action is involved:

In gennaio vado sempre in montagna   *In/every January I always go to the mountains*

3 Dates (*le date*)

The year is written as one word and the definite article is required:

Il millequattrocentonovantadue   1492

Il millenovecentosessantotto   1968

Il 1992 è un anno bisestile   *1992 is a leap year*

Notes

a) To express *in*, **in** plus the article is required:

Sono nato nel millenovecentocinquantuno   *I was born in 1951*

b) Another way of saying when you're born is to use **di**:

Di che anno sei/è? – Sono del '50/1950   *lit. of what year are you? – I'm of '50/1950.*

c) With complete dates there is no article before the year:

Sono nato il 13 agosto, 1946

d) Apart from the 1st of the month, dates are expressed with cardinal numbers:

il primo maggio   *May 1st*

il due aprile   *April 2nd*

l'otto luglio   *July 8th*

l'undici febbraio   *February 11th*

il ventun marzo   *March 21st*

il trentuno agosto   *August 31st*

e) There is more than one way of asking the date:

Qual è la data (di) oggi? – È il 3 ottobre

Quanto ne abbiamo oggi? – Ne abbiamo 3

f) To express *on*, use the article:

Arrivo il 26 ottobre

g) If you use the day with the date the article is dropped:

Arrivo giovedì 26 ottobre

h) **Ventuno** and **trentuno** tend to drop the **–o** before months beginning with consonants.

4 Centuries (*i secoli*)

B.C.: **ac** [avanti Cristo]   A.D.: **dc** [dopo Cristo]

In Italian, as in English, ordinal numbers are used:

il terzo secolo ac   *the third century* BC

From the thirteenth century on, there are two possibilities in Italian:

il Duecento	il tredicesimo secolo	13th c.
il Trecento	il quattordicesimo secolo	14th c.
il Quattrocento	il quindicesimo secolo	15th c.
il Cinquecento	il sedicesimo secolo	16th c.
il Seicento	il diciassettesimo secolo	17th c.
il Settecento	il diciottesimo secolo	18th c.
l'Ottocento	il diciannovesimo secolo	19th c.
il Novecento	il ventesimo secolo	20th c.

Note

The alternative form – **Duecento**, etc. – is especially common in art and literature. Capital letters are always used.

5 Seasons (*le stagioni dell'anno*)

la primavera	*spring*	l'autunno	*autumn*
l'estate (f)	*summer*	l'inverno	*winter*

Notes

a) The definite article is required:

Mi piace l'autunno

b) To express *in*, **in** is used, without the article:

Sono nato **in** ... primavera/estate/autunno/inverno   *I was born in spring/summer/autumn/winter*

Siamo **in** estate   *It's summer*

c) With **estate** and **inverno** only, **di** can also be used, especially where habitual action is involved:

D'estate vado al mare   *In the summer I go to the seaside*

D'inverno fa freddo qui   *In the winter it's cold here*

but:

In autunno il tempo è ancora bello   *In the autumn the weather is still fine*

III PLACE

1 Geographical position

Il nord; del nord/settentrionale	*the north; northern*
Il sud; del sud/meridionale	*the south; southern*
L'est; dell'est/orientale	*the east; eastern*
L'ovest; dell'ovest/occidentale	*the west; western*

Notes

a) To express *in*, the definite article plus **in** is used:
   Torino è nell'Italia del nord, Pescara è nell'Italia orientale
   La Finlandia è nel nord dell'Europa

b) **A** and **di** are used to express the relationship between 2 places:
   Frascati è a nord di Roma *Frascati is north of Rome*

c) **A** or **verso** express the direction:
   Bisogna andare a/verso sud *You have to go south*

2 Continents (*i continenti*)

The definite article is normally required.

l'Africa	l'Asia	l'Australasia	l'Europa	l'America
Africa	*Asia*	*Australasia*	*Europe*	*America*

Notes

a) The definite article must be combined with prepositions:
   Parla molto **dell'**Africa
   Parte **dall'**Africa

b) The article is not required with **in** to express *in* and *to*:
   Vado **in** Africa *I go to Africa*
   Vivo **in** Africa *I live in Africa*

c) The article is needed when the noun is modified:
   Vado **nell'**Africa del sud *I'm going to southern Africa*

3 Countries, regions, large islands and island groups

The article is usually required:

l'Italia **la** Gran Bretagna **il** Belgio **lo** Zaire
gli Stati Uniti **i** Paesi Bassi *but:* Israele
il Piemonte **la** Toscana **gli** Abruzzi **le** Marche
la Sicilia **la** Sardegna **la** Corsica **le** Eolie
le Tremiti

Notes

a) *In* and *to* is usually expressed by **in**, without the article:
   Vivo **in** Italia, **in** Toscana
   Vado **in** Italia, **in** Toscana
   Sono nato **in** Sicilia ma lavoro **in** Belgio

b) If the country or region is masculine, the article is sometimes used with **in**. This is less common nowadays, but some Italian regions retain the article:
   il Molise – vado **nel** Molise
   il Veneto – abito **nel** Veneto
but:
   il Piemonte – vado/abito **in** Piemonte

c) Countries or islands which are identified with their main town do not require the article and follow the rules set out in section 4 below:
   Cuba Haiti Malta Trinidad Bahrain
   Hong Kong Monaco San Marino
This is also the case with many large non-Italian islands:
   Bali Cipro Corfu Creta Malta Taiwan

d) Plural countries, regions or islands require the article:
   Quest'anno vado **nei** Paesi Bassi e **negli** Stati Uniti
   Vivo **nelle** Marche ma sono nato **negli** Abruzzi
   Ho visitato **le** Bahamas, **le** Bermuda e **le** Canarie

e) Countries, regions and islands modified by an adjective or adjectival phrases require the article:
   Vado **nell'**Italia meridionale
   Vivo **nella** Sicilia occidentale

4 Towns and small islands

The article is normally not required:
   Edimburgo Parigi Berlino
   Capri Elba Giglio Ischia Lipari Stromboli Lampedusa
Exceptions:
   L'Aia [*The Hague*] L'Aquila L'Avana [*Havana*] Il Cairo
   La Mecca Il Pireo [*Piraeus*] La Spezia

Notes

a) *To* and *in* are expressed by **a**:
   Lavoro **a** Roma e passo le ferie **a** Capri o **a** Cuba

b) Geographical names normally taking **a** require the article if they are modified:
   M'interessa **la** Berlino del secolo scorso/**la** vecchia Roma

5 Countries and nationalities

In Italian capital letters are only used for the name of the country.

	il paese	*la nazionalità*
Afghanistan	l'Afghanistan [m]	afgano
Albania	l'Albania	albanese
Algeria	l'Algeria	algerino
America (USA)	l'America gli Stati Uniti	americano statunitense
Angola	l'Angola	angolano
Argentina	l'Argentina	argentino
Australia	l'Australia	australiano
Austria	l'Austria	austriaco
Bangladesh	il Bangladesh	★
Barbados	le Barbados	★
Belgium	il Belgio	belga
Bolivia	la Bolivia	boliviano
Botswana	il Botswana	★
Brazil	il Brasile	brasiliano
Bulgaria	la Bulgaria	bulgaro
Burma	la Birmania	birmano
Cameroon	il Camerun	camerunense
Canada	il Canadà	canadese
Chile	il Cile	cileno
China	la Cina	cinese
Colombia	la Colombia	colombiano
Cuba	Cuba	cubano
Cyprus	Cipro	cipriota
Czechoslovakia	la Cecoslovacchia	cecoslovacco
Denmark	la Danimarca	danese
Egypt	l'Egitto	egiziano
El Salvador	El Salvador [m]	salvadoregno
England	l'Inghilterra	inglese
Ethiopia	l'Etiopia	etiope
Fiji	le isole Figi	figiano
Finland	la Finlandia	finlandese
France	la Francia	francese
Germany	la Germania	tedesco
Ghana	il Ghana	ganese
Great Britain (UK)	la Gran Bretagna il Regno Unito	britannico
Greece	la Grecia	greco
Guatamala	il Guatemala	guatemalteco
Guyana	la Guyana	guyanese
Haiti	Haiti	haitiano
Hong Kong	Hong Kong	★
Hungary	l'Ungheria	ungherese
India	l'India	indiano
Indonesia	l'Indonesia	indonesiano
Iran	l'Iran [m]	iraniano
Iraq	l'Iraq [m]	iracheno
Ireland	l'Irlanda	irlandese
Israel	Israele [m]	israeliano
Italy	l'Italia	italiano

Jamaica	la Giamaica	giamaicano
Japan	il Giappone	giapponese
Jordan	la Giordania	giordano
Kenya	il Kenya	keniota
Korea	la Corea	coreano
Kuwait	il Kuwait	kuwaitiano
Lebanon	il Libano	libanese
Libya	la Libia	libico
Luxembourg	il Lussemburgo	lussemburghese
Madagascar	il Madagascar	malgascio
Malawi	il Malawi	★
Malaysia	la Malesia	malese
Mauritius	Maurizio	mauriziano
Malta	Malta	maltese
Mexico	il Messico	messicano
Monaco	Monaco	monegasco
Morocco	il Marocco	marocchino
Mozambique	il Mozambico	mozambicano
Namibia	il Namibia	nambibiano
Nepal	il Nepal	nepalese
Netherlands	l'Olanda/i Paesi Bassi	olandese
New Zealand	la Nuova Zelanda	neozelandese
Nicaragua	il Nicaragua	nicaraguense
Nigeria	la Nigeria	nigeriano
Norway	la Norvegia	norvegese
Pakistan	il Pakistan	pakistano
Paraguay	il Paraguay	paraguayano
Peru	il Perù	peruviano
Philippines	le Filippine	filippino
Poland	la Polonia	polacco
Portugal	il Portogallo	portoghese
Puerto Rico	Porto Rico	portoricano
Rumania	la Romania	rumeno
Russia	la Russia	russo
San Marino	San Marino	sanmarinese
Saudi Arabia	l'Arabia Saudita	saudita
Scotland	la Scozia	scozzese
Senegal	il Senegal	senegalese
Seychelles	le Seychelles	★
Somalia	la Somalia	somalo
South Africa	il Sudafrica	sudafricano
Spain	la Spagna	spagnolo
Sri Lanka	lo Sri Lanka	★
Sudan	il Sudan	sudanese
Sweden	la Svezia	svedese
Switzerland	la Svizzera	svizzero
Syria	la Siria	siriano
Taiwan	Taiwan	taiwanese
Tanzania	la Tanzania	tanzaniano
Thailand	la Tailandia	tailandese
Trinidad	Trinidad [m]	trinidadiano
Tunisia	la Tunisia	tunisino
Turkey	la Turchia	turco
Uganda	l'Uganda	ugandese
Uruguay	l'Uruguay [m]	uruguayano
Venezuela	il Venezuela	venezuelano
Vietnam	il Vietnam	vietnamita
Wales	il Galles	gallese
Yemen	lo Yemen	yemenita
Yugoslavia	la Iugoslavia	iugoslavo
Zaire	lo Zaire	zairiano
Zambia	lo Zambia	zambiano
Zimbabwe	lo Zimbabwe	zimbabwiano

★ Adjectives of nationality are not commonly used. Reference tends to be made to **un abitante di . . .**

For more new countries, such as Estonia, see Reference, Book 2.

IV PERSONAL PRONOUN REVIEW

Below is a summary of the personal pronouns in the Course:

Subject		Stressed	
I	io	*me*	me
you	tu	*you*	te
he, she	lui, lei	*him, her*	lui, lei
you [formal]	Lei	*you*	Lei
we	noi	*us*	noi
you	voi	*you*	voi
they	loro	*them*	loro
See Systems 1, note 6, i), p. 80		See Systems 7, note 1, p. 197	

Reflexive		Direct obj.		Indirect obj.	
myself	mi	*me*	mi	*to me*	mi
yourself	ti	*you*	ti	*to you*	ti
him/herself	si	*it, him, her*	lo, la	*to him, her*	gli, le
yourself	si	*you*	La	*to you*	Le
ourselves	ci	*us*	ci	*to us*	ci
yourselves	vi	*you*	vi	*to you*	vi
themselves	si	*them*	li, le	*to them*	gli/loro★
See Systems 2, note 6, ii), p. 85		See Systems 6, note 1, p. 193		See Systems 6, note 1, p. 193	

★ **gli** is usual especially in speech. **Loro** is formal and comes after the verb.

V ADJECTIVES

I Position of adjectives

There are no hard and fast rules for this, but the following are generally applicable:

i) Before the noun

Demonstrative adjectives like **quella**:
  quella ragazza
Interrogative adjectives like **quale?**:
  quale ragazza?
Possessive adjectives like **mia**:
  la mia ragazza

Note:
In set phrases possessives can come after:
  casa mia (*my home*) colpa mia (*my fault*)

ii) After the noun

Adjectives of colour, religion, nationality and most other descriptive adjectives:
  l'esame difficile   la gonna rossa   il ragazzo italiano
  la fede cristiana

iii) Using two adjectives

The two are separated if one of them is demonstrative, possessive or interrogative:
  quell'esame **difficile**   *that difficult exam*
  la **mia** gonna **rossa**   *my red skirt*
  quale ragazzo **italiano?**   *which Italian boy?*
The same is true with many descriptive adjectives:
  una **grande** casa **antica**   *a large old house*
  un **piccolo** quaderno **giallo**   *a small yellow exercise book*
  un **nuovo** romanzo **tedesco**   *a new German novel*
  una **vecchia** sedia **rotta**   *an old broken chair*
  un **bel** vestito **nuovo**   *a beautiful new dress*
  una **brutta** maglia **vecchia**   *a horrible old jumper*

Notes: If an adverb like **molto** or **tanto** is used with an adjective, they both follow the noun. Adverbs do not agree with the noun, while adjectives do:
  una casa **molto antica**   *a very old house*
  ragazzi **tanto simpatici**   *extremely nice boys*
Sometimes two adjectives are placed together but they are usually linked by **e** – *and*. It is more common for them to go after the noun:
  un uomo **alto e bello**   *a tall handsome man*
  una donna **snella e bionda**   *a slim blonde woman*
However, they can also precede it. The effect is more emphatic:
  il **giovane e simpatico** atleta   *the charming young athlete*

iv) Variable position and changes in meaning

Many descriptive adjectives can go before the noun as well as after it. The most common are:
  antico vecchio nuovo giovane
  bello brutto buono cattivo
  grande piccolo lungo breve
  povero caro diverso

The position of some adjectives can determine slight changes in meaning. After the noun they can have a more literal meaning.

La minestra è cattiva	*The soup is horrible/bad*
È una cattiva idea	*It's a bad idea*
La carne è buona	*The meat is nice/good*
È una buona cosa	*It's a good thing*

Sometimes the changes in meaning are more than slight:

	Before the noun	After the noun
caro	*dear, lovely*	*expensive*
diverso	*several*	*different*
grande	*great*	*large*
nuovo	*another*	*new*
povero	*unfortunate*	*poor*
vecchio	*old [for many years]*	*old [age]*

È un vecchio amico di mio figlio   *He is an old friend of my son's*
Sì, il mio amico è vecchio   *Yes, my friend is old*
Ci sono diversi problemi   *There are various problems*
Ci sono problemi diversi   *There are different problems*

2 Opposites

One way of vocabulary building is to learn basic opposites:

beautiful; ugly	bello; brutto [*people/objects*]
good; bad	buono; cattivo [*food*]
good; naughty	buono; cattivo [*people*]
nice; unpleasant	simpatico; antipatico [*people*]
young; old/elderly	giovane; vecchio/anziano
big; little	grande; piccolo
fat; thin	grasso; magro
heavy; light	pesante; leggero
tall; short	alto; basso [*people*]
high; low	alto; basso [*objects/sound*]
long; short	lungo; corto [*objects*]
	breve [*book/speech*]
wide; narrow	largo; stretto
square; round	quadrato; rotondo
clean; dirty	pulito; sporco
hot; cold	caldo; freddo
wet; dry	bagnato; asciutto
sweet; dry	dolce; secco [*wine*]
greasy; dry	grasso; secco [*hair/skin*]
hard; soft	duro; morbido
loud; soft	forte; piano
fast; slow	rapido; lento/piano
sweet; bitter	dolce; amaro [*coffee, etc.*]
sweet; sour	dolce; agro
open; closed	aperto; chiuso
on; off	acceso; spento [*light, etc.*]
up; down	su; giù
upstairs; downstairs	di sopra; di sotto
inside; outside	dentro; fuori
easy; difficult	facile; difficile
happy; sad	felice; triste, infelice
pleased; displeased	contento; scontento
polite; rude	educato; maleducato

VI SPELLING AND PRONUNCIATION

I Plurals of nouns and adjectives ending in:

i) -ca, -ga

To keep the hard sound an **h** is always needed in the plurals of **-ca,/-ga** words:

l'amica simpatica   le amiche simpatiche

la strada larga   le strade larghe

ii) -co, -go

The hard sound of **-co** nouns is kept unless it is preceded by a vowel:

il mio amico polacco   i miei amici polacchi

il tedesco simpatico   i tedeschi simpatici

Exceptions include:

buco, buchi   *hole*

fuoco, fuochi   *fire* [-co preceded by a vowel, but ending is **-chi**]

porco, porci   *pig* [-co preceded by a consonant, but ending is **-ci**]

The hard sound of the **-go** ending is kept:

il lago lungo   i laghi lunghi

But if the ending is **-ologo** and the word refers to a profession, the ending tends to be **-gi**:

il biologo   i biologi   l'archeologo   gli archeologi

lo psicologo   gli psicologi

Otherwise it is **-ghi**:

il catalogo   i cataloghi   il dialogo   i dialoghi

iii) -cia, -gia

The **-i-** is usually dropped from the plural if the endings are preceded by a consonant:

l'arancia, le arance   *orange, oranges*

la spiaggia, le spiagge   *beach, beaches*

Otherwise the **-i-** is usually retained:

la ciliegia, le ciliegie   *cherry, cherries*

la camicia, le camicie   *shirt, shirts*

If a noun has a consonant preceding the **-cia** or **-gia** ending, but is pronounced with the stress on the **i**, then the **i** is retained in the plural:

l'allergia, le allergie   *allergy, allergies*

Note

You may encounter individual variations on the above rules: it is possible to spell the plural of **ciliegia, ciliege** [instead of **ciliegie**] and the plural of **provincia, provincie** [instead of **province**]. For the learner, however, it is best to use the guidelines given.

iv) -cio, -gio

There is no need for two **i**'s in the plural:

il bacio, i baci   *kiss, kisses*

l'orologio, gli orologi   *watch, watches*

v) -io

There is only one **i** in the plural:

il figlio, i figli   *son, sons/children*

lo studio, gli studi   *study, studies*

If the **i** in the singular is stressed, then there are two **i**'s in the plural:

lo zio, gli zii   *uncle, uncles*

The exception is **il tempio**   *temple*

Its plural should be **tempi**, but, in order to distinguish it from the plural of **tempo** *(time),* the form **i templi** is generally used.

2 Stress patterns

i) General guidelines

It is not always easy to know where to stress a word. As a general guideline, the stress comes on the last but one vowel and on the end of a word if this is marked by an accent:

amico   scarpe   farmacia   città   perché

Exceptions to this are numerous. It is worth marking where the stress comes when you learn new vocabulary: many dictionaries indicate stress.

ii) Accents

Rules for the use of accents exist, but by and large the convention is to use a grave accent [`] for most words apart from those ending in **-che**:

perché   *because/why*   benché   *although*

and also

né ... né   *neither ... nor*   sé   *self*

Accents are also used to distinguish between words with the same spelling but different meanings:

né ... né, *neither ... nor*	ne, *of it/them*
sé, *self*	se, *if*
tè, *tea*	te, *you*
dà, *he/she gives you give*	da, *from, by*
è, *he/she/it is*	e, *and*

Parla molto di sé   *He talks a lot about himself*

Se vieni, ci divertiamo   *If you come we'll have fun*

Mi dà un etto di formaggio?   *Can you give me 100 gr of cheese?*

Vado da mia nonna   *I'm going to my grandmother's*

VII VERBS AND PREPOSITIONS

Prepositions can be tricky for the language learner, as their meaning and use in different languages frequently differ.

I Verbs requiring no preposition in Italian

chiedere qlco.	to ask **for** s.th.
pagare qlco.	to pay **for** s.th.
aspettare qlcu./qlco.	to wait **for** s.o./th.
cercare qlcu./qlco.	to look **for** s.o./th.
guardare qlcu./qlco.	to look **at** s.o./th.
ascoltare qlcu.qlco.	to listen **to** s.o./th.
sognare qlcu./qlco.	to dream **about** s.o./th.

Notes

a) *To ask for or after* **someone** is chiedere di:
   Ho chiesto di Aldo   *I asked after Aldo*
   Di chi devo chiedere?   *Who must I ask for?*
b) *To pay for* **someone** is pagare per:
   Ho pagato io per Aldo   *I paid for Aldo*

2 Verbs with no preposition before an infinitive

i) Verbs used impersonally [See Ref. VIIIB ii and iii, p. 250 for definitions]

bastare	*to be enough*
bisognare	*to be necessary*
convenire	*to be a good idea*
importare	*to matter, to mind*
interessare	*to be interested in*
occorrere	*to need, be necessary*
piacere	*to like*
sembrare	*to seem*
servire	*to be of use*

Le conviene arrivare in anticipo   *It would be a good idea [for you] to arrive early*
Gli dispiace non venire   *He is sorry not to come*
Occorre partire presto   *It's necessary to leave early*

ii) Impersonal expressions with essere

essere ...	To be ...
semplice/facile/difficile	*simple/easy/difficult*
giusto/ingiusto	*fair/unfair*
interessante/importante	*interesting/important*
meglio/peggio	*better, best/worse*
permesso/vietato/proibito	*allowed/forbidden*
utile/inutile	*useful/useless*

È meglio partire presto   *It's best to leave early*
È facile parlare italiano   *It's easy to speak Italian*

3 Verbs and expressions with di

The following require **di** before an infinitive, noun or pronoun:

avere bisogno	*to need*
avere fretta	*to be in a hurry*
avere tempo	*to have time*
avere intenzione	*to intend*
avere paura	*to be afraid*
avere vergogna	*to be ashamed*
avere voglia	*to feel like*
essere contento	*to be pleased*
essere curioso	*to be curious*
essere felice	*to be happy*

essere stanco	*to be tired of*
essere stufo	*to be fed up with*
accorgersi	*to notice*
ammettere	*to admit*
aspettare	*to wait*
aspettarsi	*to hope, to expect to*
augurarsi	*to hope*
cercare	*to try*
cessare	*to cease, stop*
chiedere	*to ask*
credere	*to believe*
decidere	*to decide*
diffidare	*to distrust*
dimenticare/si	*to forget*
dire	*to say*
domandare	*to ask*
dubitare	*to doubt*
fare a meno	*to do without*
fare finta	*to pretend*
fidarsi	*to trust*
fingere	*to pretend*
finire	*to finish*
lagnarsi	*to complain*
lamentarsi	*to complain*
meravigliarsi	*to be surprised at*
minacciare	*to threaten*
non vedere l'ora	*to look forward to*
offrirsi	*to offer*
pensare	*to plan, think of*
pentirsi	*to regret*
pregare	*to beg*
promettere	*to promise*
rendersi conto	*to realise*
ricordare/si	*to remember*
rifiutare/si	*to refuse*
sapere	*to know*
sentirsi	*to feel like*
sforzarsi	*to try hard*
smettere	*to stop, give up*
sognare	*to dream of doing*
sperare	*to hope*
stancarsi	*to get tired of*
stufarsi	*to be fed up with*
stupirsi	*to be amazed*
temere	*to fear, be afraid*
tentare	*to try, attempt*
vantarsi	*to boast*
vergognarsi	*to be ashamed*
vivere	*to live on*

Mi fido di te   *I trust you*
Si vergogna di me   *He's ashamed of me*
Non vedo l'ora di partire   *I'm looking forward to leaving*
Ha smesso di parlare   *He stopped talking*
Mi rendo conto delle difficoltà   *I realise the difficulties*
Penso di partire domani   *I'm thinking of leaving tomorrow*
Cosa pensi del film?   *What do you think of the film?*

Note the expressions:
>   Ho detto di no/di sì   *I said no/yes*
>   Penso/credo/spero di sì   *I think/believe/hope so*
>   Penso/credo/spero di no   *I don't think/believe so, I hope not*

4   Verbs and expressions with a

i)   The following require **a** before infinitive, noun or pronoun:

abituarsi★   *to get used to*
affrettarsi   *to hurry*
aiutare   *to help*
assistere   *to attend, participate in*
assomigliare★   *to resemble, look like*
andare   *to go (and)*
annoiarsi   *to be bored*
avere ragione   *to be right*
avere torto   *to be wrong*

cominciare   *to begin*
continuare   *to continue*
convincere   *to persuade*
costringere   *to force/compel*

dare fastidio★   *to bother*
decidersi   *to make up one's mind*
dedicarsi★   *to devote oneself*
divertirsi   *to enjoy oneself*

esitare   *to hesitate*
essere deciso   *to be determined*
essere disposto   *to be prepared*
essere pronto   *to be ready*

fermarsi   *to stop*
forzare   *to force*

giocare   *to play*

imparare   *to learn*
impegnarsi   *to undertake to*
incoraggiare   *to encourage*
insegnare★   *to teach*
invitare   *to invite*

mandare★   *to send*
mettersi   *to set about, to begin*

obbligare   *to oblige/force*

parlare★   *to talk*
persuadere   *to persuade*
prepararsi   *to get ready to*
provare   *to try*

rassegnarsi   *to resign oneself*
rinunciare   *to give up*
rispondere★   *to answer, reply*
riuscire   *to succeed*
rivolgersi★   *to address oneself to*

sparare★   *to shoot at*
sopravvivere★   *to survive, to outlive*

telefonare★   *to telephone*
tornare   *to return, to do again*

voler bene★   *to be fond of, to love*

Ho pensato al problema   *I've thought about the problem*
Mi sono preparato a partire   *I got ready to leave*
Si è messa a studiare   *She began to study*
Ho provato a capire   *I tried to understand*

Notes
a) Verbs marked ★ require **a** before a person and hence an indirect object pronoun: this is not the case for the others on the list:
>   Gli insegno a leggere   *I teach him to read*
>   Le assomigli molto   *You resemble her a lot*

but:
>   Lo aiuto a leggere   *I help him to read*
>   La devi convincere a venire   *You must persuade her to come*

b) Note the following expressions:
>   andare a trovare qualcuno   *to visit someone*
>   mandare a chiamare qualcuno   *to send for someone*
>   tornare a fare qualcosa   *to do something again*

ii)   The following double object verbs require **a** before a person and hence an indirect object pronoun:

chiedere qlco. a qlcu.	*to ask s.o. for s.th.*
comprare qlco. a qlcu.	*to buy s.th. for s.o.*
consegnare qlco. a qlcu.	*to deliver s.th. to s.o.*
consigliare qlco a qlcu.	*to recommend s.th. to s.o.*
dare qlco. a qlcu.	*to give s.o. s.th.*
dire qlco. a qlcu.	*to tell s.o. s.th.*
far sapere qlco. a qlcu.	*to let s.o. know s.th.*
far vedere qlco. a qlcu.	*to show s.o. s.th.*
insegnare qlco. a qlcu.	*to teach s.o. s.th.*
inviare qlco. a qlcu.	*to send s.o. s.th.*
leggere qlco. a qlcu.	*to read s.th. to s.o.*
mandare qlco. a qlcu.	*to send s.th. to s.o.*
offrire qlco. a qlcu.	*to offer s.o. s.th.*
portare qlco. a qlcu.	*to bring s.o. s.th.*
presentare qlco../qlcu. a qlcu.	*to present s.th. or s.o. to s.o.*
prestare qlco. a qlcu.	*to lend s.o. s.th.*
promettere qlco. a qlcu.	*to promise s.o. s.th.*
proporre qlco. a qlcu.	*to propose s.th. to s.o.*
regalare qlco. a qlcu.	*to give s.th. to s.o. [gift]*
restituire qlco. a qlcu.	*to give s.th. back to s.o.*
rubare qlco. a qlcu.	*to steal s.th. from s.o.*
scrivere qlco. a qlcu.	*to write s.th. to s.o.*
spiegare qlco. a qlcu.	*to expain s.th. to s.o.*
suggerire qlco. a qlcu.	*to suggest s.th. to s.o.*

Ho chiesto un aumento al direttore   *I've asked the director for a rise*
Gli ho chiesto un aumento   *I've asked him for a rise*

5   Verbs taking a and di

Many common verbs require **a** with the person and **di** before an infinitive:

chiedere a qlcu. di	*to ask s.o. to*
comandare a qlcu. di	*to order s.o. to*
consentire a qlcu. di	*to allow s.o. to*
consigliare a qlcu. di	*to advise s.o. to*
dire a qlcu. di	*to tell s.o. to*
domandare a qlcu. di	*to ask s.o. to*
impedire a qlcu. di	*to prevent s.o. from*
ordinare a qlcu. di	*to order s.o. to*
permettere a qlcu. di	*to allow s.o. to*
proibire a qlcu. di	*to prohibit s.o. from*
proporre a qlcu. di	*to propose s.o. should*
ricordare a qlcu. di	*to remind s.o. to*

sconsigliare a qlcu. di   *to advise s.o. not to*
suggerire a qlcu. di   *to suggest s.o. should*
vietare a qlcu. di   *to forbid s.o. to*

A few verbs used impersonally are also in this category:
andare a qlcu. di   *to be fine/all right for s.o. to*
capitare a qlcu. di   *to happen to s.o. to*
succedere a qlcu. di   *to happen to s.o. to*

Ho chiesto al direttore di darmi un aumento
I've asked the director to give me a rise
Gli ho chiesto di darmi un aumento
I've asked him to give me a rise
A Lina capita qualchevolta di perdere il treno?
Does Lina ever miss the train? [lit. does it ever happen to her
    to miss the train?]
Sì, le capita ogni tanto   *Yes, it happens to her occasionally*

6   Verbs and expressions requiring da
There are not many of these and they do not often cause
confusion.

derivare **da**   *to derive from*
diverso/differente **da**   *different from/to*
difendere **da**   *to defend from/against*
dipendere **da**   *to depend on*
giudicare **da**   *to judge by/on*
indipendente **da**   *independent of*

7   Verbs and expressions requiring per
Note the following linked with place:

camminare **per** strada   *to walk **along** the street*
girare **per** il mondo   *to go **around** the world*
incontrare qlcu. **per** strada   *to meet s.o. **in** the street*
partire **per** . . . Londra   *to leave **for** London*
passare **per** . . . Londra   *to pass **through** London*

8   Verbs and expressions requiring in, su, con
The following can cause confusion with English:

entrare **in**   *to enter*
incidere **su**   *to affect*
congratularsi **con**   *to congratulate s.o.*

   Sono entrato **in** una stanza enorme
   I entered an enormous room
   Questo non incide **sulla** decisione
   This doesn't affect the decision
   Mi sono congratulato **con** lui   *I congratulated him*

VIII   VERBS

The emphasis in this section is on helping you deal with problems
and irregularities of the Present and Passato Prossimo tenses.
The regular forms, plus notes on how to use the tenses are in the
Systems sections.

A   PRESENT TENSE

I   Regular forms
See Systems 2, note 6, p. 84 for **-are** and **-ere** verbs.
See Systems 3, note 1, p. 87 for **-ire** verbs. The uses of the
present are on p. 88 [Systems 3, note 3].

i)   -ire verbs
The majority of regular **-ire** verbs take the **-isco** pattern [like
finire and **capire**]. Below is a list of the main verbs which do
not take the **-isco** pattern.

aprire	*to open*	investire	*to invest*
avvertire	*to warn, notify*	offrire	*to offer*
bollire	*to boil*	partire	*to leave*
consentire	*to consent*	pentirsi	*to regret*
convertire	*to convert*	scoprire	*to discover*
coprire	*to cover*	seguire	*to follow*
divertire	*to amuse*	sentire	*to feel, to hear*
dormire	*to sleep*	servire	*to serve, be useful*
fuggire	*to run away, escape*	soffrire	*to suffer*
		vestire	*to dress*

Notes
a) Verbs which are compounds of any of the above follow the same
pattern: e.g. riaprire, ricoprire, risalire, riscoprire, risentire.
b) Some **-ire** verbs can take either pattern. The most common of these
are:
   applaudire   *to applaud* [applaudo/applaudisco]
   assorbire   *to absorb*
   inghiottire   *to swallow*
   mentire   *to lie*
   tossire   *to cough*

2   Irregular forms

i)   -are verbs

Infinitive	Present	Meaning
andare	vado vai va andiamo andate vanno	*to go*
dare	do dai dà diamo date danno	*to give*
fare[1]	faccio fai fa facciamo fate fanno	*to make, to do*
stare	sto stai sta stiamo state stanno	*to be, to stay*

Other verbs of this type:
1. rifare   *to redo*

ii)   -ere verbs

Infinitive	Present	Meaning
Auxiliaries:		
avere	ho hai ha abbiamo avete hanno	*to have*
essere	sono sei è siamo siete sono	*to be*

Modal verbs:

dovere	devo devi deve dobbiamo dovete devono	*to have to*
potere	posso puoi può possiamo potete possono	*to be able*
volere	voglio vuoi vuole vogliamo volete vogliono	*to want*

Other:

bere	bevo bevi beve beviamo bevete bevono	*to drink*
cogliere[1]	colgo cogli coglie cogliamo cogliete colgono	*to catch, gather*
cuocere	cuocio cuoci cuoce cociamo cocete cuociono	*to cook*
muovere[2]	muovo muovi muove muoviamo muovete muovono	*to move*
parere	paio pari pare paiamo parete paiono	*to appear*
piacere	piaccio piaci piace piacciamo piacete piacciono	*to like, please*
rimanere	rimango rimani rimane rimaniamo rimanete rimangono	*to stay, to remain*
sapere	so sai sa sappiamo sapete sanno	*to know*
scegliere	scelgo scegli sceglie scegliamo scegliete scelgono	*to choose*
sedere[3]	siedo siedi siede sediamo sedete siedono	*to sit*
tacere	taccio taci tace tacciamo tacete tacciono	*to be silent*
tenere[4]	tengo tieni tiene teniamo tenete tengono	*to hold, to have*

Other verbs of this type:

1 accogliere *to welcome;* raccogliere *to pick up, to gather, pick;* sciogliere *to melt, dissolve;* togliere *to remove, take off*
2 commuovere *to move [emotions];* promuovere *to promote*
3 possedere *to possess*
4 appartenere *to belong;* contenere *to contain;* mantenere *to keep, maintain;* ottenere *to obtain;* ritenere *to claim, to maintain*

Note: For **piacere** see Systems 6, note 2, p. 193. It is possible to use parts of the verb other than **piace** or **piacciono** as follows:

Io gli piaccio *He likes me [I am pleasing to him]*
Tu gli piaci *He likes you*

iii) –ire verbs

Infinitive	Present	Meaning
apparire	appaio appari appare appariamo apparite appaiono	*to appear*
cucire	cucio cuci cuce cuciamo cucite cuciono	*to sew*
dire[1]	dico dici dice diciamo dite dicono	*to say*
morire	muoio muori muore moriamo morite muoiono	*to die*
salire[2]	salgo sali sale saliamo salite salgono	*to go up, get into*
scomparire	scompaio scompari scompare scompariamo scomparite scompaiono	*to disappear*
udire	odo odi ode udiamo udite odono	*to hear*

uscire[3]	esco esci esce usciamo uscite escono	*to go out*
venire[4]	vengo vieni viene veniamo venite vengono	*to come*

Other verbs of this type:

1 contraddire *to contradict;* disdire *to cancel*
2 risalire *to date from; to go up/to get into again*
3 riuscire *to manage, succeed*
4 avvenire *to happen;* intervenire *to intervene*

Note
Apparire and **scomparire** can also take the **-isco** ending.

iv) Verbs based on –trarre:
These all have a similar pattern:

Infinitive	Present	Meaning
attrarre	attraggo attrai attrae attraiamo attraete attraggono	*to attract*

See also: distrarre: distrarsi *to entertain, to distract, to amuse oneself;* estrarre *to extract;* sottrarre *to take away;* trarre *to draw, to pull*

v) Verbs based on –porre:

Infinitive	Present	Meaning
comporre	compongo componi compone componiamo componete compongono	*to compose*

See also: esporre *to expose;* imporre *to impose;* opporre *to oppose;* porre *to place;* proporre *to propose;* supporre *to suppose.*

vi) Verbs based on –durre:

Infinitive	Present	Meaning
condurre	conduco conduci conduce conduciamo conducete conducono	*to lead, to conduct*

See also: dedurre *to deduce;* introdurre *to introduce;* produrre *to produce;* ridurre *to reduce;* sedurre *to seduce;* tradurre *to translate*

B   PRESENT PERFECT – PASSATO PROSSIMO

Regular forms

See Systems 6, notes 3–4, p. 194.
There are notes on its use in Systems 6, note 5, p. 195.
Remember, there are two parts to the verb – an auxiliary verb and a past participle.

Which auxiliary? Essere or avere?

The majority of verbs take **avere**. If you learn the important ones taking **essere** then you can assume the others take **avere**.

I   Verbs taking essere

i)   Many intransitive verbs

andare	*to go*	morire	*to die*
apparire	*to appear*	nascere	*to be born*
arrivare	*to arrive*	partire	*to leave*
bastare	*to be enough*	pervenire	*to arrive, come to*
cadere	*to fall*	restare	*to stay*
costare	*to cost*	rimanere	*to stay*
crollare	*to collapse*	ritornare	*to return*
dipendere	*to depend*	riuscire	*to manage, succeed*
divenire	*to become*	scadere	*to run out, expire*
diventare	*to become*	scappare	*to dash, to escape*
durare	*to last*	sparire	*to disappear*
emergere	*to emerge*	stare	*to stay, be*
entrare	*to come in*	svenire	*to faint*
esistere	*to exist*	tornare	*to return*
essere	*to be*	uscire	*to go out*
intervenire	*to intervene*	venire	*to come*

Notes
a) For a definition of intransitive see Basics, note 6iv, p. 238.
b) **Beware:** do not assume that all verbs of movement take **essere**. There are some which don't. [See Ref. VIII, 2i and 3, pp. 250 and 251.]

ii)   Impersonal verbs

These verbs express actions which cannot be attributed to a specific person or thing, for example, verbs for the weather. These are always used in the *it* form [third person singular].

balenare	*to flash with lightning*	nevicare	*to snow*
diluviare	*to pour*	piovere	*to rain*
grandinare	*to hail*	tuonare	*to thunder*
lampeggiare	*to lighten*		

Note: In speech it is common to use **avere** as well as **essere** as the auxiliary. You can say **è piovuto** or **ha** piovuto. [See Profile 2, p. 221]

iii)   Verbs used impersonally

There are a number of verbs, like **piacere**, whose *it* and *they* forms [third person, singular and plural] tend to be used, often in conjunction with **mi, ti, gli, le, Le, ci, vi**.

accadere	*to happen*	mancare	*to lack, be missing*
avvenire	*to happen*	occorrere	*to be needed*
bastare	*to be enough*	parere	*to seem*
bisognare	*to be necessary*	piacere	*to like*
capitare	*to chance, happen to*	rincrescere	*to regret*
convenire	*to be advisable*	sembrare	*to seem*
dispiacere	*to be sorry*	servire	*to be needed*
importare	*to matter, to mind*	succedere	*to happen*

mi **è** piaciuto; gli **è** bastato; le **è** sembrato; Le **è** successo? ci **è** capitato, etc.

iv)   Reflexive verbs

If a verb is reflexive it always takes **essere**.

Infinitive	Passato prossimo	Meaning
alzarsi	mi sono alzato/a	*to get up*
divertirsi	mi sono divertito/a	*to enjoy oneself*
fermarsi	mi sono fermato/a	*to stop*
lavarsi	mi sono lavato/a	*to wash oneself*

Note
Beware: many reflexive verbs can also be non reflexive – and take **avere**:
alzare   ho alzato la voce   *I raised my voice*
lavare   ho lavato il pavimento   *I washed the floor*
fermare   ho fermato la macchina   *I stopped the car*

2   Essere and avere

Some verbs take **essere** if they are being used intransitively. Otherwise they take **avere**:

cominciare   finire   salire   scendere:
Il film è cominciato/finito tardi   [*intransitive*]
Sono salito in treno/sono sceso dal treno
Ho cominciato/finito il lavoro   [*transitive*]
Ho salito le scale/ho sceso le scale

i)   Other verbs of this type include:

aumentare	*to increase*	passare	*to pass, to spend [time]*
cambiare	*to change*	peggiorare	*to worsen*
correre	*to run*	salire	*to go up/get in*
dimagrire	*to lose weight, make thin*	saltare	*to jump*
		scendere	*to go down, get out of*
guarire	*to get well/cure*	volare	*to fly*
migliorare	*to improve*		

Notes
a) Transitive and intransitive verbs are defined in Basics 6 iv, p. 238.
b) A few verbs can take **avere** as well as **essere** when being used intransitively: **correre, saltare, volare** take **essere** when they express movement to a place.
sono corso a casa; **sono** volato a vederlo; **sono** saltato dal treno
However, in other intransitive expressions they take **avere**:
ho corso per due ore; **ho** saltato per cinque minuti; **ho** volato in elicottero
Like all the other verbs in the list they take **avere** when there is a direct object:
ho corso un chilometro

ii)   Modal verbs: dovere, potere, volere

These can take either **avere** or **essere**. This depends on the auxiliary required by the infinitive which follows:
ho potuto studiare   [studiare takes avere]
sono potuto/a partire   [partire takes essere]
In spoken Italian **avere** is often used instead of **essere**:
ho dovuto partire

If **dovere, potere** or **volere** are used with a reflexive verb there are two possible constructions:

With **avere**:	With **essere**:
Gina ha voluto sposarsi	Gina si è voluta sposare
Le ragazze hanno potuto divertirsi	Le ragazze si sono potute divertire

These are both used in spoken Italian.

3 Avere

Avere is used with transitive verbs. It is also used with the intransitive verbs below:

abitare	*to live*	parlare	*to speak*
brillare	*to shine*	partecipare	*to participate*
camminare	*to walk*	passeggiare	*to walk/stroll*
chiacchierare	*to chat*	piangere	*to cry*
cenare	*to have supper*	piovere★	*to rain*
collaborare	*to collaborate*	pranzare	*to have lunch*
dormire	*to sleep*	respirare	*to breathe*
esagerare	*to exaggerate*	ridere	*to laugh*
esitare	*to hesitate*	sciare	*to ski*
giocare	*to play*	sopravvivere★	*to survive*
girare	*to turn*	sorridere	*to smile*
insistere	*to insist*	starnutire	*to sneeze*
litigare	*to quarrel*	telefonare	*to 'phone*
lottare	*to struggle*	tossire	*to cough*
nevicare★	*to snow*	viaggiare	*to travel*
pattinare	*to skate*	vivere★	*to live*

★**Essere** can be used with the verbs marked ★, but it is less usual in everyday speech.

4 Past participles: 124 irregular verbs

Verbs with irregular participles are often common ones. You will need to learn them gradually:

	Infinitive	Participle	Meaning
anto	piangere	pianto	*to cry*
	rimpiangere	rimpianto	*to regret*
arso	apparire	apparso	*to appear*
	parere	parso	*to seem*
	scomparire	scomparso	*to disappear*
	spargere	sparso	*to spread*
asto	rimanere	rimasto	*to stay/remain*
aso	evadere	evaso	*to escape*
	invadere	invaso	*to invade*
	persuadere	persuaso	*to persuade*
ato	essere	stato	*to be*
	nascere	nato	*to be born*
	stare	stato	*to stay, to be*
atto	fare	fatto	*to make, do*
	soddisfare	soddisfatto	*to satisfy*
	attrarre	attratto	*to attract*
	distrarre	distratto	*to distract, entertain take mind off*
elto	scegliere	scelto	*to choose*
ento	spegnere	spento	*to turn off, put out*
	redimere	redento	*to redeem*
erso	sommergere	sommerso	*to submerge*
	perdere	perso	*to lose*
erto	aprire	aperto	*to open*
	offrire	offerto	*to offer*
	scoprire	scoperto	*to discover*
	soffrire	sofferto	*to suffer*

eso	accendere	acceso	*to light, put on*
	comprendere	compreso	*to include*
	difendere	difeso	*to defend*
	offendere	offeso	*to offend*
	rendere	reso	*to give back, to make*
	scendere	sceso	*to descend, get out of*
	sorprendere	sorpreso	*to surprise*
	spendere	speso	*to spend*
esso	succedere	successo	*to happen*
	ammettere	ammesso	*to admit*
	mettere	messo	*to put*
	permettere	permesso	*to permit*
	promettere	promesso	*to promise*
	smettere	smesso	*to stop, cease*
	esprimere	espresso	*to express*
esto	chiedere	chiesto	*to ask*
	richiedere	richiesto	*to request*
etto	contraddire	contraddetto	*to contradict*
	dire	detto	*to say*
	disdire	disdetto	*to cancel*
	costringere	costretto	*to force*
	stringere	stretto	*to squeeze, to shake [hand]*
	correggere	corretto	*to correct*
	leggere	letto	*to read*
	proteggere	protetto	*to protect*
into	distinguere	distinto	*to distinguish*
	convincere	convinto	*to convince, persuade*
	dipingere	dipinto	*to paint*
	fingere	finto	*to pretend*
	spingere	spinto	*to push*
	vincere	vinto	*to win*
iso	decidere	deciso	*to decide*
	dividere	diviso	*to divide*
	ridere	riso	*to laugh*
	sorridere	sorriso	*to smile*
	uccidere	ucciso	*to kill*
isto	prevedere	previsto	*to arrange, foresee*
	vedere	visto	*to see*
itto	descrivere	descritto	*to describe*
	iscrivere	iscritto	*to enrol*
	scrivere	scritto	*to write*
	friggere	fritto	*to fry*
	sconfiggere	sconfitto	*to defeat*
issuto	sopravvivere	sopravvissuto	*to survive*
	vivere	vissuto	*to live*
iuto	conoscere	conosciuto	*to know, meet*
	compiere	compiuto	*to undertake*
	dispiacere	dispiaciuto	*to mind, be sorry*
	piacere	piaciuto	*to like*
	tacere	taciuto	*to be silent*

ito	This regular **-ire** ending is used for a group of **-ere** verbs:		
	assistere	assistito	*to attend*
	esistere	esistito	*to exist*
	insistere	insistito	*to insist*
	resistere	resistito	*to resist*
olto	accogliere	accolto	*to welcome*
	[rac]cogliere	colto	*to pick, gather*
	togliere	tolto	*to remove*
	sciogliere	sciolto	*to dissolve*
	risolvere	risolto	*to resolve*
	rivolgersi	rivolto	*to address, speak to*
	svolgere	svolto	*to carry out, take place*
	seppellire	sepolto	*to bury*
orso	correre	corso	*to run*
	trascorrere	trascorso	*to spend [time]*
	mordere	morso	*to bite*
orto	accorgersi	accorto	*to notice, realise*
	sporgersi	sporto	*to lean out of*
	morire	morto	*to die*
oso	esplodere	esploso	*to explode*
	rodere	roso	*to gnaw*
osso	commuovere	commosso	*to move [emotion]*
	muovere	mosso	*to move*
	promuovere	promosso	*to promote*
	scuotere	scosso	*to shake*
osto	comporre	composto	*to compose*
	imporre	imposto	*to impose*
	opporre	opposto	*to oppose*
	proporre	proposto	*to propose*
	nascondere	nascosto	*to hide*
	rispondere	risposto	*to reply*
otto	introdurre	introdotto	*to introduce*
	produrre	prodotto	*to produce*
	ridurre	ridotto	*to reduce*
	tradurre	tradotto	*to translate*
	cuocere	cotto	*to cook*
	interrompere	interrotto	*to interrupt*
	rompere	rotto	*to break*
unto	aggiungere	aggiunto	*to add*
	giungere	giunto	*to arrive at, reach*
	raggiungere	raggiunto	*to reach, attain*
uso	confondere	confuso	*to confuse, muddle mix up, merge*
	diffondere	diffuso	*to spread*
	chiudere	chiuso	*to close*
	deludere	deluso	*to disappoint*
	escludere	escluso	*to exclude*
usso	discutere	discusso	*to discuss*
utto	distruggere	distrutto	*to destroy*
uto	This regular **-ere** ending is used for:		
	venire	venuto	*to come*

Index of Grammar

This index refers to the material in Systems, Troubleshooting, Basics and Reference.

LEXIS (Italian–English)

Notes:

1   The English translations apply to the words as used in the course.

2   Stress patterns: see Reference VI, 2, p. 245. Irregular stress patterns and those in words ending in two vowels are marked by a dot under the stressed vowel.

3   Abbreviations: m = masculine; f = feminine; s = singular; pl = plural; pp = past participle; inv. = invariable; pr = present; adj = adjective; adv = adverb.

4   Symbols: † = irregular present; ★ = takes **essere** [see Reference VIIIB, 1, p. 250]; ⁽★⁾ = takes **essere** and **avere**, depending on how the verb is used [see Reference VIIIB, 2, p. 250]; (pr –o) = the present tense of the **–ire** verb is like **dormire**, not **finire** [see Systems 3, note 1, p. 87 and Reference VIIIA, 1i, p. 248].

5   Countries and nationalities are listed in Reference III, pp. 242–3.

A

a   *to; at; in*
abbaiare   *to bark*
abbandonare   *to abandon; to leave*
abbandonato/a   *abandoned, left*
abbastanza   *fairly, quite*
l'abbazia   *abbey*
abbiamo   *see* avere
l'abbigliamento   *clothes*
l'abbonamento   *subscription, season ticket*
   fare un abbonamento   *to get a season ticket*
l'abbonato   *subscriber*
abbronzarsi★   *to get a tan*
l'abete (m)   *fir*
l'abitante (m/f)   *inhabitant*
abitare   *to live*
l'abito   *dress; suit*
   l'abito da sera   *evening dress*
abituarsi★   *to get used to*
gli Abruzzi   *Abruzzi (Italian region)*
accadere★   *to happen*
accanto (a)   *next to, beside*
accendere (pp acceso)   *to light; to switch on*
accettare   *to accept*
l'acciaio   *steel*
accidenti!   *bother! damn!*
accogliere (pp accolto)   *to welcome*
accomodarsi★   *to make oneself comfortable*

accompagnare   *to accompany*
accontentare   *to keep happy*
accorciare   *to shorten*
l'accordo   *agreement*
   d'accordo   *fine*
accorgersi★ (pp accorto)   *to notice; to realise*
l'acqua   *water*
acquatico/a (m pl –ci)   *aquatic*
l'acquisto   *purchase*
ad = a
adagio   *slowly*
adatto/a   *suitable*
l'addebito   *charge*
addolcito/a   *sweetened*
addormentarsi★   *to fall asleep*
adesso   *now*
adorabile   *adorable*
l'adulto   *adult*
l'aereo   *aeroplane*
aerobico/a (m pl –ci)   *aerobic*
l'aeroporto   *airport*
l'afa   *sultry heat*
gli affari (pl)   *business*
affascinante   *fascinating*
affatto   *at all*
   non ... affatto   *not at all*
affermarsi★   *to make oneself known*
affittare   *to rent*
affollato/a   *crowded*
l'affresco   *fresco*
affrettarsi★   *to hurry*
l'agenda   *diary*
l'agenzia   *agency*
l'aggettivo   *adjective*
aggiornato/a   *updated*
aggiungere (pp aggiunto)   *to add*
l'aglio   *garlic*
l'agnello   *lamb*
agro/a   *sour*
aiutare   *to help*
l'aiuto   *help*
l'albergo   *hotel*
l'albero   *tree*
l'albicocca   *apricot*
l'alcool (m)   *alcohol*
alcuni/e   *some, a few*
al di là   *beyond*
l'alimentare (m)   *grocer's*
l'allarme (m)   *alarm*
   impianto allarme   *burglar alarm*
l'allegria   *cheerfulness*
allegro/a   *cheerful, happy*
allenarsi★   *to train*
allora   *so, then, in that case*
l'alluminio   *aluminium*
allungare   *to lengthen*

almeno   *at least*
le Alpi   *Alps*
l'alpinismo   *climbing*
alpino/a   *alpine*
alto/a   *high*
altresì   *also*
altrettanto!   *the same to you!*
altrimenti   *otherwise*
altro/a   *other, another, more*
altro (inv)   *else*
   che altro   *anything else?*
   senz'altro   *definitely*
altrui   *of others, of other people*
l'alunno/l'alunna (m/f)   *pupil*
alzare   *to lift up*
alzarsi★   *to get up*
amare   *to love*
amaro/a   *bitter*
l'amaro   *bitter after-dinner liqueur*
l'amatriciana   *amatriciana sauce*
ambientale   *environmental*
l'ambiente (m)   *environment*
   la Lega Ambiente   *Environment League*
l'amico/l'amica (m pl –ci)   *friend*
l'ammiratore (m)   *admirer*
ammettere (pp ammesso)   *to admit*
l'amore (m)   *love*
l'anagrafe (f)   *registry office*
analcolico/a (m pl –ci)   *non-alcoholic*
l'analisi (f) (inv)   *analysis*
analizzare   *to analyse*
l'anatra   *duck*
anche   *also, too, as well; even*
   anch'io   *I also, me too*
ancora   *still; again; some more*
andare†★   *to go*
   come va?   *how's it going? how are things?*
   c'è qualcosa che non va?   *is something wrong?*
l'andata   *single (ticket)*
   l'andata e ritorno   *return (ticket)*
l'anello   *ring*
l'anfiteatro   *amphitheatre*
l'angelo   *angel*
l'angolo   *corner*
l'anguilla   *eel*
l'animale (m)   *animal*
   gli animali domestici   *pets*
   gli animali selvatici   *wild animals*
animato/a   *animated*
l'animazione (f)   *liveliness*
l'anno   *year*
   quanti anni hai/ha?   *how old are you?*
annoiarsi★   *to be bored*

l'anticipo (m)   *advance*
   in anticipo   *early*
antico/a   *old, ancient*
l'antipasto   *starters, hors d'oeuvre*
antipatico/a (m pl –ci)   *nasty,*
   unpleasant
antisettico/a (m pl –ci)   *antiseptic*
l'antivivisezione (f)   *antivivisection*
anziano/a   *elderly*
l'ape (f)   *bee*
l'aperitivo   *aperitif*
aperto/a   *open*
   all'aperto   *in the open*
apparire†★ (pp apparso)   *to appear*
l'appartamento   *apartment, flat*
appartenere★   *to belong*
gli Appennini   *Apennines*
l'appetito   *appetite*
   buon appetito!   *good appetite!*
applaudire   *to applaud*
applicato/a   *applied*
apprezzato/a   *appreciated*
approssimativo/a   *approximate*
l'appuntamento   *appointment*
aprile (m)   *April*
aprire (pr –o) (pp aperto)   *to open*
   aprire il rubinetto   *to turn on the*
   tap
l'apriscatole (m)   *tin opener*
l'aquila   *eagle*
l'arancia   *orange*
l'aranciata   *orangeade*
l'arancino   *rice and cheese savoury*
arancione   *orange*
l'architettura   *architecture*
l'archeologo (pl –gi)   *archaeologist*
l'arco   *bow*
   il tiro con l'arco   *archery*
l'area   *area*
l'argento   *silver*
l'aria   *air*
   all'aria aperta   *in the open air*
l'armadio   *cupboard; wardrobe*
l'armonia   *harmony*
l'aroma (m)   *aroma, fragrance*
l'arpa   *harp*
arrabbiato/a   *angry*
l'arredamento (m)   *interior design;*
   furnishings
arricchire   *to enhance, enrich*
arrivare★   *to arrive*
arrivederci   *goodbye*
l'arrivo   *arrival*
arrossire★   *to blush*
arrosto (inv)   *roasted*
l'arte (f)   *art*
l'Arte (f)   *medieval guild*
articolarsi★ (in)   *to be made up of*
l'articolo   *article*
l'artigianato   *craftsmanship*
l'artista (m/f) (m pl gli artisti,
   f pl le artiste)   *artist*
l'ascensore (m)   *lift*

l'asciugamano   *towel*
asciutto/a   *dry*
ascoltare   *to listen to*
l'asilo   *nursery*
l'asino   *donkey*
gli asparagi (pl)   *asparagus*
l'aspirapolvere (m)   *vacuum cleaner*
aspettare   *to wait*
aspettarsi★   *to hope, to expect to*
l'aspetto   *aspect*
l'aspirina   *aspirin*
assaggiare   *to taste*
assediare   *to besiege*
l'assegno   *cheque*
   la carta assegni   *cheque card*
   il libretto degli assegni   *cheque*
   book
l'Assessorato all'Ambiente (m)
   Environment Department
l'assicurazione   *insurance*
assieme = insieme   *together*
l'assistente (m/f)   *assistant*
   l'assistente sociale   *social worker*
assistere   *to attend; to participate in*
assomigliare   *to resemble, to look like*
assorbire   *to absorb*
assurdo/a   *absurd*
astemio/a   *teetotal*
l'astrologia   *astrology*
Atene   *Athens*
l'atleta (m/f)   *athlete*
l'atmosfera   *atmosphere*
attaccare   *to plug in*
attaccato/a   *attached*
attento/a   *careful*
   stare attento   *to be careful*
l'attico   *penthouse*
l'attimo   *moment*
   un attimo   *hold on (a moment)*
l'attività (inv)   *activity*
   svolgere un'attività   *to do an activity*
l'attore/l'attrice   *actor/actress*
attorniato/a   *surrounded*
attrarre† (pp attratto)   *to attract*
attraversare   *to cross*
attraverso   *through*
attrezzato/a   *well-equipped*
attualmente   *at present*
augurarsi★   *to hope to*
aumentare(★)   *to increase*
l'aumento   *payrise*
l'autista (m/f) (m pl gli autisti,
   f pl le autiste)   *driver*
l'autobus (m) (inv)   *bus*
l'automobilismo   *motor racing*
autonomo/a   *self-contained*
l'autore (m)   *author*
l'autorità (inv)   *authority*
l'autostrada   *motorway*
l'autunno   *autumn*
   in autunno   *in the autumn*
avanti   *ahead; forward*
   avanti di   *fast (time)*

   avanti di cinque minuti   *five*
   minutes fast
avere†   *to have*
   avere fame/sete   *to be hungry/thirsty*
   avere caldo/freddo   *to be hot/cold*
   avere fretta   *to be in a hurry*
   avere voglia di   *to feel like*
   avere tempo di   *to have time to*
   avere bisogno di   *to need*
   avere da fare   *to be busy, to have*
   a lot to do
l'avvelenamento   *poisoning*
l'avvenimento   *event*
avvenire†★   *to happen*
avvertire (pr –o)   *to warn, to notify*
avvicinarsi★   *to approach*
l'avvocato   *(m/f) lawyer*
avvolto/a   *wrapped*
l'azienda   *firm*
   azienda vinicola   *wine-making firm*
azzurro/a   *blue*

B

la bacca   *berry*
il bacio   *kiss*
bagnato/a   *wet*
il bagno   *bathroom*
   fare il bagno   *to have a bath*
   il bagno di servizio
   utility room
il balcone   *balcony*
ballare   *to dance*
il balletto   *ballet*
il ballo   *dance*
la bambina   *child, baby, little girl*
il bambino   *child, baby, little boy*
la banana   *banana*
la banca   *bank*
la bandiera   *flag*
il bar (inv)   *bar*
la barba   *beard*
   farsi la barba   *to shave*
il barbecue   *barbecue*
il barista   *barman*
barocco/a   *baroque*
la barriera   *barrier*
la base   *base, foundation*
   di base   *basic*
la basilica   *basilica*
la Basilicata   *Basilicata (Italian region)*
il basilico   *basil*
basso/a   *low; short*
il basso   *bass; bass guitar*
bastare★   *to be enough*
   basta così?   *is that all?*
la battaglia   *battle*
la batteria   *drums (drum kit)*
il battesimo   *christening*
beato   *lucky*
   beato/a me/te!   *lucky me/you!*
bei   *see bello*
bel   *see bello*

la bellezza *beauty*
   l'istituto di bellezza *beauty salon*
bello/a (bel) *beautiful, nice;* che
   bello! *how lovely!*
benché *although*
bendare *to blindfold*
bene *well, fine*
   va bene *okay, that's fine*
   sto bene *I'm fine*
il beneficio *benefit*
la benzina *petrol*
   finire la benzina *to run out of petrol*
bere† (pp bevuto) *to drink*
il bermuda (inv) *Bermuda shorts*
la bevanda *drink*
la biancheria *linen*
bianco/a *white*
la bibita *cold drink*
la biblioteca *library*
il bicchiere *glass*
la bicicletta *bicycle*
   con la bicicletta *by bike*
la biglietteria *ticket office*
il biglietto *ticket*
   fare il biglietto *to get a ticket*
la Bilancia *Libra*
il biliardo *billiards*
bilingue *bilingual*
il bimbo *child*
il binario *platform*
il binocolo *binoculars, field glasses*
la biografia *biography*
il biologo (m pl –gi) *biologist*
biondo/a *blond(e)*
la birra *beer*
il biscotto *biscuit*
bisognare★ *to be necessary*
il bisogno *need*
   avere bisogno (di) *to need*
la bistecca *steak*
blu (inv) *blue*
   blu scuro *dark blue*
   blu marino *navy blue*
il blu di Genova (inv) *denim*
i blue jeans (pl) *jeans*
le bocce (pl) *bowls*
la bolletta *bill*
   la bolletta del telefono *telephone
   bill*
bollire (pr –o) *to boil*
la borsa *bag; stock exchange*
il borsellino *purse*
la borsetta a tracolla *shoulder bag*
il bosco *wood*
   botanico/a *botanic*
   i giardini botanici *botanic gardens*
la bottiglia *bottle*
il bottone *button*
il box (inv) *garage*
il bracciale/il braccialetto *bracelet*
il braccio (pl le braccia) *arm*
   in braccio *in one's arms*
bravo/a *good, expert*

breve *short*
il bridge (inv) *bridge (game)*
brillare *to shine*
la brioche (inv) *croissant*
la briscola *briscola (card game)*
il brodo *broth, stock*
bruciare *to burn*
la bruschetta *bruschetta (garlic bread)*
brutto/a *ugly; nasty; unpleasant*
   fa brutto tempo *the weather's nasty*
   non è una brutta idea *it's not a bad
   idea*
bucare *to puncture*
bucato/a *punctured*
il bucato *washing*
   fare il bucato *to do the washing*
il buco *hole*
il bue (pl i buoi) *ox*
buffo/a *funny*
buio/a *dark*
il buio *dark, darkness*
buonanotte *good night*
buonasera *good afternoon; good
   evening*
buongiorno *good morning*
buono/a *good*
il burocratese *language of bureaucracy*
il burro *butter*
la bussola *compass*
la busta *envelope*
   la busta paga *wage packet*
buttare *to throw out*
   buttare la spazzatura *to throw out
   the rubbish*

C

la caccia *hunt*
il cachemire *cashmere*
cadere★ *to fall*
   lasciare cadere *to drop*
il caffè (inv) *coffee*
la caffettiera *coffee pot*
la Calabria *Calabria (Italian region)*
il calcio *football; kick*
caldo/a *hot*
   avere caldo *to be hot*
il caldo *heat*
il calendario *calendar*
il calore *warmth*
la calzamaglia *tights*
le calze (pl) *stockings*
i calzini (pl) *socks*
cambiare(*) *to change*
la camera *room, chamber*
   la camera da letto *bedroom*
   la musica da camera *chamber music*
il cameriere *waiter*
la camicia *shirt*
   la camicia da notte *nightdress*
la camicetta *blouse*
il camino *fire-place*
camminare *to walk*
la camminata *walk*

la camomilla *camomile*
il camoscio *suede*
la campagna *country(side); campaign*
la campana *bell; disposal bank*
la Campania *Campania (Italian region)*
il campanile *bell tower*
il campeggio *camping; campsite*
campestre *rural, country*
il campo *court, pitch; field; camp*
   nel campo di *in the field of*
   il campo di concentramento
   concentration camp
il canale *channel*
il cancello *gate*
il cane *dog*
la canoa *canoeing*
il canone *rule*
la canottiera *vest*
il/la cantante *singer*
cantare *to sing*
il cantautore *writer singer, singer-
   songwriter*
il cantico (m pl –ci) *canticle*
la cantina *cellar; wine-cellar*
il canto *singing; song*
la canzone *song*
la canzonetta *little poem, ditty*
CAP (codice di avviamento
   postale) *postal code*
la capanna *hut*
i capelli (pl) *hair*
capire *to understand*
   ho capito *I see*
la capitale *capital*
il capitano *captain*
capitare★ *to chance, to happen to*
il capo *boss*
il capolavoro *masterpiece*
il capolinea *terminus*
il capoluogo *regional/provincial capital*
la cappella *chapel*
il cappello *hat*
il cappotto *coat*
il cappuccino *cappuccino (white coffee)*
la capra *goat*
il carabiniere *Carabiniere (semi-military
   police officer)*
la caramella *sweet*
caratteristico/a (m pl –ci)
   characteristic
il cardigan (inv) *cardigan*
la carne *meat*
caro/a *expensive (after the noun);
   dear (before the noun)*
la carota *carrot*
la carriera *career*
la carta *paper, card*
   le carte da gioco *playing cards*
   le carte napoletane *Neapolitan
   cards*
   la carta assegni *cheque card*
   la carta di credito *credit card*
   la carta d'identità *identity card*

la cartella *briefcase*
il cartello *signpost*
la cartoleria *stationer's*
la cartolina *postcard*
il cartone *cartoon*
   il cartone animato *(film) cartoon*
la casa *house*
   a casa *at home*
   la casa di confezione *clothing manufacturer*
il casale *farmhouse*
la casalinga *housewife*
   casalingo/a *home-made*
la cascata *waterfall*
la cascina *farmhouse*
il casello *toll station*
il caso *chance*
   per caso *by chance*
la cassa *till*
il cassetto *drawer*
il cassettone *chest-of-drawers*
la castagna *chestnut*
il castagno *chestnut tree*
   castano/a *brown*
il castello *castle*
il catalogo *catalogue*
il catamarano *catamaran*
la cattedrale *cathedral*
   cattivo/a *bad*
la cattura *capture*
   catturare *to capture*
il cavallo *horse*
   a cavallo *on horseback*
   il cavallo da tiro *cart horse*
il cavatappi *corkscrew*
il cavolo *cabbage*
   c'è *see ci 2*
   ce *see ci 1*
il cedro *cedar*
il cellulare *mobile phone*
la cena *supper, dinner*
   cenare *to dine*
il centinaio (pl le centinaia) *about a hundred*
   cento *hundred*
   per cento *per cent*
il centro *centre*
il/la centralinista *telephone operator*
il centralino *exchange, switchboard*
   cercare *to look for*
   cercare di *to try to*
la cerniera *zip*
il cerotto *sticking-plaster*
   certamente *certainly*
   certo *certainly, yes indeed*
   certo/a *certain*
il cervo *stag*
il cespuglio *bush, shrub*
   cessare *to cease, to stop*
il cestino *basket*
il cetriolo *cucumber*
   che *that, which, who, whom; than*
   che? che cosa? *what?*

che! *what! how!*
   che fortuna! *what luck!*
chi *those/people who*
chi? *who?*
chiacchierare *to chat*
chiamare *to call; to telephone*
chiamarsi* *to be called*
la chiamata *call*
il Chianti *Chianti (wine)*
chiaramente *clearly*
chiaro/a *clear; light*
la chiave *key*
   chiudere a chiave *to lock*
chiedere (pp chiesto) *to ask*
la chiesa *church*
il chilo/chilogramma *kilo*
il chilometro *kilometre*
la chimica *chemistry*
il chimico (m pl −ci) *(research) chemist*
la chiocciola *snail*
   chissà *who knows*
la chitarra *guitar*
   la chitarra elettrica *electric guitar*
chiudere (pp chiuso) *to close*
   chiudere a chiave *to lock*
la chiusura lampo *zip*
ci 1 *us; ourselves; each other; to us*
ci 2 *here; there*
   c'è *there is*
   non c'è *he/she's not here*
   c'è l'hai/ha? *have you got it?*
ciao *hello, goodbye*
ciascuno/a *each, every*
il cibo *food*
   cibi transgenici *genetically modified foods*
il ciclismo *cycling*
il ciclo *cycle*
il cielo *sky*
il ciglio (pl le ciglia) *eyelashes*
la ciliegia *cherry*
   cin-cin! *cheers!*
il cinema (inv) *cinema*
la cinepresa *film camera*
il cinghiale *wild boar*
la cintura *belt*
il cioccolato/la cioccolata *chocolate*
   cioè *that is, in other words*
la cipolla *onion*
il cipresso *cypress*
la cipria *face powder*
   circa *about, around*
il circolo *club*
il citofono *entryphone*
la città (inv) *town, city*
il cittadino *citizen, townsperson*
la civetta *owl*
   civico/a *civic*
il clarinetto *clarinet*
la classe *class*
   classico/a (m pl −ci) *classic(al)*
la classifica *chart, league table*
il clavicembalo *harpsichord*

   cliccare *to click*
il/la cliente *client*
il clima (inv) *climate*
il club (inv) *club*
il cocco *coconut*
il codice *code*
   cogliere† (pp colto) *to catch; to gather*
il cognato/la cognata *brother/sister-in-law*
il cognome *surname*
la colazione *breakfast*
   fare colazione *to have breakfast*
   collaborare (con) *to collaborate, to work with*
la collaborazione *collaboration*
la collana *necklace*
i collant (pl) *tights*
il colle *hill*
il collega/la collega *colleague (m/f)*
   collettivo/a *collective, general*
il colletto *collar*
la collina *hill*
   Colonia *Cologne*
   colorato *coloured*
il colore *colour*
   di che colore? *what colour?*
la colpa *fault; blame*
   colpa mia *my fault*
il coltello *knife*
   comandare *to order*
   combattere *to fight*
   combinare *to do*
   che cos'abbiamo combinato? *what have we done?*
   come *like; as*
   come? *how? what?*
   com'è? *what's (something) like?*
   come va? *how's it going? how are things?*
   comico/a (m pl −ci) *comic*
   cominciare(*) *to start, to begin*
la commedia *play; comedy*
   commerciale *commercial, trade*
il commesso/la commessa *shop assistant*
   commestibile *edible*
il commissario *police inspector*
   commuovere† (pp commosso) *to move (emotion)*
il comodino *bedside table*
   comodo/a *comfortable; convenient*
il compact disc (inv) *compact disc, CD*
la compagnia *company*
il compagno *companion*
   compiere (pp compiuto) *to undertake*
il compito *duty, job*
   i compiti *home-work*
il compleanno *birthday*
il complesso *group, band*
   complesso/a *complex*
   comporre† (pp composto) *to compose*

comportarsi★ *to behave*

il compositore *composer*

comprare *to buy*

compreso/a *included*

il computer (inv) *computer*

comunale *municipal*

il comune *town council*

la comunicazione *communication*

la comunione *communion*

comunista (m/f) *communist*

la comunità (inv) *community*

    la Comunità Economica Europea *EEC*

comunque *however, anyhow*

con *with*

    con la bicicletta *by bike*

la concentrazione *concentration*

il concerto *concert*

concludere (pp concluso) *to end*

la conclusione *conclusion*

condannare *to condemn*

condensare *to condense*

condividere (pp condiviso) *to share*

il condominio *jointly-owned block of flats*

il condomino *joint owner*

condurre† (pp condotto) *to conduct, to lead*

il conduttore/la conduttrice *TV presenter*

confermare *to confirm*

confezionare *to pack*

la confezione *clothing; pack*

confinare (con) *to border (on)*

confondere (pp confuso) *to confuse; to merge*

confusionario/a *chaotic*

il congelatore *freezer*

la congestione *congestion*

congratularsi★ con *to congratulate*

il coniglio *rabbit*

il cono *cone*

la conoscenza *knowledge*

conoscere (pp conosciuto) *to know (someone or something); to meet*

conosciuto/a *well-known*

consegnare *to deliver, hand in*

consentire (pr −o) *to allow*

consentito/a *allowed*

il Conservatorio *state music school*

la conservazione *conservation*

consigliare *to advise*

il consiglio *advice*

consultare *to consult*

il contadino *peasant*

il contatto *contact*

    a contatto *in touch*

il conte *Count*

contenere† *to contain*

contento/a *happy*

la contessa *Countess*

contraddire† (pp contraddetto) *to contradict*

la contravvenzione *fine (formal)*

contro *against*

controllare *to check*

continuare(★) *to continue*

il contrabbasso *double bass*

convalidare *to validate*

la convenienza *convenience*

convenire†★ *to be advisable, advantageous, worthwhile*

convertire (pr −o) *to convert*

convincere (pp convinto) *to convince, to persuade*

la coppa *cup*

la coppia *couple*

coprire (pr −o) (pp coperto) *to cover*

il coraggio *courage*

    che coraggio! *how brave!*

cordiale *cordial*

coricarsi★ *to go to bed*

il corno *horn*

il coro *choir*

il corpo *corps*

correggere *to correct*

correre(★) (pp corso) *to run*

correttamente *correctly*

il corridoio *corridor, hall*

la corsa *trip, journey*

    la corsa semplice *single ride*

    la corsa campestre *cross-country running*

il corso *course*

la corte *court;* la Corte di Cassazione *Supreme Court*

cortese *courteous, polite*

corto/a *short*

la cosa *thing*

    cosa?/che cosa? *what?*

coscienzioso/a *conscientious*

così *thus, so, like this*

    basta così? *is that all?*

cosmopolita (m/f) *cosmopolitan*

costare★ *to cost*

costituire *to constitute*

costoso/a *expensive*

costringere (pp costretto) *to force*

il costume *costume, dress*

    il costume da bagno *bathing costume*

il cotone *cotton*

la cottura *cooking*

    il piano di cottura *hob*

la cravatta *tie*

la creatura *creature*

la credenza *sideboard*

credere *to believe, to think*

il credito *credit*

    la carta di credito *credit card*

la crema *egg custard*

la crisi (inv) *crisis*

crollare★ *to collapse*

il crostino *crostino (a starter)*

crudo/a *raw*

il cucchiaio *spoon*

la cucina *kitchen; cuisine*

cucinare *to cook*

cucire† *to sew*

il cugino/la cugina *cousin*

cui *which; whom; whose*

    in cui *in which*

    di cui *of which*

la cultura *culture*

culturale *cultural*

cuocere† (pp cotto) *to cook*

    fare cuocere *to cook*

il cuoio *leather*

il cuore *heart*

la cupola *dome*

la cura *treatment, care*

curioso/a *curious*

la curva *bend*

il cuscino *cushion*

D

da *by; from; since/for; at*

    da otto anni *for eight years*

    da Rita *at Rita's*

il daino *deer*

dando *giving; see dare*

il danno *damage*

la danza *dance; dancing*

dappertutto *everywhere*

dare† *to give*

    dare su *to look out on, to open onto*

    dai! *go on!*

la data *date*

il dattilografo/la dattilografa *typist*

davanti a *in front of, outside*

davvero *really*

decidere (pp deciso) *decide*

decidersi★ *to make up ones mind*

il decimo *tenth*

deciso/a *determined*

dedicarsi★ *to devote oneself*

dedicato/a *dedicated*

dedurre† (pp dedotto) *to deduce*

il delinquente *criminal*

il delitto *crime*

delizioso/a *delicious; delightful*

deludere (pp deluso) *to disappoint*

demaniale *State*

democratico/a (m pl −ci) *democratic*

il denaro *money*

il dente *tooth*

    lavarsi i denti *to brush one's teeth*

il dentifricio *toothpaste*

il /la dentista *dentist (m/f)*

dentro *in, inside*

il dépliant (inv) *leaflet*

deportato/a *deported*

il deposito *deposit*

depresso/a *depressed*

derivare *to derive*

descrivere (pp descritto) *to describe*

desiderare *to wish, to want*

il design (inv) *design*

il designer (inv)   *designer*
la destra   *right*
il dettaglio   *detail*
   devo, devi, deve, devono   *see* dovere
   di   *of; than*
      di dove sei/dov'è?   *where are you from?*
il dialetto   *dialect*
il dialogo   *dialogue*
il diamante   *diamond*
il diametro   *diameter*
il diario   *diary*
dichiarare   *to declare*
didattico/a (m pl –ci)   *teaching, educational*
dietro   *behind*
difendere (pp difeso)   *defend*
la difesa   *defence*
   il Ministero della Difesa   *Ministry of Defence*
differente   *different*
la differenza   *difference*
difficile   *difficult, hard*
la difficoltà (inv)   *difficulty*
diffidare   *to mistrust*
diffondere (pp diffuso)   *to spread*
digerire   *to digest*
il digestivo   *after-dinner drink*
digitare   *to dial, key in*
digrignato/a   *grimacing, snarling*
dimagrire(★)   *to lose weight*
dimenticare (di)   *to forget*
dimenticarsi★ (di)   *to forget*
dinamico/a (m pl –ci)   *dynamic*
il dio (pl gli dei)   *god*
il/la dipendente   *employee*
dipendere★ (pp dipeso)   *to depend*
   dipende   *it depends*
dipingere (pp dipinto)   *to paint*
il dipinto   *painting*
dire† (pp detto)   *to say, to tell*
direttamente   *directly*
diretto/a   *direct*
   il programma in diretta   *live programme*
il diretto   *average-speed stopping-train*
il direttore/la direttrice   *director, primary school head*
   il direttore/la direttrice d'orchestra   *conductor*
il diritto   *right*
disanimato/a   *inanimate*
il disastro   *disaster*
la disciplina   *regulation*
il disco   *record*
il discorso   *speech; conversation*
la discoteca   *discotheque*
discutere (pp discusso)   *to discuss; to argue*
disdire† (pp disdetto)   *to cancel*
disegnare   *to draw*
disegnato/a   *designed*
il disegno   *drawing; design*

la professoressa di disegno   *art teacher*
la disgrazia   *disaster*
il disguido   *mix-up*
il disgusto   *disgust*
disoccupato/a   *unemployed*
disordinato/a   *untidy*
dispari   *uneven (numbers)*
disperato/a   *desperate*
dispiacere★   *to be sorry; to mind*
   mi dispiace   *I'm sorry*
   Le dispiace se . . . ?   *would you mind if . . . ?*
la disposizione   *disposal*
   a disposizione   *available, at s.o's disposal*
disposto/a   *prepared, willing*
distinguere (pp distinto)   *to distinguish*
distrarre† (pp distratto)   *to entertain, to distract*
distrarsi†(★) (pp distratto)   *to have fun, to amuse oneself*
distruggere (pp distrutto)   *to destroy*
disturbare   *to trouble, to interrupt*
   la linea disturbata   *bad line*
la ditta   *firm*
il divano   *sofa*
divenire★ (pp divenuto)   *to become*
diventare★   *to become*
diverso/a   *different (after the noun); various, several (before the noun)*
divertente   *fun, amusing, entertaining*
il divertimento   *entertainment*
divertire (pr –o)   *to amuse*
divertirsi★ (pr –o)   *to enjoy oneself*
dividere (pp diviso)   *to divide*
il divieto   *prohibition, no . . .*
   il divieto di sosta   *no waiting*
   il divieto di transito   *no thoroughfare*
dobbiamo   *see* dovere
la doccia   *shower*
   fare la doccia   *to have a shower*
il documentario   *documentary*
il documento   *document*
doganale   *customs*
dolce   *sweet*
il dolce   *dessert*
il dolcelatte   *dolcelatte (cheese)*
il dollaro   *dollar*
le Dolomiti   *Dolomites*
il dolore   *pain; grief*
la domanda   *question*
   fare una domanda   *to ask a question*
domandare   *to ask*
domani   *tomorrow*
la domenica   *Sunday*
domestico/a (m pl –ci)   *domestic, household*
la donna   *woman*
dopo   *after, afterwards*
dopodomani   *the day after tomorrow*

doppio/a   *double*
   il doppio lavoro   *double work*
dormire (pr –o)   *to sleep*
il dottore/la dottoressa   *doctor*
dove?   *where?*
   dov'è?   *where is?*
dovere†(★)   *to have to, must*
dritto   *straight on*
dubitare   *to doubt*
due   *two*
dunque   *now, therefore*
il duomo   *cathedral*
durante   *during*
durare★   *to last, to go on (for)*
duro/a   *hard*

E

e   *and*
è   *see* essere
ecc.   *etc. (etcetera)*
eccetera   *etcetera*
ecco   *here is, here are*
   eccolo/la   *here it is*
   eccoli/le   *here they are*
l'ecologia (f)   *ecology*
economico/a (m pl –ci)   *cheap, economical*
ed = e
l'edicola   *news-stand*
l'edificio   *building*
l'editore/l'editrice   *publisher*
l'editoria   *publishing*
educato/a   *polite*
effettivamente   *actually; in fact*
l'effetto   *effect*
efficace   *effective*
l'elefante (m)   *elephant*
elegante   *elegant, smart*
elementare   *elementary*
   le scuole elementari   *infant and junior schools*
l'elemento   *element*
l'elenco   *list, directory*
   l'elenco telefonico   *telephone directory*
elettrico/a (m pl –ci)   *electric*
l'elettrodomestico (pl –ci)   *domestic appliance*
l'elicottero   *helicopter*
ellenico/a (m pl –ci)   *Greek*
l'email (f)   *email*
emergere★ (pp emerso)   *to emerge*
l'emigrazione (f)   *emigration*
l'emozione (f)   *emotion*
l'energetico   *energy-giving food*
l'energia   *energy*
enorme   *enormous*
entrambi/e   *both*
entrare★   *to enter, go in*
l'entrata   *entrance*
entusiasmante   *exciting*
l'Epifania   *Twelfth Night*

l'epoca   *era*
   una casa d'epoca   *period house*
equilibrato/a   *balanced*
l'equitazione (f)   *horse-riding*
erano   *see* essere
l'erba   *herb; grass*
l'errore (m)   *mistake*
   fare un errore   *to make a mistake*
esagerare   *to exaggerate*
l'esame (m)   *exam*
esattamente   *exactly*
esatto   *that's right*
esaurito/a   *out of stock/print*
escludere (pp escluso)   *to exclude*
esco, esci, esce, escono   *see* uscire
l'escursione (f)   *excursion*
   fare un'escursione   *to go on an excursion*
l'escursionista (m/f)   *walker, tripper*
l'esempio   *example*
   per esempio   *for example*
l'esemplare (m)   *specimen*
l'esercizio   *exercise*
l'esistenza   *existence*
esistere★ (pp esistito)   *to exist*
esitare   *to hesitate*
esotico/a   *exotic*
l'esperienza   *experience*
l'esperto   *expert*
esplodere (pp esploso)   *to explode*
esporre (pp esposto)   *to expose*
l'espressione (f)   *expression*
espressivo/a   *expressive*
espresso/a   *express*
   la lettera espresso   *express letter*
esprimere (pp espresso)   *to express*
essenziale   *essential*
essere†★ (pp stato)   *to be*
essi/esse   *they (m/f)*
esso/essa   *it (m/f)*
l'estate (f)   *summer*
estendere (pp esteso)   *to extend*
l'estero   *foreign countries*
   all'estero   *abroad*
estivo/a   *summer*
   le vacanze estive   *summer holidays*
estrarre† (pp estratto)   *to extract*
l'età (inv)   *age*
l'etto   *hectogramme (100 grammes)*
   all'etto   *per 100 grammes*
l'eufemismo   *euphemism*
europeo/a   *European*
evadere (pp evaso)   *to escape*
evitare   *to avoid*
evocare   *to arouse, to evoke*
evoluto/a   *advanced, highly developed*

F

fa   *ago*
   un anno fa   *a year ago*
faccio, facciamo   *see* fare
facile   *easy*

facile a   *prone to*
il faggio   *beech*
il fagiolo   *bean*
il fagiolino   *green bean*
il fagotto   *bassoon*
falso/a   *false, untrue*
la fama   *fame*
la fame   *hunger*
   avere fame   *to be hungry*
famigerato/a   *infamous*
la famiglia   *family*
familiare   *(of a) family*
famoso/a   *famous*
i fans (pl)   *fans*
la fantascienza   *science fiction*
la fantasia   *imagination*
fantastico/a (m pl –ci)   *fantastic*
fare† (pp fatto)   *to do; to make*
   fare il bucato   *to do the washing*
   fare colazione   *to have breakfast*
   fare il biglietto   *to get a ticket*
   fare un abbonamento   *to get a season ticket*
   fa bel/brutto tempo   *the weather's good/bad*
   fare vedere a   *to show*
   fare piacere a   *to please*
   fare il numero   *to dial*
   fare parte di   *to belong to*
   fare sapere a   *to let someone know*
   fare a meno di   *to do without*
   fare finta di   *to pretend*
la farfalla   *butterfly*
la farmacia   *chemist's*
il /la farmacista   *chemist*
il fascino   *fascination, attraction*
il fascismo   *fascism*
il fastidio   *annoyance*
   dare fastidio a   *to bother, to be a nuisance to*
faticoso/a   *tiring*
il fatto   *fact*
il fattore   *factor*
la fauna   *fauna*
favoloso/a   *fabulous, amazing*
il favore   *favour*
   per favore   *please*
il fax (inv)   *fax*
il fazzoletto   *handkerchief*
febbraio (m)   *February*
la fede   *faith*
la federa   *pillow-case*
la federazione (f)   *federation*
il fegato   *liver*
felice   *happy*
il feltro   *felt*
la femmina   *girl; female*
le ferie   *holidays*
feriale   *working*
   i giorni feriali   *working days, weekdays*
fermarsi★   *to stop*
la fermata   *stop*

la fermata dell' autobus   *bus-stop*
feroce   *ferocious*
il Ferragosto   *Ferragosto (August 15 Bank holiday)*
il ferro   *iron*
   il ferro da stiro   *(flat) iron*
la ferrovia   *railway*
la festa   *holiday, festival*
festeggiare   *to celebrate*
festivo/a   *holiday*
   i giorni festivi   *holidays*
la fetta   *slice*
le fettuccine (pl)   *fettucine (pasta)*
il fiammifero   *match*
il fidanzato/la fidanzata   *fiancé/fiancée*
fidarsi★ di   *to trust*
la figlia   *daughter*
il figlio   *son*
   i figli   *children*
   figli di papà   *Daddy's boys*
la figura   *figure*
   fare bella figura   *to make a good impression*
figurati!   *not at all!*
la filastrocca   *nursery rhyme, nonsense rhyme*
il film (inv)   *film*
la filosofia   *philosophy*
finalmente   *finally*
la finanza   *finance*
la fine   *the end*
   il fine settimana (inv)   *weekend*
la finestra   *window*
fingere (pp finto)   *to pretend*
finire(★)   *to finish*
fino a   *until, as far as*
il finocchio   *fennel*
finora   *till now*
il fiore   *flower*
   il fiore selvatico   *wild flower*
   a fiori   *flowered*
fiorire   *to bloom*
fiorito/a   *flowery*
Firenze   *Florence*
la firma   *signature*
firmare   *to sign*
il fitness   *fitness*
il fiume   *river*
il flacone   *small bottle*
il flauto   *flute*
la flora   *flora*
la foglia   *leaf*
folle   *mad*
fondamentale   *fundamental*
fondare   *to establish, to found*
il fondo   *bottom, base*
   lì in fondo   *right over/down there*
la fontana   *fountain*
la forchetta   *fork*
il formaggio   *cheese*
il formato   *size, format*
la formica   *ant*
la formula   *formula*

il fornello   *burner*
fornire   *to provide*
il forno   *oven*
   il forno a microonde   *microwave oven*
forse   *maybe*
forte   *strong; loud*
la fortuna   *luck*
   per fortuna   *luckily*
fortunato/a   *lucky, fortunate*
forza!   *come on!*
forzare   *to force*
la foto (inv)   *photograph*
la fotografia   *photography; photograph*
fotografico/a (m pl –ci)   *photographic*
   la macchina fotografica   *camera*
il fotografo   *photographer*
il fotoromanzo   *photoromance*
il foulard (inv)   *headscarf*
fra   *between, among, in (period of time)*
   fra poco   *soon*
la fragola   *strawberry*
la fragranza   *fragrance*
il francobollo   *stamp*
il Frascati   *Frascati (wine)*
la frase   *phrase; sentence*
il frastuono   *racket, din*
il fratello   *brother*
   il fratellino   *little brother*
la frazione   *fraction*
freddo/a   *cold*
   avere freddo   *to be cold*
il freddo   *cold*
il freezer   *freezer*
frequentare   *to frequent, attend*
frequente   *frequent*
fresco/a   *fresh*
la fretta   *hurry, haste*
   avere fretta   *to be in a hurry*
friggere (pp fritto)   *to fry*
il frigorifero   *fridge*
frizzante   *sparkling*
il fronte   *front*
   di fronte a   *opposite, in front of*
la frutta/il frutto   *fruit*
   i frutti del bosco   *forest fruits (nuts and berries)*
il fruttivendolo   *greengrocer, fruiterer*
la fuga   *(gas) leak*
fuggire*(⋆)*   *to run away, to escape*
fumare   *to smoke*
il fumetto   *cartoon comic*
il fungo   *mushroom*
la funivia   *cable car*
funzionare   *to work*
il fuoco   *fire*
fuori   *outside*
il furto   *theft*
i fusilli (pl)   *fusilli (pasta)*
la fusione   *casting*
il futbol   *football*
il futuro   *future*

G

il gabinetto   *toilet*
la galleria   *gallery*
la gallina   *hen*
il gallo   *cock*
la gamba *leg*
   essere in gamba   *to be able, capable*
le ganasce   *[car] clamps; jaws*
il garage   *garage*
il gatto   *cat*
la gelateria   *ice-cream shop*
il gelato   *ice-cream*
i gemelli/le gemelle   *twins*
generale   *general*
generalmente   *generally*
il genere   *kind, sort*
   in genere   *in general, as a rule*
il genero   *son-in-law*
generoso/a   *generous*
il genitore (m)   *parent*
gennaio (m)   *January*
la gente   *people*
gentile   *kind*
gestire   *to run, to manage*
il gettone   *telephone token*
il ghiaccio   *ice*
già   *already; that's right*
la giacca   *jacket*
   la giacca a vento   *windcheater*
giallo/a   *yellow*
   il film giallo   *thriller*
il giallo   *detective story, thriller*
il giardinaggio   *gardening*
   fare il giardinaggio   *to garden*
il giardino   *garden*
   i giardini pubblici   *public gardens*
   i giardini botanici   *botanic gardens*
gigantesco/a   *gigantic*
il gilè (inv)   *waistcoat*
la ginnastica   *gymnastics*
   la ginnastica aerobica   *aerobics*
il ginocchio (pl le ginocchia)   *knee*
giocare (a)   *to play*
il giocatore   *player*
il giocattolo   *toy*
il gioco   *game; fun*
il gioiello   *jewel*
il giornale   *newspaper*
   il giornale radio   *radio news*
giornaliero/a   *daily*
il /la giornalista   *journalist*
la giornata   *day*
il giorno   *day*
giovane   *young*
il giovane   *young man*
giovanile   *youthful*
il giovedì   *Thursday*
la gioventù (inv)   *youth*
girare   *to turn; to go round*
il giro   *tour*
   fare un giro per   *to go on a tour of*
   fare il giro di   *to go round*

la gita   *outing*
   fare una gita   *to go on an outing*
giù   *down*
giudicare   *to judge*
il giudice   *judge*
giugno   *June*
il giullare   *minstrel*
giungere *(⋆)* (pp giunto)   *to arrive, to reach*
la giustizia   *justice*
giusto/a   *right, fair*
gli 1   *the*
gli 2   *to him; to them*
lo gnocco   *gnocco (dumpling)*
la gola   *throat*
il golf (inv)   *golf; cardigan, jumper*
il /la golfista   *golfer*
la gondola   *gondola*
la gonna   *skirt*
il governo   *government*
il grado   *degree*
   essere in grado di   *to be capable of*
la grammatica   *grammar*
il grammo   *gramme*
grande (gran)   *big, large (after the noun); great (before the noun)*
grandinare*(⋆)*   *to hail*
la grandine   *hail*
grasso/a   *greasy*
gratis   *free*
grazie   *thank you*
gridare   *to shout*
grigio/a   *grey*
il grissino   *breadstick*
grosso/a   *big, large*
la grotta   *cave*
il gruppo   *group*
guadagnare   *to earn*
il guanto   *glove*
guardare   *to look at, to watch*
la guardia   *guard*
   la guardia delle finanze   *customs and excise office*
guarire*(⋆)*   *to get well; to cure*
guasto/a   *out of order*
il guaio   *trouble*
il guasto   *breakdown*
la guerra   *war*
il gufo   *owl*
la guida   *guide*
guidare   *to drive; to guide*
guidato/a   *guided*

H

hanno   *see avere*
l'hit-parade (inv)   *hit-parade*
ho   *see avere*
l'hobby (m) (inv)   *hobby*

I

i   *the*
IC   *Intercity (train)*

l'idea   *idea*
  non ho idea   *I haven't a clue*
ideale   *ideal*
l'identità (inv)   *identity*
  la carta d'identità   *identity card*
l'idraulico (pl –ci)   *plumber*
l'idromassaggio   *hydro massage*
ieri   *yesterday*
il   *the*
illimitato/a   *unlimited*
illuminato/a   *illuminated*
illustrativo/a   *illustrative*
imbarazzato/a   *embarrassed*
imboccare   *to take, turn into*
imbucare   *to post*
l'immagine (f)   *image*
l'immigrazione (f)   *immigration*
imparare   *to learn*
impazzire★   *to go mad*
  mi piace da impazzire   *I'm crazy about it*
impedire   *to prevent*
impegnarsi★   *to undertake to*
impegnato/a   *busy*
l'impegno   *engagement; commitment*
l'impermeabile (m)   *raincoat*
l'impianto   *system*
  l'impianto allarme   *alarm system*
l'impiegato   *employee*
imporre† (pp imposto)   *to impose*
importante   *important*
importare★   *to be important, to matter*
  non importa   *it doesn't matter*
impossibile   *impossible*
in   *in; into*
incamerato/a   *hidebound*
l'incendio   *fire*
incerto/a   *uncertain*
l'incidente (m)   *accident*
incidere (pp inciso)   *to affect*
includere (pp incluso)   *to include*
l'incomprensione (f)   *incomprehension*
incontrare   *to meet*
incontrarsi★   *to meet with (someone)*
incoraggiare   *to encourage*
l'incrocio   *crossroads*
l'indagine (f)   *survey*
indeciso/a   *undecided*
l'indennità (inv)   *indemnity*
indietro   *behind*
  indietro di   *slow (time)*
  indietro di cinque minuti   *five minutes slow*
indipendente   *independent*
l'indipendenza   *independence*
indiretto/a   *indirect*
indirizzare   *to aim*
l'indirizzo   *address*
indispensabile   *indispensable*
indubbiamente   *undoubtedly*
infantile   *juvenile, children's*
l'infanzia   *childhood*
infatti   *as a matter of fact, in fact*

infelice   *unhappy*
l'infermiere/l'infermiera   *nurse*
informale   *informal*
l'informatica   *information technology; computers*
le informazioni   *information*
l'infortunio   *(industrial) accident*
l'infrazione (f)   *offence*
l'ingegnere (m)   *engineer*
ingiusto/a   *unfair*
l'ingresso   *entrance; hall; admission fee*
iniziare(★)   *to begin, to start (on)*
l'iniziativa   *initiative*
l'inizio   *beginning*
innaffiare   *to water*
l'innamoramento   *falling in love*
inoltre   *besides, in addition*
l'inquilino   *tenant*
l'inquinamento   *pollution*
inquinato/a   *polluted*
l'insalata   *salad*
l'insegnante (m/f)   *secondary school teacher*
insegnare   *to teach*
insensibile   *insensitive*
insieme   *together*
  la musica d'insieme   *ensemble music*
insistere (pp insistito)   *to insist*
insomma   *in short; well*
intanto   *meanwhile*
intasato/a   *blocked up*
intelligente   *intelligent*
l'intensità (inv)   *intensity*
l'intenzione (f)   *intention*
  avere intenzione   *to intend*
intercontinentale   *intercontinental*
interessante   *interesting*
interessare   *to interest*
l'interesse (m)   *interest*
interno/a   *internal*
l'interno   *extension (telephone)*
  il Ministero degli Interni   *Interior Ministry*
intero   *whole, entire*
interrompere (pp interrotto)   *to interrupt*
l'interruttore (m)   *light switch*
l'interurbano/a   *between cities*
  la telefonata interurbana   *long-distance call*
intervenire†★ (pp intervenuto)   *to intervene*
l'intervento   *intervention; interference*
l'intervista   *interview*
intitolare (si★)   *to call (to be called: book, article, etc.)*
intorno   *around*
introdurre† (pp introdotto)   *to introduce*
l'introduzione (f)   *introduction*
inutile   *useless*
invadere (pp invaso)   *to invade*
invece   *instead, on the other hand*

inventare   *to invent*
l'invenzione (f)   *invention*
l'inverno (m)   *winter*
  d'inverno   *in the winter*
investire (pr –o)   *to invest*
inviare   *to send*
invitare   *to invite*
io   *I*
irritato/a   *irritated*
l'iscritto   *(paid-up) member*
iscritto/a   *enrolled*
iscrivere (pp iscritto)   *to enrol*
l'isola   *island*
ispirare   *to inspire*
l'istituto   *institute*
  l'istituto di bellezza   *beauty salon*
l'Italiese (m)   *anglicised Italian*
l'itinerario   *route, tour*
  l'itinerario naturalistico   *nature trail*

J

il jazz   *jazz*

K

il karatè   *karate*

L

l'   *the*
là   *there, over there*
  di là   *that way*
la; La   *her; you*
laburista   *Labour*
  il partito laburista   *the Labour party*
il ladro   *thief*
laggiù   *down there*
lagnarsi★   *to complain*
il lago   *lake*
la laguna   *lagoon*
lamentarsi★   *to complain*
la lampada   *lamp*
i lampasciumi (pl)   *wild onions*
il lampo   *lightning*
  la chiusura lampo   *zip*
il lampone   *raspberry*
la lana   *wool*
lanciare   *to throw*
largo/a   *loose; wide*
le lasagne   *lasagne (pasta)*
lasciare   *to leave*
  lasciare cadere   *to drop*
lassù   *up there*
il latte   *milk*
la lattina   *tin, can*
il lato   *side*
  a lato   *sideways*
la lauda   *medieval hymn*
la laurea   *university degree*
laureato/a in   *with a degree in*
il lavabò   *washbasin*
il lavaggio   *washing*
la lavagna   *blackboard*

264

la lavanda *lavender*
il lavandino *sink*
  lavare *to wash*
  lavarsi★ *to wash (oneself)*
la lavastoviglie *dishwasher*
la lavatrice *washing machine*
  lavorare *to work*
il lavoratore *worker*
il lavoro *work*
    il lavoro nero *moonlighting*
il Lazio *Lazio (Italian region)*
  le 1 *the; them*
  le; Le 2 *to her; to you*
la lega *league*
    la Lega Ambiente *Environment League*
  legare *to link*
la legenda *key*
  leggere (pp letto) *to read*
  leggero/a *light*
il legno *wood*
il legume *legume, pulse*
  lei *she; you*
  lentamente *slowly*
la lenticchia *lentil*
  lento *slow*
il lenzuolo (pl le lenzuola) *sheet*
la lepre *hare*
la lettera *letter*
la letteratura *litarature*
  letterario/a *literary*
il lettino *sunbed*
il letto *bed*
la lezione (f) *lesson*
  li *them*
  lì *there*
    lì in fondo *right over there*
la libreria *bookshop*
  liberare *to free*
  libero/a *free*
il libretto degli assegni *cheque book*
il libro *book*
  ligure *Ligurian*
la Liguria *Liguria (Italian region)*
il limite *limit*
il limone *lemon*
la linea *line*
    la linea disturbata *bad line (telephone)*
    rimanere in linea *to hold the line*
la lingua *language, tongue*
il linguaggio *language*
  linguistico/a (m pl −ci) *linguistic*
il lino *linen*
la lira *lira*
la lirica *opera*
  lirico/a (m pl −ci) *operatic*
  litigare *to quarrel*
  litoraneo/a *coastal*
il litro *litre*
il livello *level*
    il passaggio a livello *level crossing*
  lo *the; it*

  locale *local*
il locale *room*
la locanda *inn*
la Lombardia *Lombardy*
  Londra *London*
  lontano/a (da) *far (from)*
  loro *they; to them; their; theirs*
  lottare *to struggle*
la lottizzazione *lotting (political patronage)*
la lozione *lotion*
  lucano/a *from the Basilicata*
la luce *light; electricity*
la lucertola *lizard*
la lucidatrice *floor polisher*
  lui *he; him*
la lumaca *snail*
il lumacone *slug*
  luminoso/a *light*
il lunedì *Monday*
    dal lunedì al venerdì *from Monday to Friday*
  lungo/a *long*
    a lungo *for a long time*
il lungomare *the seafront*
il luogo *place*
    dare luogo a *to give rise to*
il lupo *wolf*
il lusso *luxury*
    di lusso *luxury*

M

  ma *but*
  macchiato/a *stained*
la macchina *car; machine*
    andare in macchina *to go in the (by) car*
    la macchina fotografica *camera*
la macedonia *fruit salad*
il macellaio *butcher*
la macelleria *butcher's*
la madre *mother*
il maestro/la maestra *primary school teacher; coach*
il magazzino *department store; warehouse*
il magistrato *magistrate*
  maggio (m) *May*
la maggiorana *marjoram*
la maglia *jumper*
    lavorare a maglia *to knit*
    a maglia *knitted*
la maglietta *T shirt*
il maglione *sweater*
  magro/a *thin*
  mai *ever*
    non ... mai *not ever, never*
il maiale *pork, pig*
  malato/a *ill*
  male *bad, unwell, badly*
    non c'è male *not bad*
    meno male! *good!*
  maleducato/a *rude*

la malinconia *melancholy*
la mamma *mum*
il mammismo *close attachment between mother and son*
il/la manager *manager*
  mancare★ *to lack*
    mancano le lenzuola *there aren't any sheets*
  mandare *to send*
  mangiare *to eat*
la manica *sleeve*
il manico *handle*
la maniera *way, style, fashion*
la manifestazione (f) *demonstration*
la mano (pl le mani) *hand*
    dare una mano *to lend a hand, to help*
  mantenere† *to keep, to maintain*
il manzo *beef*
il marafone *marafone (card game)*
le Marche *Marche (Italian region)*
il marciapiede *pavement*
il mare *sea*
  marino/a *sea, naval*
il marito *husband*
il marketing *marketing*
la marmellata *jam*
  marmorizzato/a *marbled*
  marrone *brown*
il martedì *Tuesday*
il martirio *martyrdom*
  marzo (m) *March*
il maschio *boy; male*
  massacrato/a *massacred*
la matematica *maths*
la matita *pencil*
il matrimonio *marriage, wedding*
il mattino/la mattina *morning*
  maturo/a *ripe*
il meccanico (pl −ci) *mechanic*
  medicinale *medicinal*
  medico/a (m pl −ci) *medical*
il medico (pl −ci) *doctor*
  medio/a *average*
    le medie *middle schools*
il medioevo *Middle Ages*
  meglio *better, best*
la mela *apple*
la melanzana *aubergine*
il melone *melon*
la memoria *memory*
    a memoria *by heart*
  meno *less*
    il/la meno *the least*
    le sette meno un quarto *a quarter to seven*
    meno male! *good!, thank goodness!*
la mensa *canteen*
  mentire *to lie*
  mentre *while*
  meravigliarsi★ *to be surprised at*
  meraviglioso/a *marvellous*

il mercato   *market*
il mercoledì   *Wednesday*
meridionale   *southern*
   l'Italia meridionale   *Southern Italy*
il mese   *month*
la messa   *mass*
il messaggio   *message*
il messaggio vocale   *voice message*
il mestiere   *trade, job*
la metà (inv)   *half; mid*
il metallo   *metal*
la meteo   *weather forecast*
la metropolitana   *tube (underground)*
mettere (pp messo)   *to put*
mettersi*   *to set about, to begin*
la mezzanotte   *midnight*
mezzo/a   *half*
il mezzogiorno   *midday*
mi   *me; to/for me; myself*
mica: non … mica   *not really*
la microonda   *microwave*
il miglio   *millet*
migliorare   *to improve*
migliore(*)   *better*
   il/la migliore   *the best*
mila   *see* mille
il milione   *million*
mille (pl mila)   *thousand*
minacciare   *to threaten*
minerale   *mineral*
   l'acqua minerale   *mineral water*
la minestra   *minestra (soup)*
   minestra in brodo   *pasta in clear soup*
la miniatura   *miniature*
il ministero   *ministry*
il ministro   *minister*
la minoranza   *minority*
minore   *less*
il minuto   *minute*
mio/a   *my; mine*
il miracolo   *miracle*
il mirtillo   *bilberry*
la missione   *mission*
la misura   *measurement*
misurare   *to measure*
i mobili (pl)   *furniture*
la moda   *fashion*
   l'alta moda   *haute couture*
   andare di moda   *to be in fashion*
la modella   *model*
il modello   *style*
moderatamente   *moderately*
moderno/a   *modern*
il modo   *way, manner*
il modulo   *form*
la moglie (pl le mogli)   *wife*
molto   *very; very much*
molto/a   *much, a lot (of), many*
moltissimo   *very much*
il momento   *moment*
   in questo momento   *at the moment*

mondiale   *world*
il mondo   *world*
il monolocale   *bedsit; studio flat*
monotono/a   *monotonous*
la montagna   *mountain*
il monte   *mountain*
il monumento   *monument*
la moquette   *(fitted) carpet*
la mora   *blackberry*
morbido/a   *soft*
mordere (pp morso)   *to bite*
morire†*   (pp morto)   *to die*
   mi piace da morire   *I adore it*
la mortadella   *mortadella (salame)*
mortale   *deadly*
la morte   *death*
la mosca   *fly*
la mossa   *move*
la mostra   *exhibition*
la motocicletta   *motorbike*
la mountain bike (inv)   *mountain bike*
la mozzarella   *mozzarella (cheese)*
la mucca   *cow*
la multa   *fine*
   fare la multa a   *to fine*
il municipio   *town hall*
muovere†   (pp mosso)   *to move*
il muro   *(outside) wall*
il museo   *museum*
la musica   *music*
   la musica classica   *classical music*
   la musica da camera   *chamber music*
   la musica d'insieme   *ensemble music*
   la musica pop   *pop music*
musicale   *musical*
il/la musicista   *musician*
le mutande (pl)   *underpants*
le mutandine (pl)   *panties*
il mutuo   *mortgage*

N

il nailon   *nylon*
napoletano/a   *Neopolitan*
la narrativa   *narrative; fiction*
nascere*   (pp nato)   *to be born*
nascondere (pp nascosto)   *to hide*
nascosto/a   *hidden*
il Natale   *Christmas*
la natura   *nature*
la nave   *ship*
nazionale   *national*
la nazionalità (inv)   *nationality*
la nazione   *nation*
ne   *of it, of them*
né … né   *neither … nor*
neanche   *neither, not even;*
   neanch'io   *me neither*
la nebbia   *fog*
necessario   *necessary*
il negozio   *shop*
il nemico (pl –ci)   *enemy*

nemmeno: non … nemmeno   *not even*
neppure: non … neppure   *not even*
nero/a   *black*
il neroli   *orange flower oil*
nervoso/a   *nervous; irritable*
nessuno: non … nessuno   *no-one*
neutro/a   *neutral*
la neve   *snow*
nevicare(*)   *to snow*
nevrotico/a (m pl –ci)   *neurotic*
niente: non … niente   *nothing*
   per niente   *at all*
il/la nipote   *nephew; grandson/niece; granddaughter*
no   *no*
la nocciola   *hazelnut*
il nocciolo   *heart (of the matter)*
la noce   *walnut*
   il mallo di noce   *walnut pulp*
noi   *we*
noioso/a   *boring*
noleggiare   *to hire*
il nome   *name*
nominare   *to mention*
   hai sentito nominare …?   *have you heard of …?*
il nominativo   *name [formal]*
non   *not*
il nonno/la nonna   *grandfather/ grandmother*
nonostante   *despite, notwithstanding*
il nord   *north*
il nord-est   *north-east*
normale   *normal*
nostro/a   *our; ours*
la nota   *tone; note*
la notizia   *news*
la nottata   *night (long)*
la notte   *night*
notturno/a   *night*
   la vita notturna   *nightlife*
il Novecento   *twentieth century*
novembre (m)   *November*
le nozze   *wedding, marriage*
nulla: non … nulla   *nothing*
il numero   *number; size*
   fare il numero   *to dial*
   che numero porta?   *what size do you take?*
la nuora   *daughter-in-law*
nuotare   *to swim*
il nuoto   *swimming*
Nuova York   *New York*
nuovo/a   *new*
la nuvola   *cloud*
nuvoloso/a   *cloudy*

O

l'oasi (f) (inv)   *oasis*
obbligare   *to force, to oblige*
obbligatorio/a   *obligatory, compulsory*

obiettivo/a   *objective*
l'oboe (m)   *oboe*
l'oca   *goose*
l'occasione (f)   *occasion; bargain*
gli occhiali   *glasses*
   gli occhiali da sole   *sunglasses*
l'occhio   *eye*
occidentale   *western*
occorrere★   *to be needed*
occuparsi★   *to deal with, to be interested*
  in, to be in (profession)
  mi occupo di editoria   *I'm in*
  publishing
occupato/a   *busy*
l'oculista (m/f)   *optician*
oddio!   *oh dear!*
odiare   *to hate*
odioso/a   *hateful, odious*
l'odore (m)   *smell*
offendere (pp offeso)   *to offend*
l'offerta   *offer*
offrire (pp offerto)   *to offer*
l'oggetto   *object*
oggi   *today*
ogni   *every, each*
  ogni tanto   *every so often*
  ogni quanto?   *every how often?*
l'olio   *oil*
·l'oliva   *olive*
oltre   *beyond, over*
  oltre a   *apart from*
l'ombra   *shade*
  all'ombra   *in the shade*
l'ombrellone (m)   *beach-umbrella*
onesto/a   *honest*
l'opera (f)   *work; opera*
  il teatro dell'opera   *opera house*
l'operaio/operaia (m/f)   *worker*
l'opinione (f)   *opinion*
opporre† (pp opposto)   *to oppose*
l'opportunità (inv)   *opportunity*
oppure   *or else*
l'opuscolo   *booklet*
ora   *now*
l'ora   *hour*
  che ora è?/che ore sono?   *what*
  time is it?
l'orario   *timetable*
  in orario   *on time*
Orazio   *Horace*
l'orchestra   *orchestra*
l'orchidea   *orchid*
ordinare   *to order*
ordinato/a   *tidy*
l'ordine (m)   *order*
  l'ordine pubblico   *law and order*
le orecchiette (f)   *orecchiette (ear-shaped*
  pasta)
l'orecchino   *earring*
l'orecchio (pl gli orecchi/le
  orecchie)   *ear*
organizzare   *to organise, to arrange*
l'organo   *organ*

originale   *original*
l'origine (f)   *origin*
l'orlo   *hem*
l'oro   *gold*
l'orologio   *clock; watch*
l'oroscopo   *horoscope*
l'orrore (m)   *horror*
  i film dell'orrore   *horror films*
Orsola   *Ursula*
l'orto   *garden*
l'ospedale (m)   *hospital*
ospitare   *to put someone up*
l'ospite (m/f)   *guest*
osservare   *to observe, to watch*
l'osteria   *tavern*
ottenere†   *to obtain; to achieve*
ottimista   *optimistic*
l'ottimista (m/f)   *optimist*
ottimo/a   *excellent*
l'ottone (m)   *brass*
l'ovulo   *ovule, spore (bot.)*

P

la pace   *peace*
la padella   *pan*
il padre   *father*
il padrone   *owner*
il paese   *country; village*
la paga   *pay*
  la busta paga   *wage packet*
pagare   *to pay (for)*
la pagina   *page*
  le pagine gialle   *yellow pages*
la paglia   *straw*
il paio (pl le paia)   *pair, couple*
  un paio di giorni   *a couple of days*
il palazzo   *block of flats; palace; the*
  Establishment
la palestra   *gymnasium*
la pallavolo   *volley-ball*
il pallone   *ball*
  giocare a pallone   *to play ball*
la palude   *marsh, bog*
il pane   *bread*
la panetteria   *bread shop*
il panino   *bread roll*
la panna   *cream*
il panorama (inv)   *view*
il pantaloncino   *shorts*
i pantaloni   *trousers*
il papà   *dad*
il Papa   *Pope*
il papavero   *poppy*
il paragone   *comparison, parallel*
il parapendio   *hang-gliding*
parcheggiare   *to park*
il parcheggio   *car park*
il parco   *park*
parecchio   *a lot*
il/la parente   *relative*
parere†★ (pp parso)   *to seem*
il parere   *opinion*

la parete   *(inside) wall*
pari   *equal, equivalent; even (number)*
parlare   *to speak*
il parmigiano   *parmesan (cheese)*
la parola   *word*
il parrucchiere/la
  parrucchiera   *hairdresser*
la parte   *part; side*
  da che parte?   *which way?*
  da questa parte   *this way*
  fare parte   *to form part*
partecipare   *to participate*
la partenza   *departure*
il particolare   *particular, detail*
il partigiano   *partisan*
partire★ (pr −o)   *to leave*
  a partire da   *starting from*
la partita   *match (sport)*
il partito   *party (political)*
il passaggio   *lift*
  dare un passaggio a   *to give someone*
  a lift
il passaporto   *passport*
passare(★)   *to pass; drop by*
  passare il tempo   *to spend time*
la passerella   *catwalk*
il passatempo   *pastime*
passeggiare   *to go for a stroll*
la passeggiata   *walk, stroll*
  fare la passeggiata   *to go for a walk*
la pasta   *pasta, cake*
il pasticcio   *mess, muddle*
la pastiglia   *pastille, lozenge*
il pasto   *meal*
la pasticceria   *cake shop*
la patata   *potato*
le patatine (pl)   *crisps*
la patente   *driving licence*
il patrimonio   *heritage*
il pattinaggio   *skating*
pattinare   *to skate*
la paura   *fear*
  avere paura di   *to be*
  afraid/frightened of
  fare paura a   *to frighten*
la pausa   *pause*
il pavimento   *floor*
la pazienza   *patience*
  pazienza!   *oh well! too bad! never*
  mind!
peccato   *pity, shame*
  che peccato!   *what a shame!*
la pecora   *sheep*
il pecorino   *pecorino (cheese)*
il pedaggio   *toll*
pedalare   *to pedal*
il pedone   *pedestrian*
peggio   *worse, worst*
peggiorare(★)   *to worsen*
peggiore   *worse*
  il/la peggiore   *the worst*
la pelle   *soft leather*
il pellegrinaggio   *pilgrimage*

il pellegrino *pilgrim*
la pelletteria *leather goods*
la pellicceria *fur shop*
la pelliccia *fur coat*
pendente *leaning*
il /la pendolare *commuter*
    fare il pendolare *to commute*
penetrato/a *penetrated*
la penisola *peninsula*
la penna *pen*
    le penne *penne (pasta)*
pensare *to think*
    quando pensa di partire? *when are you thinking of leaving?*
    penso di sì *I think so*
la pensione *pension; guest house*
    in pensione *retired*
pentirsi★ (pr –o) *to regret*
il pepe *pepper (spice)*
il peperone *pepper*
il peperoncino *hot pepper, chilli*
per *for; in order to; through; around; by; because of*
    per esempio *for example*
    per strada *in the street*
la pera *pear*
perché? *why?*
perché *because*
la percentuale *percentage*
percorrere (pp percorso) *to go along*
perdere (pp perduto or perso) *to lose*
    perdere il treno *to miss the train*
perfetto *perfect*
il pericolo *danger*
pericoloso/a *dangerous*
la periferia *outskirts, suburbs*
    abitare in periferia *to live in the suburbs*
periodico/a *periodic*
il periodo *period*
permesso *allowed*
permettere (pp permesso) *to permit, to allow*
però *but, however*
la perplessità (inv) *perplexity, bewilderment*
le persiane (pl) *blinds*
persistente *long-lasting*
la persona *person*
personale *personal*
il personale *staff*
persuadere (pp persuaso) *to persuade*
pervenire†★ (pp pervenuto) *to arrive, to come to*
pesante *heavy*
pesare *to weigh*
la pesca 1 *peach*
la pesca 2 *fishing*
il pescatore *fisherman*
il pesce *fish*
il peso *weight*
pessimistico/a *pessimistic*
pettinarsi★ *to do one's hair*

il pezzo *piece*
    pezzettini *small pieces*
piacere†★ (a) *to please; to like*
    mi piace *I like*
    fare piacere a *to please*
piacere *how do you do? pleased to meet you*
    per piacere *please*
piacevole *pleasant*
piangere (pp pianto) *to cry*
il /la pianista *pianist*
piano *softly; slow*
il piano *floor*
    al primo piano *on the first floor*
il piano di cottura *hob*
il pianoforte *piano*
la pianta 1 *plant*
la pianta 2 *map*
il pianterreno *ground floor*
il pianto *weeping*
la pianura *plain*
il piatto *plate, dish*
la piazza *square*
piccante *hot, spicy*
piccolo/a *small, little*
il picnic: fare un picnic *to go on a picnic*
il piede *foot*
    a piedi *on foot*
    andare/venire a piedi *to walk*
pieno/a *full*
la pietà (inv) *compassion, pity*
la pietra *stone*
il pigiama *pyjamas*
pignolo/a *particular, precise*
pigro/a *lazy*
il /la pilota *pilot (m/f)*
la pinacoteca *art gallery*
il ping-pong *table-tennis*
il pino *pine*
il pinolo *pine-nut*
la pioggia *rain*
    sotto la pioggia *in the rain*
il piombo *lead*
il pioppo *poplar*
piovere(★) *to rain*
il pipistrello *bat*
la piscina *swimming-pool*
i piselli *peas*
il pistacchio *pistachio*
pittorico/a *pictorial*
più *more; most; plus*
    il/la più *the most*
    di più *more/best*
    in più *in addition*
    non … più *no longer*
il piumino *duvet*
la pizza *pizza*
la pizzeria *pizzeria*
il pizzo *lace*
la plastica *plastic*
plastificato/a *plastic-coated*
il platano *plane (tree)*

il plenilunio *full moon*
un po' *a little; some*
    un altro po' *a bit more/a few more/some more*
    poco *little, not much (adj.); not very (adv.)*
la poesia *poetry; poem*
il poeta/la poetessa *poet*
    poetico/a *poetic*
    poi *then*
la poliammide *polyamide*
la polizia *police*
    la polizia doganale *border/customs police*
    la polizia stradale *road police*
poliziesco/a *of the police*
    il film poliziesco *thriller*
il poliziotto/la poliziotta *policeman/policewoman*
il pollo *chicken*
la poltrona *armchair*
la pomata *cream, ointment*
    la pomata antisettica *antiseptic cream*
il pomeriggio *afternoon*
il pomodoro *tomato*
il pomolo *knob*
il pompelmo *grapefruit*
il ponte *bridge*
popolare *popular*
la popolazione *population*
il porcino *porcino mushroom, cep*
il porco *pig*
porre† (pp posto) *to put*
la porta *door*
il portafoglio *wallet*
il portamonete *purse*
portare *to wear; to bring*
portatile *portable*
il portico (pl –ci) *arcade*
il portone *front door*
possedere† *to possess, to own*
possibile *possible*
posso, possiamo *see potere*
le poste *Post Office*
il poster (inv) *poster*
il postino *postman*
il posto *place; seat; job*
    prenotare un posto *to book a seat*
    da due posti letto *which sleeps two*
potente *powerful*
potere†★ *to be able to*
povero/a *poor (after the noun); unfortunate (before the noun)*
pranzare *to have lunch*
il pranzo *lunch*
    a pranzo *at lunchtime*
praticamente *virtually, basically*
il/la praticante *participant*
praticare *to practise*
    praticare uno sport *to play a sport*

pratico/a (mpl –ci)   *practical*
preferire   *to prefer*
preferito/a   *preferred*
il prefisso   *code (telephone)*
pregare   *to beg*
prego   *don't mention it, go ahead*
il preludio   *prelude*
premere   *to press*
il premio   *prize, award*
prendere (pp preso)   *to take; to collect; to have (to) eat/drink*
cosa prendi/e?   *what will you have (to eat/drink)?*
prendere la macchina/il treno   *to take the car/train*
prenotare   *to book*
preparare   *to prepare*
prepararsi★   *to get ready to*
la presa   *socket*
presentare   *to present; to introduce*
il /la preside   *head-teacher*
presso   *care of*
prestare   *to lend*
presto   *quickly; early; soon*
a presto   *see you soon*
il prêt-à-porter   *ready-to-wear fashion*
prevedere (pp previsto)   *to predict; to envisage, to foresee*
prezioso/a   *precious; valuable*
il prezzemolo   *parsley*
il prezzo   *price*
la prigionia   *imprisonment*
prima (di)   *before*
la prima colazione   *breakfast*
la primavera   *spring*
in primavera   *in the spring*
primeggiare   *to dominate*
primo/a   *first*
il primo   *first course*
principale   *principal*
principalmente   *principally*
il principio   *principle*
privo/a   *devoid of*
probabilmente   *probably*
il problema (pl i problemi)   *problem*
non c'è problema   *no problem*
la problematica   *problems (pl)*
il prodotto   *product*
produrre† (pp prodotto)   *to produce*
profano/a   *profane, secular*
professionale   *professional*
la scuola professionale   *vocational school*
la professione   *profession*
il professore/la professoressa   *professor, teacher*
la profumeria   *perfumery*
il profumo   *perfume*
il progetto   *project*
il programma (pl i programmi)   *programme; routine*
proibire   *to prohibit*
il promemoria   *memo*

promesso/a   *promised*
I Promessi Sposi   *'The Betrothed' (novel)*
promettere (pp promesso)   *to promise*
promuovere† (pp promosso)   *to promote*
pronto   *hello (on the telephone)*
pronto/a   *ready*
proporre† (pp proposto)   *to propose*
la proposta   *proposal, suggestion*
la proprietà (inv)   *ownership; property*
il proprietario   *owner*
proprio   *really; precisely, exactly*
proprio/a   *one's own*
il proposito   *subject*
a proposito di   *about, on the subject of*
prosciugato/a   *dried up*
il prosciutto   *ham*
la prossimità   *proximity, nearness*
prossimo/a   *next*
proteggere (pp protetto)   *to protect*
la protezione   *protection*
Prov. (la provincia)   *province*
la prova   *rehearsal; test*
provare   *to try; to try on*
provenire† (pp provenuto)   *to originate from*
la provincia   *province*
lo psicologo (pl –gi)   *psychologist*
pubblicare   *to publish*
pubblico/a (m pl –ci)   *public*
i giardini pubblici   *public gardens*
le pubbliche relazioni   *public relations*
la Puglia   *Puglia (region)*
pugliese   *from Puglia*
pulire   *to clean*
pulito/a   *clean*
il pulsante   *button*
la puntata   *episode*
il punto   *point*
il punto di vista   *point of view*
puramente   *purely*
pure   *also; by all means*
puro/a   *pure*
purtroppo   *unfortunately*

Q

qua   *here*
di qua   *this way*
il quaderno   *exercise-book*
quadrato/a   *square*
i quadretti   *small squares*
a quadretti   *checked*
il quadro   *picture*
qualche   *some, a few*
qualche volta   *sometimes*
qualcosa   *something*
qualcosa da bere   *something to drink*
qualcuno   *someone*
quale?   *which (one)? what (one)?*
qualsiasi   *any*

quando   *when*
la quantità (inv)   *quantity*
quanto/a?   *how much how many?*
quanti anni hai?   *how old are you?*
da quanto tempo?   *for how long?*
ogni quanto?   *every how often?*
quant'è?   *how much is it? how much is that?*
il quartiere   *district*
il quarto   *quarter*
un'ora e un quarto   *an hour and a quarter*
quasi   *almost*
quattordicesimo/a   *fourteenth*
quello/a   *that (one)*
la quercia   *oak tree*
questo/a   *this (one)*
questi/e   *these (ones)*
la questione   *question*
per la questione di . . .   *about the . . .*
la questura   *police station*
qui   *here*
quindi   *so, therefore*
quinto/a   *fifth*

R

raccogliere† (pp raccolto)   *to pick; to collect; to gather*
la raccolta   *picking, gathering; collection*
il racconto   *short story*
il radicchio   *radicchio lettuce*
la radio (inv)   *radio*
raffinato/a   *refined*
la ragazza   *girl*
il ragazzo   *boy*
raggiungere (pp raggiunto)   *to reach; to attain*
la ragione   *reason*
avere ragione   *to be right*
il ragioniere/la ragioniera   *accountant*
il ragno   *spider*
il rame   *copper*
il ramo   *branch*
il ramoscello   *twig*
la rana   *frog*
rapidamente   *quickly*
rapido/a   *fast*
la rapina   *armed robbery*
rappresentare   *to represent*
raramente   *rarely*
il raso   *satin*
rassegnarsi★   *to resign oneself*
il ratto   *rat*
razionale   *rational*
reagire   *to react*
realizzare   *to create; to accomplish*
reale   *royal; real*
il reato   *crime*
recitare   *to act*
redimere (pp redento)   *to redeem*
refrattario/a   *refractory*

regalare   *to give (as a present)*
il regalo   *gift, present*
il reggiseno   *bra*
regionale   *regional*
la regione   *region*
il /la regista   *producer*
registrare   *to record*
il regno   *kingdom*
regolarmente   *regularly*
la relazione   *relation*
rendere (pp reso)   *to render, to make*
rendersi★ conto   *to realise*
la repubblica   *republic*
resistere   *to resist*
la Resistenza   *Resistance*
respirare   *to breathe*
responsabile   *responsible*
il responsabile   *the one responsible, in charge*
restare★   *to stay*
restituire   *to give back*
il resto   *rest; change (money)*
restringere (pp restritto)   *to take in*
la rete   *net*
la retorica   *rhetoric*
il riadattamento   *renovating*
riagganciare   *to hang up (phone)*
riaprire (pr −o) (pp riaperto)   *to reopen*
ricco/a   *rich; lavish*
il riccio   *curl*
la ricerca   *search*
ricercato/a   *sought-after*
il ricercatore/la ricercatrice   *researcher*
la ricetta   *recipe*
ricevere   *to receive*
il ricevimento   *reception; welcome*
il ricevitore   *receiver (telephone)*
richiamare   *to call back*
richiedere (pp richiesto)   *to request*
riconoscere   *to recognise*
ricoprire (pr −o) (pp ricoperto)   *to cover*
ricordare   *to remember; to remind*
ridere (pp riso)   *to laugh*
ridicolo/a   *ridiculous*
ridurre† (pp ridotto)   *to reduce*
la riduzione   *reduction*
riempire (pr −o)   *to fill in (form)*
rientrare★   *to get back*
il rifugio   *hut*
rifiutare   *to refuse*
i rifiuti   *waste, refuse*
la riga   *stripe*
a righe   *striped*
rilassante   *relaxing*
rilassarsi★   *to relax*
rimandare   *to postpone*
rimanere★ (pp rimasto)   *to stay, to remain*
rimettere (pp rimesso)   *to put back*
rimettere a posto   *to tidy*

rimpiangere (pp rimpianto)   *to regret*
rinascimentale (adj)   *Renaissance*
rincrescere★ (a)   *to regret*
ringraziare   *to thank*
rinunciare   *to give up*
rinviare   *to postpone*
riparare   *to mend*
ripetere   *to repeat*
riposarsi★   *to rest*
riprendere (pp ripreso)   *to resume*
il riscaldamento   *heating*
il rischio   *risk*
riscoprire (pr −o) (pp riscoperto)   *to rediscover*
risentire (pr −o)   *to hear again; to feel again*
la riserva   *reserve*
la riserva naturale   *nature reserve*
il riso   *rice*
risolvere (pp risolto)   *to resolve; to solve*
il risotto   *risotto*
risparmiare   *to save*
rispettare   *to respect*
rispettivamente   *respectively*
rispondere (pp risposto)   *to answer, to reply*
il ristorante   *restaurant*
ristrutturato/a   *modernised*
il risultato   *result*
il ritardo   *lateness, delay*
essere in ritardo   *to be late*
ritenere†   *to claim; to maintain*
ritornare★   *to return, to come back*
il ritorno   *return*
l'andata e ritorno   *return (ticket)*
la riunione   *meeting*
riuscire†★   *to succeed; to manage to*
la rivista   *magazine*
rivolgersi★ (pp rivolto)   *to apply to, to contact*
la roba   *things, stuff, belongings*
il rock (inv)   *rock music*
rodere (pp roso)   *to gnaw*
il rognone   *kidney*
romagnolo/a   *from Romagna*
romano/a   *Roman*
il romanzo   *novel*
il romanzo rosa   *romantic fiction*
rompere (pp rotto)   *to break*
il rompiscatole   *nuisance, pest*
rosa (inv)   *pink*
la rosa   *rose*
il rospo   *toad*
il rossetto   *lipstick*
rosso/a   *red*
rotondo/a   *round*
rovesciare   *to spill*
rubare   *to steal*
mi hanno rubato il portafoglio   *I've had my wallet stolen*
il rubinetto   *tap*

aprire il rubinetto   *to turn on the tap*
la rubrica   *column (in newspaper)*
il rumore   *noise*
rumoroso/a   *noisy*
il ruscello   *stream*
il rustico (pl −ci)   *cottage*

S

il sabato   *Saturday*
il sacchetto   *(small) bag*
il sacchetto di plastica   *plastic bag*
il sacco   *sack, bag*
il sacco a pelo   *sleeping bag*
il sacerdote   *priest*
il saggio   *essay*
la sagra   *village festival*
la sala da pranzo   *dining-room*
il salame   *salami*
il salario   *wage*
il saldo   *the balance (financial)*
il sale   *salt*
salire†★   *to get into (vehicle), to go up*
il salotto   *sitting-room*
la salsa   *sauce*
la salsiccia   *sausage*
saltare(★)   *to jump*
salutare   *to greet, say hello/goodbye*
Salute!   *Your health! Cheers!*
salvato/a   *saved*
San Marco   *Saint Mark*
San Pietro   *Saint Peter*
il sandalo   *sandal*
il sanguinaccio   *pork blood sausage*
sano/a   *healthy*
sapere†★   *to know; to know how to*
sai guidare?   *can you drive?*
non lo so   *I don't know*
sapiente   *masterly*
la sapienza   *wisdom*
il sapone   *soap*
la Sardegna   *Sardinia*
il sarto   *tailor*
la sartoria   *tailor's workshop*
il sasso   *rock, stone*
il sassofono   *saxophone*
sbagliare   *to make a mistake, to get it wrong*
sbagliare numero   *to dial a wrong number*
sbagliato/a   *wrong*
la camera sbagliata   *the wrong room*
sbattuto/a   *beaten*
gli scacchi (pl)   *chess*
scadere★   *to expire, to run out*
lo scaffale   *shelf, bookshelf*
la scala   *stairs*
lo scaldabagno   *water heater*
la scampagnata   *country outing; picnic*
lo scantinato   *basement*
scappare★   *to flee, to dash off*
scarico/a (m pl −ci)   *flat (battery)*

la scarpa *shoe*
lo scarpone *ski/walking boot*
la scatola *box, packet*
lo scatto *unit (phone)*
scegliere† (pp scelto) *to choose*
la scelta *choice*
la scena *scene*
scendere(★) (pp sceso) *to come down, to get out (vehicle)*
lo sceneggiato *TV serial*
la scheda *card*
    la scheda telefonica *telephone card*
lo scheletro *skeleton*
lo schermo *screen*
lo scherzo *joke*
schiacciare *to press, to crush*
la schiena *back*
la schiera *group*
    a schiera *terraced (houses)*
lo schifo *disgust*
    fare schifo a *to disgust*
lo schizzo *sketch*
lo sci *skiing*
    sciare *to ski*
la sciarpa *scarf*
scientifico/a (m pl −ci) *scientific*
lo scienziato/la scienziata *scientist*
sciogliere† (pp sciolto) *to melt; to dissolve*
lo scioglilingua *tongue-twister*
lo sciopero *strike*
    fare sciopero *to strike*
lo scippo *(handbag) snatching*
lo scoiattolo *squirrel*
scomodo/a *uncomfortable*
scomparire†★ (pp scomparso) *to disappear*
sconfiggere (pp sconfitto) *to defeat*
sconsigliare *to advise not to*
scontarsi★ *to expiate, to pay for*
scontento/a *dissatisfied, discontented*
lo sconto *discount*
lo scontrino *ticket, receipt*
sconvolto/a *overcome, disturbed, troubled*
lo scopo *aim*
scoppiare★ *to break out*
scoprire (pr −o) (pp scoperto) *to discover*
scorso/a *last*
scozzese *Scottish; tartan (material)*
lo scritto *writing*
lo scrittore/la scrittrice *writer*
scrivere (pp scritto) *to write*
    scrivere a macchina *to type*
lo scultore/la scultrice *sculptor*
la scuola *school*
    le scuole elementari *infant and junior schools*
    le (scuole) medie *middle schools*
    la scuola superiore *upper school*

scuotere (pp scosso) *to shake*
scuro/a *dark*
scusare *to excuse*
    scusa!/scusi!/ scusate! *excuse me!/sorry!*
la sdraia *deck-chair*
se *if*
sé: se stesso *himself, herself, yourself, itself*
secco/a *dry*
il secolo *century*
secondo *according to*
    secondo Lei *in your opinion*
il secondo *second ; main course*
il sedano *celery*
la sede *seat; centre; HQ*
sedersi†★ *to sit*
la sedia *chair, seat*
sedurre† (pp sedotto) *to seduce*
il segnale *signpost*
segnare *to mark*
il segno *sign*
la segretaria *secretary*
la segreteria telefonica *telephone answering machine, Ansaphone*
segreto/a *secret*
seguire *to follow*
il seguito *sequence*
    in seguito *subsequently*
selvatico/a (m pl −ci) *wild*
il semaforo *traffic light*
sembrare★ *to seem*
il seminterrato *basement*
semplice *simple; single*
    una corsa semplice *a single ride*
la semplicità *simplicity*
sempre *always*
senese *Sienese*
sensibile *sensitive*
il senso *sense*
    aver buon senso *to have common sense*
il sentiero *path, track*
il sentimento *feeling*
sentire (pr −o) *to feel, to hear*
    senti/senta! *listen!*
sentirsi (pr −o)★ *to feel like*
senz'altro *definitely*
senza *without*
seppellire (pp sepolto) *to bury*
la sera *evening*
serale *evening*
    il corso serale *evening class*
sereno/a *clear*
il serpente *snake*
la serie (inv) *series*
serio/a *serious*
la serra *greenhouse*
servire (pr −o)(★) *to serve; to be needed*
    serve altro? *do you need anything else?*

il servizio *service*
    il bagno di servizio *cloakroom/ spare bathroom*
il sesso *sex*
la seta *silk*
la sete *thirst*
settembre (m) *September*
la settimana *week*
    il fine settimana (inv) *weekend*
settimanale *weekly*
settimo/a *seventh*
il settore *sector*
sferico/a (m pl −ci) *spherical; round*
sfidare *to defy; to challenge*
sforzarsi★ *to try hard*
sfruttare *to exploit, take advantage of*
sfumare in *to blend into*
lo shampoo (inv) *shampoo*
si *oneself; yourself; yourselves; herself; himself; itself; themselves; (to) each other; one*
sì *yes*
sia: sia ... che *both ... and*
siamo *see essere*
la Sicilia *Sicily*
sicuramente *surely*
la sicurezza *safety*
sicuro/a *sure*
    sicuro di sé *confident*
la sigaretta *cigarette*
il sigaro *cigar*
la sigla *signature tune*
la signora *lady, Mrs, madam*
il signore *man, Mr, sir*
signorile *elegant*
la signorina *young lady, Miss*
il silenzio *silence*
silenzioso/a *silent*
il simbolo *symbol*
simile *similar*
simpatico/a (m pl −ci) *nice, pleasant*
il sindaco *mayor*
la sinfonia *symphony*
la sinistra *left*
    a sinistra *on the left*
sintetico/a (m pl −ci) *synthetic*
SIP *Italian Telephone Company*
il sistema (pl i sistemi) *system*
sistemare *to put; to arrange*
la situazione *situation, position*
lo slip *briefs*
smettere (pp smesso) *to stop; to give up*
    smettere di fumare *to give up smoking*
l'SMS (m) *text message*
snello/a *slim*
so *see sapere*
sociale *social*
    l'assistente sociale *social worker*
socialista (m/f) *socialist*
la società (inv) *society; company*
il socio *member*

soddisfare† (pp soddisfatto) *to satisfy*
la sofferenza *suffering*
la soffitta *attic*
il soffitto *ceiling*
soffrire (pr −o) (pp sofferto) *to suffer*
il soggiorno *stay; sitting-room*
sognare *to dream*
il sogno *dream*
il soldato *soldier*
i soldi (pl) *money*
il sole *sun*
   c'è sole *it's sunny*
solito/a *usual*
   di solito *usually*
la solitudine *solitude*
sollecito/a *prompt*
solo *only*
   da solo *by oneself*
soltanto *only*
la soluzione *solution*
sommergere (pp sommerso) *to submerge*
il sonno *sleep*
   aver sonno *to be sleepy*
sono *see essere*
sopra *above*
   di sopra *upstairs*
il soprano (inv) *soprano*
soprattutto *above all, chiefly*
sopravvivere(*) (pp sopravvissuto) *to survive*
la sorella *sister*
la sorellina *little sister*
sorpassare *to overtake*
sorprendente *surprising*
sorprendere (pp sorpreso) *to surprise*
la sorpresa *surprise*
sorridere (pp sorriso) *to smile*
la sosta *halt*
   il divieto di sosta *no waiting*
sotto *under, beneath*
   di sotto *downstairs*
la sottoveste *petticoat, slip*
sottrarre† (pp sottratto) *to take away, remove*
sovietico/a (m pl −ci) *Soviet*
S.p.A. (Società per Azioni) *Joint-Stock Company*
la spada *sword*
gli spaghetti *spaghetti*
sparare *to shoot*
spargere (pp sparso) *to spread*
sparire* *to disappear*
lo spazio *space*
spazioso/a *spacious, roomy*
la spazzatura *rubbish*
lo specchio *mirror*
la specialità (inv) *speciality*
specialmente *especially*
la specie (inv) *species*
spedire *to send; to post*
spegnere (pp spento) *to put out, to extinguish; to turn off*

spendaccione *extravagant*
spendere (pp speso) *to spend*
sperare *to hope*
   sperare di trovare *to hope to find*
la spesa *shopping*
   fare la spesa *to go shopping*
spesso *often*
lo spettacolo *show; performance*
la spiaggia *beach*
   in spiaggia *on the beach*
gli spiccioli *small change*
lo spider (inv) *convertible sports-car*
spiegare *to explain*
la spilla *brooch*
la spina *plug*
gli spinaci *spinach*
spingere (pp spinto) *to push*
splendido/a *splendid, magnificent*
sporco/a *dirty*
sporgersi* (pp sporto) *to lean out of*
lo sport (inv) *sport*
sportivo/a *sporting*
sposarsi* *to get married*
sposato/a *married*
   sposato con *married to*
gli sposi *married couple*
   I Promessi Sposi 'The Betrothed' *(novel)*
lo spot (inv) *TV advert*
la spremuta *freshly squeezed juice*
lo sprint (inv) *sprint*
lo spumante *sparkling wine*
lo spuntino *snack*
   fare uno spuntino *to have a snack*
la squadra *team*
lo squash *squash*
   giocare a squash *to play squash*
squillare *to ring (telephone)*
squisito/a *delicious*
staccare *to unplug*
lo stadio *stadium*
la stagione *season*
stamattina *this morning*
la stampa *press*
stancarsi* *to be tired of*
stanco/a *tired*
la stanga *shaft*
la stanza *room*
la star (inv) *star (celebrity m/f)*
stare†* *to be; to stay*
   come stai/sta? *how are you?*
   stare attento *to be careful*
   stare zitto *to be quiet*
   stare bene a *to suit*
starnutire *to sneeze*
stasera *this evening*
statale *(of the) state*
lo statale *state employee, civil servant*
gli Stati Uniti *United States*
lo stato *state*
la statua *statue*

la stazione *station; resort*
lo stereo *stereo*
la sterlina *pound (money)*
lo stesso/la stessa *the same*
   sé stesso/a *himself, herself, yourself, itself*
lo stile *style*
lo /la stilista *designer (m/f)*
lo stipendio *salary*
   stiro: il ferro da stiro *(flat) iron*
lo stivale *boot*
la stoffa *material*
lo stomaco *stomach*
   il mal di stomaco *stomach-ache*
la storia *history; story*
la stracciatella *clear soup with egg*
la strada *road*
straniero/a *foreign*
lo straniero, la straniera *foreigner*
strano/a *strange, unusual*
straordinario/a *exeptional*
straziante *excruciating*
stressante *stressful*
stretto/a *tight; narrow*
la stringa *lace*
stringere (pp stretto) *to squeeze; to shake (hand)*
lo strumento *instrument*
lo strutto *lard*
lo studente/la studentessa *student*
studiare *to study*
lo studio *studio*
stufo/a *bored, fed up*
stupido/a *stupid*
stupirsi* *to be amazed*
su *on, upon; up*
subito *straight away, at once, immediately*
succedere* (pp successo) *to happen*
   che cos'è successo? *what's happened?*
successivo/a *successive, following*
il successo *success*
il succo di frutta *fruit juice*
   il succo d'arancia *orange juice*
suddetto/a *afore-mentioned*
suggerire *to suggest*
suicidarsi* *to commit suicide*
suo/a *his; her; hers; its; your; yours*
il suocero/la suocera *father-/mother-in-law*
suonare *to play (an instrument); to ring (telephone)*
il suono *sound*
superare *to exceed*
la superficie *surface*
superiore *superior, upper*
il superlativo *superlative*
il supermercato *supermarket*
il supplemento *supplement*
supporre† (pp supposto) *to suppose*
lo svago *entertainment; relaxation*
lo svantaggio *disadvantage*

la sveglia   *alarm-clock*
svegliarsi★   *to wake up*
svenire†★ (pp svenuto)   *to faint*
svolgere (pp svolto)   *to carry out;*
  svolgere un'attività   *to carry out an*
  activity

T

il tabaccaio   *tobacconist*
la tabaccheria   *tobacconist's shop*
il tacco   *heel*
il taccuino   *note book*
tacere† (pp taciuto)   *to be silent*
la taglia   *size (clothes)*
tagliare   *to cut*
le tagliatelle   *tagliatelle (pasta)*
il tailleur (inv)   *(woman's) suit*
talmente   *so (adv)*
tanti/e (adj)   *so many*
tanto (adv)   *so much; such a lot; anyway*
  tantissimo   *lots*
tanto/a (adj)   *such a lot (of), so much*
  ogni tanto   *every so often*
il tappeto   *carpet, rug*
tardi   *late*
  a più tardi   *see you later*
il tartufo   *truffle*
la tasca   *pocket*
il tassì (inv)   *taxi*
il/la tassista   *taxi-driver*
il tasto   *key*
la tastiera   *keyboard*
il tavolo/la tavola   *table*
la tazza   *cup*
il tè (inv)   *tea*
il teatro   *theatre*
  il teatro dell'opera   *opera house*
il telecomando   *remote control*
il telefilm (inv)   *TV film*
telefonare a   *to telephone*
la telefonata   *telephone call*
  la telefonata interurbana   *long-distance call*
  la telefonata urbana   *local call*
il telefonino   *mobile phone*
il telefono   *telephone*
il telefono fisso   *landline phone*
il telegiornale   *TV news*
il telegramma (pl -i)   *telegram*
la telenovela   *'soap'*
la televisione   *television*
il televisore   *television set*
il tema (pl i temi)   *theme*
il tempio   *temple*
il tempo   *time; weather*
  da quanto tempo?   *how long?*
  avere tempo   *to have time*
  da molto tempo   *for a long time*
il temporale   *storm*
la tenda   *curtain; tent*
tenere†   *to hold; to keep*
tenersi†★ in forma   *to keep fit*

il tennis (inv)   *tennis*
tentare   *to try, to attempt*
il termosifone   *radiator*
la terra   *earth*
  la terra rossa   *clay*
la terracotta   *terracotta*
il terrazzo   *(roof) terrace*
terribile   *terrible*
il terrore   *terror*
  avere il terrore di   *to be terrified of*
il terzo   *third*
il tesoro   *treasure*
la tessera   *ticket, card*
  tessera club   *club membership*
  avere la tessera per   *to belong to, to have a ticket for*
il tessuto   *textile, fabric*
il tetto   *roof*
il Tevere   *Tiber*
ti   *you; to/for you; yourself*
il tifoso   *fan (sports)*
il tinello   *dining-room*
il tipo   *kind, type; chap*
tirare   *to pull*
  tira vento   *it's windy*
tirchio/a   *tightfisted, mean*
il tiro   *shooting*
  il tiro con l'arco   *archery*
  il cavallo da tiro   *cart-horse*
il toast (inv)   *toasted sandwich*
togliere† (pp tolto)   *to remove*
tollerante   *tolerant*
tonificante   *toning*
il topo/il topolino   *mouse*
tornare★   *to return, to go/come back; to do again*
  tornare indietro   *to turn back/round*
il torneo   *tournament*
il toro   *bull*
la torre   *tower*
il torrente   *river, stream*
la torta   *cake*
i tortelli   *tortelli (pasta)*
i tortellini   *tortellini (pasta)*
il torto   *wrong*
  avere torto   *to be wrong*
toscano/a   *Tuscan*
tossico/a (m pl –ci)   *toxic*
tossire   *to cough*
il totale   *total*
  in totale   *in total*
totalmente   *totally*
la tovaglia   *table-cloth*
il tovagliolo   *napkin*
tra   *see fra*
tradizionale   *traditional*
la tradizione   *tradition*
tradurre† (pp tradotto)   *to translate*
la traduzione   *translation*
il traffico   *traffic*
la tragedia   *tragedy*
il traghetto   *ferry*
la trama   *plot*

il tramezzino   *sandwich*
il tramonto   *sunset*
tranne   *except*
la tranquillità   *tranquillity, calm*
tranquillo/a   *quiet, peaceful*
trarre† (pp tratto)   *to pull, to draw*
il transito   *thoroughfare*
  il divieto di transito   *no entry*
trascorrere (pp trascorso)   *to spend, to pass*
  trascorrere il tempo   *to use time*
il trasporto   *transport*
trattare (con)   *to deal with*
il trattato   *treaty*
la trattoria   *trattoria (modest restaurant)*
traversare   *to cross*
il Trebbiano   *Trebbiano (wine)*
il Trecento   *fourteenth century*
tredicesimo/a   *thirteenth*
il trekking   *hiking*
il treno   *train*
  prendere il treno   *to take the train*
  il treno delle 7.53   *the 7.53 train*
il trentino   *person from Trento*
trifolato   *truffled (sliced and cooked with oil, garlic and parsley)*
triste   *sad*
la tristezza   *sadness*
la tromba   *trumpet*
il trombone   *trombone*
il tronco   *(tree) trunk*
troppo   *too much*
trotterellare   *to trot*
trovare   *to find*
  andare a trovare   *to visit (person)*
trovarsi★   *to be (somewhere); to find oneself*
il trucco   *make-up*
il trullo   *trullo (ancient conical house in Puglia)*
le truppe   *troops*
tu   *you*
il tuffo   *dive*
tuo/a   *your; yours*
il tuono   *thunder*
turchese   *turquoise*
turchino/a   *dark blue*
il /la turista   *tourist*
turistico/a (m pl –ci)   *tourist*
  l'ufficio turistico   *tourist office*
il turno   *shift, duty*
tutelare   *to protect*
tutto   *all, everything*
  in tutto   *altogether*
tutti/e   *all, everyone*
  tutti e due   *both*

U

l'ubicazione (f)   *location*
l'uccello   *bird*
uccidere (pp ucciso)   *to kill*
l'ufficio   *office*

ulteriore *further (adj.)*
ultimo/a *last; latest*
  l'ultimo piano *top floor*
l'umanista (m/f) *humanist*
l'umanità *humanity*
un, un', uno, una *a, an, one*
  è l'una *it's one o'clock*
unico/a *only; unique*
  sono figlio unico *I'm an only child*
l'unione (f) *union*
unire *to join; to unite; to enclose*
l'unità (inv) *unit*
unito/a *united*
l'università (inv) *university*
gli Unni *the Huns*
l'uomo (pl gli uomini) *man*
l'uovo (m) (pl le uova) *egg*
  uova sbattute *beaten eggs*
urbano/a *city, urban*
  la telefonata urbana *local call*
usare *to use*
uscire†★ *to go out, to exit*
  uscire di casa *to leave the house*
l'uscita *exit*
l'usignolo *nightingale*
utile *useful*
utilizzare *to use*
l'utopia *utopia*
l'uva *grapes (pl)*

V

va bene *okay, that's fine*
  mi va bene *that suits me*
la vacanza *holiday*
  in vacanza *on holiday*
la vacca *cow*
vado, vai, va, vanno *see andare*
vagare *to wander*
  vagare per *to wander through*
la valigia *suitcase*
la valle/la vallata *valley*
i valori *valuables*
  il deposito valori *safety deposit*
la vaniglia *vanilla*
il vano *room*
il vantaggio *advantage*
  vantaggioso/a *advantageous*
  vantarsi★ *to boast*
il vaporetto *waterbus*
vario/a *various, different*
il vascellaro *vatmaker*
il vaso *vase*
vecchio/a *old*
vedere (pp visto *or* veduto) *to see*
  fare vedere a *to show*
  non vedere l'ora *to look forward to*
vedersi★ (pp visto *or* veduto) *to see one another; to meet*
  ci vediamo! *see you!*
vegetariano/a *vegetarian*
la veglia *(night) watch*

la vela *sail*
velenoso/a *poisonous*
il velluto *velvet, corduroy*
veloce *fast*
velocemente *quickly*
vendere *to sell*
il venerdì *Friday*
Venezia *Venice*
vengo, vieni, viene, vengono *see venire*
venire†★ (pp venuto) *to come*
ventidue *22*
la ventina *about 20*
il vento *wind*
  tira vento *it's windy*
veramente *really*
il verbale *statement*
verde *green*
la verdura *vegetables*
la vergogna *shame*
  avere vergogna *to be ashamed*
vergognarsi★ *to be ashamed*
il verme *worm*
i vermicelli *vermicelli (pasta)*
vero? *true? right?*
versare *to pour*
verso *towards; at about*
la vespa *wasp*
la vestaglia *dressing-gown*
vestire (pr −o) *to dress*
vestirsi★ (pr −o) *to get dressed*
il vestito *dress*
la vetrina *shop-window*
vi *you (pl); to/for you; yourselves*
la via *street*
viaggiare *to travel*
il viaggio *journey*
il vicino/la vicina *neighbour*
vicino *nearby, close*
  qui vicino *near here*
il video *video*
il videoregistratore *video*
vietare *to forbid*
vietato/a *forbidden*
  è vietato fumare *it is forbidden to smoke*
il/la vigile *traffic policeman/woman*
la villa *detached house*
il villaggio *village*
la villetta *cottage*
il villino *cottage*
vincere (pp vinto) *to win*
vinicolo/a *(relating to) wine*
il vino *wine*
viola (inv) *purple*
la viola 1 *viola*
la viola 2 *violet*
il /la violinista *violinist*
il violino *violin*
il violoncello *cello*
la vipera *adder, viper*
la virgola *comma*

la visione *vision*
visitare *to visit (place)*
il viso *face*
la vista *view*
  il punto di vista *point of view*
  a prima vista *at first sight*
la vita *life*
il vitello *veal; calf*
vivace *lively*
vivere(★) (pp vissuto) *to live*
vivo/a *alive*
la voce *voice*
la voglia *desire, wish*
  avere voglia di *to feel like*
voglio, vogliamo, vogliono *see volere*
voi *you (pl)*
volare(★) *to fly*
volentieri *willingly, with pleasure*
volere†★ *to want*
  voler bene *to be fond of, to love*
volgare *vulgar, coarse*
il volo *flight*
la volpe *fox*
la volta *time*
  a volte *sometimes*
il volto *face*
volto/a *turned to*
il volume *volume*
vostro/a *your (pl); yours (pl)*
votare *to vote*
il voto *mark*
vuoi, vuole *see volere*
vuotare *to empty*
vuoto/a *empty*

W

il waltzer (inv) *waltz*
il water (inv) *toilet*
il weekend (inv) *weekend*
il western (inv) *western film*
il whisky (inv) *whisky*
il windsurfing *windsurfing*

Y

lo yoga *yoga*

Z

lo zabaglione *zabaglione, syllabub (dessert)*
lo zaino *rucksack*
la zanzara *mosquito*
la zia *aunt*
lo zio *uncle*
la zip *zip*
zitto/a *quiet, silent*
  stare zitto *to be quiet*
lo zoccolo *clog*
lo zodiaco *zodiac*
la zona *area, district*
lo zoo (inv) *zoo*
lo zucchero *sugar*
la zucchina/lo zucchino *courgette*

Picture Credits

BBC Languages would like to thank the following for providing photographs and for permission to reproduce copyright material. Every effort has been made to trace and acknowledge all copyright holders but if there are any omissions, the publishers will be pleased to make the necessary arrangements at the earliest opportunity.

Imagestate/Alamy page 17; **Robert Harding Picture Library/Alamy** page 33; **Frank Chmura/Alamy** page 38; **Peter Adams/Alamy** page 49; **Stock Italia/Alamy** page 57; **Frank Chmura/Alamy** page 65; **Sc Photos/Alamy** page 111; **Peter M. Wilson/Alamy** page 143; **Paul Almasy/Corbis** page 151 (*top*); **Vittoriano Rastelli/Corbis** page 151 (*bottom*); **Imagebroker/Alamy** page 159; **CuboImages srl/Alamy** page 160; **Ken Walsh/Alamy** page 167 (*bottom*); **Peter Adams/Alamy** page 167 (*top*); **Robert Mullan/Alamy** page 175; **Vittoriano Rastelli/Corbis** page 176; **Fergus MacKay/Alamy** page 184 (*bottom*); **Julius Lando/Alamy** page 184 (*top*); **World Pictures** page 127; **PhotoDisc** page i; **Julian Baldwin** pages 2 (*top*), 3 (*left*), 10, 18 (*bottom*), 34, 48, 58, 73, 120, 136 (*bottom*), 144, 145, 152, 153, 162 (*left*), 176 (*bottom*), 178, 185 and 186; **Chiappini family** pages 107 and 108; **Giangiacomo Feltrinelli Editore, Milano** page 24; **Robert Harding Picture Library** page 135 (Giulio Veggi); **Image Bank** page 146 (Giuliano Colliva); **Andrew Oliver** pages 32 and 174; **Jeremy Orlebar** pages 2 (*bottom*), 19, 43, 51, 52, 66, 73, 136 (*top*), 137, 162 (*right*), 168 and 177; **Picturepoint** page 70; **Scala** pages 109 and 223; **Spectrum** page 78; **Mick Webb** pages 72, 76, 221 and 222; **Zefa** page 142; **Denise De Rôme** page 9.

The following photographs were taken for the BBC by:
Benedict Campbell pages 24, 118 and 192; and **Daniel Thistlethwaite** page 11 (*top left*).

Front cover photo: **Donald Nausbaum/Alamy**
Back cover photos: **PhotoDisc**

Notes

Keep on Talking Italian!

If you would like to continue to improve your Italian, BBC Languages has an extensive selection of other course books and resources. *Italianissimo 2* will take you to the next level of fluency using a combination of print, audio and online, while the Italian Dictionary, Grammar and Get By language and travel guide serve as invaluable references that are easy to use at home, on holiday or in the classroom.

Don't Stop Now!

You can add another language to your repertoire with the extensive range of BBC Languages course books and resources. The *French Experience* (1 & 2) and *Sueños* (1 & 2) can take you from beginner's level to a high standard using a combination of print, audio, TV and online.

For more information and our complete catalogue, log on to www.bbclanguages.com or phone us today on 08705 210292

Italian Grammar and Dictionary

Concise and compact, both are excellent references that are easy to use at home or in the classroom.

Provides clear and accessible examples illustrating the language as it is actually used

Contains over 78,000 up-to-date translations together with cultural notes

288 pp course book;
4 audio CDs or 4 x 75 minute audio cassettes; 20 part TV series; free online activities

288 pp course book;
4 audio CDs or 4 x 75 minute audio cassettes; 20 part TV series; free online activities